Martin Luther King, Jr.,
and the Theology of Resistance

Martin Luther King, Jr., and the Theology of Resistance

RUFUS BURROW, JR.

Foreword by Dwayne A. Tunstall

McFarland & Company, Inc., Publishers
Jefferson, North Carolina

ALSO BY RUFUS BURROW, JR.

James H. Cone and Black Liberation Theology
(McFarland 1994; paperback 2001)

Frontispiece: Martin Luther King, Jr., 1964
(Library of Congress, *World Telegram & Sun* photograph
by Dick DeMarsico, LC-USZ62-126559)

LIBRARY OF CONGRESS CATALOGUING-IN-PUBLICATION DATA

Burrow, Rufus, 1951–
Martin Luther King, Jr., and the theology of resistance /
Rufus Burrow, Jr. ; foreword by Dwayne A. Tunstall.
p.   cm.
Includes bibliographical references and index.

ISBN 978-0-7864-7786-9 (softcover : acid free paper) ∞
ISBN 978-1-4766-1732-9 (ebook)

1. King, Martin Luther, Jr., 1929–1968.   2. United States—History—20th
century.   3. United States—Church history—20th century.   I. Title.
BX4827.K53B87 2015   230'.61092—dc23   2014042029

BRITISH LIBRARY CATALOGUING DATA ARE AVAILABLE

On the front cover:
The Reverend Dr. Martin Luther King, Jr., 1960s (Photofest)

Printed in the United States of America

McFarland & Company, Inc., Publishers
Box 611, Jefferson, North Carolina 28640
www.mcfarlandpub.com

To the memory of my oldest sister,
Miss Linda Kaye Burrow (1950–2014).
She was, to use the word coined
by the poet Maya Angelou, my shero.

Table of Contents

PART III: WHERE DO WE GO FROM HERE?

Acknowledgments

Over the past twenty years I have written and published many articles on various aspects of the life, ideas, and socio-ethical practice of Martin Luther King, Jr. Although I have published in a number of different journals, it is fair to say that the vast majority of the publications on King were submitted to my journal of choice, *Encounter*, the faculty journal at Christian Theological Seminary in Indianapolis, Indiana, where I have taught theological social ethics for more than thirty years. I have intentionally published most of my articles in this journal both because the editors have always encouraged faculty members to submit their work, and because I always felt that I had the freedom to essentially say what I wanted to say. Moreover, I have felt comfortable to introduce new ideas in *Encounter*. There was a kind of tacit agreement that these ideas would always be well documented and supported by good, solid research. Indeed, publishing in *Encounter* gave me the opportunity to find my own niche in King Studies, which turned out to be what I call the man of ideas and ideals genre. This area of King Studies stresses the ongoing dance between European, European American, and black southern, religious, familial, and cultural influences on King. The focus on specific ideas and ideals that King himself brought to the table, and how they impacted what he was introduced to from college through doctoral studies, is seen to be an important key to understanding the real Martin Luther King, Jr. By the time King had his Ph.D. in hand, he was not simply the product of European and European American influences. Rather, he was an amalgam of black family, black southern cultural and black religious influences that were intricately intermingled with the ideas and ideals of great Western thinkers and the best of Western cultural traditions. This made him unashamedly both black *and* American.

The most recent editor of *Encounter*, Professor Ronald James Allen, was one of two people who encouraged me to think about publishing a collection of my journal articles on King in a book. A former teacher, Dean Emeritus James Earl Massey, was the other person. I am grateful to both men for cheering my work over many years. I have had the good fortune of having Dean Massey read a number of my publications in manuscript form and to make (what Lewis V. Baldwin calls) "diplomatic criticisms" and suggestions for improvement. He has also been kind enough to encourage me in my teaching and scholarship over many years.

Professor Randall Auxier of Southern Illinois University in Carbondale, Illinois, has been very helpful in providing an outlet for my work on King and personalism, whether through publications in *The Personalist Forum* (for which he served as editor for several years, before it was renamed *The Pluralist*), or through inviting me to give, or respond to, papers presented to the Eastern Division of the American Philosophical Association (The Personalistic

Discussion Group). I have found Randy to be a kindred spirit in both personalist and King Studies. I shall forever be grateful to him for making it possible for my work on King and personalism to be acknowledged and honored at a meeting of the Personalistic Discussion Group in Chicago in 2010. The papers presented were published in *The Pluralist* (The Journal of the Society of the Advancement of American Philosophy) in the spring issue of 2011. Professors Lewis V. Baldwin and Dwayne Tunstall of Vanderbilt University and Grand Valley State University, respectively, read excellent papers on various aspects of my work on King, and I responded to them. White male academicians do not get better than Randy Auxier when it comes to supporting, using, and applauding the work of colleagues across racial-ethnic-cultural lines.

My most significant, and deeply respected dialog partner in King Studies over many years is recently retired Vanderbilt University professor, Lewis Velvet Baldwin, who I can only characterize as King scholar extraordinaire, and arguably the top King scholar in the world today. He is this, not merely because of his voluminous writings on King, but because of the sheer quality and thoroughness of his work, as well as his own witness to, and application of, King's ideas. In addition, there is the matter of the genuineness of Baldwin's commitment to teaching an entire generation about the witness and sacrifice of the true Martin Luther King, Jr. and what that must mean for us today, rather than to allow an invented King, e.g., the King of secular and religious right wing conservatives, to gain ascendancy. Lewis Baldwin has been the consummate scholar, and more, my friend.

I was quite intentional about asking Professor Dwayne A. Tunstall to write the foreword to this collection. Even before I met Tunstall some years ago, his doctoral advisor (Randall Auxier) had boasted to me about a bright, energetic, rising personalist who happened to be one of his top Ph.D. students in philosophy, and was black. I discovered this, and much more, to be true when I heard Tunstall, then working on his dissertation, read a paper on the beloved community concept in Josiah Royce and Martin Luther King, Jr., at a meeting of the American Philosophical Association meeting in Chicago. I had the good fortune to be a respondent to his paper. Our paths crossed a number of times thereafter, and I became increasingly impressed with his sharpness of mind and his careful interpretations of King's ideas and personalist philosophy (the philosophy that King took as his own). I have no doubt that Dwayne Tunstall is a rising star in both personalist and King Studies, who has already begun to make his mark in both. I am truly honored and thankful that he agreed to introduce this volume.

In addition to the articles published in *Encounter* approximately one third of the chapters in this book were first presented at King Day celebrations, or delivered in classroom settings at various colleges and theological schools. I wish to thank each of those communities for inviting me to speak, but more so, I thank the members of each school for having patiently listened to what I had to say, particularly those instances in which I was more interested in learning from them during the discussion periods. I thank them for allowing me to bounce ideas off them, as well as the benefits gained from their contributions.

Nearly another third of the chapters were written solely for this book. Although I did not initially intend to do this, I believe the collection is better for having done so. When I first conceived the idea for this book, I was frankly skeptical that any publisher would be interested in it. I was both surprised and delighted when one did express interest in the manuscript proposal. I had in fact published my first book with this publisher twenty years earlier: *James H. Cone and Black Liberation Theology*. There is a certain amount of gratification that comes from receiving a second contract from my first publisher. I am thankful for the close, careful eyes of my editors, their patience, and their amazing ability to help me say more clearly what I really wanted to say.

I would like to acknowledge the contributions of my students, particularly those who enroll in my courses on Martin Luther King, Jr., and Prophetic and Ethical Witness of the Church. Both are my all-time favorite courses. By now, it is no secret that many of my ideas for writing projects come from interactions with my students, especially in the two courses cited. Indeed, my students are generally the first to be exposed to ideas I might have for writing projects on King, and what Mary Alice Mulligan and I call *ethical prophecy* in our book, *Daring to Speak in God's Name* (2002). Many of these ideas are generated through the courses themselves. Ideas may arise when a student asks a particularly intriguing or provocative question, or when one takes issue with something I said, and then is able to get me to see the significance of their idea. I am grateful for all of this, in addition to the students' willingness to put up with my efforts to make sense of what may be going through my mind on any given class day. Mostly, I am appreciative for the uncanny ability, and the willingness of some students to help make my own ideas clearer to me. This is a reminder to me of just how precious is the human mind, and why we should put it to better use, than we do.

This book is dedicated to the oldest of the ten children reared by my parents. Only eight of those ten were actually born to our mother; two were grandchildren to my parents but were raised as their own, because their mother, my oldest sister Linda Kaye Burrow, was too young to do so herself. She lost her way for a few years during young adulthood, but had the good fortune of finding her way to a life sustaining path, and upon the death of our loving mother, she assumed the role of matriarch of the Burrow clan. No one was better suited for that role. Although her formal education ended after high school in 1969, I always knew that her sharpness and quickness of mind transcended my own, and that she could have been anything she wanted. After all, our mother had drilled this into us, the two oldest of her children. In everything I did that might be deemed good and noble, she cheered me, indeed, was the wind beneath my wings, always reminding me that I could do it even better, if I stay with it. Because of her, and her witness, I vow to stay with it, until I too fall out of the line of march. Until then, I am happy to dedicate this book to her memory.

I hope that readers of this book will learn some things about Martin Luther King, Jr., that they did not already know, or that things they thought they already knew will gain more clarity than was heretofore the case. More than anything, I hope the book will lead many to want to read and study more carefully the life, ideas, ideals, and practice of the greatest civil rights leader of the twentieth century. What did he really stand for, and what does it mean for the world today and tomorrow, that Martin Luther King, Jr., lived, espoused the ideas and ideals he did, and relentlessly applied them in an effort to make the world better than it was when he was born into it?

Foreword
by Dwayne A. Tunstall

To adequately appreciate Rufus Burrow, Jr.'s writings on Martin Luther King, Jr., in general and his writings on King's theological social ethics in particular, one first needs to appreciate Burrow as a master teacher-scholar. That is to say, Burrow is the kind of scholar whose teaching informs his scholarship, and he is the kind of teacher whose scholarship informs his pedagogy. As a master teacher, Burrow taught courses on King's theological social ethics at Christian Theological Seminary for over two decades. In those courses he introduced students to King as a social activist, a theologian, a Boston personalist, and, most importantly, a Baptist minister rooted in the early and mid-twentieth century black southern church. He took these classroom lessons and made them available to a wider audience with his book, *Martin Luther King, Jr. for Armchair Theologians* (2009). His courses on King provided him numerous opportunities to familiarize himself with King's own writings and with the relevant secondary literature on King. That familiarity with King's writings and the relevant secondary literature on King led to him writing several scholarly articles and book chapters about King's personalism and social activism. It also has led him to write two scholarly monographs on King's personalism and social activism: *God and Human Dignity: The Personalism, Theology, and Ethics of Martin Luther King, Jr.* (2006) and *Extremist for Love: Martin Luther King, Jr., Man of Ideas and Nonviolent Social Action* (2014).

Yet, Burrow hasn't written a book in the voice of a master teacher-scholar until now. This is because he hasn't written a book where he would let himself write in that voice. If one wanted to hear or read Burrow, the master teacher-scholar, one would need to read or listen to his public lectures and his spoken commentaries on other scholars' works. I have listened to him speak in that voice twice in person: First, on April 29, 2005, when Burrow commented on my first foray into writing about King's personalism, and, second, on February 20, 2010, when Burrow graciously commented on a presentation where I honored his work in personalist ethics while criticizing his strong moral realism. I haven't forgotten how he conducted himself on those two occasions. I admired how his careful reading of other scholars' works and his knowledge of the secondary literature on King's personalism was coupled with an earnest desire to promote social justice and a willingness to teach a young scholar how to read one's fellow scholars charitably and sympathetically. I think these qualities are present in his other published writings on King's personalism, but not to the same extent that they are in this book. Unlike his other published writings, this book best retains the spirit of his public lectures and his spoken commentaries.

With that said, dear reader, I contend that what you have before you is a personal book, more specifically, a book that functions as a testament to Burrow's decades-long commitment to promoting social justice in the vein of Martin Luther King, Jr.'s theological social ethics. This book also is a personal one because Burrow explains King's *theological* social ethics in almost a conversational tone, using a series of occasional pieces aimed at different audiences. This format gives readers numerous opportunities to learn about King's theological social ethics. Here are some of the lessons waiting for you.

First, as with Burrow's other writings on King, he weaves together King's early familial roots in black southern and Baptist culture and his initial exposure to personalism at Morehouse College and Crozer Theological Seminary with his formal graduate studies at Boston University where he wrestled intellectually with Walter Rauschenbush, Reinhold Niebuhr, and Mohandas Gandhi amongst others and his later career as a minister and social ethicist.

Second, Burrow examines the significance of theological social ethics to understanding King's social activism. Third, Burrow reminds us how we can extend King's social activism and promotion of social justice to groups King himself neglected—namely, women's rights and rights for lesbians, gays, and transgendered people.

Fourth, Burrow explains what it means for Martin Luther King, Jr., to be a theological social ethicist. That is to say, King should be seen as someone who practiced a God-centered social ethics. This ethics is guided by King's commitment to living a life in accordance with God's love for us and his belief that the beloved community ought to be the standard by which we evaluate our current sociocultural and historical circumstances.

Fifth, as a theological social ethicist, King thinks that promoting social justice ought to involve identifying specific social problems in local communities, and not overemphasize battling "racism in general" or "oppression in general." If one were to apply King's approach to promoting social justice today, one would, for example, identify specific problems in many black communities, for example, intraracial crime committed by young black youth. Rather than simply condemning the offenders and criticizing them for their lack of personal responsibility, one first would need to identify the social, cultural, and economic roots of intraracial crime in black communities. One then would need to formulate solutions to these specific problems, for example, establishing local programs or funding already existent local programs that have a record of addressing these problems by respecting the somebodiness of black people, especially the somebodiness of young black men.

Sixth, Burrow reminds readers that King was a flawed person who performed some extraordinary feats with the help of others. He also reminds readers even though King was flawed, like all human beings are, that shouldn't lessen his symbolic image as a champion of social justice.

The beauty of Burrow's explication of King's theological social ethics in this book is that he reminds the reader that one doesn't need to be a Christian to promote social justice. One just needs to believe in critically examining "*what is* in light of *what ought to be*, according to the norm of agape love.... That is, once one investigates and determines that racism [or sexism or classism or homophobia] exists in one's work place or in one's church, for example, she is then required to reflect on the meaning of agape and what it requires in the face of such a state of affairs." In an era where state legislatures can pass bills allowing businesses to deny services to gay and lesbian customers on religious grounds and where young black men are haunted by the specter of being subjected to arbitrary state-sanctioned violence or even extra-juridical violence owing to their very bodies being considered dangerous, I think Burrow's demand that we respect the somebodiness of *all* people is timely and *necessary*. I also think that his King-inspired, prophetic call "to reflect on the meaning of agape and what it requires in the face of such a state of affairs" is perhaps the most effective means of promoting social justice in our fallen world. Indeed, that prophetic call, resounding in our ears as we dwell and toil in a fallen world, is the living spirit of King's theological social ethics. I would even claim that one should, nay ought to, read the fifteen chapters of this book as different yet related articulations of that spirit. I hope that by reading this book, those with ears to hear and eyes to see will heed the call and take up King's social activism as a way of life.

Dwayne A. Tunstall is an assistant professor of philosophy and African and African American studies at Grand Valley State University. He is the author of *Yes, But Not Quite: Encountering Josiah Royce's Ethico-Religious Insight* (2009) and *Doing Philosophy Personally: Thinking about Metaphysics, Theism, and Antiblack Racism* (2013) and also several book chapters on Martin Luther King, Jr., and on ethical personalism.

Introduction

By his own account, Martin Luther King, Jr. (1929–1968), was many things: father, husband, preacher, civil rights leader, author, recipient of a Ph.D. and dozens of honorary degrees, the Nobel Peace Prize, etc. But more important than all of these he made it crystal clear that he was fundamentally a Baptist preacher; a Christian minister; a man of the cloth in whom the fundamental principles of the Christian faith had deep roots. At the very center of King's life and civil rights ministry was his religious faith and theological convictions, most particularly his sense of God as personal and loving creator, and the source of the inviolable sacredness of every human being (without exception). The deepest foundation of these convictions may be found in his black Baptist upbringing and his rootedness in the black southern culture that was so dear to him. Although this book takes that stance for granted, its focus is on Martin Luther King, Jr., as a Christian theologian who not only loved ideas, but was committed from the very beginning of his civil rights ministry to applying them in efforts to address and eradicate the racism and economic injustice that hounded and dogged his people from the time of their enslavement in this country to his arrival in Montgomery, Alabama, in 1954, as senior minister of the Dexter Avenue Baptist Church.

This book examines the idea of Martin Luther King as a theologian and social ethicist who, because of his love for personalist and Christian ideas, relentlessly resisted social injustice through organized nonviolent direct action. In this regard, he was truly the quintessential theologian of resistance. (In this book "theologian of resistance" is taken to be synonymous with "theological social ethicist.") The focus, therefore, is on some of the basic personalist ideas that were important to King as he lived out his civil rights ministry. These ideas include, but are not limited to: the idea of God as personal, the sacredness of persons, the fundamental morality of the universe, the significance of moral laws, and freedom. Ideas such as these helped King to ground his thinking and socio-ethical practice theologically and philosophically.

The book also examines what it means to be a personalist in one's day to day living and what is required of one who desires to be a disciple of the type of personalism espoused by King.[1] And if one truly believes what is required by such a personalism, what is her moral responsibility to self and community, indeed, to self-in-community? As a theological social ethicist, Martin Luther King was never satisfied with the existence of injustice in the United States and the world. In speeches and writings, therefore, he frequently addressed the question: Where do we go from here? In his responses he generally included an element of imagination or visioning about what ought to be, indeed *can* be, if human beings in all spheres of society exhibit the will to make it happen, and then set out to do what they can to make it a reality.

5

Consequently, this book is also devoted to an examination of where King's basic Christian and personalist ideas must lead one who follows in his path, even if King himself fell short in some ways, e.g., in the matter of sexism.

Martin Luther King did not love ideas solely for the sake of loving ideas or of wanting to be seen as some kind of erudite academic. Although his doctoral training was in systematic theology, it was not long after beginning the work in the Montgomery, Alabama, bus boycott in December 1955 that he found himself eagerly doing the work of the social ethicist.[2] He soon found that his love for ideas played an important part in the stride toward freedom and liberation. His love affair with ideas dated back to his childhood in Atlanta where, around age six, he also promised his father that he would do all he could to help him address and eradicate the race problem. So it is not difficult to see that from an early age Martin Luther King had an appreciation for ideas as well as the need to apply them in the struggle for social justice. From college onward, he developed a sense of the intricate interrelationship between ideas and nonviolent direct action to set at liberty the oppressed. We see this dual emphasis on ideas and resistance in King from the beginning of his civil rights ministry in Montgomery, to its end in Memphis. In practice, these were not separate, unrelated emphases. Rather, for King they were integrally interrelated; they fed on, informed, and drove each other.

Martin Luther King was not the typical theologian who gave abstract lectures and wrote abstruse books that seemed to have little or nothing to do with how human beings behave toward each other and the world and what God required of them. As a theologian he loved ideas, but his experiences of racism and his understanding and interpretation of the Christian faith through the lens of his oppressed people forced him to essentially redefine what it meant to be a theologian. Writing books and giving lectures was an important but small part of it. One who spent so much of her time thinking about God, human beings, the world, and their interactions had also to take the lead in doing what God requires—put so poignantly by the prophet Micah—namely to do justice, love kindness, and walk humbly with God (Micah 6:8). The theologian—regardless of religious affiliation, but particularly Christianity—is obligated to do all she can to insure that justice is done in God's world. In a word, the theologian, accord-ing to Martin Luther King, must always be ready to resist anything and everything that under-mines the dignity and worth of human beings, individually and collectively. She must be a *theologian of resistance*, as well as possess a deep appreciation for ideas and their relevance for making the most of human beings and the world. Without question, Martin Luther King was the chief exemplar of the theologian of resistance. Moreover, such a one is a social ethicist in the best sense, a discovery that King himself made in the early months and years of his min-istry.

Martin Luther King loved ideas because he believed that the right ones, when creatively and relentlessly implemented, could help human beings and the world to be better than they were. Ideas, to be truly meaningful to King had to *do* something, had to be of use in the struggle to establish the community of love. This stance had as much to do with the seriousness with which King took the ethical prophetic tradition of the Jewish and Christian traditions than anything else. Such traditions placed much less emphasis on theories of justice, for example, than actually doing justice in the world. This is what the God of the Hebrew prophets required—that justice be done, not that theories of justice be devised, studied, and lectured about, although King surely understood that these latter have their place in the wider scheme of things. When used rightly, he believed, ideas could take us a long way toward building the beloved community in which the dignity of every human being will be acknowledged, cele-brated, and respected solely because they are human beings. As a theologian, however, Martin

Luther King added the significant dimension that human beings are inalienably and inviolably sacred because summoned into existence, sustained, enhanced, and loved by the God of the Hebrew prophets and Jesus Christ. By adding this dimension, King effectively grounded both his social ethics and his doctrine of human dignity, theologically.

As a lover of ideas and ideals, King operated fundamentally out of the personalist conceptuality. There is nothing hypothetical about this, since King himself declared that personalism—the doctrine that God is personal and persons are endowed with inviolable dignity—was his fundamental point of departure.[3] It is quite possible that King was first introduced to the term "personalism" during his student days at Morehouse College. It is known with certainty that he was introduced to the philosophy of personalism more formally and substantively at Crozer Theological Seminary, and read and studied it systematically at Boston University where he earned the Ph.D. The truth is that Martin Luther King was already a personalist by the time he arrived at Crozer, but he was not yet conscious of it. Unknown to him at the time, he had been introduced to personalist ideas throughout his upbringing in Ebenezer Baptist Church where his father was senior minister, and also in his home where his parents and maternal grandmother stressed the ideas of God as personal and loving, as well as the sacredness of all persons because they belong to and are loved by God. To the younger King, these were simply Christian ideas. He had no way of knowing at the time that they were also two of the fundamental tenets of the philosophy of personalism that he would study in seminary and graduate school. So important were these two personalist ideas (as well as personalism's emphasis on freedom and the moral foundation of the universe) for King that they appear in one form or another in the vast majority of his speeches, sermons, interviews, and writings.

Martin Luther King was more than a theoretical personalist. Unlike his personalist forebears at Boston University (where personalism was systematized and made a going concern by Borden Parker Bowne and his disciples), he distinguished himself by trying to *live* the personalist faith by applying its fundamental principles to the civil rights movement. King did this not as an academician like his personalist teachers, but through literally initiating and leading organized nonviolent direct action campaigns in the South and North in an effort to arouse the conscience and "save the soul of America" (as he liked to say) and to create the community of love where his people would no longer be victims of structural and other forms of racism and economic deprivation, but would be admitted to a state of equality with their white counterparts. As theologian of resistance, Martin Luther King literally put his life in the line of fire every time he led or participated in a nonviolent demonstration for freedom and justice. This book examines King's love of ideas, his commitment to applying them toward the establishment of his dream of the beloved community, and his sense of what was possible when human beings relentlessly exert their will.

I have been a professor of theological social ethics for over thirty years at Christian Theological Seminary in Indianapolis, Indiana. Having done my doctoral work at Boston University where Martin Luther King went because he wanted to study the philosophy of personalism under the premier personalist at the time, Edgar S. Brightman, I was, not surprisingly, required to take a course on the life, teachings, and work of King. This was at a time when dissertation after dissertation, book after book, was being written on King. Before completing doctoral studies I had concluded that so much had already—and was being—written on King that there could not possibly be anything I could contribute to King Studies. This, in large part, is why I did not teach or attempt to write on King in the early years of my tenure in the theological academy. The field, I believed, was already saturated with writings on King, which I naively took to mean that all that needed to be said about King was in fact being said, and said well.

Throughout much of the 1980s, then, I read very little on King, and made little effort to revisit his writings that I had read and studied under John J. Cartwright in graduate school at Boston University in the mid–1970s.

It was in a course I was teaching on the church and racism that I re-read King's writings on the 1963 Birmingham, Alabama campaign. Afterward, I became intrigued with what King had said about the racism of white liberals and white moderates. Soon thereafter, around the late 1980s, I decided to try my hand at writing an article on the subject and submitted it for publication. It was a couple of years before I heard back from the editor, who said that the journal was interested in publishing the article, *if* I would be willing to include relevant ideas from the Pulitzer Prize–winning books, *Bearing the Cross: Martin Luther King, Jr., and the Southern Christian Leadership Conference* (1986), and *Parting the Waters: America in the King Years 1954–1963* (1988), by David J. Garrow and Taylor Branch, respectively. I opted not to follow through on the editor's offer, partly because I felt that the assessment of the article should have been based solely on published scholarship at the time I submitted it, and also because by then my interest in King Studies had once again waned. Then, several years later (1992), I was reading what was premier King scholar Lewis V. Baldwin's second book on King, *To Make the Wounded Whole: The Cultural Legacy of Martin Luther King, Jr.*, when I discovered that he had read the manuscript I wrote on King, white liberals and white moderates. During Baldwin's research in Atlanta, he discovered a copy of the manuscript in the files of the journal, read it, and referenced ideas from it in his book.[4] Because Baldwin implied that I might have something to offer King Studies, I decided to begin reading the most recent scholarship on King, as well as his published and unpublished writings. In addition, I decided to offer an annual course on King, which meant that I would need to be aware of the most recent scholarship on King. I found this to be a monumental challenge, since the publications on King were constant. In any case, before long I began writing articles on King. Although the vast majority of these were published in the theological journal *Encounter*, I also published in *The Western Journal of Black Studies*, *The Lexington Theological Quarterly*, *The Personalist Forum*, etc. In addition, I began receiving invitations from religious organizations, universities, and seminaries, to speak and lecture on King, generally for King Day celebrations, during Black History Month, and also in classes on King at various colleges and seminaries.

About ten years ago, both a colleague at the seminary, and a former teacher, Ronald James Allen and James Earl Massey, respectively, recommended that I think about publishing a collection of these speeches and lectures. This is how the idea for the present collection came about. In some sense, a common theme runs through most of my writing on King, and the same can be said for this collection. I have been interested in King as one who loved ideas and ideals who devoted his life as civil rights minister to showing what this could mean concretely in efforts to establish the beloved community. King was convinced that such a community could be established only through organized nonviolent resistance. In my mind, at least, the term *theologian of resistance* best characterizes the Martin Luther King who has emerged from my studies and reflections. This is a King for whom ideas and relentless resistance to injustice are integrally related in ways that make for good and justice in the world. Indeed, for King as man of ideas and ideals (and as one who was truly educated), it necessarily followed that he also be devoted to changing or transforming the world in ways that are consistent with God's requirement that love and justice be done.

This book is comprised of three parts, with a total of fifteen chapters, a third of which were written expressly for this book. Others were presented as lectures at King Day celebrations at churches, seminaries, and colleges, and like those published in theological journals, have undergone extensive revision and updating (where appropriate) for this book. Because of the nature of the selections, the dates and contexts in which they were presented, it has been virtually impossible to avoid all redundancy, but I have succeeded at keeping it at a minimum.

The six chapters in Part I (Man of Ideas and Ideals) establish and examine the meaning of Martin Luther King as theologian of resistance, who loved ideas and ideals, and who, although his doctoral training was in systematic theology, came to think of himself as a theological social ethicist. King was, in the truest sense, a theologian of organized nonviolent resistance. He was one whose understanding of theology developed in horrendous conditions of racial oppression and who, by virtue of this fact and who he was as person, essentially had no choice than to be a theologian of resistance who loved ideas and ideals for what they could contribute toward the elimination of oppression and the establishment of justice.

Part I focuses on key personalistic themes and ideas that had a major impact on King's thought and practice. Chapter 1 defines and discusses the importance of King's conviction that the universe hinges on a moral foundation, or the idea that the universe is fundamentally moral, and thus is friendly to all efforts to achieve good, value, and justice in the world. It is an idea that has roots deep in the history of idealistic philosophy, Christian history, and the black religious tradition. What could the conviction that the universe is fundamentally moral mean for those who engage in efforts to dethrone injustice and establish the community of love? The chapter addresses this and related questions. Indeed, I think it is not possible to adequately understand King's social ethics in general, and his doctrine of nonviolent resistance in particular, if one fails to take seriously his faith that the universe is fundamentally moral, which is not the same as saying that we experience the day to day world this way. Rather, it is to say that from the foundation of the world, God infused the world with morality. That God also called persons into the world with freedom within limits to make choices is a reminder to us that despite the fundamental morality of the universe, human beings may—indeed frequently do—choose against what is best and most consistent with a value-fused universe and God's expectation that justice and righteousness be done in the world.

Martin Luther King frequently spoke and wrote about his deep love for the church. That is the focus of Chapter 2. It was because he loved the church as deeply as he did that he was among its staunchest critics. This was especially the case whenever the church failed to be the voice of the voiceless and the voice of conscience. The church, he said, "must be reminded that it is not the master or the servant of the state, but rather the conscience of the state. It must be the guide and the critic of the state, and never its tool.... If the church does not participate actively in the struggle for peace and for economic and racial justice, it will forfeit the loyalty of millions and cause men everywhere to say that it has atrophied its will."[5] In his famous "Letter from Birmingham Jail," King wrote of weeping over the failure of the church to be the moral thermostat of society, and yet he affirmed that his were tears of love. "There can be no deep disappointment where there is not deep love."[6] He loved the church. It was in his blood. After all, he said, he was the son, grandson, and great grandson of Christian ministers. "Yes, I see the church as the body of Christ," he declared. "But, oh! How we have blemished and scarred that body through social neglect and through fear of being nonconformists."[7] Without question, Martin Luther King believed the church has a major role to play in the world, particularly where social problems and matters of injustice are concerned. In his view, the church is obligated to give the moral lead based on the Christian ethical imperative of love-justice. King's deep faith that the universe hinges on a moral foundation is grounded not only in his personalist philosophy, but equally important, in his understanding of the church and what it means to be a Christian minister.

Chapter 3 turns to a consideration of the meaning of human dignity and how this doctrine influenced King and his civil rights ministry. The only doctrine more important to King than human dignity was his conviction that God is personal and loving creator, for God, according to King, is the ground of human worth. Human beings are of innate inestimable value because they are created and loved by God. King's way of putting it is different from philosophers he studied, e.g., Immanuel Kant, who argued that human beings possess innate dignity by virtue of being human beings. King added the theological element, claiming that human beings possess absolute dignity because they are imbued with the image of God and are loved and sustained by God. Therefore, persons possess inherent dignity by virtue of relatedness to God. The chapter examines some of the socio-ethical implications of King's doctrine of dignity, including whether there were areas in his practice that contradicted the personalistic theory of dignity that meant so much to him.

The subject of Chapter 4, King's personalism and moral laws, reminds us that unlike most post-modernists today, King was staunchly committed to the idea that God inserted universal moral laws at the seat of the universe that are discoverable by any rational being who seeks them. Such laws, he believed, are relevant to all rational human beings anywhere in the world. Moreover, King was convinced that the world functions rightly only when people strive to live in accordance with moral law. How did King define moral law, and where do we see evidence of such laws in his work? This chapter addresses these matters and is a good segue to Chapter 5, which tries to give the reader a sense, not merely of the type of philosophical personalism that influenced King, but of what he himself brought to that type of personalism. The main focus, then, is on what I refer to as the King type of personalism. What are similarities to the personalist ideas he learned at home (e.g., God as personal, and the sacredness of persons) and were reinforced through teachings in Sunday school, as well as sermons preached by his father and other black ministers in the Deep South? How was this *homespun personalism* similar to the personalism he studied in seminary and during doctoral studies? How was it different? What was King's greatest contribution to the personalist way of thinking and living in the world? These and related issues are discussed in Chapter 5.

How may we characterize Martin Luther King as theological social ethicist? Chapter 6 examines this and similar questions, and introduces ideas and principles that characterize his theological social ethics. The chapter addresses such questions as: What is the significance of God in Kingian social ethics? This is an important question, since I refer to King not as Christian social ethicist, but theological social ethicist. Although it is true that Jesus Christ has a place of centrality in King's thought, my designation of him as theological social ethicist places the emphasis on God. How did King, as theological social ethicist, differ from the likes of Walter Rauschenbusch and Reinhold Niebuhr, both of whom were (in their own right, but different from King) theologians of resistance who significantly influenced his theological development? What is the place of nonviolent direct action in King's social ethics? What is expected of one who claims to be influenced by King's theological social ethics?

There are six chapters in Part II (Pursuing the Dream). Chapter 7 focuses on Martin Luther King as human being and his vigilance in pursuing his dream. King was not a saint by any stretch of the imagination, and was the first to say so on more than one occasion. He realized that he had weaknesses and limitations like all human beings, and that even Christians sin and misses the mark. If we are to truly understand Martin Luther King and his contribution to making the world better than it was before he was born into it, it is imperative that we remember that he was thoroughly human, susceptible to all of the limitations and strengths as other human beings. In any case, the object, for King, was to remain faithful to God's call, and to exhibit an unswerving determination to do all one can to help realize the community of love. Chapter 7 examines these and other ideas related to King's pursuit of the dream.

A central idea in King's theological social ethics was his concept of the beloved community; a core ideal for all that he sought to do as theologian of resistance. What is the meaning of "beloved community" and how deeply is the idea rooted in philosophy, theology, and black religious thought and experience? To what extent was King influenced by Josiah Royce's doctrine of the beloved community? How did Royce express the doctrine, and what were points of convergence and divergence between him and King? What are the basic characteristics of the beloved community ideal, and to what extent are we, particularly those who are proponents of King's understanding of theological social ethics, obligated to actualize it? Is the beloved community achievable in history? Chapters 8 and 9 attends to these and related questions.

Chapter 10 provides reflections on King's famous "I Have a Dream" speech and its meaning for us fifty years later. The occasion for this speech was the March on Washington for Jobs and Freedom, August 28, 1963, which brought an estimated 250,000 Americans of all racial-ethnic backgrounds to the nation's capital. We learn that this was not the first time that American citizens either marched or planned to march on Washington, and that in no case was they welcomed with open arms by Washington politicians. Leaders of Corey's Army of the jobless were arrested and jailed when they arrived in Washington in 1894. Thousands of World War I veterans in the Bonus Army were tear-gassed and driven out of town by soldiers commanded by General Douglas MacArthur in 1932. Then, in 1941, when a surge in military spending began lifting white Americans out of the Depression, while the needs of unemployed blacks were ignored, Asa Philip Randolph, founder of the Brotherhood of Sleeping Car Porters, threatened Franklin D. Roosevelt's administration with a mass march of more than 100,000 blacks if they were not given equal employment opportunity in the defense industry. When the president issued an executive order that led to the establishment of the Fair Employment Practices Commission, Randolph did not cancel, but *postponed* the March on Washington. In addition to examining reasons that led Randolph to call for the famous march in 1963, Chapter 10 also considers the role and response of black women and the sexism they experienced throughout the planning of the march. Moreover, on the eve of the march, King met for several hours with a group to get ideas to go into his speech. No women were present. The chapter also discusses the question of whether Martin Luther King actually stole the Dream speech (as charged by one claimant) and how phrases and ideas of the famous speech were articulated in King's sermons and speeches as early as the mid to late 1950s. We learn that King actually gave two earlier versions of the Dream speech in Rocky Mount, North Carolina, and Detroit, Michigan, in November 1962 and June 1963, respectively. The chapter then examines the aftermath of the Dream speech, then and now.

Martin Luther King never claimed to be the movement, or to have even started it, despite what various entities in the media seemed to imply during movement days. King always acknowledged his awareness that the Montgomery bus boycott and the civil rights movement would have occurred even had he not been born. Moreover, he was also quick to point out that much good work had been done by many very good and committed people locally and nationally to prepare the way for the civil rights ministry he was able to do in Montgomery and beyond. He acknowledged that a chief contributor to the movement (from the beginning) was young people, whose struggle for freedom he was able to witness first hand. From Montgomery to Memphis black children and youths, and increasing numbers of white college youths, contributed much to the struggle for civil rights. Chapter 11 provides a sense of King's admiration and respect for the contributions of young people in the movement. Indeed, in this chapter we will see that he was much in awe not only of the accomplishments of youths affiliated with SCLC, but the student activists in SNCC as well (and these possibly even more so). King had many positive things to say about the student sit-ins and freedom rides, as well as the very dangerous Freedom Summer Project in the Mississippi Delta in 1964, and the Summer Community Organization and Political Education (SCOPE) Project the following summer. Reflecting on the Freedom Summer and SCOPE projects, King said that it was white youths, more than white adults, who were on the right side of the freedom struggle, and willing to sacrifice even their lives for that cause. Notwithstanding the mutual admiration and respect between King and youth activists, there were also periodic disagreements and conflicts which led inevitably to disappointment and divisiveness.

In Chapter 12 we are introduced to what is arguably one of King's most provocative and frequently misunderstood convictions, namely, that unmerited or "unearned suffering is redemptive." Womanists and a variety of other feminist thinkers have reacted sharply and critically to King's conviction. But what precisely did King mean by this claim? Did he mean, as some critics contend, that suffering as such is redemptive? What did he see as the relation between suffering due to systemic oppressions of various kinds, as well as efforts to eradicate the suffering? This chapter seeks to clarify King's sense that unearned suffering is redemptive, and reflects on whether all suffering caused by oppression is redemptive, or whether something must happen to make it so. The chapter also responds to the criticism and concern raised by womanists and feminist thinkers.

As a theological social ethicist, Martin Luther King knew the importance of understanding and being able to articulate the immediate state of affairs relative to some social, political, or economic condition, and how it affected those counted among the least of these. He also understood that it is one thing to be able to describe a particular state of affairs that crush massive numbers of people, but it is quite another to have the imagination and strength of character to say what should—indeed ought—to come next, and to suggest ways of making it happen. In other words, one should be able to say where we go from here, and what steps will need to be taken to get there. This is the general theme of Part III (Where Do We Go from Here?), and the three chapters that comprise it.

Chapter 13 turns to the issue of King's sexism and establishes that it was a contradiction of his doctrine of dignity, his personalism, as well as his understanding of the Christian faith. A consistent personalism requires that one respect the dignity of persons as such, as well as every individual person. (I put it this way because Fyodor Dostoevsky reminds us of the human tendency to love human beings in general, but not to love individual human beings very much at all.[8] I think the same holds regarding the idea of respect for human beings in general.) This is to be evident not merely in verbal expressions of respect for human dignity, but in concrete behavior, which is where the breakdown generally occurs. That Martin Luther King was sexist is clear evidence of his failure to be consistent with his ethical personalism and his understanding of the Christian faith. Among other things, this chapter reflects on what led to King's sexism, evidences of it, and whether he was aware of it. How did he respond to those women (usually black) who took offense with his male chauvinism? What does a consistent Kingian ethic require?

Chapter 14 addresses an issue that was very close to King's moral sensitivities, as well as the author's. To a large extent, this is attributed to the fact that each man is or was (in King's case) a son of the black community. A number of times, from Montgomery to Memphis, Martin Luther King found himself reacting to exorbitantly high rates of intra-community black violence and homicide. Even in his first book, *Stride Toward Freedom: The Montgomery Story*

(1958), we find him reflecting on and criticizing the high incidence of black-against-black violence. In the last book published before he was assassinated, *Where Do We Go from Here: Chaos or Community?* (1967), we find King lamenting the fact that on weekends the emergency rooms in far too many hospitals in inner cities are filled with victims of black-on-black violence. It is the tragic phenomenon of intra-community black violence and homicide, particularly as it affects young black males between the ages of 16–25, that is the concern of this chapter. In the mid–1980s the Centers for Disease Control in Atlanta declared young black males in this age category to be "an endangered species." Although the violence and homicides in black communities during King's day had not escalated to where they are today, the problem was serious enough even then that King was compelled to acknowledge the severity of it and urged that the violence cease, and that blacks assume responsibility for the specific acts of violence committed. Recognizing that blacks are responsible for such individual acts, King was just as adamant that there were environmental causes of this tragedy which were not completely in blacks' control, e.g., the consequences of long years of systematic racial discrimination and economic deprivation which has caused such unprecedented and exorbitantly high rates of underemployment and unemployment in black communities and all of the ugly and devastating social problems that have resulted. Among other things, this chapter considers whether there may be reasonable solutions to the phenomenon of intra-community black violence and homicide, i.e., to what is really a state of emergency in black communities and the nation.

One of Martin Luther King's toughest, most persistent challenges throughout his civil rights ministry was the failure of courage among white liberals and white moderates in the South and the North and their insistence on gradualism in the civil rights struggle. Chapter 15, the final chapter in this book, looks at King's reactions to liberals and moderates and considers and discusses his recommendations of what they should be doing. To what extent are white moderates and white liberals one and the same, and to what extent have they stepped up to the moral plate relative to issues of race in the 21st century? What needs to happen, and what may be good ways forward? This final chapter attends to these and kindred matters of concern.

Not nearly enough has been written that focus on the personalist social ethics of Martin Luther King and what this entails both theoretically and practically. Although not a systematic treatment of this, the present book at least attempts to provide some broad outlines. I believe that one is better positioned to understand King as social ethicist if he also understands that King was not merely a man of persistent nonviolent direct action, but a man of ideas, who actually loved ideas and contributed much to the world of ideas and ideals. From the time he was a boy, King loved not only "big" words, but also ideas. Around the age of six he told his father that he would do all he could to help him address and eradicate the race problem. He soon came to recognize the important role that ideas could play in such efforts, which helps to explain his seriousness as a student in seminary, and later during doctoral studies. In any case, any attempt to understand King's social ethics must also include a serious consideration of his love of ideas.

Although not much has been written and published on King as social ethicist, I think it appropriate to mention two sets of books that have in one way or another impacted my own scholarly approach to King studies. The first group include books that focus primarily on religious, theological, and philosophical ideas that influenced King's intellectual development: Ernest Shaw Lyght, *The Religious and Philosophical Foundations in the Thought of Martin Luther King, Jr.* (1972); Kenneth L. Smith and Ira G. Zepp, Jr., *Search for the Beloved Community: The Thinking of Martin Luther King, Jr.* (1974); Ervin Smith, *The Ethics of Martin*

Luther King, Jr. (1981); and John J. Ansbro, *Martin Luther King, Jr.: The Making of a Mind* (1982). None of these espouse the thesis of King as man of ideas, which is a primary focus of much of my prior work on King. In addition, they do not expressly present King as man of ideas *and* theologian of nonviolent resistance. Instead, the focus in each of these books is on the theological and philosophical ideas that influenced King in a substantial way. This is important for my own work, but I have the added interest of presenting King as one who not only loved ideas (as espoused by others), but brought his own ideas to the table when examining those of others. In making the ideas of others his own, King filtered those ideas through his own socio-cultural and mental grid.

Although these are excellent books in terms of what they each try to do, I find that a major limitation of the Kenneth Smith and Ira Zepp text and that of John Ansbro is their failure to include the black church, family, and southern black cultural influences on King's intellectual development, and thus do not place enough emphasis on the centrality and importance of his religious faith and family upbringing. Ernest Shaw Lyght and Ervin Smith both acknowledge the black church and southern black cultural influences on King, and thus are aware of the central place of his family and religious faith. However, neither of these authors examines deeply enough the idea of King as man of ideas, and like the others, they do not intentionally link this with my concern and emphasis on King as theologian of nonviolent resistance. Frederick L. Downing has probably given the most systematic attention to the centrality of religious faith for King in *To See the Promised Land: The Faith Pilgrimage of Martin Luther King, Jr.* (1986).

The second set of influential books include: Noel Leo Erskine, *King Among the Theologians* (1994), Richard Wayne Wills, Sr., *Martin Luther King, Jr. and the Image of God* (2009), and the edited collection by Robert E. Birt, *The Liberatory Thought of Martin Luther King, Jr.: Critical Essays on the Philosopher King* (2012). Significantly, in their own way each of these three texts make the argument for King as theologian, philosopher, or as thinker, which for my purpose, implies the authors' sense that King was a lover of ideas. Erskine does an excellent job of characterizing what for King is the chief theological task in the condition of oppression: 1) The need to work from within the struggle against oppression to apply the Christian faith to the blood and guts conditions that actually affect human beings. This is an acknowledgement that the theologian is obligated to apply basic Christian principles to solving social injustice. 2) The need to be committed to actual participation within the struggle against human oppression and be willing to give one's life if necessary. This is the closest that any of the authors named comes to declaring the need for the theologian to be more than a writer and lecturer on abstract concepts that are hard for people to grasp. Unfortunately Erskine does not do enough to flesh out just what it means to view King as theologian of resistance. 3) Recognize that the aim of liberation work is the reconciliation of alienated human beings and God; and 4) Strive to creatively join faith and praxis. By delineating these four theological tasks and citing the importance of applying one's faith to striving to eradicate oppression and to literally involve oneself in the struggle against injustice, Erskine comes close to what I want to do in my book. However, he does not focus on the significance of personalist ideas that ground King's theology of resistance or social ethics, nor does he raise and address issues that are addressed in various chapters in my book. Not unlike Erskine, Richard Wills also depicts King as theologian or one who loved ideas. He does an admirable job of presenting King as thinker, discussing his theological anthropology, and clarifying the conclusions and implications that King drew about the image of God. He does not come close to shedding light on King as theologian of nonviolent resistance, however. The collection of sixteen essays by mostly trained and teaching philosophers edited by Robert Birt does an excellent job of exploring various facets of King's legacy as philosopher and his relevance as thinker-activist. King is presented as a philosopher who both influenced and was influenced by Western philosophical tradition. Some of the essays present King as man of ideas, and some present him as the model nonviolent social activist, but none of the essays focus on King as man of ideas *and* theologian of resistance as depicted in my book. In short, what we find in Erskine, Wills, and the Birt anthology is all great stuff, but it falls short of what I try to do in this book.

PART I

MAN OF IDEAS AND IDEALS

1

The Universe as Fundamentally Moral[1]

It is indisputable that the keystone of Martin Luther King, Jr.'s theological social ethics was his *beloved community* ideal. The philosophical roots of this term can be traced to the work of the Absolutistic Personalist, Josiah Royce (1855–1916).[2] Royce viewed the beloved community as the criterion of all morality. Moreover, all morality is to be judged by its standards. Accordingly, every action is to be tested by whether it contributes to actualizing such a community.[3] Indeed, the "principle of principles" in Christian ethics, according to Royce, is that one does whatever she can to contribute to the establishment of the beloved community.[4] There is no question that in King's work as in Royce's, the beloved community is synonymous with the Kingdom of God ideal. This ideal dates back to the time of Jesus. Social gospel leader Walter Rauschenbusch argued that the Kingdom ideal was "the last social ideal of Christendom" and that it was at the center of Jesus's teachings.[5] King credited Rauschenbusch with providing him with a sound theological foundation for the passion for social concerns he grew up with.[6]

In a seminal essay, "Black Christians in Antebellum America: In Quest of the Beloved Community," Lawrence N. Jones has argued that blacks have been searching for the beloved community for as long as they have been in this country.[7] He further maintains that during slavery blacks primarily appealed to the Declaration of Independence and the Bible as they sought to ground their desire for the actualization of the beloved community.[8] These documents were their primary sources of authority on the matter. Jones's point is not that the term "beloved community" was known during the antebellum period. Instead, he sought to show that from the time of American slavery blacks have always sought inclusion in the type of society represented by what came to be known as the "beloved community"—a society based on justice, respect for self and others, and equality of opportunity to be the best that one can be.

Martin Luther King was utterly captivated by the beloved community ideal and how best to actualize it in the world, notwithstanding the fact that he nowhere writes systematically about it. One has to read the corpus of his published and unpublished writings, sermons and speeches, in order to piece together his philosophy, theology, or ethics of the beloved community. But important as this idea was for King, I want to focus on the significance of some of his basic personalistic doctrines (which also have implications for his beloved community ideal), their ethical implications for personal-communal living today, and how or whether they undergird the keystone of his theological social ethics, i.e., the beloved community ideal. Since

I devote chapters 8 and 9 to King, Royce, and the beloved community, I do not examine the concept fully here.

King grew up with a number of personalistic ideas. Of course, he did not know the term personalism at the time. At least four personalistic ideas had considerable influence on the young King: ultimate reality (God) is personal; persons are the highest intrinsic values; reality is social or relational; and the existence of an objective moral order at the center of the universe. That these ideas so quickly appealed to King in seminary and during doctoral studies at Boston University and helped him toward rational clarity regarding some of his fundamental faith claims is a testament to the family and religious values instilled in him during his childhood and adolescent years. Each of these personalistic ideas has important bearing on King's beloved community ethic. Among other things they give us important insight into the ground of this ethic and why King interpreted it as he did. For the purpose of this discussion, I focus on one of these ideas, namely, King's conviction that there is an objective moral order. He also expressed this in the idea that the universe hinges on a moral foundation. Since this is a basic personalistic doctrine, it is important to first establish the place of personalism in King's thought development. What follows is a cursory treatment of personalism, since Chapter 4 devotes significant space to it, and the entirety of Chapter 5 focuses on what I call the King type of personalism.

Homespun Personalism

To the extent that it is possible to say it of one whose life *was* the civil and human rights struggle, Martin Luther King, Jr., was a thoroughgoing personalist. In this sense he sought to reason personalism out to its logical conclusions in metaphysics, epistemology, the philosophy of religion, and ethics. Long before he was introduced to the term "personalism" or any of its chief representatives, King was introduced to some of its basic ideas through the teachings and example of his parents and grandparents (especially his live-in maternal grandmother, Jennie Celeste Williams).

As a little boy, King learned from his mother that he was as good as anybody, regardless of race; indeed, that he was *somebody*. He was somebody because he was a child of God. He was a being of infinite worth to God; precious and sacred beyond all measure. This was reinforced by his father who modeled for him what it meant to be in touch with one's own sense of dignity. Daddy King (as Martin Luther King, Sr. was called) refused to allow white racists to insult his personhood with impunity. Therefore, he always stood up for himself and his people—at times in the presence of his young son![9] King also learned from his parents a corollary of this principle, namely, that persons should love and respect each other as children of God. In addition, as a boy, King learned from the example of his father and maternal grandfather the need for his people to work together cooperatively and with God in order to assert their humanity and dignity and to demand that they be treated accordingly. He was taught by them the necessity of social protest and struggle if one desired to gain her rights as a human being and citizen of the United States. King was introduced by his father and grandfather to a basic Hegelian principle, namely that progress and growth come through struggle.[10] Years later he would critically examine this principle as a graduate student at Boston University. Like the previous principles, he would recite it in numerous speeches, sermons, and writings. King also received from his upbringing a strong belief in a personal and loving creator God who cares about the wellbeing of persons in the world and who is always present and working on their behalf.

As important as Boston University was for King's theological development, it did not make him a personalist. And yet, what it did do was critical for his subsequent work in the civil and human rights movement. King's study with prominent personalists at Boston University, e.g., Edgar S. Brightman and L. Harold DeWolf, provided for him a sound philosophical basis for the homespun personalistic convictions cited above.

It is unquestionably the case that Martin Luther King was what we might characterize as a personalist in the rough long *before* he went to Crozer Theological Seminary and Boston University. That is, his personalism was initially spun in his parent's home, in Sunday school classes and worship services at Ebenezer Baptist Church (pastored by his father), in courses under the instruction of Benjamin E. Mays and George Kelsey at Morehouse College, and in other areas of the black community. Early on, King's was a home and church grown personalism that was thoroughly mixed with strong family and black southern community values.

Through the formal personalistic framework provided by Brightman and DeWolf, King was able to critically reflect on the meaning and value of his homegrown personalism. In addition, the teaching of Brightman and DeWolf enabled him to draw out the deeper implications of the meaning of human dignity, the need for self-love and respect for others, belief in the existence of an objective moral order, the necessity of mutual cooperative endeavor between persons and God while working to achieve the beloved community, and his long held conviction that God is personal. Therefore, the formal study of personalism contributed much to King's overall theological and philosophical development.

Before proceeding with the discussion on King's conviction that the universe is grounded on a moral foundation and that its source is divine, it will be helpful to clarify the formal influence of personalism on his thought, inasmuch as a number of King scholars have sought to undermine its significance.

King and the Formal Influence of Personalism

At Boston University, Martin Luther King was a student under the premier personalist philosopher, Edgar S. Brightman, for a brief period only. King even wrote of Brightman's strong influence on his character development.[11] Since King also studied under DeWolf, who became his major advisor when Brightman died suddenly in 1953, there is no question that he was familiar with all of the basic concepts of personalism and its chief proponents. Indeed, what Brightman and DeWolf did was to give King a name for ideas conveyed to him by his parents, grandparents, and college professors. They also instructed him on the deeper philosophical, theological, and ethical implications of these ideas. Since King himself acknowledged personalism or personal idealism as his fundamental philosophical stance,[12] it is reasonable to say that he was, in the academically formal sense, a personalist.

While in graduate school, King wrote papers on the Bowne-Brightman type of personalism, comparing and contrasting it with that of other types, e.g., the atheistic personalism of John M.E. McTaggart.[13] He also compared Brightman's personalism to the philosophies of other thinkers, e.g., William Ernest Hocking (who was a friendly critic of personalism).[14] King wrote other papers like this, a practice which culminated in his dissertation: "A Comparison of the Conceptions of God in the Thinking of Paul Tillich and Henry Nelson Wieman" in 1955. He chose to write on the doctrine of God because of the central place it occupies in religion and because he believed it to be one of the perennial issues begging for further clarification.[15] He selected Tillich and Wieman primarily because they represented vastly different philosophical standpoints, which was conducive to his desire to compare and contrast at least two theological systems. Although King learned much from his study, Tillich and Wieman were essentially foils for highlighting the significance of a personalistic conception of God. Indeed, (the personalist) Borden P. Bowne's was for him the more reasonable doctrine of God. Arguing that God is both omnipotent, and omnibenevolent, Bowne's view was closest to that of the vast majority of black religionists, and thus to King's.

King was influenced by personalism's doctrine of the personal God of love and reason,[16] as well as the emphasis in personalistic ethics on moral laws and the inherent sense of the dignity and worth of persons as such. In light of this it is baffling to note that King scholars of the caliber of David J. Garrow[17] and Keith D. Miller[18] try to undermine the importance of personalism as a major influence on him. They imply that personalism played but a minor role in King's theological development.

Garrow is quite right to criticize early King scholars for their failure to stress the black church and familial influences on King's development, for these laid the foundation for what was to come during his formal seminary and doctoral studies. But Garrow could have made his criticism without also downplaying the influence on King of personalistic idealism. In any event, there is no question that King was both a metaphysical and an ethical personalist. That is, he believed in a personal God who is the ground of all things. He was also a staunch believer in the dignity and sacredness of all persons. "Every man is somebody because he is a child of God," King said. ... "Man is a child of God, made in His image, and therefore must be respected as such."[19] King maintained that persons have inviolable dignity because created, loved, and sustained by God.

Despite the tendency of some King scholars to downplay the significance of personalism in King's intellectual development, an examination of his writings confirms its importance for him. Garrow[20] and Taylor Branch[21] have pointed out that a number of King's speeches and essays were ghostwritten. For Garrow this means, in part, that we should not give much weight to references in many of King's speeches and writings to the key role of personalism in his theological development. In addition, Garrow argues that a serious limitation of much early scholarship on King was the failure to give serious—indeed any!—attention to the more formative or pre-academic influences such as the importance of being brought up in a black family under a father who was an outstanding pastor of one of the largest churches in Atlanta. So rather than begin, as most early studies on King did, with the written and formal academic influences on him, Garrow argues for the need to begin much earlier, i.e., with his childhood Bible instruction and his youthful and adolescent years observing his father as pastor of a large black Baptist church.[22] I find this to be one of Garrow's most important contributions to King studies.

No reasonable person can doubt the importance of this aspect of Garrow's concern. What I take issue with, however, is Garrow's implication that because a number of King's speeches and writings were ghostwritten, we should be apprehensive about accepting as truth his published claims about the importance of personalism for his theological and philosophical development. The problem with this part of Garrow's criticism is that long before King became so popular and busy that he needed others to write speeches, articles, and chapters in his books, he had already spoken and written of the fundamental role of personalism in his intellectual development.

In addition, there is no evidence that Martin Luther King ever denied the importance of personalism for his way of thinking about and doing theology and social ethics. King was a very good and incisive thinker. It would therefore be preposterous to think that he would not have challenged the accounts of ghostwriters regarding his basic philosophical standpoint if they in fact misrepresented him. Were he in basic disagreement with ghostwritten statements in this regard he would very likely have taken issue with them personally and through his own writings. There is no evidence that he disagreed with written statements about the influence of personalism on his thought. Not only did King acknowledge personalism as his fundamental philosophical starting point, but his wife wrote that he was "wholeheartedly committed"[23] to it.

Furthermore, one also gets a sense of the significance of personalism for King from papers he wrote as a seminary and graduate student. After all, had he not gone to Boston University precisely for the purpose of studying personalism under Brightman?[24] In addition, his doctoral dissertation is but a foil to highlight the importance of personalism. For example, in the dissertation we find him rejecting the view of Paul Tillich and Henry Nelson Wieman that God is "supra-personal."[25] Instead, King agreed with chief proponents of personalism that there is one of two ways to characterize God: as *impersonal* or *personal*. In addition, King insisted against Wieman and Tillich that the term "personality" as applied to God is theomorphic, not anthropomorphic. It is in God, not in human beings, that we get our best idea of the essence of *person*. The human person gives us our best clues to the meaning of *person*, to be sure. But the true essence of *person* is to be found only in God or the Absolute.[26] Following Bowne, King maintained that essential *person* is not commensurate with corporeality. Rather, *person* essentially "means simply self-consciousness and self-direction."[27] In God these reach a perfection that far surpasses that of human persons, who are but faint images of essential personhood.

God, in this regard, is the chief exemplification of what it means to be *person*. In addition, and also in his dissertation, King quoted approvingly from Knudson a statement that Thomas Aquinas made about God and essential *person*. "As Thomas Aquinas says: 'The name *person* is fittingly applied to God; not, however, as it is applied to creatures, but in a more excellent way (*via eminentiae*).'"[28]

The point of all this is that during his formal theological and graduate studies and the writing of his dissertation, King was unquestionably influenced by personalism. Furthermore, there is no evidence in anything that he said or wrote after graduate school that suggests a diminished influence of personalism in his life, thought, and work. And yet, King's personalism transcended that of his teachers.

Transcending the Personalism of His Teachers

Although he was to a large extent a thoroughgoing personalist, Martin Luther King's personalism transcended that of his personalist teachers in two major respects. First, his personalism was formed and forged in a hostile environment, and therefore against the odds. King's personalism developed in a social context that was not friendly to either his own nor the humanity of his people. Although his family was well off in comparison to many other blacks, all were victims of racism. All of this affected the contours of his personalism, giving it a qualitatively different look than that of his teachers. What King learned about human dignity, the need for self-love, and cooperative endeavor, he learned from the Bible, from behavior modeled by his parents and grandparents, and from what he knew of the black struggle and the contributions of black fore parents since slavery. These things were not learned primarily through reading philosophy and theology books and listening to highly refined lectures. NO. They were etched into King's soul and being while he was in the hot cauldron of human oppression.

There is an important corollary to this. King's personalism was hammered out in a hostile environment that was fused with social activism. Both his father and maternal grandfather were pastors who lived and modeled the conviction that the church is morally obligated to do all that it can to help the people to attain their full stature and rights as persons created in God's image. Ministry for them was not a 9–5 job. It was a vocation to which pastors are *called* by God. It requires that pastors be available to address the people's needs whenever they arise. These men believed that if the people are suffering under the iron feet of oppression the church is obligated to do all that it can to liberate them and help to restore them to wholeness. This leads to the second important way that King's personalism differed from that of his personalist teachers.

While also a metaphysical personalist, Martin Luther King was *fundamentally a social-activist personalist* inasmuch as he spent his entire professional life applying personalistic principles to solutions to the triple menaces of racism, economic injustice, and militarism. The meaning of King's personalism was worked out in the scorching heat of blacks' struggle for justice and regaining their lost sense of dignity, rather than in the relative comfort and safety of the classroom or in a cozy study. From the Montgomery, Alabama bus boycott to the sanitation workers' strike in Memphis, Tennessee, King lived with and through the constant threat of death. This was the context in which he forged his personalism, and why his was undoubtedly the most vibrant and relevant of the varieties of personalisms in existence during that period. I now turn to a more explicit consideration of King's conviction that the universe hinges on a moral foundation.

Objective Moral Order

An objective moral order is one that is relevant for all being. In this sense it is not relative (subjective) to the feelings of a single individual for who value is not in the nature of things. To speak of an objective moral order is to refer to that which is universal; that which can be experienced by all. It says something about the structure of reality as well as the universe itself. On this view, reality is so structured that value is its key ingredient. Any person who thinks reasonably is capable of acknowledging and sharing objective values. But in addition, an objective value is valid not only for individuals and groups, but for the universe.[29] The structure of the universe is grounded in moral values.

King came to the formal study of personalism with a deeply ingrained conviction that the structure of the universe is on the side of justice and righteousness; that there is a higher law than human law, and that persons violate it at great risk. The conviction that the universe is value-fused may be dated to a sermon that King gave at Morehouse College in his senior year. Samuel DuBois Cook, a classmate of King's at Morehouse, recalls that senior sermon delivered in the Morehouse chapel. "I remember, as if it were yesterday, M. L.'s great oratorical flourish. He asserted that there are moral laws in the universe that we cannot violate with impunity, anymore than we can violate the physical laws of the universe with impunity.... He electrified us."[30] Because of this homespun personalistic conviction, King could easily resonate to Brightman's doctrine of the existence of an *objective moral order* in the universe which persons ought to obey. The existence of an objective moral order is as real to one's moral experience as the objective physical order is to one's sense experience. Brightman made this point, saying: "Idealists hold that moral experience points to an objective moral order in reality, as truly as sense experience points to an objective physical order, and most idealists believe that the objective existence of both orders can be understood rationally only if both are the activity or thought or experience of a supreme mind that generates the whole cosmic process and controls its ongoing."[31] That persons have moral experience at all implies both that a moral order exists, and that it has a source. For the theist-creationist, that source is God. Therefore, to violate moral law places one in jeopardy with God and the universe. For, to violate moral law is to go against the grain of the universe, which is to disregard God's law. There can be nothing but grave consequences for violation of moral law, just as if one violates a physical law, e.g., the law of gravity. King was quite familiar with these ideas, inasmuch as Brightman formulated them in *Religious Values* (1925), and most systematically in *Moral Laws* (1933). King was familiar with both texts during doctoral studies.[32]

For Brightman as for King, the source of both the physical and the objective moral orders is God. King's belief in the existence of a moral order can be seen in a number of his speeches and sermons. For example, in one sermon he said: "God walks with us. He has placed within the very structure of this universe certain absolute moral laws. We can neither defy nor break them. If we disobey them, they will break us."[33] One cannot violate moral law without also having to contend with the consequences. In the same sermon King declared: "There is a law in the moral world—a silent, invisible imperative, akin to the laws in the physical world—which reminds us that life will work only in a certain way. The Hitler's and Mussolinis have their day, and for a period they may wield great power, spreading themselves like a green bay tree, but soon they are cut down like the grass and wither as the green herb."[34] This statement clearly reflects the influence of Brightman's view of the existence of an objective moral order in the universe which requires that persons live together in ways that are consistent with moral laws. These laws require respect and love for persons both as individuals and as members of communities. If persons choose not to live in harmony with these laws, all efforts to achieve the highest good both for self and for the common good will be unnecessarily hampered. For both persons and the universe are so structured that fundamentally there is in them a nisus or an inherent urge toward harmonious and communal living based on mutual respect, love, and sharing. This point is of no small importance for the beloved community ideal. Reality itself draws persons toward such an ideal. To disregard this is to severely jeopardize the quality of personal-communal living.

Violation of physical laws of the universe, such as the law of gravity, could mean severe consequences. We may expect the same when there is violation of the moral law on which all reality hinges. King, following Brightman, maintains that moral law in the universe is as absolute and permanent as physical law. If one intentionally jumps off the Bank One Tower in Indianapolis, Indiana, he violates the law of gravity. Unless he is incredibly lucky, he will either be severely injured or instantly killed. If he violates the law of gravity he can generally count on suffering the consequences. So too, are there consequences when one violates the moral law, which is also absolute and ingrained in the universe by God. We do not have to look far to see the consequences of human beings' violations of the law of love.

King maintained that because reality is value-fused, persons live in a moral universe. There was no doubt in his mind that in such a universe there are some things that are right, and some things that are wrong. In this regard there is no in between. Because there is a law of love in this value-fused universe, hatred, for example—and anything else that is contrary to love, according to King—is considered to be absolutely wrong. To disobey the law of love in a value friendly universe means that one is out of step with the beat of the universe and must face the consequences. And because love is a social category there will be consequences for both the individual and the community. To hate an individual or a group has consequences not only for the hater and the hated, but for the entire community, inasmuch as the social nature of reality means that persons are interdependent. In addition, to violate the law of love is to disobey God, since God is the author of moral law and that highest of moral laws.

King frequently quoted a line from the nineteenth century abolitionist preacher Theodore Parker: "The arc of the moral universe is long, [but] it bends toward justice."[35] By this, King was pointing to his fundamental conviction that no matter how much injustice exists in the world; no matter how badly one is treated by outside forces, there is something at the very center of the universe which sides with good and justice. The basis of this conviction is King's belief in the existence of an objective moral order created and sustained by the God of his faith.

To say that reality is value-fused may be interpreted to mean that there is a fundamental goodness at the core of the universe such that all being has an essential goodness, notwithstanding the capacity of human beings to behave in ways that are contrary to, or thwarts, goodness. At any rate, Martin Luther King believed that the universe is friendly rather than unfriendly to values and the achievement of value in the world. This means that everything that human beings do in the world has value implications. Therefore, there is no such thing as moral neutrality. In this regard, no person or group is allowed to escape the moral hook. The conviction that reality hinges on a moral foundation means that there are no moral holidays in the face of injustice, oppression, or other practices that undermine the dignity of human beings.

Because human beings are created in freedom, and thus are self-determining beings, they can choose to obey or disobey moral law. The rational awareness that reality is grounded on a moral foundation is not in itself sufficient to guarantee that persons will necessarily and always behave accordingly. God therefore creates persons with freedom of will (within limits). Persons are not only capable of knowing that the universe is friendly to values, but have the potential power to orchestrate their lives in ways that are consistent with such knowledge. In the area of morality there is no place for fence straddling. One stands for right, or she stands for wrong. There is nothing else.

King's conviction that the universe hinges on moral foundations means that persons ought, at all times, to live and relate to each other in ways that exhibit respect for their own and each other's humanity and dignity. The invisible eternal moral laws are a reminder that there are some things that are right and some things that are simply wrong, whether someone sees us do those things or not.

In King's view, God instilled value in the universe, and thus it may be said that the universe itself is on the side of all who endeavor to achieve and sustain the highest personal-communal values. "God has made the universe to be based on a moral law...,"[36] said King. The progress of humanity is therefore dependent on its willingness to come to terms with, and abide by, the conviction that the universe is grounded on a moral foundation, and God is its author and sustainer.[37] This was King's way of theologically grounding his firm belief that reality is value-fused.

King's many references to his belief that freedom fighters have cosmic companionship, was an outgrowth of, and a further solidification of, his conviction that the grain of the universe is on the side of right and justice. Those who are outraged at injustice and oppression, and who fight and strive toward the establishment of justice, have the assurance of being in harmony with the moral law and with God's will. Because human beings have constant cosmic companionship they—and most especially the poor and the oppressed—need never be dissuaded from their struggle against the forces of evil and injustice. King possessed an unqualified trust in this cosmic companionship.

Theologian J. DeOtis Roberts once criticized King for having "trusted the conscience of the white man, believing that the white conscience would be responsive to his nonviolent militant movement."[38] This was surely true of King during the early part of the Montgomery bus boycott, an admission that he himself made.[39] Indeed, looking back on that experience, King reflected on his naiveté during one of the early meetings with that city's white leadership. "I had gone to the meeting with a great illusion. I had believed that the privileged would give up their privileges on request."[40] Such an expectation could only have been based on an unwarranted optimism regarding human nature. King had assumed the basic liberal perspective that human nature is fundamentally good. He therefore believed that if one is essentially good and also an adherent of the basic principles of Christianity, he would willingly do the right thing when asked, and when made to see that injustice was being done. King did not, in this case, account for human sin, selfishness, and pride. Although he said that he learned a valuable lesson,[41] it is also the case that King sometimes, perhaps unwittingly, reverted to that earlier optimism regarding the white man's conscience. We see an indication of this in "Letter from Birmingham Jail," in which he admits his deep disappointment in the behavior of white moderates and pastors.[42] That he was disappointed implies momentary lapses when he again "trusted" the white man's conscience.

Nevertheless, a close examination of King's writings and speeches suggests that *he trusted God more than he trusted the conscience of whites*; trusted God more than he trusted that whites would respond positively and humanely to nonviolence and his beloved community ethic. Undoubtedly, King *wanted* to trust the conscience of at least well-meaning white moderates and liberals.[43] However, after the bus boycott experience he was realistic enough to know that frequently there was no basis for such trust. And yet, because King believed that all persons are children of God, he possessed a general optimism and trust that people of any race are at least *capable* of doing the right thing; *capable* of making themselves worthy of being trusted. King believed that human beings have the innate capacity to be better than they are at any given period of their mature lives. But because of his conviction that sin exists on all levels of human existence, and because of his awareness of the prominence of human greed and selfishness, King knew that mere appeals to the conscience of whites would not be sufficient to move most of them to do justice. At least there is no historical evidence that this has been the case. He was especially cognizant of this after the Albany, Georgia and Chicago campaigns where he experienced racism in some of its most blatant and vicious forms. Therefore, we may conclude that King was not as naive about such matters, and about the abuse of power, as Roberts maintained.[44]

At the end of the day, what really mattered to Martin Luther King was not that God is perfectly powerful, but that God is able to achieve God's purpose in the world through cooperative endeavor with willing human beings. King's firm conviction that such cooperation between persons and God is needed in order for blacks to regain their sense of dignity and their freedom also points to the hypothesis that he did not adhere to the classical view of divine omnipotence. For a God who possesses either all, or perfect power, does not need the assistance of created persons to actualize this or that aspect of God's purpose in the world. That is, if we understand ourselves and are serious when we say that God possesses absolute and perfect power, we must see that God does not *need* human cooperation in order to accomplish God's purpose in the world. A God who possesses perfect power can accomplish all divine purposes without human participation. And yet, very much of Jewish and Christian history reveals God, and human beings of faith, working together toward the achievement of divine purpose.[45]

Unquestionably, it was King's conviction that God's purpose is best achieved when human beings and God work together cooperatively. An infinitely loving God of "matchless" or "boundless" power, but not absolutely perfect power, would want and need the cooperation of free self-determined individuals in the struggle to overcome injustice and to achieve (as nearly as possible!) the great "World House" or the "Beloved Community." As human beings cooperatively strive toward the actualization of the beloved community, God works unceasingly with them.[46]

Martin Luther King believed that blacks have a major role in the struggle for human dignity and freedom, which is why he was so adamant about the importance of black self-determination, a point he made after the passage of the severely watered down Civil Rights Act of 1957.[47] For King, the world's salvation will be brought about by neither God nor created persons alone, but by their mutual cooperation. In this regard he said that, "both man and God, made one in a marvelous unity of purpose through an overflowing love as the free gift of himself on the part of God and by perfect obedience and receptivity on the part of man, can transform the old into the new and drive out the deadly cancer of sin."[48] In addition to King's insistence on the need for cooperative endeavor between persons and God in the struggle to actualize the beloved community, what are some ethical implications for his belief that the universe is friendly to value and thus hinges on a moral foundation?

Ethical Implications for Today

Martin Luther King's most original and creative contribution to the personalist tradition was his relentless persistence in translating personalism into social action by applying it to the trilogy of social problems he vowed in seminary to focus on throughout his ministry—racism, poverty/economic exploitation, and militarism.[49] By focusing on socio-ethical personalism, King was only following the precedence set by the black John Wesley Edward Bowen (1855–1933). But more than any other personalist, King forged the concept of the dignity of the person in the fire of nonviolent demonstrations, which often pitted demonstrators—including children and youths—against vicious and venomous racists, high-powered fire hoses, and vicious attack dogs.

That King was a member of a race of people who have been systematically discriminated against from the time of American slavery to this writing, is reason in itself that he would be the premier social-activist personalist in this country. It would not have been enough for him to merely study the philosophy and theology of personalism and then write monographs on the subject to satisfy the intellectual curiosity of those who do not suffer under—but benefit from—the iron feet of oppression and injustice. For King, it was never enough to simply know the chief tenets of personalism. King was from a long tradition of blacks who believed that *to know* obligates one morally. That is, to know the truth necessarily means to do what it requires. *To have the truth is to do the truth*, a view that has not been popular in white western civilization. For King, the truth may be an end in itself only if to have access to it means also that one is required to do what possessing the truth demands. King was not consoled by simply having the truth for the sake of having the truth. Therefore, he could not merely accept as truth the personalistic conviction that God is personal and loving; that persons are ends in themselves, and thus possess infinite dignity, without also applying the meaning of these convictions to the everyday affairs of concrete flesh and blood human beings.

But something else pushed and pulled King toward social-activist personalism, and would not let him be content with a theoretical or abstract personalism that did not address human beings' everyday lives. I have shown that he believed that there was something about the nature of reality itself that places on all persons a moral onus to act to eliminate injustice and oppression in whatever forms they are manifested. That is, King believed that the "stuff" of reality is of the nature of value or that which is moral. Reality is grounded on a moral, rather than an immoral or even amoral, foundation. This has important implications for individual and communal living in the world.

Indeed, not only does it have implications for personal-communal living, but for how persons relate to all aspects of God's creation. For the conviction that reality hinges on moral foundations must be applicable to the entire creation, not merely to that which pertains to persons and their communities. In other words, the conviction that the universe is grounded on value means that any viable personalism must be *ecopersonalism*. That is, it must acknowledge not only the intrinsic worth of all life forms—human and nonhuman—but must be concerned about how they interrelate and contribute to the wellbeing of other areas of creation. Ecopersonalism also will be concerned about how to insure respect and appreciation for every life form. It will be concerned about the moral relations between persons and the natural world.

What does it mean for our personal-communal living when it is said that the universe is friendly to value, or that it hinges on a moral foundation? We can be certain that when Martin Luther King made this declaration he was saying something deep and profound about the fundamental nature of the universe and the way(s) human beings ought to be, and live in, the world. He was saying that the universe, indeed reality itself, is based on a moral foundation. This, he believed, has everything to do with how human beings should think and relate to themselves, other persons, and the rest of creation. King's declaration means that every life form, human and nonhuman, has intrinsic value, although life forms do not all have the same degree of worth. A person, for example, has more value than a dog, although this is not always evident in the way we humans treat each other in relation to how we treat dogs. The point is that, although we may rank the worth of life forms on a scale, all life forms have value in themselves.

The claim that there is an objective moral order and that the universe is grounded on moral values also says something quite profound about the nature of the Creator. King was both a theist and a creationist. He lived by the conviction that as Creator, God is personal. Minimally, any personal being has the capacity for rationality or intelligence and for self-determination. As Creator, then, God would be both the supreme exemplification of rationality and self-determination. In addition, the source of these traits in all human beings must be attributed to God.

If God is supremely intelligent and self-determining, it is reasonable to conclude that God thoughtfully and willingly established the universe on a moral foundation. This not only implies God's essential love and goodness, but it says something about how God expects persons to treat each other in the world. It also says something about how God must expect persons to behave in the world, individually and communally.

If one is really serious when she says that the universe is friendly to value, it must be the case that whatever else she may do, she simply cannot intentionally violate her own or the personhood of others. One cannot intentionally adhere to a racist, sexist, heterosexist, or classist lifestyle if he truly believes in the existence of an objective moral order whose source is the God of Martin Luther King. For this God requires that justice be done in the world, and that it be done in ways that both respect and enhance the dignity of human beings. This God requires that individuals live in communities where respect for the dignity of persons and love of persons is the rule rather than the exception.

The universe is created in such a way that everybody ought to be treated with dignity and respect just because they are. For the claim being made here is that the universe is charged with value, or that which is moral. Since the universe is value-fused, moral agents such as human beings are obligated to acknowledge, respect, and appreciate the value of all life forms. And now, more specifically, what does it mean for our personal-communal living when it is said that the universe is friendly to value, or that it hinges on a moral foundation?

For one thing, it means that every person, regardless of gender, race, class, health, sexual orientation, and age is imbued with the image, fragrance, and voice of God. Because God is both rational and self-determining we may say that God thoughtfully and willingly calls every person into existence. No person exists by accident. God calls every person into existence, and, as blacks like to say, called each one of us by name! Thus, every person has absolute and infinite value, for every person belongs (in the best sense) to God. Martin Luther King was fond of saying that every human being is somebody, because every single one is a child of God.[50] Every person has infinite worth, because every person is created and loved by God.[51] As such, we owe self and each other respect. Indeed, whenever and wherever any two or more persons meet in the world, they owe each other respect and good will.[52] In addition, no person or group should be easily sacrificed for the wellbeing of another, considering that each is equally imbued with the image of God. King put it poetically. "There are no gradations in the image of God. Every man from a treble white to a bass black is significant on God's keyboard, precisely because every man is made in the image of God."[53]

The conviction that the universe hinges on a moral foundation also implies the need to exert a strong sense of *self-determination* in the face of dehumanizing and oppressive practices. In such cases, human beings are obligated to exert to the fullest their will to overcome injustice and demeaning practices. Although blacks are not responsible for their oppression, King, not unlike Malcolm × and a host of black ancestors, was convinced that they are responsible for how they respond to what has been (and is being) done to them. They are responsible for their liberation and empowerment. No matter how violently their personhood is assaulted by powerful and racist whites, for example, it is within blacks' power as persons to accept such treatment or not; to fight to eradicate it, or not. King did not excuse what racist whites had done and were doing. His primary focus was on the recovery of his people and the conviction that they themselves possessed the key to their recovery and freedom. He was confident that because of the long history of the African protest tradition, his people had in them what it takes to regain their sense of dignity and worth. Indeed, they are morally obligated to do this because the universe stands on a moral foundation.

King said that there was no lack of human and other resources to solve the problems that were created to undermine black personhood. What was lacking, he believed, was the will to make the effort. In this, he sounded much like Bowne, who argued that the basic deficit in ethics is the will to do the right thing.[54] But also like Bowne, King conceded that the mere possession of a good will would not in itself solve social problems. And yet, such a will must be the basis of all ethics—a necessary prerequisite to solving social maladies; a necessary element in the enhancement of human dignity. If one has the will to do the right thing he can usually find a way to do it. But it will require both effort and courage. King himself held firm to the conviction that human progress never rolls in on the wheels of inevitability.[55] Progress occurs when human beings believe that the grain of the universe is on the side of right, justice, and righteousness, *and* when they set about to work cooperatively with each other and with God to achieve justice and the common good.[56]

Martin Luther King was convinced that his people would not regain their lost sense of dignity, nor their freedom, without a staunch determination and willingness to struggle to overcome and to stand up. He frequently reminded his people that a new sense of dignity would come about only through determined struggle and hard work. The awareness that there exists an objective moral order, and that the universe hinges on a moral foundation is not sufficient in itself to guarantee that human beings will behave in ways that are consistent with, and honors such a conviction. But there is consolation in the faith that the universe itself is so constructed by God that human beings will live and prosper only if they live in ways that encourage living together respectfully as sisters and brothers. God has infused the universe and all being with value. Therefore, when human beings and groups intentionally strive to live according to the highest moral principles, they live in obedience to moral law.

Finally, another implication of the claim that the universe is friendly to value is that human beings and communities have to own responsibility for what happens or is allowed by them to happen. The faith that the universe is infused with value does not undermine the existence in human beings of moral agency. Persons are free within limits to make choices. This means that individuals must also own responsibility, and be willing to face the consequences, for the choices made. That the universe hinges on a moral foundation implies that persons are created with the capacity to do what is good, just, and noble. And although people also have the capacity to do the opposite, in the end they are responsible for the direction chosen.

2

The Church and a
Value-Fused Universe[1]

In the opening sentence of the conclusion to his famous *Critique of Practical Reason*, Immanuel Kant declares that the more one reflects on two things, the mind is filled with ever more admiration and awe: the starry heavens above, and the moral law within.[2] I too am awed by these phenomena. However, there is yet another phenomenon that fills me with even deeper admiration and awe.

Whenever I consider the seemingly infinite ways that we humans choose to disrespect and destroy life—most particularly human life—I am absolutely speechless and awed when I think about this third phenomenon, and indeed, I wonder why Kant himself did not include it when he made his famous statement. When I consider the history of blacks and how they were ripped and stolen from the African continent, making them *not* "unwilling immigrants," as Marvin Scott erroneously claimed at the 2004 Republican National Convention, but rather the only group of Americans who came to these shores not by choice, but by force, I am awestruck by this third phenomenon. When I consider the near total genocide of the native peoples of this country; when I remember the events leading to, and the aftermath of the Treaty of Guadalupe Hidalgo in 1848 that led to the United States' acquisition of approximately one-half of Mexico for a measly $15 million, and then think about this third phenomenon, I am filled with both admiration and awe.

When I think about the tragic phenomenon of black-against-black violence and homicide among young black males between the ages of fifteen and twenty-five in many cities throughout the United States; when I consider the plight of young Latinos; the verbal, physical, and other kinds of abuse inflicted upon women and children in virtually every city in this nation; when I remember that tens of thousands of children in this country and around the world die of preventable disease, hunger, inadequate housing, and unsafe neighborhoods every year; when I am reminded that various elements in the church and its institutions have added their signature of support to war (murder); when I consider that otherwise racist segments of this society and the church consider themselves to be morally superior to those whose sexual orientation is different from theirs, I must say that I am absolutely awed, and indeed overwhelmed, by this third phenomenon, which is that the God of this great universe, the God of the eighth-century prophets, of Jesus Christ, and Martin Luther King loves you and me, both *because of us, and in spite of us.* I am filled with awe and admiration when I reflect that the great God of the universe loves you and me.

I am even more awed by this when I remember the utterly savage things human beings do to each other.

There was a man whose deepest faith was in this great God of the universe, a man whose steady conviction was that the universe is fused with value, or, as he often declared, the universe "hinges on a moral foundation."[3] Or, stated differently, the universe itself is friendly toward value, toward every effort to achieve good, love, and justice in the world. Few have understood the significance of this declaration and faith, and how it served in moments of deepest despair, depression, fear, and uncertainty to propel Martin Luther King forward, enabling him to stay the course, and to remain in the margin with those counted among the least of sisters and brothers.

Without question, Martin Luther King was also awed by "the starry heavens above, and the moral law within." But I submit that he was even more awestruck by the Jewish and Christian affirmation that God loves us. So much and so deeply did King believe this that he could not support capital punishment,[4] nor could he support the Vietnam War, one of the most controversial conflicts of the twentieth century. For King, the biblical commandment, "You shall not Kill," did not mean, "You shall not murder," for this would imply that the state, for example, has the right to kill its internal and external enemies by lethal injection or preemptive strike. Rather, for King, "You shall not kill," means *You shall not kill!* This implies that to kill under any circumstance whatever, whether in self-defense, or to preserve a state or nation, means that one must ultimately answer to the God of this great universe.

Dietrich Bonhoeffer was one of the few people in history who understood this as well as Martin Luther King. A pastor and theologian of resistance like King, Bonhoeffer participated in a plot to assassinate Adolf Hitler. When the plot failed, Bonhoeffer and others were discovered, imprisoned, and ultimately hanged. Before he was marched off to the gallows, Bonhoeffer had ample opportunity to reflect on his involvement in the attempt to get rid of Hitler. While he clearly wanted the plot to succeed, he was almost devastated by heaviness of heart regarding his own participation in the failed attempt. He recognized that notwithstanding Hitler's massive brutality against millions of God's children, Hitler too belonged to the same God, and thus was loved by that God, although God too must have grieved uncontrollably over the monstrosity of the crimes against humanity committed by Hitler and his henchmen. Bonhoeffer believed, just as King did, that God gives life, that all life belongs to God, and therefore no man, woman, state, or nation has the right to take a life. Anyone who does so or even successfully plots to do so—regardless of the reason—must at least be left with extreme heaviness of heart and conscience akin to what Bonhoeffer experienced.

Any who would follow Bonhoeffer's path must remember what his close friend and biographer, Eberhard Bethge, reported. Bethge reminds us that Bonhoeffer had no interest or desire to defend his involvement in the plot to assassinate Hitler, but he desired to take responsibility for his own actions. Although he kept many notes of his involvement in the failed plot, he believed that only God could provide justification (or not!) for his actions.[5] Indeed, Bonhoeffer himself admitted:

Those who in acting responsibly take on guilt—which is inescapable for any responsible person—place this guilt on themselves, not on someone else; they stand up for it and take responsibility for it. They do so not out of a sacrilegious and reckless belief in their own power, but in the knowledge of being forced into this freedom and of their dependence on grace in its exercise. Those who act out of free responsibility are justified before others by dire necessity [Not]; before themselves they are acquitted by their conscience, but before God they hope only for grace.[6]

So horrific were Hitler's crimes against the Jewish people in particular, and humanity in general, that Bonhoeffer felt compelled to do whatever was necessary to stop him. And yet, so deep was his conviction that all life belongs only to God and is precious to God, that he knew he would have to answer to God personally for the attempt on Hitler's life, as that life also belonged to God.

This is what too many politicians and religious people do not know or want to know: the God of the Hebrew prophets and Martin Luther King has created human beings such that they are all members of one family. They are all sisters and brothers, under God, whether they like it or not. Former President George W. Bush and Osama bin Laden were brothers, no matter how much they despised and wanted to kill each other and thousands of innocent people in the process. In King's view, there are no outsiders in God's family. In this regard, everybody belongs, unless, of course, the words we find in Ezekiel 18:4 are little more than a misprint. Here God puts into the mouth of the prophet the words: "Know that all lives are mine; the life of the parent as well as the life of the child is mine." Therefore, there are no outsiders. Every person is an insider in God's family. This means black, brown, red, gold, and white folk alike. It means rich and poor, gay and straight, Jew and Arab, Palestinian and Israeli.[7] All belong to the same family and the One God of the universe.

Retired Anglican Archbishop Desmond Tutu argues that it is a significant aspect of God's dream for humanity that we behave as brothers and sisters, or a family. Family is God's gift to each of us,[8] and what God gives, no human being can take away. This means that no matter what cruel acts a person commits, she remains our sibling, part of God's family, forever. This reminds me of something my late brother, Jeffrey, used to say when there was tough goings among family members. "The thing about family members," he would say, "is that you can't get rid of them. You're stuck with them, no matter what. You're stuck with them for life."

The Christian ethic is a very tough ethic by which to live, individually, and most especially, collectively. Most people have no clue just how radical the claim is that all persons are members of God's family, and that whether we like it or not, we are created for God and each other. Archbishop Tutu put it this way:

> If we could but recognize our common humanity, that we do belong together, that our destinies are bound up in one another's that we can be free only together, that we can survive only together, that we can be human only together, then a glorious world would come into being where all of us lived harmoniously together as members of one family, the human family, God's family. In truth a transfiguration would take place. God's dream would become a reality.[9]

And God's dream is for the achievement of the beloved community, that community in which every person—regardless—is respected and treated as the sacred and precious one that she is. The Bible teaches that persons are essentially created by God in community, for community. Therefore, no person can be all she can be without other persons. We are made for community, for relationship, for each other, and *not* to be alone. Moreover, inasmuch as every human life is sacred before God, it should be understandable why the commandment says, "You shall not kill."

One who feels compelled to kill—whether presidents, prime ministers, dictators, state executioners, religious leaders, or individual citizens (even in self-defense)—should be left with unbearable heaviness of heart and conscience, as well as a sense of the assurance that inasmuch as God disapproves, they will have to answer for the destruction of human life. And yet, tragically, we know that most often this is not the case. Human life is frequently destroyed almost as a matter of course, and with virtually no pangs of conscience experienced by the killer. Have you ever been stunned senseless, as I have, as to how easily many politicians, as well as professing Christians, proclaim the need to track down and kill "the terrorists"? Rarely is a single thought given to the theological affirmation that we are all sisters and brothers under God, and that this affirmation includes the terrorists too.

I can't help wondering what would likely be Martin Luther King's message to us today regarding such a matter. While we cannot know with absolute certainty what King would say since he no longer lives, I am certain that we may gather clues from how he thought about the church and the role of ministers in the social struggle. In addition, we may surmise what he might say to us when we consider implications of his firm conviction that the universe is built on justice and morality. Before examining this, however, I want to say a word about King's staunch realism regarding the church and those who profess a call to ministry.

The Church and the Minister

The very first thing we have to know about Martin Luther King is that he was, first and last, a Baptist preacher. "This is my being and my heritage," he said, "for I am also the son of a Baptist preacher, the grandson of a Baptist preacher and the great-grandson of a Baptist preacher."[10] In spite of his stature as civil and human rights leader, orator, and lecturer, as well as his numerous academic, humanitarian and other awards including the Nobel Peace Prize, King was, at the end of the day, "a preacher by trade."[11] He was a preacher of the gospel before he became a civil rights leader. Ministry was his first, most important calling, and to the end remained his "greatest commitment." Moreover, King declared that everything he did in the civil rights movement he did because he considered it part of his ministry. He said, "I have no other ambitions in life but to achieve excellence in the Christian ministry."[12] King seemed to have a sense of ministry as the greatest vocation in the world, one that required the absolute best that a person had to give. Ministry was, for him, a matter of life and death, as it should be for anybody who claims to be called by God.

The true Christian minister is neither in the entertainment business nor in the business of appeasing and placating well to do and privileged church members in their wrongdoing. The true preacher of the gospel understands clearly what God expects, namely, that followers of God promote justice, love mercy, and walk humbly with God. By virtue of being called by God, the minister knows that she is called not to be successful in a material sense, but to be faithful to God's expectation that she be a voice for the voiceless in the face of injustice, rather than conform to the expectations of politicians and others who turn a deaf ear to the cries and pain of the poor and oppressed among us. Indeed, King had this in mind when he preached against the tendency of ministers to be conformists rather than radically transformed noncon-formists.

Furthermore, King did not hesitate to criticize his colleagues in ministry who seemed to value personal success and church growth—"jumboism" he called it[13]—more than securing justice for those counted among the least of the sisters and brothers. If only more of today's ministers would follow his example. In this regard King admonished:

> We preachers have ... been tempted by the enticing cult of conformity. Seduced by the success symbols of the world, we have measured our achievements by the size of our parsonage. We have become showmen to please the whims and caprices of the people. We preach comforting ser-mons and avoid saying anything from our pulpits which might disturb the respectable views of

the comfortable members of our congregations. Have we ministers of Jesus Christ sacrificed truth on the altar of self-interest and, like Pilate, yielded our convictions to the demands of the crowd?[14]

Who among us can deny that many sectors of the church, historically, have easily conformed to the worst ideas and practices of society, whether racism, sexism, heterosexism, homophobia, ageism, or ableism? Indeed, King believed that nowhere is such conformity a more tragic tendency than in the church. In this regard he said:

> The erstwhile sanction by the church of slavery, racial segregation, war, and economic exploitation is testimony to the fact that the church has hearkened more to the authority of the world than to the authority of God. Called to be the moral guardian of the community, the church at times has preserved that which is immoral and unethical. Called to combat social evils, it has remained silent behind stained-glass windows. Called to lead men on the highway of brotherhood and to summon them to rise above the narrow confines of race and class, it has enunciated and practiced racial exclusiveness.[15]

Martin Luther King was quite aware that from its inception, the early church contained prophetic elements in its body, and he was essentially calling for the church of his day—as we must demand of the church today—to recapture its prophetic zeal. The consequence of the failure of most churches in this regard is obvious, inasmuch as they have already become what King characterized in 1963 as irrelevant social clubs "without moral or spiritual authority."[16] The rare church that has not lost its prophetic edge and zeal eagerly and actively speaks God's truth to the powers that be, and leads the way in the social struggle, instead of waiting for that leadership to come from politicians, business and industry, or educational institutions. The early church was a countercultural community, not the status quo organization many congregations have become. By the church recapturing its historic mission of speaking and acting passionately, "fearlessly and insistently in terms of justice and peace, it will enkindle the imagination of mankind and fire the souls of men, imbuing them with a glowing and ardent love for truth, justice, and peace. Men far and near will know the church as a great fellowship of love that provides light and bread for lonely travelers at midnight."[17]

Here was a preacher who, despite his deep disappointment with the church, and his shedding of many tears because of its failure to advance the work of justice, actually deeply loved the church. King's tears were "tears of love. There can be no deep disappointment where there is not deep love,"[18] he said. Notwithstanding this, King knew that the church, as the body of Christ, had been "blemished and scarred" as a result of failing to be nonconformist.[19]

My own sense about this is that the church is in much more trouble in this regard than it was during the period of social upheaval in the 1960s and 1970s. A case in point: How many of our pastors preach from and about the Hebrew prophets, those most peculiar personalities to have crossed the stage of history? Upon entering the office and library of our pastors, how many commentaries and other books do we discover on and about the prophets of the eighth century BCE? Surely one must wonder, as I do, why so many pastors literally refuse to preach from the prophets, those persons who relentlessly and fearlessly proclaimed, "Thus says the Lord!" to their own members, let alone the powers that be. Most pastors barely mention the names of the Hebrew prophets, let alone preach from them, and endeavor to connect their message to what is happening in society, the nation, and the world. For if they did, they would immediately be convicted and propelled to a deeper sense of faith and commitment to God and to those counted among the least of these.

Martin Luther King rightly believed that it is virtually impossible to talk seriously about ministry and the church without also stressing as fundamental the prophecy represented by the likes of Amos, Micah, Jeremiah, and Isaiah. In his speech at Mason Temple on the night before he was assassinated, King said:

> Who is it that is supposed to articulate the longings and aspirations of the people more than the preacher? Somehow the preacher must have a kind of fire shut up in his bones, and whenever injustice is around he must tell it. Somehow the preacher must be an Amos, who said, "When God speaks, who can but prophesy?" ... Somehow the preacher must say with Jesus, "The spirit of the Lord is upon me, because He has anointed me, and He hath anointed me to deal with the problems of the poor."[20]

King's good friend and supporter, Rabbi Abraham Joshua Heschel, was convinced that the Hebrew prophets had a strong sense of "the monstrosity of injustice,"[21] of whatever type. God requires that the minister of Jesus Christ be as outraged over seemingly minor injustices as the major ones. Any injustice, whether in Indianapolis, Indiana where I live, throughout the United States, or the world, that comes to the attention of any minister of Jesus Christ, regardless of his racial-ethnicity, sexual orientation, or class, should lead to nothing short of vociferous moral outrage and protest. Injustice must always summon the strongest possible rebuke by one who claims to be called by God. In words that could have been King's own, Rabbi Heschel declares: "The distinction of the prophets was in their remorseless unveiling of injustice and oppression, in their comprehension of social, political, and religious evils."[22]

In truth, this is not a function merely of those called to parish ministry. Rather, it is the responsibility of all who claim to be children of God. In other words, all people, not just prophets, ordained ministers, and judges are called to seek justice, to undo oppression, and to defend the weak and the poor (Isa. 1:17). Heschel tells us that such a one is "an advocate or champion, speaking for those who are too weak to plead their own cause. Indeed, the major activity of the prophets was *interference*, remonstrating about wrongs inflicted on other people, meddling in affairs which were seemingly neither their concern, nor their responsibility.... The prophet is a person who is not tolerant of wrongs done to others, who resents other people's injuries. He even calls upon others to be the champions of the poor."[23]

Such people, i.e., prophets, try to see the world and all that happens in it through the eyes of God and what God expects to be happening in the world. God despises anything beautiful, such as religious liturgies, if it occurs while longstanding injustices are not acknowledged and addressed. Make no mistake about it. According to Martin Luther King, the heart of God goes out, not to the rich and the privileged, but to the lowly and downtrodden. Indeed, "The prophets proclaimed that the heart of God is on the side of the weaker. God's special concern is not for the mighty and the successful, but for the lowly and the downtrodden, for the stranger and the poor, for the widow and the orphan."[24]

Martin Luther King understood his ordination to the ministry as signifying that he was both commissioned and forever committed to bringing to bear the ethical principles of the Jewish and Christian faiths on socio-economic, political, and other evils.[25] Ordained ministry was, for King, a vocation, a calling, a way of life. As such, ministry has to be devoted to the care of the whole person. The gospel, in this sense, is social, or it is nothing. This is radically different from those people in the church who claim to uphold family values, for example, while simultaneously supporting politicians and policymakers who oppose health care legislation for children and the poor, livable housing and safe neighborhoods for them, healthy food, and safe and challenging learning environments.

Martin Luther King saw as clearly as anybody the weaknesses and limitations of the church, and yet he loved the church and refused to give up on it, or even on those he believed to be "un-Christian Christians." "I am too much the preacher to doubt the power of God to call men to repentance," he said.[26] Moreover, he declared: "The Church today is the same Church which John called 'lukewarm' from the island of Patmos, and which Paul and the Disciples struggled so vigorously to save from their own sin. If such as these and our Lord can give their lives to the Church and to the redemption of un–Christian Christians, we can do no less."[27] King maintained to the very end that the church dare not be indifferent or silent in the face of injustice and social evil. But all too often he found himself voicing his deep disappointment in the church and its ministers. We must ask ourselves whether the church, in all honesty, has progressed very far since that 30.06 slug tore away the right side of King's jaw in the early evening of April 4, 1968, as he stood on the balcony of the Lorraine Motel in Memphis, Tennessee.

The Universe as Fundamentally Friendly

I want now to briefly discuss King's long time faith that the universe is fundamentally friendly—friendly toward every effort to do and achieve good in God's world. And this *is* God's world, despite the fact that many of us behave as if it is ours, as if *we* have had a hand in creating and sustaining it. At any rate, even as a student at Morehouse College, King had a sense that there are objective moral laws operative in the world and that God is the ground or source of these. The most important of these laws, King believed, is love. In numerous speeches and sermons he declared that only one who loves has the key to unlock not only the mysteries of the universe, but the solutions to the social ills that devastate human and nonhuman life.[28]

Human beings have nothing to do with the existence of the moral laws. According to King, God expects only that they be obeyed. Only when human beings obey the moral laws will the world function as it should. When human beings disobey the law of love, when we fail to remember that we are one family under God, and that the destiny of any one of us is inextricably linked with the destiny of the rest of us, we condemn ourselves to endure tragic events such as those before, during, and after September 11, 2001. When we choose not to remember that we are one under the God of Esther and Priscilla, we give young black boys a kind of license to take the lives of other young black boys and other innocent people in black communities. When we work as hard as we do *not* to remember that each one of us is God's child, we give certain segments of humanity a kind of permission to engage in activities such as gay bashing. The errant assumption here is that God loves straight people, who might also be racist, sexist, and classist, more than gay people who might also be racist, sexist, and classist.

These failings take place when human beings do not obey the moral laws of the universe. Martin Luther King was quite clear on the matter. "There is a law in the moral world," he said, "which reminds us that life will work only in a certain way."[29] These laws are given by God. Indeed, God has implanted them "within the very structure of this universe. We can neither defy nor break them," King maintained. "If we disobey them, they will break us."[30] What does this mean? It means that wickedness and injustice done to children may reign supreme for a day. It means that the abuse of sexual oppression suffered by women, regardless of race and class, may have its day in the sun. It means that the forces of evil may conquer truth for a day, but at the end of the day, God's truth will triumph. Is this not what James Russell Lowell meant in one of his famous poems?

Though the cause of Evil prosper, yet 'tis Truth alone is strong,
And, albeit she wander outcast now, I see around her throng
Troops of beautiful, tall angels, to enshield her from all wrong....
Truth forever on the scaffold, Wrong forever on the throne,—
Yet that scaffold sways the future, and, behind the dim unknown,
Standeth God within the shadow, keeping watch above his own.[31]

Lowell seems to have understood that the universe is constructed such that truth, love, and justice will prevail when all is said and done. This was also a fundamental metaphysical and theological conviction for Martin Luther King. The critical point is not how human beings behave moment by moment in the world, for experience and history remind us of how devastatingly cruel and monstrous we can be toward human and nonhuman life. Rather, the doctrine that the universe hinges on a moral foundation and thus is fundamentally good, means that we have been created to behave in ways that are pleasing to God, in ways that are consistent with agape, and in ways that honor and respect the dignity of life in general, and human life most especially. Because God created us in freedom with the capacity to choose between good and evil, there is obviously no guarantee that any particular human being will in any moment choose to live as God desires.

But no matter how creatively cruel we discover we can be, the faith that the universe is founded on morality means that such behavior will not have the last word in God's world. Whether as individuals, groups, or nations, behaving in defiance of this universal moral foundation will result in the ultimate detriment to all. The annals of history provide a clear pattern to this effect. When human beings persistently behave in ways that are contrary to God's design and will, in ways that defy truth, love, and justice, we are assured of the existence of life-defying, humanly contrived, social evils.

God has created the world to function in a certain way, that is, in a way that makes for good, truth, love, and justice for everybody, or for nobody. For the God of the Hebrew prophets and Jesus Christ is the God of everybody, or nobody. Martin Luther King's basic conviction was that God had created the universe in such a way that ultimately the highest values will conquer the lesser or lower values. Creation, as history seems to suggest, possesses an inherent urge or straining toward goodness and justice.

Nations that choose to circumvent this innate urge inevitably decline. The nineteenth-century abolitionist and Unitarian preacher, Theodore Parker, said in an 1850 Thanksgiving Day sermon that the greatest nations die because of their persistent pattern of doling out injustice and trampling under foot, the masses of God's people. Parker said, "They would make unrighteousness their law, and God wills not that it be so. Thus they fall; thus they die."[32] Reflecting on the cause of the demise of nations because of their failure to acknowledge God's requirement that justice be done, Parker had this to say about the fall of the Roman Empire:

Oh, manly and majestic Rome, thy sevenfold mural crown, all broken at thy feet, why art thou here [in the graveyard of fallen nations]? It was not justice brought thee low; for thy great book of law is prefaced with these words, justice is the unchanging, everlasting will to give each man his right! [To this Rome responded:] "It was not the saint's ideal: it was the hypocrite's pretence! I made iniquity my law. I trod the nations under me. Their wealth gilded my palaces,—where thou mayest see the fox and hear the owl,—it fed my courtiers and my courtesans. Wicked men were my cabinet-counsellors, the flatterer breathed his poison in my ear. Millions of bondmen wet the soil with tears and blood. Do you not hear it crying yet to God? Low, here have I my recompense, tormented with such downfall as you see! Go back and tell the newborn child, who sitteth on the Alleghanies, laying his either hand upon a tributary sea, a crown of thirty stars about his youthful brow—tell him that there are rights which States must keep, or they shall suffer wrongs! Tell him there is a God who keeps the black man and the white man, and hurls to earth the loftiest realm that breaks His just, eternal law! Warn the young Empire that he come not down dim and dishonoured to my shameful tomb! Tell him that justice is the unchanging, everlasting will to give each man his right. I knew it, broke it, and am lost. Bid him to know it, keep it, and be safe!"[33]

To my mind, there is an ominous familiarity and trend of behavior when I reflect on the past and recent history of these United States of America. And while I want to believe that there is still time to change our ways and direction as a nation, I am also reminded of Martin Luther King's insistence that we take seriously "the fierce urgency of now," for our time is winding up. "We are now face with the fact that tomorrow is today,"[34] he said. There is no time in the future for our salvation. The time to do right, to do justice, is now.

The universe, according to King, is fused through and through with morality, love, and justice. Although by the mid–1960s King was saying that his dream had turned to a nightmare,[35] in 1957 he was certain that a new age was emerging in the South. He believed that this revealed much about the nature of the universe itself. He said, "It tells us something about the core and heartbeat of the cosmos. It reminds us that the universe is on the side of justice."[36] It was a reminder that those who struggle for justice, freedom, and reconciliation do not struggle alone, but have cosmic companionship with the God who struggles alongside them. Accordingly, King said:

> This belief that God is on the side of truth and justice comes down to us from the long tradition of our Christian faith. There is something at the very center of our faith which reminds us that Good Friday may occupy the throne for a day, but ultimately it must give way to the triumphant beat of the drums of Easter. Evil may so shape events that Caesar will occupy a palace and Christ a cross, but one day that same Christ will rise up and split history into AD and BC, so that even the life of Caesar must be dated by His name.[37]

The wicked may triumph for a moment—but *only* a moment.

Most of us may not live to see the promised land or the establishment of the beloved community, but the doctrine that the universe is founded on morality and goodness supports the conclusion that such a community will someday exist, and sooner rather than later, *if* we choose to work cooperatively with each other and with God toward that end. History teaches us that nothing can stop the advance of justice. It may be delayed by the forces of evil, but it cannot be stopped. Thomas Jefferson seemed to be cognizant of this when he reflected on slavery in *Notes on Virginia.*

> And can the liberties of a nation be thought secure when we have removed their only firm basis, a conviction in the minds of the people that these liberties are of the gift of God? That they are not to be violated but with His wrath? Indeed I tremble for my country when I reflect that God is just; that his justice cannot sleep forever; that considering numbers, nature and natural means only, a revolution of the wheel of fortune, and exchange of situation is among possible events; that it may become probably by supernatural interference! The Almighty has no attribute which can take side with us in such a contest.[38]

King's way of expressing this idea is seen in one of his favorite sayings: "The arc of the moral universe is long, but it bends toward justice."[39] This was his way of reminding people that social evil, wickedness, and injustice will prosper only for a season, for at the heart of the universe are God's eternal, unshakable moral laws. God has placed at the center of the cosmos "the pole-star of the world"—Justice.[40] Furthermore, God has created persons in such a way that they have an innate mechanism, namely conscience, to guide them on the path to justice if they would but choose to follow it.[41]

Conclusion

Now, what does all this mean for the church, the synagogue, the mosque, and other religious institutions? Most especially, what does it mean for those who claim to be called by God to various ministries? What does it mean for every proponent of the Christian faith? Knowing, now, what Martin Luther King thought about the church, ministry, preachers, and the significance of a universe thought to be morally infused, what would he say God requires of us today? I want to suggest five possibilities, all of which are consistent with King's ideas.

First, the church, its members, and its ministers must come to the sense that God did not establish the church nor call persons into ministry in order for them to seek material and other forms of success in a capitalist political economy such as that in the United States. God calls the church and all its members to be faithful to God's requirement that justice be done in the world, even if by doing so pastors are forced from their pulpits or local churches are forced to close their doors. King would admonish that we remember that the church neither exists as an end in itself, nor to serve itself and its leaders. The church's purpose, rather, is to glorify and serve God, to care for those who are systematically forced into the muck and mire of the world with little to no hope of relief. In addition, the church is charged with the responsibility of facing up to the powers and principalities to declare God's requirement that justice be done in righteous ways. Indeed, the church is charged with being the voice of those who have no voice.

Second, one of the implications of King's ideas is that it is imperative that the church lead this nation and the world from a "thing-oriented" society and world to a "person-oriented" one.[42] Let us learn to be driven in ministry not by the profit motive and protecting endowments as the first order of business. Rather, let us be driven by the ethics of the absolute dignity and sacredness of persons. The Christian faith teaches that while nonhuman beings and inanimate objects of nature have intrinsic value by virtue of God valuing them, persons have supreme value to God, and therefore we should treat ourselves and others as the precious ones we are.

Third, Martin Luther King would say to us that we should cease our easy willingness and practice of *adjusting* to injustice and other social evils. We too easily allow ourselves to get used to a certain amount of injustice and wrongdoing. We can live with just a little bit of injustice. We can tolerate a little bit of blatant and subtle racism, sexism, heterosexism, abelism, or classism. We can live with the news that only a few of the chronically homeless slept under overpasses and on the streets in last night's sub-zero temperature. We can tolerate reports that only a few blacks and Hispanics are now being stopped by the police for DWB—Driving While Black or Brown. We have become so immune to moral scandals that we are not disturbed to the point of moral outrage and taking steps to resist them through direct action of some kind. Too frequently we are at best indifferent, which is an even greater evil. "We are getting used to scandals, to outrage, even to terrible danger,"[43] Rabbi Heschel reminded us. King himself lamented "our proneness to adjust to injustice...,"[44] and charged us with the responsibility of confronting a hostile and unjust world by "declaring eternal hostility to poverty, racism, and militarism."[45] One must wonder whether much poverty, racism, and war would cease if religious institutions of all kinds would declare in one relentless voice—Basta! Enough!

At any rate, Martin Luther King's legacy challenges us to "recapture the revolutionary spirit and to directly challenge every instance of injustice and human degradation. For King, like the Hebrew prophets, no amount of injustice is acceptable or tolerable. Heschel made the point well: "To us injustice is injurious to the welfare of the people; to the prophets it is a deathblow to existence; to us, an episode; to them, a catastrophe, a threat to the world.... To the prophets even a minor injustice assumes cosmic proportions."[46]

Fourth, Martin Luther King would challenge us to form what he called "a grand alliance"[47] of blacks, Latinas/os, whites, Native Americans, Asian Americans, and others as we begin to take more seriously than ever before the challenge of moving more intentionally toward the establishment of the beloved community. It seems to me that such efforts must be made in local communities across this nation. We can begin right where we are, each on the corner on which she happens to be standing. But we must know that this will be very difficult work, for before a grand alliance can be formed, it will be necessary to develop at least a modicum of trust, which, quite frankly, will take a great deal of courage and risk, especially on the part of blacks, so-called Native Americans, and Latinos/as. For, by virtue of the history of the relationship of these groups with white Americans, there is little reason for them to trust that they will not be betrayed one more time.

And yet, those who take seriously Martin Luther King's legacy must also recognize that because the ultimate faith of blacks must be, not in white people, nor even in each other, but in the God of this vast universe, we must find, indeed *make* ways, to begin the hard work of trusting each other enough so that we might get on with the business of forming that grand alliance. For, none can argue that without such a committed collective effort, not even our children's children will likely see the establishment of the beloved community. For what is becoming increasingly clear is that no matter who has been the major culprit in dishing out injustice, no single group can solve the problems and suffering which devastate such large sectors of the human community. "Few are guilty," Rabbi Heschel taught, "but all are responsible."[48] For example, blacks are not guilty of causing and sustaining racism and unearned white privilege. However, blacks, well-meaning white people, and others are morally responsible for how they respond to it. There will be challenges in the effort to form meaningful alliances, but somehow we must find the means to do it.

Finally, we learn from Martin Luther King's witness that the God of the Hebrew prophets and Jesus Christ will not do for us what we can do for ourselves. All social problems and injustices in the world are in some form or fashion humanly contrived, which means that the human factor is necessarily a chief element in any proposed solution. God is not the moral author of racism and unearned white privilege, nor of heterosexism, black-against-black violence and homicide among young black males, nor hunger and homelessness on a massive scale in the richest nation in the world. These and so many others are humanly contrived problems that, to a large extent, can and must be solved by human beings. And yet, because of the gravity of many of these social problems and the massive and complex unexpected consequences, it is also clear that we will need divine assistance to solve them. Nevertheless, it is crucial that we remember that neither we nor God can do it alone. There must be what King called "cooperative endeavor" between human beings and God. King put it this way: "The belief that God will do everything for man is untenable as the belief that man can do everything for himself. It, too, is based on a lack of faith. We must learn that to expect God to do everything while we do nothing is not faith, but superstition."[49] Neither God nor human beings can do it alone. Rather, it will take cooperative endeavor between God and human beings to transform this society and the world into a more gentle, and loving place.

3

Doctrine of Human Dignity

Dignity is from the Latin word *dignus*, which means worth or value. When the term is applied to human beings one is saying something about their worth or value. What is a human being worth? What is the value of this or that person?

In numerous places in his writings, speeches, and sermons Martin Luther King stresses his conviction about the absolute dignity or preciousness of human beings to God. God, he maintains, is always in search of human beings,[1] a point which says much about how precious they are to God. This chapter is a reflection on King's doctrine of dignity and its implications for today. Since King frequently linked human dignity to God it is important to say at the outset that he grounded his doctrine of human worth theologically.

The following discussion on King's doctrine of dignity—a key component of his philosophy of personalism—aims to remind us of our own moral obligation to live and behave in ways that exhibit respect not only for human beings in general, but for every concrete individual, no matter their race-ethnicity, gender, sexual orientation, class, age, or health. This means, minimally, that we will have to be witnesses to the true meaning of human dignity as something concrete, and not merely theoretical or abstract. To be a witness means not only to see and report clearly. In the black tradition and that of eighth-century Hebrew prophecy, to be a witness also means to be a disturber of the peace; a disturber of the way things are when they are not in compliance with divine expectations. But to be a witness also means to be courageous enough to speak the truth about what can, and ought, to be. It means that in the face of injustice, for example, one does not merely *suggest* that justice be done. Rather, one admonishes, even demands, that justice be done.

Literary artist James Baldwin captures the point about being a witness when he writes: "In the church in which I was raised you were supposed to bear witness to the truth."[2] The witness not only sees or experiences firsthand what went down. For the sake of the innocent ones and those who come after her, the witness must also report truthfully what she saw or experienced. She must speak the unadulterated truth, no matter the consequences. In this very sense, Martin Luther King was a witness, and for this, he was assassinated in Memphis, Tennessee, April 4, 1968. Since witnessing, in the best sense, is risky business, and requires moral fiber and courage (key missing ingredients in the lives and behavior of far too many Christians and people of other faiths), I can only hope that the following discussion will inspire readers to work at developing the courage to be witnesses to the truth about human dignity.

Martin Luther King grew up in a well to do family in Atlanta, Georgia. Notwithstanding this, he did not escape indirect and direct encounters with one of the cruelest enemies of human dignity—racism. As a young boy, King witnessed the racist mistreatment of his father by a white shoe salesman, and by a white policeman.[3] Around the age of six, when he had started school, he was told by the parents of his white friend that he could no longer play with him because he was a "Negro." King recalled this as his first encounter with racism.[4] At about eight years of age, he was at a downtown Atlanta store when a white woman slapped him and said: "You are that nigger that stepped on my foot."[5] A number of times young King saw members of the Ku Klux Klan riding through black neighborhoods trying to intimidate the residents. In addition, he had witnessed police brutality, "and watched Negroes receive the most tragic injustice in the courts."[6] Moreover, while in high school, there was the nasty incident on a return bus trip from Dublin, Georgia where he won an oratory contest. Because of segregation laws, he and his teacher were disrespectfully ordered by the bus driver to give their seats to white patrons. When King hesitated, the driver began cursing at him and his teacher. Urged by his teacher to get up, because it was the law, King recalled that they stood all the way back to Atlanta. He reflected: "That night will never leave my memory. It was the angriest I have ever been in my life."[7] As if this were not enough, King recalled that just before he entered Morehouse College, he spent the summer working on a tobacco farm in Connecticut. He was thrilled by the fact that he could move about freely and eat wherever he wanted. However, it was hurtful to have to return to a segregated South. He recalled how it made him feel to have to move to a Jim Crow car on the return trip to Atlanta.

> It was hard to understand why I could ride wherever I pleased on the train from New York to Washington and then had to change to a Jim Crow car at the nation's capital in order to continue the trip to Atlanta. The first time that I was seated behind a curtain in a dining car, I felt as if the curtain had been dropped on my selfhood. I could never adjust to the separate waiting rooms, separate eating places, separate rest rooms, partly because the very idea of separation did something to my sense of dignity and self-respect.[8]

We will see later that it is important to note that King did not say that being forced to sit behind that curtain *destroyed* his dignity and self-respect. It adversely affected his *sense* of dignity and self-respect, but it did not, indeed could not, destroy it. I return to this important point subsequently. For now, suffice it to say that it is not difficult to understand why King confessed to having come "perilously close to resenting all white people."[9]

Without question, money and status served as a bit of a buffer for King when he was growing up, but they did not completely shield him from the degradation caused by racism. King's own early encounters with racism and the utter disgust that resulted, helps us to understand why he was so devoted to fighting for the dignity of persons as such, and that of his own people in particular. As a boy, King learned from his parents and teachings at his father's church that every person is a child of God, and therefore is sacred and infinitely valuable to God. However, he also knew that because of the enslavement of his people and the continued practice of racial discrimination, the *sense* of human dignity was marred, and even lost, in large numbers of his people. Get the distinction here. Blacks' *sense* of dignity was marred, and in too many instances it was completely lost, as a result of the debilitating consequences of racism. As tragic as this was, it was not the same as saying that their dignity as such was destroyed, for dignity is not given, or in any way created by, human beings. Dignity, then, is not something that human beings can give away, or have taken away from them. The reason this claim is made is because King's deepest understanding of human dignity had its source in the God of his faith. Human beings have infinite, inviolable worth because they are created, sustained, and loved by God. God is the source of human dignity, and therefore there is nothing that any human being can do to divest self of it, or have it taken away or otherwise destroyed. All kinds of things can transpire to tamper with one's *sense* of dignity; to cause in her a *sense* of declining dignity, for example. But because God has imbued human beings with dignity, there is nothing any human being can do to destroy it; nothing human beings can do to give it away, or take it away from another. Therefore, much of King's civil rights ministry was devoted to helping to restore in his people their lost sense of dignity. Although there are a number of themes that appear repeatedly in King's published and unpublished writings, speeches, and sermons, a case could be made that the two themes that appear most often have to do with God, and human dignity. As a pastor and theological social ethicist, King believed God to be the fundamental source of human worth or dignity. "The basic thing about a man," he declared, "is his dignity and his worth to the Almighty God."[10] Consequently, King believed that persons have inviolable worth because they are created, loved, and sustained by the God of the Hebrew prophets and Jesus Christ. "Christianity at its highest and best has always insisted that persons are intrinsically valuable,"[11] he said. Christians, thus, are required to love human beings precisely because God loves them.

Although Martin Luther King discovered the theological ground for his doctrine of dignity in his conception of God, he grounded it metaphysically in the philosophy of personalism. There is evidence that he first encountered this philosophy as a student at Morehouse College, although it is not known (at this writing) whether he only heard the term "personalism" at that time,[12] or whether he was exposed to a lecture on it. However, it is known that his first serious encounter with personalism occurred when he was a seminary student at Crozer Theological Seminary, and more especially during doctoral studies at Boston University. Although the doctrine of human dignity was instilled in King by his parents and through religious teachings at Ebenezer Baptist Church, the later introduction to the philosophy of personalism provided the intellectual framework for him to ground that doctrine in a formal way. In any case, from the time King was a boy, and especially after the encounter with the parents of his white friend, he had a profound sense of his own, and the dignity of others. This chapter, therefore, focuses on the meaning of King's doctrine of human dignity, and what it requires of us today. Since King was first and last a Christian minister,[13] the focus is especially on the relevance of human dignity for Christians, and how they should behave in light of it.

The phenomenon of self-inflicted genocide, what Cornel West calls the "nihilistic threat,"[14] is pervasive among young black males in the urban centers—and increasingly in suburban and rural areas—of this nation. Indeed, at this writing it is one of the most effective means of depopulating black communities and crushing the spirits of the remaining inhabitants. As a theological social ethicist, it is increasingly difficult for me to take seriously those in the academy and church who do their work in a way(s) that does not reflect the sense of urgency prompted by the daily murders of young black males by other young black males, or by the police. Welfare agencies, schools, and even churches tend to participate in this tragedy through silence, and looking the other way. If it is true that persons are precious and have inviolable dignity by virtue of being created in God's image, then the work of the theological social ethicist—indeed all scholars, regardless of academic discipline—should reflect the influence of the tragic phenomenon of black against black violence and murder among young black males.

The Humanity of Martin Luther King, Jr.

Martin Luther King was as human as you and me. Like every human being, he was an earthen vessel. As such, he had strengths as well as limitations or weaknesses. His sister, Christine King Farris, has made this point repeatedly in her writings about him.[15] It is, after all, human beings that God uses to achieve God's purposes in the world. No matter what one's race, ethnicity, gender, class, sexual orientation, age, or health, she is at bottom a being created by the One God of the universe. Every person is therefore imbued with the image and fragrance of God, and it is this that bonds us all together in what we call the human race. King was quite certain that no person or group has more or less of the image of God than any other. This speaks to the fundamental equality of all persons, an equality bestowed by God for all time. In his sermon, "The American Dream" (1965), King said: "There are no gradations in the image of God. Every man from a treble white to a bass black is significant on God's keyboard, precisely because every man is made in the image of God.... We will know one day that God made us to live together as brothers and to respect the dignity and worth of every man."[16] Every person possesses a fundamental equality and dignity with every other, which implies, at the very least, that human beings ought to be treated a certain way. At the bare minimum, every person ought to be respected and treated like a being of infinite worth.

Martin Luther King was not a saint, and left no evidence that he ever wanted to be. He was limited by his blindness to sexism, as evidenced by his failure to include women in leadership positions in the Southern Christian Leadership Conference (SCLC). Only grudgingly did he allow Ella J. Baker to be the first director of SCLC, while providing her virtually no monetary and other support. He engaged in extra-marital relations. He used the ideas of others, but did consistently follow the standard practice of documenting what was borrowed.[17] All of this is to say, that he was a human being. The appeal to his humanity excuses none of his limitations. It is merely a reminder to us that King was a flesh and blood human being like the rest of us, and consequently, was no more or less susceptible to human error. I have argued that what set King apart was his sense of call, and his extraordinary and unswerving efforts to liberate the oppressed, while trying to establish the community of love. In this regard, I like to say that Martin Luther King was an ordinary human being who did some extraordinary things to make the most of human beings and what he referred to as the world house.

As a human being, Martin Luther King made many of the same mistakes that you and I make. He did not pretend to be perfect. He had hopes and dreams and aspirations. He got tired. He cried. He brooded. There were times when he was admittedly afraid. He suffered moments of depression. He wished for the day that he could relax and get some respite; when he could just take some time to think, really think, about all that was happening in his life and in the civil rights movement, and what were the most reasonable next steps. We get a sense of how heavily this sometimes weighed on him when he told Alex Haley in the famous and important *Playboy* interview in January 1965: "I feel urgently the need for even an hour of time to get away, to withdraw, to refuel. I need more time to think through what is being done, to take time out from the mechanics of the movement, to reflect on the meaning of the movement."[18] Although King was absolutely committed to the struggle for the total liberation and empowerment of blacks and other oppressed peoples, there were also times when he longed for the day he could leave the struggle and leisurely teach theology in a seminary or university.[19] Prior to 1965, he had tried co-teaching a philosophy course with Samuel Williams (his former teacher) at Morehouse College, but the pressures of the movement made it impossible for him to continue.

King was not a god, and he knew it. He was, through and through, a human being, with feelings and emotions, hopes, dreams, failures, accomplishments, and disappointments. In my way of thinking this was one of the most significant things about Martin Luther King. It is a reminder of just how extraordinary ordinary people can be. I have always told students in my course on King that he was an ordinary human being, who did some very extraordinary things; did these things because of his sense of commitment to God's call, and his strong and relentless faith in God, as well as his conviction that in the end, God will prevail.

What a person he was!, a human being, just like you and me, but a human being who devoted his life to making human beings and the world better than they were. King was so committed to the total liberation of blacks and the poor that he sacrificed his personal hopes and aspirations, including his family life, and devoted his entire adult life to the achievement of their freedom. His devotion was grounded in the theological conviction that God is concerned not merely about the survival, liberation, and empowerment of blacks, but the entire human race.[20]

The Nature of Dignity

We saw earlier that dignity means worth or value. Garth Baker-Fletcher's book, *Somebodyness: Martin Luther King, Jr. and the Theory of Dignity*,[21] was the first attempt to systematically address King's doctrine of dignity. King frequently used the term *somebodyness* early in his civil rights ministry.[22] Nearer the end of his life he increasingly used the term as a way of naming the new sense of self-respect, self-worth, or dignity that blacks were gaining as a result of their relentless direct nonviolent protests against racism and economic exploitation.[23] As previously observed King named God as the cause or source of the inherent dignity and preciousness of human beings. In this, King went beyond the philosopher Immanuel Kant, who argued that persons are ends in themselves by virtue of being persons. There was no necessary connection to God. Human beings possess inviolable worth just because they are human beings. Martin Luther King accepted this Kantian stance, but he added to it by insisting that God must be the central figure in the equation, such that God is the source or ground of human dignity. This means that King had a theological interpretation of human dignity or somebodyness. Every person possesses intrinsic dignity and is significant because they are loved by God.[24]

From this, we may conclude that every person is somebody, because every person is a child of God; is related to God. As such, every person ought to be treated with dignity and respect. Moreover, human beings should not respond passively and nonchalantly when their dignity is threatened or undermined. Every person is sacred and possesses infinite worth because the image of God is stamped on their being. Martin Luther King reasoned that every person ought to be respected because God loves each and every one. What is more, King held, "Human worth lies in relatedness to God."[25] A person has value because she is valued by God. Since God is the source of human dignity, it is not something that can be given or taken away. We may argue the point as to whether persons have value and worth solely because they are valued by God,[26] or whether they have value apart from God. However, there is no question that King's doctrine of dignity was chiefly theistic, and thus has its foundation in a supremely personal, loving, and creator God. It is therefore not difficult to understand why King also believed in the relational quality of life. "All life is interrelated," he asserted. "All men are caught in an inescapable network of mutuality, tied in a single garment of destiny."[27] Similarly, King frequently recited the words, "out of one blood God made all men to dwell upon the face of the earth."[28] He was therefore led to the conviction that there is no fundamental difference between human beings such that it can be said that one has more value than another. All have equal value and are equally precious to God. One does not want to say or hear it, but on this view

Adolf Hitler as human being was as valuable to God as Mahatma Gandhi. In this regard, the personalist John Wright Buckham argued, and King would have agreed, that there is even worth in the hard to love,[29] and if we humans do not know or accept the fact, God does. Even those who are too mean to love or be loved, have in them the "root of righteousness," which must mean that even they have *potential* worth.[30] This, of course, is a metaphysical, not an ethical claim, meaning that not every individual chooses to behave like beings who possess infinite worth.

At least from the time of Borden P. Bowne (1847–1910), the father of American personalism (who systematized it and made it into a philosophical method), the essence of the personal is *self-consciousness*, *self-knowledge*, and *self-direction*. The personal is that which is self-conscious, and thus self-aware, and is capable of determining its own direction. Although Bowne did not expressly name *self-worth* or *dignity* as a central element of the personal as John Wright Buckham did,[31] it seems to me that this trait is implied in Bowne's understanding of the personal. My preference is that dignity be explicitly stated as a chief trait of personality or the personal. The personal has a sense of its own worth, a point to which King would adhere. On the ethical side, personalism holds that persons possess infinite dignity and worth because created and loved by the Supreme Person of the universe. I would say that it follows that the Supreme Person has a keen awareness of its supreme worth, and as the One who imparts dignity to other personal beings. Concretely, Bowne was adamant that wherever any two persons meet anywhere in the universe, they owe each other respect or good will.[32] In addition, making it clear that persons have the right of way, Bowne further argued that no person should be used as fuel to warm society.[33] This is a reflection of the Kantian principle that persons are ends in themselves and should not be treated as means only.

As observed before, another important principle of personalism is the communal or relational. From the time of Bowne, personalists have underscored the importance of relationality or mutuality; the fact that all beings are conditioned in their activities by all other beings, such that no being exists in isolation. On the human plane this means that all persons are conditioned by other persons, and therefore cannot be all they can be in isolation, calling to mind the African traditional concept: "I am because we are; and since we are, therefore I am."[34] One discovers what it truly means to be a person-in-community; discovers her "full personality in group relationships."[35] Writing on the communal nature of reality, Bowne said: "If all its activities and properties are conditioned, it implies that the thing cannot exist at all out of its relations."[36] There is, then, no absolute, unrelated existence. Beings, more specifically, human beings exist in relation or community. An important corollary to this is King's belief (also found in African traditional thought[37]) that no person can really be a person without other persons. I can be a human being only *with* other human beings. This is what South African Archbishop Desmond Tutu has in mind when he frequently speaks and writes about *Ubuntu* as "the first law of our being."[38] Based on the relational principle, Ubuntu essentially means "that we are set in a delicate network of interdependence with our fellow human beings and with the rest of God's creation.... It is the essence of being human. It speaks of the fact that my humanity is caught up and inextricably bound up in yours. I am human because I belong."[39] I can't be what I can be, if you are not what you can be, and if we do not do all we can to assist each other in being the best that we can be as human beings. In other words, human beings need each other!

Similarly, Martin Luther King held that the very structure of the universe is such that things do not work out right if persons do not persist in their concern for the well being both for self and for others.[40] Moreover, what I do affects the next person, and vice versa, directly or indirectly. More concretely, what happens to black boys on the streets of major urban centers and in other places in this country happens to you, and to me, as well. And since King's doctrine of dignity is fundamentally theological, we must also say that God too is affected by what happens to young black males and how the rest of us respond. For, whether we like it or not, we are a part of each other, and are summoned into existence by God for communal living. This means that we are a part of black children and teens who have known nothing but injustice, deprivation, fear, and uncertainty in their young lives. Most of these are young people who don't even know what it means to love, trust, and hope (in themselves or in others); who do not value themselves, let alone others. Consequently, far too many have no concept or expectation of a constructive future, because they do not expect to live beyond their teens or early twenties at most. Tragically, it is the case that too many young black boys do not ask the question that more privileged and protected children ask, namely, "What do you want to be when you grow up?" Rather, they are frequently heard asking the question—itself a devastating commentary on this nation: "What do you want to be *if* you grow up?"

Historically and biologically, the blood of blacks flows in the veins of white people, a fact supported by the thousands of African women who were raped by white men during, and long after, blacks' enslavement in this country. On the historical and biological levels, then, blacks and whites are forever related by blood and history. In this sense, we are all brothers and sisters, one people, inextricably bound together forever, whether we like it or not. And yet, there is also a basic theological reason for speaking of the interrelatedness of persons. No professional theologian himself, James Baldwin wrote as cogently about this idea as any academic theologian or philosopher. He wrote that we all have male and female traits, "not only because we are all born of a woman impregnated by the seed of a man but because each of us, helplessly and forever, contains the other—male in female, female in male, white in black and black in white. We are a part of each other. Many of my countrymen appear to find this fact exceedingly inconvenient and even unfair, and so, very often, do I. But none of us can do anything about it."[41] Baldwin was making a fundamental metaphysical claim that is supported by his understanding of the Bible and the best in his experience as a black person. Similarly, Martin Luther King knew better than most that if the idea of the fundamental interdependence of persons ever caught on, human beings would not exploit other human beings, would not "trample over people with the iron feet of oppression," and would no longer take delight in killing other human beings.[42] According to King, the rational human being who truly understood what it meant to adhere to the view that he and other human beings are integrally bound together under God as one family, would be hard pressed to devise a rational reason to cheat, exploit, or destroy another human being(s).

The question we must ask is: What does Martin Luther King's theory of the dignity and worth of human beings mean in the most concrete sense for black children who are victims of institutional and structural racism, the "nihilistic threat," and self-imposed genocide? What does a responsible ethic of dignity require behaviorally, particularly for those who claim to be Christians?

It is one thing to say, as King did, that the idea of the dignity of persons roots deep in the political and religious heritage of the United States.[43] He saw this emphasis in the spirit of the Constitution of the United States, and especially in the Declaration of Independence where we find the words: "All men are created equal and endowed by their Creator with certain inalienable rights." King was pleased that Frederick Douglass sought to show in his speech on the Constitution and slavery that both the Constitution and the Declaration contained the rights not only of white people, but of black people as well. Speaking in Glasgow, Scotland on March 26, 1860, Douglass told his audience:

> Its language is "we the people"; not we the white people, not even we the citizens, not we the privileged class, not we the high, not we the low, but we the people; not we the horses, sheep, and swine, and wheel-barrows, but we the people, we the human inhabitants; and, *if Negroes are people*, they are included in the benefits for which the Constitution of America was ordained and established.[44]

It is important to note my emphasis on the phrase "if Negroes are people." For if they were considered people, then Douglass was correct about their rights being contained in the Declaration and the Constitution. But the truth is that during that period blacks were not considered by many whites to be fully human. This was, in fact, the stance of the framers of the Constitution. Nothing so clearly demonstrated this than American slavery, the unusually brutal and inhumane forms it took, and the fact that the framers did not outlaw it (and why would they, since most presumed to own Africans?). Indeed, this was also Alexis de Tocqueville's observation when he was sent by the French government to the United States in 1831 to examine the prison system. Tocqueville wrote about the condition of blacks, and whites' perception of them, in his classic work, *Democracy in America* saying:

> ... we scarcely acknowledge the common features of humanity in this stranger whom slavery has brought among us. His physiognomy is to our eyes hideous, his understanding weak, his tastes low; and *we are almost inclined to look upon him as a being intermediate between man and the brutes*.[45]

Indeed, Tocqueville went on to say that he did not believe the black and white races would ever co-exist on the basis of equality, especially in the United States,[46] where the democratic principle reigns. The tragedy of this view is exacerbated by the fact that it is not just historical. Whether Tocqueville's prophecy that blacks and whites will never co-exist on the basis of equality is ever found to be wrong or not, what we do know is that nearly two centuries later blacks and whites in the United States still do not co-exist on the basis of equality; still do not live in a racism-free society where equal opportunity exists for all as a matter of course. We also know that in 1857 Chief Justice Roger B. Taney declared in the famous Dred Scott case that blacks had no rights that the white man was bound to respect,[47] a claim that reverberates loudly in the ears of blacks even at this writing.

Andrew Hacker has shown in his instructive and provocative book, *Two Nations: Black and White, Separate, Hostile, Unequal* (1992), that "*there persists the belief that members of the black race represent an inferior strain of the human species*."[48] No other people of color, no other racial-ethnic strain in this country suffers from the "presumptions of inferiority" associated with the continent of Africa and American slavery. Based on Hacker's observation and the experience of countless blacks, vast numbers of whites and neo-conservative blacks need to reassess the unfounded view that racism is a thing of the past; that it was essentially eradicated during the civil rights movement; and that only an insignificant number of whites are racists today. How can this be the case when it is still true that every white person in America continues to benefit immensely from white privilege, whether they admit their racism or not, and whether they admit that they benefit from racism or not? In any event, the point to be conveyed here is that it is still highly questionable whether the basic human rights documents of the United States considers black people to be full-fledged human beings deserving all the rights thereto pertaining. It is therefore questionable whether blacks should look to those documents in support of their claim to basic human rights.

Christians and non Christians alike resist acknowledging that racism is still a significant factor in religious and secular communities in the United States. And yet, there is no unanimity of agreement among theologians and social scientists regarding this matter. In fact, it is most disturbing that more often than not, theologians and religious ethicists seldom even discuss—not just mention in passing—the matter of race in their classes, public lectures, and published writings. Although there is vigorous discussion among social scientists, it is clear that some agree with the thesis proposed by William J. Wilson in the late 1970s that since the civil rights movement racism is of declining significance in the way things are done in this country. The more fundamental issue, he argued, is economics.[49] Indeed, many, like Dinesh D'Souza, claim that there is no racism,[50] implying that talk of its existence today is nothing short of an imagined state of affairs. Persons such as D'Souza often support the basic socio political and economic structures of this society, essentially arguing that they are fundamentally sound, and need little more than an adjustment or reform here and there. However, many other social scientists, such as Manning Marable,[51] Joe R. Feagin,[52] and C. Eric Lincoln[53] conclude what is consistent with the experience of vast numbers of blacks, namely that racism is alive and well and is deeply and intricately embedded in both the basic human rights documents of the United States as well as the structures of society.[54] Without question, Martin Luther King was in the camp regarding the ongoing significance of racism, not only in the United States, but throughout the international community as well.[55]

During the early 1960s, King came increasingly to believe that the basic socio-economic structure of the United States was corrupt and unjust, and thus was in need of more than a mere cosmetic makeover. Furthermore, there was no question in his mind that racism remained deeply entrenched in the very fabric of this nation and its religious and secular institutions. King himself said that racism "is so imbedded in the white society that it will take many years for color to cease to be a judgmental factor."[56] He declared that, "white America must recognize that justice for black people cannot be achieved without radical changes in the structure of our society."[57] Repeatedly, near the end of his life, King admonished that the American nation "must be born again,"[58] by which he meant that its very structures must be radically altered and reconstituted if there is to be hope of the emergence of the beloved community. The preponderance of the evidence and the testimonies of numerous blacks reveal conclusively that racism is still alive and well in churches, seminaries, universities, courtrooms, government at all levels, and other institutions. King himself was forthright in asserting that, "the American people are infected with racism."[59] This suggests the need for radical transformation in both individuals and institutions, as well as a transvaluation of values. In part, King meant that there is a need to move from a "thing-oriented society," to a "person-oriented society," where the emphasis will be placed less on property rights and material things, and more on human values.[60]

Martin Luther King saw clearly the interconnection between racism, economic injustice, and militarism.[61] By the time he entered seminary he had already determined that these would be the three social evils he would focus on throughout his ministry. Although in later years he focused heavily on economic exploitation and war, he was just as adamant that racism did not take a backseat, for he understood better than most that it was implicated in the problems of poverty and war.

King pointed the way to the elimination of the dreaded evil of racism and suggested that the fundamental prerequisite for genuine racial equality is "a humble acknowledgement of guilt" on the part of white Americans. As a nation, however, no such acknowledgement had ever been made. In King's way of thinking, honest confession serves to purge the self and prepare one for participation in the liberation and reconciliation processes. And yet, honest confession is the one thing that very many whites, especially white men, find very difficult to do. Rather than confess wrongdoing, their general tendency is to merely acknowledge that something needs to be done. Indeed, many go as far as to suggest solutions, but never once do they publicly own their racism or acknowledge their unearned privilege and how this may have contributed to the problem in the first place. If this society—and more particularly the churches and other religious bodies—truly desire to eliminate racism, there must first be an honest acknowledgement of its existence. According to King, the church, as one of the assumed moral and spiritual leaders of the nation and world, should take the lead. To the Jewish rabbis at the meeting of the Rabbinical Assembly on March 25, 1968, King said: "However difficult it is to hear, however shocking it is to hear, we've got to face the fact that America is a racist country. We have got to face the fact that racism still occupies the throne of our nation. I don't think we will ultimately solve the problem of racial injustice until this is recognized, and until this is worked on....I think religious institutions in society must really deal with racism."[62] However difficult it is to hear and accept in the twenty-first century, the United States, its religious, political, economic, and educational institutions are not yet in a position to boast of clean hands regarding the issue of racism. White Christians in particular, and other whites of good will, must take this seriously, for theirs may be the most important role of all in solving the problem of racism and massive unearned white privilege.

What Should Christians Be Doing?

The novice who is introduced to Christian principles, and then is permitted to observe the actual behavior of long time professing Christians will easily conclude that most are Christian in name only. For, one of the things the newcomer to the faith will observe is that most Christians display little regard for the humanity and dignity of other people, especially those who are different from themselves. She observes that professing Christians do not live according to their own beliefs, e.g., that one supremely loving Creator-God calls every person into existence and stamps each with the divine image; that all persons are children of the same God; that God loves every person without qualification; and that every person has infinite and inviolable worth precisely because God loves them. However, when the newcomer observes the behavior of many of these professing Christians, she is taken completely aback when she sees them behaving toward others just as non–Christians and non-religious people do. Indeed, she sees that the latter often behave in more humane fashion toward others than professing Christians. This notwithstanding, we may be assured that a basic core belief of any Christian who understands what it means to be Christian, must be that every person is heir to a legacy of absolute dignity and is deemed to be infinitely precious to God. This was a basic assumption for Martin Luther King, and he did not allow professing Christians to forget it. Indeed, King seldom spoke or wrote about God without also mentioning the inherent sacredness of persons as such. Moreover, often when he spoke or wrote about the dignity of persons, he referenced God as the source.

The first thing that the ethics of dignity requires of professing Christians is a *commitment to the principle of the absolute dignity and worth of persons as such.* Theologically, to say that persons have absolute dignity is to say that their value is inextricably linked to their relationship with God. Interestingly, many people pretend to have difficulty knowing who is a person and who is not. Moreover, at a time when blacks are still victimized by racism and treated like they are less than persons, some scholars have expanded the concept of person to include non-human animals such as coyotes and chimpanzees.[63] Part of their rationale for this has to do with their hope that by thinking of non-human life forms as persons, there will be an increased likelihood that human beings will acknowledge the inherent dignity of such life forms and treat them with respect. But considering that human beings have long exhibited difficulty respecting other human beings, I find it difficult to accept the likelihood that they will respect the dignity of non-human beings until they first learn to respect the dignity of human beings. In other words, until human beings learn to respect other human beings, especially those who are in some way(s) different from themselves, I do not see the likelihood that they will respect non-human life forms and the environment. Environmentalists and animal rights activists who are racists, sexists, classists, and heterosexists are at best living a contradiction when they argue for acknowledgement of the dignity of non-human life forms, while failing to acknowledge the humanity and dignity of blacks and other historically mistreated groups. For if it is true that all life is interrelated and God is the source of life, one cannot reasonably respect some life forms while disrespecting or disregarding others. One cannot pretend to respect non-human life forms while disrespecting certain groups of human beings and disregarding their inherent dignity. Many of us, regardless of where we live in the United States, have read of animal rights activists who have exhibited outrage over the mistreatment of dogs and cats, for example, while remaining virtually silent regarding racial profiling and police brutality against young blacks and Latinos.

In any case, I am not here making a case against the idea of the dignity of non-human life forms and the need to value, respect, and care for them, since their source is also the One God of the universe. *All* life belongs to God, and thus is valuable in itself and to God. Nor am I arguing against the idea that some non-human beings may in some sense be considered persons, a point which King, the personalist, would have been familiar.[64] Rather, the state of emergency which exists relative to the plight of young black males, forces me to focus on what it means to be a human person, and most especially, a black human person under the age of twenty-five, since those in this category have been characterized as "an endangered species."[65] To be sure, there is also a state of emergency relative to the environment and non-human life forms. Indeed, the best ecological theorists and activists are adamant that although all life forms have intrinsic value, they do not have the same value. Therefore, it is reasonable to speak of a "gradation of intrinsic value," which implies "a diversity of rights."[66] Those life forms with the greater potential richness of experience have greater rights. Furthermore, those in this group who have had their rights systematically trampled upon are obligated to find ways to assert their rights as human beings.[67] For the earlier reference to "absolute dignity" was intended to convey the idea that inasmuch as it is *given* by the Creator and sustainer of all life, it can neither be given nor taken away. Since dignity is a birthright, i.e., part of what it means to be a human being, this obligates persons to fight to preserve and enhance it both in self and other human beings.

Any who has difficulty determining which beings are human beings and which are not, may be helped by remembering that as a Christian and a personalist, Martin Luther King believed that any being who is conscious, potentially self-aware, self-directed, and has a sense of innate worth; whose basic anatomy is like yours and mine; who has limbs, eyes, ears, and nose; who walks and runs in an upright manner; who smiles, laughs, and cries; who exhibits the same weaknesses and strengths; who sins and strives to achieve value; who forgives and desires forgiveness; and who inevitably seeks relationships, is nothing less than, or more than, a person.

Secondly, the ethics of dignity requires that persons *develop the highest possible conception of the worth and value of persons as such*. That is, one is to make no distinction whatever between human beings in this regard. One's highest possible estimate of the value of human beings applies to all, or to none, for God is the Creator of all human beings, or of none. In order to insure that persons will be treated like human beings, this conception is a necessary conditioning factor for all ethical principles, e.g., love, justice, and mercy. Without a sense of the highest estimate of the worth of persons, it is conceivable that even one who espouses the highest ethical principles may condone practices that are oppressive, dehumanizing, and otherwise morally repugnant.

For example, Plato was one of the greatest philosophers and ethical theorists in the West. Yet he considered infanticide and killing off the elderly to be compatible with his ethical theory. For example, Plato thought it permissible to secretly dispose of children born defective or otherwise deemed to be inferior.[68] This might mean either hiding them away from public view, or actually killing them.[69] In addition, it was acceptable to Plato that children born of incestuous relations should be disposed of "on the understanding that no such child can be reared."[70] Likewise, Aristotle saw nothing wrong with slavery and believed the enslaved to be without the capacity to reason.[71] What is more, he believed women to be inferior to men and thus should be ruled by them.[72] Aristotle also believed that "a modest silence" is the glory of women.[73]

Some scholars have argued that the problem with Plato and Aristotle was not their ethical insight and espousal of fundamental ethical principles, but the fact that each had a low estimate of the worth and value of human beings as human beings.[74] The personalist Ralph Tyler Flewelling argued that this was also the trouble with Kant, Fichte, and Hegel, who each failed "to connect with the vital problems of human beings."[75] Their treatment of persons in their philosophies was, according to Flewelling, too impersonal, abstract, and unrelated to the existential, blood and guts issues that confront human beings.[76] Indeed, Flewelling might also have added that Kant,[77] following David Hume,[78] expressed no appreciation for the humanity and dignity of black people, but instead considered them to be the inferiors of whites, intellectually, morally, and culturally.[79]

In the end, the way we treat human beings will have more to do with our estimate of their worth, than with our espousal of formal ethical principles or our claims to be Christian or adherents of some other religious faith. A low conception of the sacredness or dignity of human beings or a particular group of human beings will generally result in corresponding treatment,[80] despite one's insistence that she adheres to highly revered ethical principles. In addition, we mistreat non-human life forms because of our low estimate of their worth; because of their relative insignificance to us. Furthermore, if we believe a group of people to be fundamentally inferior to our own, it matters little what religious and moral principles we espouse, for we will likely treat that group with the utmost disrespect. This is clearly a major consideration in race, gender, sexual orientation, and class relations in the United States of America.

Thirdly, any adequate ethics of dignity (especially relative to racism) *requires that the contending black and white groups do some intra-group house cleaning*. This may require a kind of temporary separation between the two groups, although this would be very difficult to achieve today, considering that whites and blacks are so intimately and integrally involved in each other's history and culture. They are bound together that way, whether they like it or not. At any rate, both groups will need the space and time to address internal problems that militates against the achievement of the racial brotherhood that King promoted throughout his civil rights ministry. This state of affairs between blacks and whites will never exist as long as racism and the refusal to acknowledge unearned white privilege festers in the white community and white religious institutions; as long as the behavior and practices of whites say that they believe blacks to be inferior; as long as even the most liberal white person refuses to acknowledge that he receives numerous unearned privileges by virtue of his white skin. The issue is not whether some whites are not in fact racists; King himself acknowledged that there were some individual whites who were not racists, a claim that is consistent with this writer's experience as well. So the issue is not whether some whites are or are not racists. The issue is that all whites—whether racists or not—possess unmerited privileges by virtue of historic and present day systematic racial discrimination. Since racism emanates from the white community, only committed, well meaning white people can effectively root it out. *This* is the cross that otherwise well-meaning white people must bear and risk being nailed to, and not many have been willing to bear that cross.

On the other hand, racism has caused so much familial and communal damage to past, present, and future generations of black Americans that there are tremendous internal problems confronting the black community; problems that must initially be dealt with internally and without the assistance or counsel of whites. It is absolutely ludicrous to preach and teach black-white unity when there is so much disunity and destructiveness within the black community. Indeed, even the fact that blacks are generally more willing to forgive white racist behavior than to forgive each other their mistakes is part of that destructiveness.

Earlier, I referred to the family and community-destroying phenomenon of self-inflicted genocide and the fact that the number one cause of death among young black males is homicide at the hands of another black male. On one level, this tragedy is caused by a pervasive sense of lovelessness, hopelessness, and absence of a sense of dignity and self-worth among young black males. In part, it might well be that an underlying cause of this overwhelming sense of nihilism in black communities, is the lessening sense among a historically religious people of the existence of a good and loving God who cares for them, and is in control of the ultimate outcome of the universe. At bottom, then, the self-inflicted genocide to which I refer is a deep-rooted spiritual problem.

But it must also be added that the practice of centuries of American slavery, systematic racial discrimination, and economic exploitation effectively prepared the way for the genocidal tendencies of many young black males. Cornel West does not go far enough when he identifies what he calls "the nihilistic threat" as the major destructive factor in the black community. Indeed, talk about such a threat does not make sense unless it is understood that its seeds were planted and very carefully and methodically nurtured in the deadly soil of white supremacy, greed, and the ongoing systematic theft of black labor. Notwithstanding this, the point is that the tragic phenomenon of self-inflicted violence and murder among young black males must be addressed and solved by the black community. There is nothing in the history of blacks' presence in this country that supports the naïve belief of some that whites either will, or must, solve this problem, even though racism is a root cause. The rate of depopulation among black male youths through murder, imprisonment, and drug abuse demands that the problem be solved forthwith. The memory of black ancestors and their emphasis on black self-dignity demands it, as does their belief—historically at least—that God cares about all human beings.

At this point, the primary concern should be finding solutions to the problem of black-against-black violence and murder. In the broader sense, all persons, regardless of race and ethnicity, are morally obligated to work in this direction. But from a strategic standpoint, the black community must take the lead in resolving this problem. Black youths have fewer meaningful, life-enhancing choices than their white counterparts. Moreover, many of the choices at black youths' disposal make no sense at all. Given the status of life-chances for blacks, why should black youths remain in school, especially when the quality of education in most public school systems is at an all-time low? Why remain, when indicators are that there will be no living wage jobs available to them when they finish? In addition, why work dead end jobs in the fast food and other service industries when your peers make tremendous amounts of money selling drugs or engaging in other illegal activities? Whichever of these options one chooses will likely lead to consequences that are life-threatening, which is to say that young black males have very few to no options that make sense. Virtually any one they choose will have devastating, even life-threatening, consequences.

This effectively means that young black males are daily confronted with what Helmut Thielicke refers to as *borderline situations*. These, Thielicke maintains, are without question the crucial tests of ethics.[81] From the ethical standpoint, the borderline situation is where the rubber hits the road. As in the case of the biblical Abraham, one confronts a borderline situation when she is forced by circumstances to choose between what amounts to two or more forms of sinning. Not only does one *have* to choose, but there appears to be no way of escape.[82] And yet, she must then face the consequences, regardless of the alternative chosen. The problem is that there are generally only life-threatening consequences for any choice made in the borderline situation.[83] Borderline situations generally arise due to an *extreme emergency*. Is this not precisely the type of situation that confronts vast numbers of young black males? And yet, black adults have the difficult—often impossible—task of helping these young men to understand that as autonomous agents they are responsible for the individual choices they make, including the impossible choices they are forced to make. They must pay for the choices they make, e.g., drive-by shootings that too often end in the severe maiming or death of innocent bystanders. A major part of the ethical messiness of all this is that young black males are not guilty of the racial, economic, political, and other environmental factors that cause the conditions that lead them on paths of self-destruction and destruction of others in their communities. But precisely here, is the rub. *They are responsible for how they respond to what has been and is being done to them by external forces.* And by and large, it is the black community that should mete out the punishment for internal crimes against itself, which might well mean *being ready to do wrong in order to prevent even more devastating wrongs*.[84] This is essentially what led theologian Dietrich Bonhoeffer and others in the German resistance movement during World War II to try to assassinate Adolf Hitler. What we have here is a fairly radical form of situation ethics, a type of ethical response that was not foreign to enslaved blacks who sometimes opted to keep their truth from whites during the period of American enslavement, if to do so might mean their successful escape from slavery or the protection of others who were trying to escape.[85] The idea of keeping the truth from another might well be considered by some to be a "dubious principle" at best, for it implies that the end justifies the means. Thielicke reminds us that any who appeals to and acts on such a principle must also be ready to shoulder the legal and moral responsibility for it.[86] In the case of the fore parents of blacks and many in the black community today, shouldering such responsibility is itself a moral responsibility, considering the obligation to protect and enhance one's own humanity and dignity.

One of the things that adult blacks must do is to teach black children that not only is a mind a terrible thing to lose, but a body—*their* body—is also a terrible thing to lose. This means there is need to teach them to love their whole self, most especially their body. One does not injure, maim, and kill what one truly loves. Indeed, Alice Walker reminds us that anything that one truly loves can be saved.[87] In a passage in her book *Beloved* (that Martin Luther King would have praised and celebrated), Toni Morrison captures the spirit of this need for blacks to learn to love their whole self.

"Here," she said, "in this here place, we flesh; flesh that weeps, laughs; flesh that dances on bare feet in grass. Love it. Love it hard. Yonder they do not love your flesh. They despise it. They don't love your eyes; they'd just as soon pick em out. No more do they love the skin on your back. Yonder they flay it. And O my people they do not love your hands. Those they only use, tie, bind, chop off and leave empty. Love your hands! Love them. Raise them up and kiss them. Touch others with them, pat them together, stroke them on your face 'cause they don't love that either. *You* got to love it, *you*! And no, they ain't in love with your mouth. Yonder, out there, they will see it broken and break it again. What you say out of it they will not heed. What you scream from it they do not hear. What you put into it to nourish your body they will snatch away and give you leavins instead. No, they don't love your mouth. *You* got to love it. This is flesh I'm talking about here. Flesh that needs to be loved."[88]

Few have understood as clearly as Martin Luther King that when speaking of the sacredness of human beings, especially those who have been systematically oppressed, one must have in mind the entire person, mind *and* body, and not merely the more spiritual aspects, as if to imply that the body itself has no worth of its own. Well aware of the systemic oppression of his people and how white racists from slavery to more contemporary times abused their bodies as a matter of course, Martin Luther King understood the significance of the worth of the body, and insisted that it too is loved and seen as precious, by God. He saw the body as good because it was created by God, and he was not hesitant to appeal to the passage in the Book of Genesis (1:31) that declares that all that God created is good.[89] King rejected the Platonic doctrine of human beings, saying:

The Greeks under the impetus of Plato felt that the body was something inherently depraved, inherently evil, and that somehow the soul could not reach its full maturity until it had broken aloose [*sic*] from the prison of the body. But this was never the Christian doctrine. The Christian doctrine did not consider the body as the principle of evil; Christianity says the will is the principle of evil. And so in Christianity the body is sacred. The body is significant. This means that in any Christian doctrine of man we must forever be concerned about man's physical well-being.[90]

When King appealed to the cross, and declared that "Christ has bound all men into an inextricably [*sic*] bond of brotherhood, and stamped on all men the indelible imprint of preciousness,"[91] his reference was to the preciousness or sacredness of the whole person, body and mind.

Finding ways to radically reduce black-on-black teen violence and homicide will take blacks a long way toward re-establishing and developing unity within the black community. Until there is indisputable evidence that those who preach, teach, and write about such unity are also willing to give their all to make it a reality, their words cannot be taken seriously. When there is unity in the black community; when the next generation of black youths have been taught and have internalized the necessity of loving and respecting themselves, their heritage, and their community, only then will blacks be positioned to think about and create coalitionist activities and black-white unity. I realize that what I am saying has implications for all kinds of things, not least the role of black faculty and students in predominantly white university and seminary settings. However, we have seen that borderline situations are extreme ethical situations that require solutions that may also be extreme and distasteful.

Martin Luther King lived by the faith that blacks must take their destiny into their own hands, in the sense of not making the mistake of passively waiting for others to take up their cause. Indeed, even white social ethicist Reinhold Niebuhr cautioned blacks not to uncritically trust the moral sense of the white man[92] who, as James Baldwin frequently reminded us, too often fails to honor his own moral professions.[93] Instead, blacks will need to work relentlessly toward the development of a deeper sense of self dignity and pride, especially in light of the nihilistic threat in the black community. Although blacks are Americans, they are also Africans. This is their inescapable "great dilemma," King held. It does not help to pretend to be merely one or the other, African *or* American. Instead, blacks are always and forever what W. E. B. DuBois characterized as a "double consciousness."[94] Black people in the United States are an amalgam of Africa and America. Martin Luther King was adamant that whether his people like it or not, and whether white racists understand it or not, they are at once, and forever, the children of two cultures, an amalgam of black and white.[95]

If blacks expect to gain full liberation and empowerment, it is necessary that they begin to highlight the African side of their heritage, no matter who might be displeased by the effort. It is necessary to work in the schools, homes, churches, and in places of employment in order to eradicate self doubt, and to manage repressed rage and anger enough to create openings to recapture the true meaning of that now forgotten slogan of the late 1960s, "I'm Black and I'm proud!" Influenced by the emerging Black Consciousness Movement near the end of his life, Martin Luther King himself counseled: "We must stand up and say, 'I'm black and I'm beautiful,' and this self-affirmation is the black man's need, made compelling by the white man's crimes against him."[96]

What this all comes down to is that blacks must not shy away from being *race persons*, which for our purpose only means that they must be lovers of things African. They must love themselves, their culture, and their heritage. Furthermore, they must teach black children— while they are very young—to do the same. To be a race person does not mean that one is anti-white, anti–Jewish, or anti- any other group. But it does mean that one is anti-oppression, anti-dehumanization, and pro-black.

Part of what I gather from Martin Luther King's later view of dignity is that this sense of black pride must be intentionally instilled in black children from the time they are able to recognize the meaning of symbols and words. By saying this I am also implying that it may already be too late for many present day black youths. It is virtually impossible to turn many of these youths around, so thoroughly and intricately ingrained is their sense of being nobody and of having no meaningful future in sight. And yet, because every black child is precious beyond measure, it is important that black adults keep trying. Teaching pride to black children must be an ongoing process until it becomes so deeply woven into their psyche that they naturally live, think, and act black, and never exhibit the characteristic of being ashamed of being black.

Martin Luther King said that black Americans "have been patient people, and perhaps they could continue being patient with but a modicum of hope; but everywhere, 'time is winding up ... corruption in the land, people take your stand; time is winding up.'"[97] So, whatever black and white allies intend to do to eradicate racial injustice, economic deprivation, and other forms of human oppression that diminish the sense of dignity in blacks, they had best get on with it. As James Baldwin reminded us, there is no time in the future for our salvation and that of our children.[98] We have only today to do what we know needs to be done. We must seize this moment—today!—to do love and justice. Let us heed King's passionate reminder: "We are now faced with the fact that tomorrow is today. We are confronted with the fierce urgency of now. In this unfolding conundrum of life and history there is such a thing as being too late. Procrastination is still the thief of time."[99]

If the reader's heart and entire being cries, as does mine, over the senseless intra-community homicides of black boys and girls all over this country, then one must understand what I mean when I say that there is no tomorrow where this issue is concerned. We have only today to put an end to this horrific tragedy, and everything we do from this moment onward, must reflect this sense of urgency.

No matter how pessimistic some of what has been said may appear, I am deeply committed to the idea that human beings of whatever hue, gender, sexual orientation, or class can do a much better job of relating and living together than we presently do. We can be better than we are, if we would only develop the will and tenacity to do so.

My conviction, consistent with Martin Luther King's, is that because the universe rests on a moral foundation or hinges on morality, as he liked to say, it is on the side of goodness and justice. Moreover, the best forces in the universe are always striving toward fuller, richer values. At birth human beings are candidates for rationality, humanity, and morality. When we will to do so; when we commit our entire being and best resources to achieving these, we can. James Baldwin, in words not at all unlike ideas preached and taught by Martin Luther King, was quite adamant that:

> ... this country is going to be transformed. It will not be transformed by an act of God, but by all of us, by you and me. I don't believe any longer that we can afford to say that it is entirely out of our hands. We made the world we're living in and we have to make it over.[100]
>
> Everything now, we must assume, is in our hands; we have no right to assume otherwise.... If we do not now dare everything, the fulfillment of that prophecy, re-created from the Bible in song by a slave, is upon us: *God gave Noah the rainbow sign, No more water, the fire next time.*[101]

Indeed, we are frightfully close to the point of having to declare, *the fire right now*!

4

Personalism and Moral Laws

Martin Luther King was not the first black person to study the philosophy of personalism at Boston University. However, he is the black person most often associated with this philosophical tradition. Indeed, had he not written in his application to Boston University Graduate School that he wanted to study there, both because Edgar S. Brightman (1884–1953) was teaching personalism there, and because one of his professors at Crozer Theological Seminary (a Boston University alumnus) encouraged him to do so?[1] King earned the Ph.D. in systematic theology[2] at that institution in 1955. While there, he was much influenced by Brightman and his former student, L. Harold DeWolf (1905–1986). Due to Brightman's sudden death, King had limited but quality time with him.

DeWolf wrote of his own influence on King, saying: "At nearly all points his system of positive theological belief was identical with mine, and occasionally I find his language following closely the special terms of my own lectures and writings."[3] King's most original and creative contribution to the personalist tradition was his relentless persistence in translating personalism into nonviolent social action by applying it to the trilogy of social problems—racism, poverty/economic exploitation, and war—that he believed plagued this country and the world.[4] While in seminary he vowed to focus on these social evils throughout his ministry. By focusing on social-ethical personalism, King, although unknowingly, was only following the precedence set by John Wesley Edward Bowen (1855–1933), the first black academic personalist,[5] and Francis J. McConnell (1871–1953), also a student under Bowne.

This chapter seeks to do three things: First, to assess the impact of personalism on King. Because some King scholars, e.g., David Garrow, downplay the importance of personalism on King's formal theological development,[6] it is critical that we remember at all times that King himself affirmed that personalism or Personal Idealism was his fundamental philosophical point of departure. "This personal idealism remains today my basic philosophical position. personalism's insistence that only personality—finite and infinite—is ultimately real strengthened me in two convictions: it gave me metaphysical and philosophical grounding for the idea of a personal God, and it gave me a metaphysical basis for the dignity and worth of all human personality."[7] Notice that King did not say that he first came to believe in a personal God and the dignity of persons through his study of personalism, as if to imply that he developed these convictions only after he arrived at the predominantly white Boston University. These were beliefs that were instilled in him through his family upbringing and teachings at the Ebenezer Baptist Church where his father was the senior minister. Therefore, these were convictions that King brought to the formal study of personalism, which in turn provided the metaphysical grounding he sought. Indeed, Susan Harlow brings a sharp clarity to the point in a paper she wrote on King: "The church of his parents and grandparents had imparted an understanding of God and of the purposes of Christian ministry that could not be displaced by theological sophistication. *His study of personalism reinforced his beliefs, rather than supplanted them.* It gave him a metaphysical basis for the dignity and worth of all persons."[8]

Second, I examine King's contribution to what may be cautiously referred to as "Boston personalism." I say "cautiously" because it implies that all who attended and taught at Boston University accepted the personalist faith. Or, equally problematic, the designation "Boston personalism" implies that proponents were in agreement about all aspects of personalism. "Boston personalism" must be taken to mean that advocates were in agreement with the basic outline of personalism, but differed in their understanding of various topics, e.g., God, time, and axiology. Third, this chapter considers the meaning of King's personalism for the black community today. I begin with a brief discussion of the meaning and development of personalism, followed by a consideration of several of its chief traits, and how King interpreted them. There is also further examination of King's belief in the existence of an objective moral order and the moral law system. These and related beliefs contributed to King's relentless faith that the *beloved community* would be actualized. He believed nonviolence to be the only means to this end. He thought of nonviolence not primarily as a strategy, but as a philosophy or way of life. Finally, I briefly discuss implications of the King type of personalism for the tragic phenomenon of intra-community black violence and murder among young black males. I discuss this phenomenon more fully in Chapter 14.

Meaning and Development of Personalism

What is personalism? In a nutshell, it is the view that reality is personal, and human beings are the highest—not the only!—intrinsic values. Personalism is a type of idealism which maintains that *person* is the supreme philosophical principle—that principle without which no other principle can be made intelligible. The type of personalism here considered, and which prompted Martin Luther King to claim it as his basic philosophical stance,[9] maintains that the universe is a society of interacting and intercommunicating selves and persons with God at the center. Personalism provided for Martin Luther King a philosophical framework to support his long held belief in a personal God; the idea of the absolute dignity and worth of persons[10]; and his belief in the existence of an objective moral order.

The term *personalism* was first coined by the German theologian Friedrich Schleiermacher in 1799, although he did not develop it philosophically. Both English and American scholars[11] used the term in their writings in the mid-nineteenth century. However, like Schleiermacher, they did not develop its philosophical meaning.

Personalism was made a going concern in the United States by Borden Parker Bowne, who is remembered as "the father of American personalism." Bowne was called to Boston University in 1876. Vigorously reacting against impersonalistic and naturalistic philosophies of the likes of Herbert Spencer,[12] Bowne argued persuasively and relentlessly that the personal can never be derived from an impersonal "Unknown," and that only mind or intelligence can produce intelligence. Indeed, for Bowne the most acute argument for theism is the argument from intelligibility.[13] Much influenced by the idealism of René Descartes, Bishop George Berkeley, and Immanuel Kant, Bowne gave primacy to self-certainty; the immaterialism of all phenomenal objects (which led to the view that all objects in nature are the manifestation of God's will and thought); the practical reason; a dualistic and activistic epistemology; the primacy of the good will; and the intrinsic dignity of the person.

Bowne's systematic development of personalism as a worldview, and as a way of living in the world led to the characterization of his philosophy as "systematic methodological personalism."[14] This meant that Bowne, more than any of his contemporaries, with the possible exception of George Holmes Howison,[15] pushed the personalistic argument to its logical conclusions in metaphysics, epistemology, philosophy of religion, and ethics. As a result of Bowne's leadership, Boston University was known as the great bastion of personalistic studies until (roughly) the end of the 1960s. For my purpose, I date the decline of personalism by the year of King's assassination in 1968. I do so because King was the chief social personalist in this country who explicitly identified himself as a personalist, was devoted to applying personalist principles to the civil rights movement, as well as addressing social problems.

King and Personalism

There is not one, but nearly a dozen types of personalisms.[16] Yet, even within the most systematically developed type, namely, *theistic personalism* (which King studied at Boston University), there are divergent viewpoints. For example, not all in this type of personalism accept the idea of an omnipotent-omnibenevolent God. Nor do all adhere to the idea of the temporality of God. But differences notwithstanding, personalism has a number of distinguishing features shared by all proponents (not least those affiliated with Boston University).

First, personalism maintains that *person* is prominent, both metaphysically and ethically. This means that the Supreme Reality (i.e., God) is both personal and the cause and sustainer of human and non-human life forms. This idea has important implications for the treatment of human beings in the world, for it implies that because the Supreme Person *chooses* or wills to create human beings, they are of infinite value to the Creator, and thus should be respected and treated like beings who possess infinite dignity. King often said that persons should be loved and respected precisely because God loves them. "The worth of an individual," he said, "does not lie in the measure of his intellect, his racial origin, or his social position. Human worth lies in relatedness to God. An individual has value because he has value to God."[17] Persons as such possess a fundamental sacredness because they are created and loved by God. For King, the biblical tradition of the Jewish and Christian faiths points to the quality of innate dignity in persons, an idea he believed to be implicit in the concept of *the image of God*. This led him to conclude: "This innate worth referred to in the phrase the image of God is universally shared in equal portions by all men. There is no graded scale of essential worth; there is no divine right of one race which differs from the divine right of another. Every human being has etched in his personality the indelible stamp of the Creator."[18] King believed that every person has not only an inborn sense of worth, but is of inestimable value to the Creator. This necessarily implied for him the obligation of persons to treat self and others with respect. The idea of an inborn ideal of worth is prominent in the ethical system of Bowne,[19] the black church tradition, and the Jewish and Christian traditions, each of which influenced King.

Second, the type of personalism that appealed to Martin Luther King is *theistic*. Personalists believe in a Personal God who is the creator and sustainer of the created order. In theistic personalism, we find metaphysical grounding for the biblical teaching that in God we live and move and have our being. Such a God is perceived as infinitely loving, caring, responsive, active, righteous, and just. We get a sense of the thoroughgoing nature of theistic personalism in

Bowne's contention that God is the only foundation of truth, knowledge, and morals.[20] Although he argued that it is impossible to demonstrate (i.e., prove) the existence of God, Bowne was eager to show that the problems of the world and life cannot be solved without God as the fundamental assumption.[21]

There is no question that King believed the universe to be under the guidance of a personal and loving Creator God. Nowhere did he express this more poignantly and movingly than when he reflected on some of the hardships and threats made against he and his family during the civil rights movement. "I am convinced that the universe is under the control of a loving purpose, and that in the struggle for righteousness man has cosmic companionship. Behind the harsh appearances of the world there is a benign power. To say that this God is personal is not to make him a finite object besides other objects or attribute to him the limitations of human personality; it is to take what is finest and noblest in our consciousness and affirm its perfect existence in him."[22] King believed God to be "a Personal Being of matchless power and infinite love," and that "creative force" in the universe who "works to bring the disconnected aspects of reality into a harmonious whole."[23]

Third, in addition to holding that reality is personal, personalism is *freedomistic*. In fact, the two organizing principles of personalism are person, and freedom. Accordingly, all being is both personal and free. To be is to be free, and to act, or have the potential to do so. Indeed, at bottom, to be free is what it means to be a person; to be a person is to be free, or an agent capable of acting, whether for good or evil. This sense of self-determination is what the Creator intends, a view which has important implications for the ethical and political freedom of human beings in the world, and what they ought to be willing to do to assert, protect, and defend their essential freedom.

Persons are not first created, and then *given* freedom. Rather, the nature of person is freedom. That is, it is the intention of the Creator that persons come into existence as free beings with the capacity to be self-determined moral agents. That some persons lack moral agency because they are mentally and otherwise challenged raises the theodicy question. That the extent of the existence of moral agency in some individuals is questionable because of the denial of basic life-chances also raises fundamental difficulties that have both moral and socio-political implications. For example, to what extent can we say that young black males who engage in intra-community violence and murder are *morally* responsible? There is no question that the one who pulls the trigger in a drive-by shooting is legally responsible; but morally? This is a most intriguing and important issue, but it must be set aside for now. At any rate, personalism maintains that in the most fundamental sense, to be is to be free. It is because of this essential freedom (the nature of what it means to be a human being) that *all* persons who are moral agents[24] are morally obligated to resist fiercely anybody and anything that undermines or seeks to crush that freedom.

Martin Luther King said three things about this essential freedom. First, freedom is the capacity to be self-determined and self-directed; "to deliberate or weigh alternatives." One can deliberate and weigh alternatives because she has sufficient intelligence and maturity to do so. I cannot help wondering about the extent of these in many young black males who, through no fault of their own, have been denied adequate training of the intellect and development of the socialization needed to reasonably insure their ability to deliberate and make responsible decisions. Second, freedom "expresses itself in decision." Once one chooses a particular alternative, she necessarily cuts off other possible choices. And third, King held that freedom implies responsibility. Once one makes a choice she is responsible both for the choice made, and its most foreseeable consequences.[25] It may also be reasoned that any practice that threatens one's freedom is also a threat to her personhood and impinges on her ability to weigh alternatives, to make decisions, and to be responsible for the choices made.

Freedom was so important to King that he concluded with Brightman that without it there can be no persons. Freedom is a capstone of personalism. Following Brightman and Bowne, King emphasized both the ethical as well as the speculative significance of freedom. Without freedom, he held, neither morality nor knowledge is possible, since each depends on the capacity to deliberate and choose. During doctoral studies at Boston University, King wrote an essay on the personalism of the British philosopher, John M.E. McTaggart (1866–1925). He argued against McTaggart's rejection of freedom. "In rejecting freedom," he said, "McTaggart was rejecting the most important characteristic of personality."[26] For King, in agreement with his personalist teachers, but also with existentialists such as Paul Tillich and Jean Paul Sartre,[27] freedom is an abiding expression of the higher spiritual nature of persons. "Man is man," he said, "because he is free to operate within the framework of his destiny.... He is distinguished from animals by his freedom to do evil or to do good and to walk the high road of beauty or tread the low road of ugly degeneracy."[28] In the deepest sense, freedom is what it means to be a human being; to be a human being is what it means to be free. "Man, says Paul Tillich, is man because he is free," King said.[29]

Finally, personalism conceives of *Reality as through and through social*, relational, or communal. Accordingly, it views the universe as a society of selves and persons who interact and are united by the will of God. The individual never experiences self in total isolation. Rather, the self always experiences something which it did not invent or create, but finds or receives from his "interaction and communication with other persons."[30] This idea is similar to the African traditional worldview which emphasizes the importance of the relational or communal, rather than the isolated individual. The focus is on *WE*, rather than *I*.[31] No person exists in isolation, but in community.

In any event, the emphasis on the communal nature of reality has been present in personalism since the time of Bowne. The focus on the personal was never intended to point to the idea of individuals in a vacuum. Instead, in the Bowne type of personalism the reference has always been to "persons set in relations to one another, which relations are as much a fact as is the separate existence of the individuals."[32] Third generation personalist social ethicist Walter G. Muelder, dean of Boston University School of Theology and mentor to King, expressed this idea in the term *persons-in-community*. He writes that "man is a socius with a private center...."[33] This description effectively holds in tension the primacy of both the person and the community, neither of which can be adequately understood apart from the other.

King's idea of the communal nature of reality and persons, and his idea of *the beloved community* were grounded in his doctrine of God. Although King followed more closely Bowne's more traditional concept of God than Brightman's, he had deep affinity with the latter's view that while God does not need us for God's existence as we need God for ours, God is love, and love is a social category. Persons cannot love to the fullest in isolation. Human beings are created to live together and can be fully human only in community. Brightman seemed to have this in mind when he wrote: "The maxim, 'Think for yourself,' is basic; but the further maxim, 'Think socially,' must be added if philosophy is to do its whole duty."[34] This implies that the nature of persons is such that we need relationship with like beings, and thus possess *a natural urge toward community*.

Martin Luther King was in agreement with personalism's view that this is what is required of Christians. "The real Christian world," wrote Albert C. Knudson, "is a world of mutually dependent beings. It is a social world, a world of interacting moral beings; and in such a world love is necessarily the basic moral law."[35] For King, love is the essence of the Christian faith. "I have discovered that the highest good is love," he said. "This principle is at the center of the cosmos. It is the great unifying force of life. God is love. He who loves has discovered the clue to the meaning of ultimate reality; he who hates stands in immediate candidacy for nonbeing."[36] Since love is at the center of the universe, so too, is the idea of community. Indeed, the relational idea roots deep in the black American familial, religious, and cultural heritage. Personalism helped King to ground this view philosophically.

King frequently expressed the idea of the interrelatedness of all life, and his sense that persons are by nature social. We see in his thought both a focus on the centrality of the person, and of community. "All life is interrelated," he said. "All men are caught in an inescapable network of mutuality, tied in a single garment of destiny."[37] This led King to reason that what affects one person directly, affects all persons indirectly. "We are made to live together because of the interrelated structure of reality,"[38] he frequently said. To treat even a single human being unjustly, therefore, is an affront to *all* human beings, including God.

Moral Law and the Moral Law System

In the literature on personalism, a moral law is defined as a principle which is intended to be *universal in application*. It applies to all cases and is valid for all human beings. It was Brightman who first developed the *moral law system*. He acknowledged that the system may be improved,[39] and this in fact occurred at the hands of some of his followers.[40] Brightman intended that this system be relevant and meaningful in every culture. However, he seemed to recognize and appreciate that cultural difference may require certain adaptations of the respective laws. This is what I take Brightman to mean when he writes that, "moral law is not intended to be universal in the sense of being binding on human beings at every stage of evolution and development, any more than it is binding on apes; it is universal for moral beings such as we know ourselves to be."[41]

Brightman distinguished moral law from civil, religious, natural, and logical law.[42] Moral law has two necessary conditions. First, it must be a universal principle or norm. Second, it must apply to the obligation of the will in choosing.[43] Because it is a universal norm it is a law. Because it requires the will to choose, it is moral. Accordingly, Brightman held that no act is moral merely because it conforms to a social code. An act is moral only if it conforms to moral law.[44] Therefore, every code is subject to critique by moral law.

According to Brightman, the moral law system is regulative, not prescriptive. That is, it does not tell us what specific moral choices to make. The laws are intended to guide us as we endeavor to make responsible moral choices. Because it is a "system," the use of the laws requires intention and effort on the part of those who use it. For, in order to accomplish what Brightman intended, the moral law system must be seen in its totality, and one must be aware at all times of the place and role of each law, as well as their interrelationship with each other and the entire system.

Brightman's moral law system is comprised of three sets of laws: *Formal Laws* (Logical Law, Law of Autonomy); *Axiological Laws* (Axiological Law, Law of Consequences, Law of the Best Possible, Law of Specification, Law of the Most Inclusive End, Law of Ideal of Control); and *Personalistic Laws* (Law of Individualism, Law of Altruism, Law of the Ideal of Personality). Each category, and the laws in it, presupposes the law which came before, and anticipates or points to the law which follows in the line of progression toward the most concrete law in the system (i.e., the last law in each group). Each law beyond the Logical Law (the first law in the system) includes more content than the one that precedes it. Brightman sums up the contribution of each set of laws to the system. "The Formal Laws deal solely with the will as a subjective fact. The Axiological Laws deal with the values which the will ought to choose. The Personalistic Laws are more comprehensive; they deal with the personality as a concrete whole."[45] In the Personalistic Laws the emphasis is on the person and persons in relationship as the subjects of the preceding laws. The Law of the Ideal of Personality is, for Brightman, the summary law of the entire moral law system. It states: "All persons ought to judge and guide all of their acts by their ideal conception (in harmony with the other Laws) of what the whole personality ought to become both individually and socially."[46]

King and Moral Law

Martin Luther King may have first heard of Brightman's personalism during his student days at Morehouse College.[47] It is significant that during his student days at Crozer Theological Seminary in Chester, Pennsylvania (1948–51), King took a third of his courses with George Washington Davis[48] in theology and philosophy of religion. Under Washington's careful guidance, King was introduced to the personalism of both Brightman and DeWolf.

When King matriculated as a doctoral student at Boston University, he was a student of Brightman's for only a brief period, for the teacher died less than two years after King began his work. King wrote of Brightman's strong influence on his character development.[49] Since he also studied under DeWolf (who became his major advisor when Brightman died), there is no question that he was familiar with Brightman's moral law system. Indeed, we have seen that during his first year of graduate study he wrote a paper in DeWolf's class on personalism entitled, "The Personalism of J.M.E. McTaggart Under Criticism." At several points King contrasted McTaggart's views with Brightman's. In the discussion on the significance of freedom King cited passages in Brightman's *Moral Laws*, to support his criticism of McTaggart's rejection of freedom. At one point he wrote: "As Brightman has cogently put it: 'If choice is not possible, the science of ethics is not possible. If rational, purposive choice is not effective in the [control] of life, goodness is not possible.'"[50] King believed that without freedom, persons would be little more than automatons. And then, in a passage reminiscent of Bowne's emphasis not only on the ethical, but the speculative significance of freedom,[51] King again cited *Moral Laws*, approvingly. "Without freedom, we are not free to think, for the power to think means that the individual can impose on himself the ideal of logic or scientific method and hold it through thick and thin."[52] This requires self-determination or power of will.

It may be argued that long before his formal study of personalism, Martin Luther King had developed the conviction that the structure of the universe itself is on the side of justice and righteousness; that there is a higher law than human law, of which human beings violate at great risk. Because of this, King easily resonated to Brightman's view of the existence of an *objective moral order* in the universe which people ought to obey. Said Brightman: "Idealists hold that moral experience points to an objective moral order in reality, as truly as sense experience points to an objective physical order, and most idealists believe that the objective existence of both orders can be understood rationally only if both are the activity or thought or experience of a supreme mind that generates the whole cosmic process and controls its ongoing."[53] For Brightman, as for King, the cause of both the physical and the objective moral orders is God. King's belief in the existence of such an order can be seen in a passage in his sermon,

"Our God is Able." "There is a law in the moral world—a silent, invisible imperative, akin to the laws in the physical world—which reminds us that life will work only in a certain way."[54] Similarly, he said in another sermon, "How Should a Christian View Communism?," that the Christian faith "sets forth a system of absolute moral values and affirms that God has placed within the very structure of this universe certain moral principles that are fixed and immutable."[55] Indeed, reflecting on the Montgomery bus boycott, King said: "There is something in the universe that unfolds for justice and so in Montgomery we felt somehow that as we struggled we had cosmic companionship. And this was one of the things that kept the people together, the belief that the universe is on the side of justice."[56] King believed with Brightman that the moral laws are "just as abiding as the physical laws" of the universe, and when they are violated the consequences will be no less severe than the violation of the law of gravity or other physical laws.[57]

King's fundamental faith was that no matter how much injustice exists in the world there is something at the seat of the universe which sides with good and justice. The basis of this faith was his belief in the existence of an objective moral order created and sustained by God, (before whom every knee shall bow). His many references to his conviction that freedom fighters have cosmic companionship further solidified his faith that the very grain of the universe is on the side of right and justice.

One who knows the moral law system of Brightman, and has read King's writings will be able to detect King's appropriation of these laws. What one should not look for in King, however, is explicit reference to or naming of the individual laws, although there is clear evidence that his moral reasoning was influenced by Brightman's moral law system. Furthermore, unlike Brightman and other moral law theorists, King sought to apply and work out these laws in the context of his civil rights ministry. So, while he did not specifically name the moral laws to which he appealed, he often cited the basic principle of a given moral law. For example, when he works through the practical application of the Logical Law, he does not cite the Logical Law as such. Rather, we find him citing the principle involved, namely, "logical consistency."[58]

Both Walter Muelder and John Ansbro have provided instructive discussions on the moral laws in the work of King. Although Kenneth Smith and Ira Zepp, Jr., examined the influence of the existence of an objective moral law on King's thinking, they did not discuss his appropriation of the moral law system as such.[59] However, Muelder and Ansbro did an admirable job in this regard.[60]

Ansbro suggests that in several instances King appropriated the moral laws differently than Brightman. Consideration of how King utilized two of these moral laws will have to suffice for our purpose. Although King appealed to both the *Law of Individualism* and the *Law of Altruism*, Ansbro suggests that he identified more with the latter law. This implies that there was in King's ethics a stronger other-regarding sentiment than we find in Brightman. The Law of Individualism points to the idea of the individual as the basic moral unit and thus the importance of self-love. It expresses what Bowne meant when he said that no person should ever be used as fuel to warm society.[61] King accepted the validity of the Law of Individualism, but seemed to place less emphasis on it than did Brightman. Instead, King focused more on regard for the other, or the ethics of agape. This ethic emphasizes the need of the other, not of self.[62] And yet, because he was a Christian and a personalist, King also saw the significance of self-love in any authentic interpretation of the Christian ethic.

According to King, agape "is the love of God working in the lives of men. When we love on the *agape* level," said King, "we love men not because we like them, not because their attitudes and ways appeal to us, but because God loves them."[63] It is this understanding of love which led King to the controversial conviction that "unearned suffering is redemptive."[64] But King went further. "Now I pray that, *recognizing the necessity of suffering*, the Negro will make of it a virtue. To suffer in a righteous cause is to grow to our humanity's full stature."[65] As for the need to abide by the philosophy of nonviolence, King pointed to one of its chief characteristics, namely, "a willingness to accept suffering without retaliation, to accept blows from the opponent without striking back."[66] He quoted Gandhi approvingly in this regard. "Rivers of blood may have to flow before we gain our freedom, but it must be our blood."[67] There was no question in King's mind that "suffering ... has tremendous educational and transforming possibilities."[68] We will see in Chapter 12 that womanist and other feminist thinkers find King's emphasis on redemptive suffering to be problematic.

Ansbro contends that King "was convinced that *agape* may at times demand even the suspension of the law of self-preservation so that through our self-sacrifice we can help create the beloved community."[69] King did not believe that such self-sacrifice necessarily precludes self-respect and self-love, although one surely wonders about this when it is known that he frequently placed the moral onus on those who are actually suffering oppression and injustice. That is, more often than not, King expected the oppressed to make sacrifices in order to love their oppressors. In one place he said that "there will be no permanent solution to the race problem until oppressed men develop the capacity to love their enemies. The darkness of racial injustice will be dispelled only by the light of forgiving love."[70] King believed that in the best interest of the redemption of others and the establishment of the beloved community, it is sometimes necessary for individuals to sacrifice everything for such an end. Ansbro rightly concludes that more than Brightman, King's application of the Law of Altruism was more open to self-sacrifice.[71]

This is an interesting point, since in personalism the self is the basic moral unit. A necessary precondition of respect, and regard for others, is that one respect and love self. Accordingly, Bowne wrote: "The condition of owing anything to others is to owe something to myself. The humanity which I respect in others, I must respect in myself. I am not permitted to act irrationally toward myself any more than toward others."[72] In this regard, duties to self are not of secondary, but primary importance. Bowne believed such duties "must take first rank in ethics," and that one is never more responsible for others than for self. This, he believed, is important because of the social or communal implications. "Every one must be a moral object for himself, and an object of supreme importance; for *he is not simply the particular person, A or B, he is also a bearer of the ideal of humanity*, and its realization depends pre-eminently upon himself."[73]

Personalistic ethics condemns not self-interest, but selfishness. Since the time of Bowne, this type of ethics has sought a balance between self and other-regarding interests. Just as the individual is not to disregard the needs and interests of society, society is not to unduly sacrifice the individual for its ends either. Both the individual and society have values that must be respected.[74]

As the basic moral unit, the individual always has rights against others and society. However, some seem more likely to sacrifice this principle than did Brightman or Bowne. It seems to me that this is a logical conclusion of the King-Gandhi principle that the nonviolent resister accepts violence of various kinds without retaliating in any way. As noble as this principle appears on the surface, it is not one that should be accepted uncritically, especially by those who have known nothing but the iron hands and feet of racial and other types of oppressions. For, one wonders how it can be expected that such a person can even have proper regard for others if she lacks such regard for self; if she places the needs or desires of the oppressor before her own. If I have little or no regard for myself, it is inconceivable to me that I will have a healthy regard for the neighbor, let alone for those who oppress me and demean my humanity. And while it may be conceded that it is difficult to maintain a good balance between the Law of Individualism and the Altruistic Law, I would say that for a period of time, it behooves groups like young black males, to place more emphasis on healthy regard for self. Because they have never been taught the importance and meaning of love of self, I understand perfectly why so many of them seem to live only to be killed or to kill others in their community. The need for a much higher regard for self among young black males is absolutely critical in light of the alarmingly high incidence of black-on-black violence and homicide. Yet, I want to be careful not to suggest that King was not aware of the need for self-love among young black males, for he most assuredly was. This is why—even during his pastorate in Montgomery, Alabama—he was so critical about the high rate of crime in the black community.[75] King was also very much aware—and troubled by—the phenomenon of black-against-black violence. Pointing out that blacks had not murdered innocent children in church bombings, and had not forcibly removed a black child from the home of his uncle, savagely beat and murdered him and dumped him in Mississippi's Tallahatchie River, King also acknowledged that blacks were not saints who were free of the violence spirit. "Unfortunately," he wrote, "a check of the hospitals in any Negro community on any Saturday night will make you painfully aware of the violence within the Negro community."[76] Life, he said further on, "is too precious to be destroyed in a Saturday night brawl, or a gang execution."[77]

Conclusion

What is the meaning of King's personalism in light of intra-community violence and murder perpetrated by young black males? Indeed, what might one under the influence of King's personalism say to the black community regarding this problem?

Martin Luther King was aware that the quantity and quality of the choices available to young black males are so limited that no matter what they choose, the consequences tend to be self-defeating and demeaning. When King took the movement to Chicago in 1966, he lived in a slum apartment. There he met and talked with many of the angry young black males who had no sense of hope or purpose because this society offered them nothing of substance. As a result, many of these young men resorted to violence against each other and other members of the Chicago black ghetto. Reflecting on this experience King said:

> I met these boys and heard their stories in discussion we had on some long, cold nights last winter at the slum apartment I rent in the West Side ghetto of Chicago. I was shocked at the venom they poured out against the world. At times I shared their despair and felt a hopelessness that these young Americans could ever embrace the concept of nonviolence as the effective and powerful instrument of social reform.
>
> All their lives, boys like this have known life as a madhouse of violence and degradation. Some have never experienced a meaningful family life. Some have police records. Some dropped out of the incredibly bad slum schools, then were deprived of honorable work, then took to the streets. To the young victim of the slums, this society has so limited the alternatives of his life that the expression of his manhood is reduced to the ability to defend himself physically. No wonder it appears logical to him to strike out, resorting to violence against oppression. That is the only way he thinks he can get recognition.
>
> And so, we have seen occasional rioting—and, much more frequently and consistently, brutal

acts and crimes by Negroes against Negroes. In many a week in Chicago, as many or more Negro youngsters have been killed in gang fights as were killed in the riots here last summer.[78]

King was unquestionably familiar with the phenomenon of intra-community violence and homicide among young black males.

One who takes King's personalism seriously would have to emphasize at least three things that necessarily must happen if we expect, realistically, to put a stop to the day to day incidents of black-on-black violence. I know that at some point it will be necessary to take on the powerful and privileged who controls the structures of this society and even benefit from intra-community black violence and homicide. But it seems to me that the first order of business is to send these three interrelated messages to the black community.

First, because God is the Creator and sustainer of all persons or of no persons, every human being, regardless of gender, race, class, health, age, or sexual orientation has been stamped with the image, fragrance, and voice of God. Because God willingly creates human beings every single one has absolute and infinite value, which means that all owe respect to each other and to self. No person or group should be easily sacrificed for the wellbeing of another.

Martin Luther King himself would remind black adults (many of whom have forgotten) and inform black youths (many of whom have never known!) of their infinite worth. He would emphasize that it is not merely the spiritual aspect of the black person that is so precious and valuable to God, but the *whole* person. He would stress the fact that mind and body are two sides of a single coin, and that both needs the other in order for either to exist in human form. Created persons are not disembodied selves, and cannot exist in this world without either mind or body. In addition, the best in the Jewish, Christian, and black American traditions suggests (against the classical Platonic-Aristotelian view!) that mind is not superior to the body, nor is the body intrinsically evil. King would stress the infinite worth of the whole black person—mind *and* body.

The Kingian personalist would say, especially to young black males today, that the body is sacred and precious.[79] Indeed, it is through the body that human beings come to know and understand life; that they know about emotions; are able to see, hear, touch, receive, give, fuse, separate, procreate, etc. The human being has no better means, no better instrument for communicating love (or anything else for that matter) than the body. That God created the human body and then breathed into it the breath of life, suggests its worth and sacredness. Robert Bruce McLaren rightly observes that God's action in this regard "clarifies that a human being is not essentially a soul inhabiting a body [as if to say with Plato that it is imprisoned by the body], but a body made to live by God. This eliminates the dualism of classical philosophy."[80]

One influenced by the King type of personalism would drive home the point that the bodies of black folk have an inviolable sacredness of their own, and therefore should be cared for and protected. Black youth should love, care for, and respect not only their bodies, but those of others. Black youth—all youth really—should be taught to reject the idealistic philosophical notion that the body is "a kind of casing over what I considered my real self," as literary author Alice Walker put it.[81]

Love your body! This is also a way of stressing the importance of caring for one's entire self, first, so that she may dare to learn how to care for others. "That's what makes the caged bird sing," Maya Angelou admonishes.[82] That's the message of the King type of personalism to young black males today; the message that all of us—regardless of race-ethnicity or class—

must try to convey to them, and it must be done when they are very young. And then it must be modeled for them, day in and day out, until the message gets home.

A second point is necessarily related to the first. Black youth must learn, celebrate, and be proud of their heritage and their race. Once they are shown how to develop a healthy sense of the dignity and worth of their mind-body, this will open the way to self-esteem and being proud—and not ashamed—of their blackness. This can only lead to a heightened sense of self-love, which means less temptation to abuse either one's self or others in the black community. No one who truly loves self, people, and heritage, perpetrates and perpetuates their own, and the destruction of their people. In his final presidential address to the Southern Christian Leadership Conference, King challenged those in attendance, saying, "...we must massively assert our dignity and worth. We must stand up amidst a system that still oppresses us and develop an unassailable and majestic sense of values. We must no longer be ashamed of being black."[83] This admonition implies the need to make a conscious effort to learn about black history, including both African and American contributions. For King insisted that whether we like it or not, and even if white racists do not understand it, black Americans (and white Americans too!) are an amalgam of Africa and America.[84] But realistically, we can be certain today that black youth will not learn about their heritage and history in this nation's educational institutions. This means that the responsibility of so educating them falls to the black community and its civic and religious institutions.

That King urged blacks to be proud of their blackness also implies his awareness that they are endowed with the capacity for developing such pride. What is needed is *the will* and *the effort* to develop it. In addition, what is important is not what those outside the black community think about blacks. On this point, King would join with Malcolm × in saying that it is necessary that blacks look to themselves, first and foremost. "We've got to change our own minds about each other," said Malcolm. "*We have to see each other with new eyes. We have to see each other as brothers and sisters. We have to come together with warmth so we can develop unity and harmony that's necessary to get this problem solved ourselves.*"[85]

Finally, the King type of personalism, which will be addressed in depth in the next chapter, points to the *need for the black community to own responsibility for all that happens therein.* This raises the issue of *moral agency* that has been so difficult for blacks to discuss openly and publicly, for fear that the whites will use what is said to appease their own consciences, and to diminish their sense of responsibility for creating the conditions that have made young black males an endangered species. Yet, I think that the Kingian personalist would say that there is too much at stake for blacks to remain silent about moral agency and owning responsibility for the many specific acts of violence and homicide in the black community. Therefore, it is critical for blacks to risk breaking silence on the question of moral agency.

Black Americans can, and *should*, blame the powerful and privileged (who manage and control racist institutions) for the conditions that have created in so many black youths a sense of hopelessness, lovelessness, and mean-spiritedness. But as for the specific acts of violence blacks must find in themselves the courage and the wherewithal to proclaim that inasmuch as black boys pull the trigger that maims or takes the lives of others in their community, they must answer, *not to White America!*, but to the black community. For both they and their victims belong to the black community. On the other hand, inasmuch as black adults allow incidents of black-on-black violence and homicide to continue unabated, they must be able to say that, "*WE* are responsible, and *WE* alone can put a stop to the violence. *WE* alone can, and must, take back the streets of our neighborhoods from our boys."

No matter how bad things may get, we must be willing to say with Malcolm × that we are at bottom the "masters of our own destiny." *We may not be responsible for what has caused our condition, but we are responsible for how we respond to it*. This keeps us in the moral field of responsibility. During an interview with Kenneth Clark in 1963, Malcolm × said emphatically that no one framed him when he was arrested and incarcerated prior to joining the Nation of Islam. "I went to prison," he said, "for what I did...."[86] "For what *I* did!" Malcolm owned responsibility for what he did that led to his imprisonment, even though he knew without question that the American legal system was unjust and racist. Indeed, the Kingian personalist would say that until blacks come to terms with their own responsibility for intra-community black violence and murder among black boys, the problem will be with them for many years to come.

5

The King Type of Personalism[1]

Although Martin Luther King claimed that Yale University was his preference for graduate school, he said that he was not admitted because of failure to take the Graduate Records Examination.[2] He also applied to Edinburgh University in Scotland and received a letter of acceptance.[3] However, it is strange indeed that he asserted that Yale was his school of preference, since he also said that he wanted to study the philosophy of personalism. Boston University was then the leading center for personalistic studies in the United States. In his letter of application to Boston University, King made it clear that a primary reason that he wanted to attend there was because (while a student at Crozer Theological Seminary) he had been influenced by the personalist ideas of Edgar S. Brightman, and wanted to study under him.[4] Brightman was an advocate of the theistic idealistic personalism that was developed and systematized by his teacher, Borden P. Bowne. When King applied to BU, Brightman was the premier personalist philosopher in the country. As a doctoral student at BU, King came to accept the Bowne-Brightman type of personalism as his basic philosophical stance.

Once King earned his doctorate and began the grueling and dangerous work of the civil rights movement, his personalism took on a form that went beyond that which he studied in school. The purpose of this chapter is to show how King came to personalism as his basic philosophical standpoint. To this end I want to do several things. First, to define personalism and provide a brief discussion of some of the early proponents in the United States, including early black Americans. Second, to provide a brief discussion of what I characterize as the "homespun" or homegrown contributions to King's personalism. Thirdly, to list and briefly discuss five key personalist ideas in the mature thought and practice of King. It is important to examine the King type of personalism, both because he himself named personalism as his basic philosophical point of departure, and because more explicit attention needs to be devoted to it.

About Personalism

Personalism, the oldest surviving American philosophy that still has a following, would not have meant as much to Martin Luther King had he not believed that its basic principles demands that proponents apply, live, or practice them, in efforts to achieve the *beloved community*, a term that absolutistic personalist Josiah Royce introduced and developed in his book, *The Problem of Christianity* (1913).[5] *Beloved community* was a popular term in the hallways and classrooms at Boston University School of Theology when King was a doctoral student

71

there. As far back as 1957, not long after the Montgomery bus boycott, King talked about the coming of the "new world" which was essentially what he had in mind when he spoke of the beloved community. The following is a paraphrase of what King said: The beloved community is one in which human beings will live together as brothers and sisters; in which they will beat their swords into ploughshares and their spears into pruning hooks; in which they will no longer take necessities from the masses to give luxuries to the classes; a community in which all human beings will respect the dignity and worth of all human personality.[6]

Inasmuch as the curricula at Crozer Theological Seminary and Boston University were essentially Eurocentric, Martin Luther King primarily studied and pondered the ideas of white men. Consequently, when he reflected on his intellectual journey in the two versions of "Pilgrimage to Nonviolence,"[7] we see no reference to the formal academic influences of blacks. Notwithstanding this, we can be certain about two important things. First, King filtered the ideas of white theologians and philosophers through his own mental and socio-cultural grid, which was the only way that he could make those ideas his own. Second, he was much more influenced by teachers and mentors at Morehouse College, including President Benjamin E. Mays and Professor George Kelsey, than he and commentators on his work, tell us. However, some King scholars, such as Lewis V. Baldwin, Luther Ivory, James H. Cone, David J. Garrow, Garth Baker-Fletcher, Michael G. Long, Clayborne Carson, and this writer have been quite intentional about trying to uncover some of those influences, as well as family and black church influences, in order to show how they were related to ideas that King later took as his own in seminary and during doctoral studies.

It was not difficult for Martin Luther King to find himself on the path to personalism. After all, he had grown up in a staunchly religious home and his father, maternal grandfather, and maternal great grandfather were preachers. What King was taught throughout his childhood, and what was modeled for him at home and in church, all confirmed for him that Christianity at its best stressed four things: 1) the value of persons as beings of supreme worth; 2) the value of the world; 3) the value of life itself; and 4) the importance of working to enhance and increase value in the world.[8] Unknown to the boy King and those who taught and modeled basic Christian principles for him, these emphases on the value of human beings, life, and the world were also basic foci of the philosophy of personalism. Consequently, by the time King first heard the term "personalism" (most likely) at Morehouse College, was introduced to its basic ideas at Crozer Theological Seminary, and then studied it systematically at Boston University, he was already solidly in the personalist camp; had grown up with some of its basic ideas, but did not know the term "personalism" at the time.

The later, mature King, would not have disagreed with Albert C. Knudson's claim that: "Personalism is *par excellence* the Christian philosophy of our day,"[9] or John Wright Buckham's statement that, "it can hardly be gainsaid that Christianity has closer and more complete affiliations with personalism than with any other philosophy. Its theory, as well as its very life, is bound up with the emphasis upon the person and personal values, as related to man and God."[10] Indeed, King would have cheered Buckham's claim that personality is "the master principle."[11] For both Christianity and personalism, the central feature is personality. In this sense, we may say that to be Christian is to also be personalist, if only a minimalist, i.e., one who believes God is personal, and that human beings possess inalienable worth.

When we think of Martin Luther King as personalist we need to remember that he adhered to a particular type of personalism, for there are at least a dozen of these, including but not limited to: the atheistic personalism of John McTaggart, the absolutistic personalism of Mary Calkins and Josiah Royce, the realistic personalism of Georgia Harkness, and the theistic personalism of Borden Parker Bowne, Edgar S. Brightman, and their disciples. Previously we saw that, as a seminary and doctoral student, King was introduced to and studied the theistic personalism of Brightman, was much influenced by it, and by his own admission, took it as his fundamental philosophical stance. Personalism gave him the philosophical and metaphysical basis for his long held beliefs in a personal-creator God, and the absolute dignity or sacredness of human beings.[12]

By rigorously and vigilantly applying the basic principles of the Bowne type of personalism to the civil rights movement, King unwittingly helped to forge another type of personalism—what I have called *Afrikan American personalism*.[13] This is a thoroughly social activist type of personalism that requires that one be unswervingly committed to acting against social injustice, with the aim of eliminating it. No one surpassed Martin Luther King in this regard. Indeed, more than his personalist teachers at Boston University, King consistently applied the principles of personalism to the problems encountered in the civil rights movement. By doing so, the personalism to which he adhered during his days as a doctoral student and the first months of his ministry as senior pastor at the Dexter Avenue Baptist Church in Montgomery, Alabama, took on a much different texture and look. Indeed, King was truly the quintessential *social activist personalist*.

Morehouse College and King's Personalism

Before proceeding, it will be instructive to say a brief word about the Morehouse College contributions to King's developing personalism. I know of no other instance in which efforts have been made to uncover the Morehouse roots of King's personalism, nor is the undertaking here intended to be exhaustive. For our purpose, I am particularly interested in the personalist contributions of the late president of that historic institution, Benjamin Elijah Mays (1894–1984). Indeed, the most cursory examination of writings, speeches, and sermons by Mays easily reveals a man who was steeped in personalist ideas and practice, even though he was not a personalist in a doctrinaire or thoroughgoing sense. Indeed, on closer examination, even the student of King will see that a number of personalist ideas frequently espoused by King were in fact borrowed (without attribution) from Mays. One illustration will have to suffice.

In a 1946 publication Mays wrote: "The destiny of each individual wherever he resides on the earth is tied up with the destiny of all men that inhabit the globe."[14] King was in his second year at Morehouse College at this time, and might well have even heard these or similar words in one or more of Mays' weekly chapel talks. A few years later, Mays enhanced the statement, saying (in a 1954 sermon at Bucknell University): "The destiny of each man is tied up with the destiny of another. We are so interlaced and interwoven that what affects one touches all. We are all bound together in one great humanity."[15] By this time King had completed the formal requirements for his doctorate and had been appointed senior pastor at the Dexter Avenue Baptist Church in Montgomery, Alabama.

Years later, King popularized Mays' statement in various speeches and writings, not least his famous "Letter from Birmingham Jail" in 1963, where he reminded his fellow white clergymen: "We are all caught in an inescapable network of mutuality, tied in a single garment of destiny. Whatever affects one directly, affects all indirectly."[16] In "A Christmas Sermon on Peace" (preached barely four months before he was assassinated), he added to that statement saying: "We are made to live together because of the interrelated structure of reality."[17] King did not cite Mays as the source of this idea, but we know from the previous quote from Mays that this idea was his. And yet, to his credit King, as was frequently his habit, added words and phrases that made the words of Mays (or others) fit his own rhythm, timing, and oratory. In this way he made the words as much his own as was possible. Although not to be taken as an excuse, even when King appropriated the words or ideas of others without attribution, his adjustments and his amazing oratory not only made them sound better, but gave them even deeper meaning.

Personalism is a fundamentally relational or communal philosophy that argues for the interrelated or interdependent structure of reality. Accordingly, in one way or another all things interact, affect, and are affected by all others. This implies a dependence of all things on all others, and is what Bowne seems to have meant as far back as 1887. When discussing the unity of the World-Ground, Bowne said that the idea of "interaction implies that a thing is determined by others, and hence that it cannot be all that it is apart from all others. If all its activities and properties are conditioned, it implies that the thing cannot exist at all out of its relations."[18] Without question, King early had a sense of this fundamental personalist idea, which arose, in part, because of ideas espoused by Mays. King's systematic study of personalism at Boston University solidified the relational idea by giving him the metaphysical foundation for it. This would become the basis of King's global outlook at a time when the term "globalization" was not in vogue. Long before most people, he was declaring the unity and oneness of the world, claiming that neither individuals nor nations can live alone. The destiny of India (which he had visited in 1959), he said in his commencement address at Lincoln University in 1961, is tied up with the destiny of the United States and every other nation. He affirmed the interrelatedness of all life, followed by the very familiar refrain:

> We are caught in an inescapable network of mutuality; tied in a single garment of destiny. Whatever affects one directly, affects all indirectly. As long as there is poverty in this world, no man can be totally rich even if he has a billion dollars. As long as diseases are rampant and millions of people cannot expect to live more than twenty or thirty years, no man can be totally healthy, even if he just got a clean bill of health from the finest clinic in America. Strangely enough, I can never be what I ought to be until you are what you ought to be. You can never be what you ought to be until I am what I ought to be. This is the way the world is made. I didn't make it that way, but this is the interrelated structure of reality.[19]

According to King, this was the handiwork of God. King went on to tell the graduates that in order to achieve the American dream it would be necessary to nurture and "cultivate this world perspective."[20] In recent studies on King, scholars such as Lewis V. Baldwin and Paul R. Dekar,[21] and Thomas Mulhall[22] have begun to give systematic attention to the globalization theme and its ethical implications in King's work, a theme easily identifiable from near the very beginning of his civil rights ministry. Indeed, Lewis Baldwin makes this very point in his second of many books on King, *To Make the Wounded Whole* (1992), a theme he continued to focus on in subsequent writings on King.[23] King was careful to name God as the source of the interrelated structure of the world.[24] This idea was implanted in King's mind when he was a student at Morehouse College. He uncovered the metaphysical basis for the idea during his systematic study of personalism as a doctoral student.

What Is Personalism?

In the simplest and broadest terms, personalism is any philosophy that makes mind or personality the ultimate reality or principle of explanation, while also stressing the innate and absolute dignity of human beings. The first part of this definition is important because it means that even the atheist can be a personalist, as was the case of John McTaggart, who held that personality is the ultimate reality. However, McTaggart had no use for God. For him, somehow, personality simply exists, apparently without cause. Of course, Martin Luther King believed firmly in a personal God, and thus was a theist. Therefore, it would be reasonable for the theist to define personalism as the philosophy that God is personal, and persons possess infinite, inviolable dignity because imbued with the image of God. This provides theological grounding for this latter idea.

The type of personalism to which Martin Luther King adhered is essentially a metaphysic. That is, it maintains that reality is a society of interacting selves and persons with a Supreme Person (God) at its center. (Notice the emphasis on reality as social or relational.) According to Bowne, "A world of persons with a Supreme Person at the head," is what we come to with this type of personalism.[25] Indeed, we come to the idea of "a Supreme Rational Will, which forever founds and administers the order of the world."[26] More explicitly, and in King's own words, personalism means "that there is a creative personal power in this universe who is the ground and essence of all reality...."[27] For King, as for his personalist teachers, personality is the fundamental principle of explanation, capable of explaining all other principles (as far as they can be explained), except itself.

Just think about this. In order to do any explaining or discoursing at all, one has to *assume* mind, intelligence, or personality, which itself says something about the significance and value of personality. This is why it is not uncommon for personalists to speak of personality as the *assumption of assumptions*. It is that principle to which few can be compared, and without which no principle can be compared. For, personality is that principle without which no other principle matters, or can even be known. Personality, on this view, is "the supreme philosophical principle," which means that in the quest for reasons and causes for things it is to personality that one must look for explanation. This is another way of saying that personality is the key to the mysteries of the world and the universe, or there is no key.[28]

What is important for our purpose is the emphasis that personalism places on personality or mind. Personality is significant metaphysically because it is thought to be the ultimate explanation of all things. But it is also significant ethically, inasmuch as it says something about how persons ought to be treated, by virtue of being persons. For, if personalists are right in their claim that human beings possess inherent and inviolable dignity, it follows that they ought to be treated accordingly.

Borden P. Bowne

Borden Parker Bowne (1847–1910) was the father of American personalism. He was called to Boston University in 1876 to teach in the philosophy department, and was later appointed dean of the graduate school. Interestingly, although known as the one who systematized and made personalism a philosophical method in the United States, Bowne did not refer to his philosophy as "personalism" until very late in his career (about five years before his death).

Initially, Bowne referred to his philosophy as *objective idealism*, the view that the object of perception is independent of the subject perceiving it. This implies that something in reality exists that human beings find, but do not make or create. That something is given, which means that human beings are not all there is in existence. In other words, there is something in existence (not ourselves) that conditions us and creates other things as well. This implies an objective ground of our sensations, which in turn suggests (to some thinkers at least) the existence of an Author or Creator.

As Bowne's thinking matured, he next referred to his philosophy as *transcendental empiricism*. This is the view that experience or nature depends on the categories of mind (e.g., space, time, number, motion, purpose, and freedom) rather than the other way around. The categories "are to be understood through the mind's living experience of itself."[29] In other words, it is the mind that makes and interprets experience and nature. Essentially this means that all thought about reality must be rooted in experience, or more specifically, the active self-experience of mind or intelligence.

Transcendental empiricism, according to Bowne, is the view that "all thought about reality must be rooted in experience and that apart from experience we never can be sure whether our conceptions represent any actual fact or not."[30] Just as in objective idealism, we can see in transcendental empiricism an increasing emphasis on the importance of personality, mind, or self. Bowne moved progressively from the *objective idealism* stage (roughly 1874–1895), to *transcendental empiricism* (about 1896–1904), and finally to the *personalism* stage (approximately 1905–1910). Bowne's student, and biographer, Francis J. McConnell, said that he first heard him refer to his philosophy as personalism in 1905.[31] Having read each of Bowne's books and dozens of his articles, I first saw his use of the term in his 1905 publication, *The Immanence of God*.[32] In each stage personality became more central, such that Bowne saw it as capable of explaining everything (that can be explained) but itself.

BOWNE AND BLACK AMERICANS

John Wesley Edward Bowen (1855–1933) was the first black person to study under Bowne for the Ph. D. As dean of the graduate school, it was Bowne who admitted Bowen. However, we should not assume too much about Bowne's racial views, for one looks in vain for evidence in his published works for where he really stood on the question of race relations. Unfortunately, the whereabouts of Bowne's unpublished papers—if any remain—is not known at this writing.[33]

Despite Bowne's reticence on race, it is without question that no one wrote more eloquently and passionately about the need to affirm the infinite, inviolable dignity of human beings in general, than Bowne. Indeed, two key statements in his famous book, *The Principles of Ethics*, stand out in this regard. "Whenever any two persons meet anywhere in existence," Bowne wrote, "they owe each other good will."[34] This implies that every person has intrinsic worth, and thus should never be treated as an impersonal object, a point that Bowne makes in the second statement: "The individual may never be regarded as fuel for warming society."[35] The person is not a means to an end, but an end in herself. However, it is not clear that Bowne actually included blacks in these statements, as he nowhere explicitly applies them to the race question. In addition, during Bowne's day it was not uncommon for many whites to view blacks as nonpersons, or at best subhuman. Thus, it was possible to view the abstract "human beings" as ends in themselves, while not applying the principle to a specific concrete group of human beings. This brings to mind words that Dostoevsky's character, Father Zosima, heard a doctor say (in *The Brothers Karamazov*): "'I love mankind,' he said, 'but I find to my amazement that the more I love mankind as a whole, the less I love individual people.'"[36] The more he loved human beings in general, the less he loved particular concrete human beings. The more he hated particular individuals, the more he loved human beings in general.[37] It is easy to love generally, universally, or in an abstract sense. If love means anything at all, the requirement must be to love concrete, specific, blood and guts human beings. This writer has known too many people who love humanity in general or universally, but who despise this or that group because of their difference, whether of culture, race, gender, sexual orientation, class, health, etc. Based on my close reading of the Bowne corpus, I have no doubt that he loved and respected humanity in general, and that this was a key idea in his philosophical scheme. I am more concerned about Bowne's specific stance on race, of which no record has been left or discovered to this point.

Bowne's student, John Wesley Edward Bowen, essentially devoted his life to academic administration and therefore did not write much. He did not use personalist nomenclature in what he did write, nor did he refer specifically to Bowne. However, some of his writings refer frequently to personalist ideas that are easily traceable to Bowne.[38] In addition, when I did research on Bowen I located notes that he took in courses with Bowne on theism. Bowen studied under Bowne during his objective idealism stage.

Gilbert Haven Jones was another black person who was much influenced by the personalism of Bowne. I had not been aware of Jones until his name came to my attention in an email from Robert Wesley Munro (a doctoral candidate at Michigan State University) who was writing his dissertation on Jones, and has read his German dissertation. Jones was not a student under Bowne at any point, but was clearly familiar with, and influenced by, his personalism. He was the first black man to earn the Ph.D. in philosophy from the University of Jena, where Rudolph Eucken served as his advisor. Near the end of his life, Bowne developed a friendship with Eucken, who he wrote twice. Bowne had obligations in Germany, and the two men planned to get together in Jena in June of 1910. Bowne suggested this in his second letter. However, Bowne died in April, and to date there is no known record of Eucken's response.[39] Jones received his degree in 1909, a year before Bowne's death. He wrote his dissertation on the philosophy of Rudolph Hermann Lotze and Borden P. Bowne. Bowne studied under Lotze in Germany in 1873. In any event, Gilbert Jones intended for his work on Lotze and Bowne to be a contribution to the philosophy of personalism, particularly as it was developing in the United States.

Edgar S. Brightman

Borden Parker Bowne had a number of outstanding students who also became university professors, and first rate scholars. Two of these (who would also gain appointments at Boston University) were Albert C. Knudson (1873–1953) and Edgar S. Brightman (1884–1953). Knudson followed closely Bowne's line of thinking, so much so, that when one reads his many books on philosophy and theology she might just as well be reading Bowne. Knudson did not advance much beyond Bowne's platform in personalistic thought, as he seemed to see no reason to criticize and otherwise challenge the views of his teacher.

It was an entirely different story with Brightman, who was not one to follow the party line, so to speak. Unashamedly and firmly in the personalist camp, he was determined to follow truth wherever it seemed to lead. He therefore challenged his teacher's thought at a number of points, not least his orthodox view of an omnipotent God. Brightman, who initially accepted this view, came to reject it as a result of his appeal to more empirical facts through both the biological and psychological sciences, as well as his insistence that personalism should be informed by more of William James's pragmatism and his emphasis on *doing* and *action*. Brightman also embarked on a renewed study of Charles Darwin and later evolutionary theorists, which influenced his revised thinking about God and evil. In addition, he lived through the slow, painful death of his young wife due to cancer, and also had to live with the knowledge of the tragic spinal injury suffered by a friend during a swimming accident that left him a paraplegic. Moreover, Brightman was much influenced by the idea that the universe is not static, but is essentially processive, creative, dynamic, and developing, as well as the idea that God is limited by the temporal structure of God's experience. Brightman was therefore led to reject his earlier adherence to Bowne's (and traditional theism's) view of God as omnipotent. In its place, Brightman substituted his controversial hypothesis of the *finite-infinite God.* By combining the previous elements and experiences along with the painful awareness of the presence of tragedy amid beauty in the world, Brightman developed the theory that God's power is limited by an uncreated internal factor he called the non-rational Given, while God's goodness and justice are infinite. Without question, Brightman was much more creative in the use of Bowne's ideas than Knudson, and as we have seen, he was willing to both criticize his ideas and then courageously follow the evidence where it seemed to lead.

BRIGHTMAN AND BLACK AMERICANS

Two black persons of note earned their Ph. D. under Brightman. One was James Hudson (1903–1980), who earned his degree in 1946. Hudson was without question much influenced by Brightman's personalism and his social thought. He was an academician, pastor, theologian, and civil rights activist in Tallahassee, Florida where he led protests and boycotts against segregated department stores, the local bus company, and Tallahassee Memorial Hospital.

Hudson's civil rights activism in Tallahassee occurred concurrently with that of the other black who chose to go to Boston University precisely because he wanted to study personalism under Brightman. I refer, of course, to Martin Luther King. There was mutual acquaintance between King and Hudson.

According to Professor Larry Rivers of Augusta State University, Hudson and other black leaders in Tallahassee sought King's advice during the boycott of the busses in that city. They surreptitiously brought King to town on a number of occasions to assist in the planning of their boycott strategy. King was also a guest in Hudson's home a number of times.[40] Hudson is credited with calling the meeting of the Interdenominational Ministerial Alliance and urging the members to join the boycott of the busses that was initiated by students at Florida Agricultural and Mechanical College when two female students were forced to give their seats to white patrons.[41] During the same period, King was already leading the Montgomery bus boycott and being advised on the nonviolent techniques of Gandhi by Bayard Rustin of the War Resister's League, and Glenn Smiley of the Fellowship of Reconciliation.

Contributions from Home

I now want to give brief consideration to personalist ideas to which King was exposed at home and during his black church upbringing. Although there are a number of personalist ideas that King was exposed to during this period, I here name and examine three: *Dignity of Persons; God as personal and creator; Self-Determination and the need to protest injustice.*

ABSOLUTE DIGNITY OF PERSONS

Most people who are familiar with Martin Luther King's upbringing are aware of the incident involving him and a white playmate. As preschoolers the boys played together regularly. When they reached school age, the white boy's parents forbade the two to play together. When young King inquired as to why, the reason given was that he was a "Negro." Confused and devastated, he told his parents about the incident, and they in turn had the painful and impossible task of trying to explain to the young boy what was behind what occurred. In a word, they had to give him a lesson in the history of race relations, as if any of this would make sense to a six year old.

King's mother placed him on her lap and told him about the history of the enslavement of his people and the remnants of that tragedy in the form of racial discrimination in the south and the rest of the country. Mrs. King also told and impressed upon her son that because the Kings were Christian people, it was not permissible to hate others because they were racists. Rather, Christians were required to return love for hate. His mother then told him what countless black parents told their children: "You are as good as anybody," a point that was regularly reinforced by both of King's parents and his maternal grandmother, Jennie Celeste Williams. The point of this was to awaken and strengthen the boy's sense of being somebody who was of inestimable value. His mother told him that he must never allow racism and discrimination to make him feel inferior. Because he was a child of God, was loved by God, and was imbued with God's image, he was deemed by God to be sacred and precious.

As might be expected, the boy could not understand how it was possible to love people who hated him because of the color of his skin. Looking back many years later, King said that he was determined to hate all white people, and that this attitude did not begin to subside until he enrolled at Morehouse College and joined an interracial organization called the Intercollegiate Council, where he discovered that not all white people were like the parents of his boyhood friend. King reflected that his involvement in this group "convinced me that we had many white persons as allies, particularly among the younger generation. I had been ready to resent the whole white race, but as I got to see more of white people," he said, "my resentment was softened, and a spirit of cooperation took its place."[42]

To have been loved by his parents, and reminded throughout his childhood that he was a child of God, infused with the image of God, that he was somebody, and that he was as good as anybody, made it easy for King to accept the personalist idea of absolute dignity and worth during his formal intellectual training.

GOD AS PERSONAL AND AS CREATOR

Martin Luther King grew up in the black church and was the son, grandson, and great grandson of southern Baptist preachers. Indeed, King recalled that while growing up he and his siblings spent so much time in church that it was like their second home. This means that they received heavy and regular dosages of fundamentalist black Baptist teachings in Sunday school, church, youth groups, and other church related activities. In addition, the King children were required to recite Bible verses at the dinner table. This was supplemented by frequent Bible story telling by their live-in grandmother. They would have learned much about the Fatherhood of God and the love of God through these stories. Reinforcement of these and related religious teachings was provided by their parents.

In addition to learning about God as Creator, King also learned from his church and home teachings that the God of Christians is personal. While growing up, he would have understood this in the religious sense, but not philosophically. The religious sense of God as personal has more to do with individual relationship with God, than with the philosophical meaning of a personal God. While growing up, King learned from the Bible and his father's sermons that each individual has her own personal relationship with God, in the sense that God has numbered every hair on her head and knew her by name, even before God summoned her into existence. Because God calls every person by name, each belongs to God and thus has her own special relationship with God (Isaiah 43:1). Religiously, young King knew from the Bible that every person belongs to the God of the universe (Ezekiel 18:4), which means that there is one Supreme Parent of all people (Malachi 2:10). This latter idea has strong implications for the unity or solidarity of human beings as one family under God. It is also suggestive of the interrelatedness or interdependence of all life. This means that even before entering More- house College and hearing chapel addresses by Benjamin E. Mays, the idea of the relational nature of life had already been implanted in King by his religious upbringing.

The boy King learned that God is personal in the sense that each human being is unique and special to God and can have his own unique relationship with God. While growing up, and prior to entering seminary, King would have known nothing about how the idea of God as personal was related to the philosophy of personalism. Because he learned much through teachings and example in the home and at church about the religious meaning of God as per- sonal, this made it possible for him to easily and comfortably adopt the personalistic view of God as personal during his formal academic training.

IMPORTANCE OF SELF-DETERMINATION AND OBLIGATION TO RESIST INJUSTICE

Both self-determination and the sense of the need to protest injustice are prominent themes in King's family lineage. The staunchly religious members of King's family did not, like many of their white counterparts, separate religion from socio-ethical behavior. For the Kings, to be religious affected how one lived one's day to day life, and required that one resist social evil and injustice. This was a chief theme of the Hebrew prophets and Jesus Christ, who declared God's expectation that justice and righteousness be done in the world.

King's paternal grandparents, James and Delia King, were not disposed to uncritically, silently, and passively endure injustices against them, and especially their children, without resisting, even violently. When King, Jr.'s father was growing up in Stockbridge, Georgia, a white mill owner beat him one day when he was on an errand for his mother. When he returned home in bloodied condition, his mother returned (with him) to confront the mill owner, man- aged to take him to the ground, and beat him, declaring simultaneously that anybody who harms her children will answer to her. During that period in the Deep South this was a very dangerous move on Delia King's part. For her to have even looked at the white mill owner a certain way could have led to her own or the flogging or lynching of other members of her family. Nevertheless, her action revealed her willingness to resist such mistreatment—violently if necessary—regardless of the possible consequences. When James King heard about the inci- dent he got his rifle and went looking for the white mill owner. King, Jr., obviously did not inherit the nonviolent spirit from his paternal grandparents, but he did inherit from them the spirit of the obligation to resist social evil with all one's might.

King's maternal grandparents, Adam Daniel (A. D.) and Jennie Celeste Williams, also pro- tested social injustices, but *only* through nonviolent means. When the newspaper editor of *The*

Georgian made derogatory statements about Atlanta's black community, many blacks wanted to burn down the building. A. D. Williams, pastor of Ebenezer Baptist Church and president of the local chapter of the NAACP insisted that violence was not the way. Instead, Williams first met with the editor, who insulted him, refused to issue an apology, and then demanded that he leave his office. Williams then called a meeting of black pastors and organized a boycott of the newspaper. No apology was forthcoming. So determined were the boycotters that within a few months *The Georgian* went out of business due to low sales. Here we have an instance of both the spirit of protest and the appeal to nonviolent direct action as the most reasonable means to addressing injustice. This double emphasis was the legacy from the maternal side of King's family. Historically, the belief in God as personal and as loving creator who imbues all persons with the image of God, caused blacks to believe that Christians have a moral obligation to resist collective evil.

What is important for our purpose is that each of these three themes: that every person is an heir to a legacy of absolute dignity by virtue of their relatedness to God; the conviction that God is personal and creator; and that human beings are morally obligated to resist social injustice, are fundamental religious themes that made a deep impression on the boy King and made him amenable to the formal teachings of the philosophy of personalism.

Characteristics of the Mature King's Personalism

Although there is some overlap with characteristics of King's *homespun* personalism, I want now to examine five of the basic traits of the mature King's personalism: Belief in a Personal God; Significance of Freedom; Absolute Dignity; Interrelatedness of Persons; and the faith that the universe is value-fused and under a loving purpose. These are all basic tenets of the King type of personalism.

BELIEF IN A PERSONAL GOD

We saw earlier that King's personalism and his Christian faith assured him that a Personal, creative, and loving power is the source of reality. What precisely did King mean when he referred to God as personal? He sometimes spoke and wrote about this in philosophical terms. At other times he did so in more religious, concrete terms.

When King talked about a personal God philosophically he was without question influenced by the personalist Bowne. Nowhere is this clearer than King's distinction between what he characterized as his earlier philosophical conception of a personal God that "was little more than a metaphysical category that [he] found theologically and philosophically satisfying,"[43] and the personal God of his faith who, as "a living reality," was present in his day to day struggles during the Montgomery bus boycott. He expressed the following philosophical view of God as personal:

> I am convinced that the universe is under the control of a loving purpose, and that in the struggle for righteousness man has cosmic companionship. Behind the harsh appearances of the world there is a benign power. To say that this God is personal is not to make him a finite object besides other objects or attribute to him the limitations of human personality; it is to take what is finest and noblest in our consciousness and affirm its perfect existence in him. It is certainly true that human personality is limited, but personality as such involves no necessary limitations. *It means simply self-consciousness and self-direction.*[44]

This characterization clearly reflects King's reading of Bowne's book, *Personalism*. In that text Bowne wrote: "The essential meaning of personality is selfhood, self-consciousness, self-control, and the power to know. ... *Any being, finite or infinite, which has knowledge and self-consciousness and self-control, is personal*; for the term has no other meaning."[45] (This is without doubt the view expressed above by King.) By definition then, corporeal or physical attributes are not part of the philosophical meaning of personality. Consequently, Bowne writes (what we also see reflected in King's statement): "In thinking ... of the Supreme Person we must beware of transferring to him the limitations and accidents of our human personality, which are no necessary part of the notion of personality, and think only of the fullness of power, knowledge, and selfhood which alone are the essential factors of the conception."[46] In a 1956 sermon, King, clearly influenced by Bowne, said that to say that God is personal means: "God can think; God is a self-determined being. God has a purpose. God can reason. God can love."[47]

Having found this way of thinking about God as personal to be philosophically satisfying during his student days, King discovered early in his leadership of the Montgomery bus boycott that this was not fully satisfying and did not provide the trust and comfort level needed for the dangerous work in which he was engaged. The threats to his life and that of his wife and children during and beyond the Montgomery bus boycott caused him to draw closer to the personal God of his religious faith.

Prior to Movement work, Martin Luther King had always believed in a personal God, although mostly from a philosophical standpoint. With the threats to his and the lives of his family, and the bombing of his house in Montgomery, he needed the personal God that his parents and maternal grandmother told him about when he was a boy. This all came to a head for the young minister one late night after a few weeks into the Montgomery bus boycott. King had gone to bed, and just as he was dozing off, the telephone rang. As King remembered it: "An angry voice said, 'Listen, nigger, we've taken all we want from you; before next week you'll be sorry you ever came to Montgomery.'"[48] He had received numerous similar threats before, but that particular night it was too much to bear. He couldn't get to sleep, so he left the bedroom and began to pace the floor. King tells us what happened next.

> Finally I went to the kitchen and heated a pot of coffee. I was ready to give up. With my cup of coffee sitting untouched before me I tried to think of a way to move out of the picture without appearing a coward. In this state of exhaustion, when my courage had all but gone, I decided to take my problem to God. With my head in my hands, I bowed over the kitchen table and prayed aloud. The words I spoke to God that midnight are still vivid in my memory. "I am here taking a stand for what I believe is right. But now I am afraid. The people are looking to me for leadership, and if I stand before them without strength and courage, they too will falter. I am at the end of my powers. I have nothing left. I've come to the point where I can't face it alone."
>
> At that moment I experienced the presence of the Divine as I had never experienced Him before. It seemed as though I could hear the quiet assurance of an inner voice saying: "Stand up for righteousness, stand up for truth; and God will be at your side forever." Almost at once my fears began to go. My uncertainty disappeared. I was ready to face anything.[49]

In a later version of this incident, King said that as he paced the floor he tried—to no avail—to get comfort from some of the philosophical and theological ideas he had studied in school as he tried to make sense of the existence of sin and evil.[50]

If we sometimes wonder whether King ever experienced fear during and beyond Montgomery, the answer is yes. In an interview by Martin Agronsky in 1957, King said that "there were points and there were times that I moved around, actually afraid within."[51] On June 21, 1966, King gave a speech on the steps of the courthouse in Longdale, Mississippi, on the second year anniversary of the murders of the young civil rights activists, James Chaney, Andrew Goodman, and Michael Schwerner. Immediately behind King was Deputy Cecil Price, one of the murderers. King told the crowd: "I believe the murderers are somewhere around me at this moment."[52] Deputy Price immediately responded: "you damn right..., they're right behind you."[53] Although King went on to say that he was not afraid, he later expressed his fear to a reporter, saying, "This is a terrible town, the worst I've seen. There is a complete reign of terror here."[54] Nevertheless, King believed that as time went on he experienced fewer moments of fear, primarily because he had submitted to total dependence on God. The vision at the kitchen table that late January night during the Montgomery bus boycott was for him "a deep religious experience" which prepared him for what was to come. In that same interview King told Agronsky: "I had come to feel, at that time, that in the struggle, God was with me, and through this deep religious experience, I was able to endure and face anything that came my way. Now, I think that still stands with me. After a long process of really giving my whole life to a religious way and to the will of God, I came to feel that, as we struggle together, we have cosmic companionship."[55] Such a stance enabled King to confront the fears, refusing to allow them to incapacitate him.

In any case, it is quite likely that the experience at the kitchen table is what led to King's overwhelming sense of trust and dependence on the personal God of his faith. In a provocative statement, David J. Garrow has written that the night of King's vision at the kitchen table was "the most important night of his life, the one he always would think back to in future years when the pressures again seemed to be too great."[56] Each time he seemed to gain new energy, strength, and courage. King learned that his faith had to become real for him. It was not enough that his mother, father, and grandmother had such faith. He came to see that he had to know God for himself—not philosophically, not through the experience of family members. He had to know God personally. This was the personal God he would now depend on for the rest of his life.

Martin Luther King came to see that he could not say about his philosophical conception of a personal God what he could say about the personal God of his faith; the God he discovered at the kitchen table; the God who would stand with him, as murderers stood behind him. About this God he could later say: "God has been profoundly real to me in recent years. In the midst of outer dangers I have felt an inner calm. In the midst of lonely days and dreary nights I have heard an inner voice saying, 'Lo, I will be with you.' When the chains of fear and the manacles of frustration have all but stymied my efforts, I have felt the power of God transforming the fatigue of despair into the buoyancy of hope."[57] This was what King meant when he spoke of a personal God in the religious sense. He said that this God "does not leave us alone in our agonies and struggles," but "seeks us in dark places and suffers with us and for us in our tragic prodigality."[58] This is the God who "is a light unto our path," who "imbues us with the strength needed to endure the ordeals of Egypt," and who "gives us the courage and power to undertake the journey ahead."[59] Because God is personal, i.e., has both feeling and will, God receives, understands, and responds to human beings' prayers.[60]

The personal God of King's faith was not Alfred North Whitehead's "Principle of Concretion" (although King most assuredly would have warmed to Whitehead's characterization of God as "the great companion—the fellow-sufferer who understands"[61]); not the "Absolute Whole" of Hegel and Spinoza; not the "Architectonic Good" of Plato; nor the "Unmoved Mover" of Aristotle. King said that one need not know philosophy or what philosophers have said about God, particularly if one knows God for oneself. In this way, King said, blacks in particular know well that their ancestors were right: "Because they did know [God] as a rock in a weary land, as a shelter in the time of starving, as my water when I'm thirsty, and then my bread in a starving land. ... 'He's my everything. He's my sister and my brother. He's my mother and my father.'"[62] It doesn't get anymore *personal* than this. King's concept of a personal God clearly means that one can actually depend on God in a way and to an extent that he cannot depend on the God of philosophy. For King, the God of personalism was similar to the God that his parents, maternal grandmother, and the black Baptist church told him about. This was the God who revived his soul and helped him to live through his fears during his most difficult times during the civil rights movement. *This* God was his balm in Gilead.[63]

SIGNIFICANCE OF FREEDOM

When Martin Luther King talks about freedom philosophically, one can again hear the influence of Bowne, who he read and studied in the course on personalism that he took under L. Harold DeWolf during his doctoral studies. In the final examination for that course, King described Bowne as "the forthright champion of freedom," and said that it was his "most characteristic emphasis."[64] He acknowledged that for Bowne freedom had both epistemological and ethical significance; that without freedom both reason and morality would be shipwrecked.

Years later, in his speech, "The Ethical Demands for Integration," we again find King talking about freedom in ways that unquestionably reveal the influence of Bowne's personalism. Discussing the nature and significance of freedom King said:

> The very character of the life of man demands freedom. In speaking of freedom at this point I am not talking of the freedom of a thing called the will. The very phrase, freedom of the will, abstracts freedom from the person to make it an object; and an object almost by definition is not free. But freedom cannot thus be abstracted from the person, who is always subject as well as object and who himself still does the abstracting. So I am speaking of the freedom of man, the whole man, and not one faculty called the will.[65]

King was speaking of the freedom of the concrete flesh and blood human being; the freedom of the whole person, and as we will see below, what he said was without question influenced by Bowne.

Apart from his final examination in the class on personalism, King did not cite Bowne in his later post-doctoral discussions on freedom, and yet Bowne's ideas were present. For Bowne also rejected the idea of an abstract freedom existing by itself.[66] Rather, Bowne characterized freedom as the power of self-direction in human beings, a view that King made his own. For Bowne—and again similar to King—freedom was not merely a question of ethics, but of reason or rationality as well. Without freedom both ethics and reason are impossible— "shipwrecked" Bowne liked to say.[67] There can be no ethical responsibility without freedom. Nor can there be a distinction between truth and error. The King type of personalism contends for the essential truth of our faculties; that they were constructed for truth. We have error because we are free to misuse our faculties or to disregard them. Although constructed for truth, our faculties have not the power to insure that we will use them to acquire truth. The fact that we have error must mean that we appeal to our freedom to do things other than what the faculties or reason was made for.[68] If reason had right and power, as it has authority, it would rule the world.[69]

According to King, freedom means essentially three things: the power to deliberate or weigh alternatives; to come to decision; and to be responsible for the decision or choice made.[70] Again, this view is not different from Bowne's contention that freedom is "the power of self-direction, the power to form plans, purposes, ideals, and to work for their realization."[71] For both Bowne and King, freedom is something of the vitamin A of what it means to be a human being. Freedom, Bowne held, "seems to be involved in the very thought of a personal and rational life."[72] Freedom is what it means to be a person; a person is what it means to be free. King observed that "we are all free in the sense that freedom is that inner power that drives us to achieve freedom."[73]

Regarding the latter idea about the essential quality of freedom in human beings, King was in agreement with not only his personalist forbears at Boston University, but with existentialists, especially Paul Tillich (on whom he wrote half of his doctoral dissertation[74]) and Jean Paul Sartre (whose ideas he first encountered in seminary[75]). King often cited Tillich's idea that "man is man because he is free...,"[76] and was certain that the focus on human freedom is "one of the permanent contributions of existentialism."[77] Furthermore, King was certain that: "Freedom is that vital, intrinsic value which determines ones selfhood. It is worth suffering for; it is worth losing a job for; it is worth going to jail for. I would rather be a poor free man than a rich slave."[78] Arguing that indecision is still decision,[79] King was in clear agreement with Sartre's view that human beings are "condemned to be free,"[80] another way of saying that it is impossible for human beings not to choose. "I can always choose," writes Sartre, "but I ought to know that if I do not choose, I am still choosing."[81] Clearly with Sartre in mind, King himself declared that human beings "must choose, that we are choosing animals; and if we do not choose we sink into thinghood and the mass mind."[82] King was convinced that freedom is that vital intrinsic value that determines one's personhood.[83] Take away one's freedom, and you take away that which is vital to what it means to be a human being; in effect, King held, you "rob him of something of God's image."[84]

ABSOLUTE DIGNITY

Martin Luther King accepted implicitly the personalist view that human beings are both the highest in the animal kingdom, *and* the children of the Highest, made in God's image.[85] There is no unanimity of agreement as to the precise meaning of the *imago dei* or image of God. Suffice it to say that it has been interpreted in terms of fellowship, freedom, love, responsiveness, creativity, relationality, reason, and conscience, expressions of human beings' higher spiritual nature. King tried to clarify this when he said: "Man is more than flesh and blood. Man is a spiritual being born to have communion with the eternal God of the universe. God creates every individual for a purpose—to have fellowship with him. This is the ultimate meaning of the image of God. It is not that man as he is in himself bears God's likeness, but rather that man is designated for and called to a particular relation with God."[86]

Because all human beings are infused with something of the Divine, all equally possess intrinsic worth and are equally valued by God. For King, and other theistic personalists, this and the relatedness to God is what give each human being her uniqueness and dignity. In his second year in seminary, King wrote of how enslaved Africans in the United States were insulted and demeaned on a daily basis, but found solace in their religious gatherings. "But as they gathered in these meetings," King wrote, "they gained a renewed faith as the old unlettered minister would come to his triumphant climax saying: 'you—you are not niggers. You—you are not slaves. You are God's children.' This established for them a true ground of personal dignity."[87] In a message written for the National Council of Churches' thirty-fifth annual observance of Race Relations Sunday on February 10, 1957, King said:

All men, created alike in the image of God, are inseparably bound together. This is at the very heart of the Christian gospel. This is clearly expressed in Paul's declaration on Mars Hill: "...God who made the world and everything in it, being Lord of heaven and earth,..." again it is expressed in the affirmation, "There is neither Jew nor Greek, there is neither slave nor free, there is neither male nor female; for you are all one in Christ Jesus." The climax of this universality is expressed in the fact that Christ died for all mankind.

This broad universality standing at the center of the Gospel makes brotherhood morally inescapable. Racial segregation is a blatant denial of the unity which we all have in Christ. Segregation is a tragic evil that is utterly un–Christian.[88]

Not only is every human being made to live together in community, but every single one is infinitely precious to God, a point that King sought to convey when he quoted the scripture: "There is joy in heaven over one sinner"[89] (Luke 15:7). This, he held, is precisely why we must resist and fight against racism, segregation, and every other attitude and practice that alienates and separates human beings from each other and from God.

We need also to remember that when personalists such as Martin Luther King talk about the dignity or sacredness of human beings, the reference is not merely to the spiritual side of their being, but to the whole person—mind, spirit, and body. God calls human beings into existence as *en-souled bodies* and *embodied souls*, so that on this side of the grave, at least, we are at once and always a spiritual *and* biological being. Because both soul and body are thought to be the creation of God, both are intrinsically good; both are sacred. This is a view that could have come straight out of the Book of Genesis where we are told that all that God created is *very* good (Genesis 1:31). The body is not inherently evil, but is sacred, because created by God.

INTERRELATEDNESS OF PERSONS

We have seen that King's personalism contends that reality is a society of interrelated and interacting selves and persons with God (the Supreme Person) at its center. Such beings are dependent on, but not a part of, God. In any event, according to personalism the basic structure of experience is social. King's personalist teacher, Brightman, held that, "For personalism ... reality is social through and through. Every personal experience includes something which the person did not invent or create, but which he received from his interaction and communication with other persons."[90] For personalism, then, "social categories are ultimate," which means that human beings are essentially relational beings, or individuals-in-relationship.

Martin Luther King pointed to the interrelatedness of human beings and communities in many of his writings and speeches, not least his famous "Letter from Birmingham Jail." He also stressed the indivisibility of justice, and rejected the idea that any community any place in the world exists in isolation. Instead, he reminded all of the interrelated nature of reality and the world.[91] What affects one, affects all directly or indirectly. Stressing the idea that human beings are made to live together because of the interdependent quality of the structure of reality, King gave the example of how dependent we each are on people in other parts of the world.

Did you ever stop to think that you can't leave for your job in the morning without being dependent on most of the world? You get up in the morning and go to the bathroom and reach over for the sponge, and that's handed to you by a Pacific islander. You reach for a bar of soap, and that's given to you at the hands of a Frenchman. And then you go into the kitchen to drink your coffee for the morning, and that's poured into your cup by a South American. And maybe you want tea: that's poured into your cup by a Chinese. Or maybe you're desirous of having cocoa for breakfast, and that's poured into your cup by a West African. And then you reach over for your toast, and that's given to you at the hands of an English-speaking farmer, not to mention the baker. And before you finish eating breakfast in the morning, you've depended on more than half of the world. This is the way our universe is structured, this is its interrelated quality.[92]

King was convinced that until we acknowledge and take serious the interrelated structure of the universe and what this means for human relations, love, justice, and peace will not prevail in the world. Moreover, we saw earlier that this led him to the conviction that he could not be what he ought to be, if the next person is not what she ought to be, and vice versa. God made the world this way. King was unquestionably arguing against an "I-centered" ethic, and in favor of a "we-centered" one. This, he was convinced, is more consistent with how the universe is structured. If all life is truly involved in a single process as King believed, then whatever is done to Rebecca is done to me. Injustice to Gay, Lesbian, Bi-Sexual and Transgendered people is injustice to heterosexual people. "Injustice anywhere," King loved to say, "is a threat to justice everywhere."[93]

Conviction That the Universe Is Value-Fused

Martin Luther King was always reminding his audiences that there is something basic or fundamental about the universe that justified his faith that the universe itself is on the side of justice and righteousness; that at the end of the day, good will triumph over evil; that the vitriolic words and deeds of racists and segregationists will not have the last say; that one dies morally when she fails to stand up for justice.[94] Noting the similarity to Christian principles, King said: "This belief that God is on the side of truth and justice comes down to us from the long tradition of our Christian faith. There is something at the very center of our faith which reminds us that Good Friday may occupy the throne for a day, but ultimately it must give way to the triumphant beat of the drums of Easter. Evil may so shape events that Caesar will occupy a palace and Christ a cross, but one day that same Christ will rise up and split history into AD and BC, so that even the life of Caesar must be dated by His name."[95] This is but a reminder to human beings "that God ultimately rules history" and "the forces of evil and injustice cannot survive."[96]

Martin Luther King lived by the faith conviction—not proof, for it is not possible to mathematically prove or disprove his position—that there is something at the core of the universe that supports the claim of the nineteenth-century abolitionist-preacher Theodore Parker that, "the arc of the moral universe is long, but it bends toward justice"; that supports the claim of the Bible that you will reap what you sow; the claim of Thomas Carlyle that "no lie can live forever"; the claim of William Cullen Bryant that, "truth crushed to earth will rise again"; the claim of James Russell Lowell that, "Truth forever on the scaffold, wrong forever on the throne, yet that scaffold sways the future, and behind the dim unknown, stands God within the shadow, keeping watch above his own."[97] This was one of King's favorite mantras, and he repeated it frequently in speeches and sermons.

According to Martin Luther King, goodness, love, and justice are at the center of the universe. For any who believes this, there is always reason for hope. To believe that love, justice, and good will ultimately triumph means that every seeming defeat is only temporary as long as one persists in trying to overcome. To believe that God is the source of love, justice, and good is to also believe that one has cosmic companionship as she fights for justice in the world.

Personalism declares that it is right that all things should support the good will on its way to doing what is just and right. "The moral government of the universe means just this, among other things," said Bowne, "that all things are working together to secure for the good will the perfect life it seeks."[98] King himself declared on numerous occasions that God has created the universe such that it hinges on a moral foundation,[99] and that "there is a law in the moral world—a silent, invisible imperative, akin to the laws in the physical world—which reminds us that life will work [well] only in a certain way. The Hitlers and Mussolinis have their day," said King, "and for a period they may wield great power, spreading themselves like a green bay tree, but soon they are cut down like the grass and wither as the green herb."[100]

Not unlike his personalist teachers at Boston University, Martin Luther King believed deeply in the existence of objective moral laws on which all human or civil laws should be based. Bowne had this in mind when he wrote: "Back of both the individual and the collective will is the fixed nature of things, the moral law, the natural rights of the person, and the constitution of the objective world; and all that men or nations do must finally be referred to these as their warrant and foundation."[101] Because King believed with Bowne and other personalists that moral law is an expression of God's will, he was adamant that it applies to all people, and that it cannot be mocked or defied without severe consequences. He often reminded his audiences that if we defy moral law it will break us. There will be consequences. There may be times when it seems that evil carries the day, and even seemingly conquers truth. Nevertheless, King was convinced that in a moral universe truth and justice, not evil and injustice, will have the last word.

Conclusion

Why was personalism so appealing to Martin Luther King? Larry Rivers has provided an excellent summary of its significance for King and its relationship with various Jewish and Christian ideas.[102] Personalism appealed to King in the following ways:

- In personalism he found a philosophy of religion that fit well with his pre-existing beliefs in the black church's prophetic tradition, Gandhian nonviolence, the Social Gospel, and liberal theology.
- Personalism fulfilled his need for an explanation of a personal God, the sacredness of persons, and the meaning of life that went beyond evangelicalism's dogmatic boundaries but remained true to their roots in the black church.
- Personalism helped King to reconcile his scientific mind with the reality of the evangelical surroundings in black Southern churches.
- Personalism is grounded in reason, but its emphasis on the love ethic and the prophetic message of Jesus, as well as its openness to divine providence give it common ground with the more supernaturally-oriented and Biblically-centered form of Christianity that continues to be dominant in the black church.[103]

In "Pilgrimage to Nonviolence," Martin Luther King said that personalism appealed to him on two levels, thereby strengthening his two long held convictions: (1) it provided a sound metaphysical basis for his belief in a personal-creator God, and (2) it provided a solid philosophical grounding for his belief in the infinite, inviolable dignity of human beings. These were convictions that were instilled in him through his family and black church upbringing. They were elements of his organic or homegrown personalism. Although King did not explicitly say so, the student of personalism knows that this conceptuality also provides a sound metaphysical basis for his strong belief in the centrality of freedom, the relational character of God, persons, and the universe, and his conviction that the universe is value-fused, or hinges on a moral foundation.

The King type of personalism is a social activist personalism that requires not only one's adherence to the principle of the absolute dignity of persons generally, but an unswerving determination to resist any attempt to demean or undermine the dignity of concrete flesh and blood human beings. Martin Luther King knew that it was not enough to declare one's respect for human dignity in general. One has to go beyond the abstraction of human beings in general, and take actions intended to positively impact the dignity of concrete human beings.

6

Reflections on King as Theological Social Ethicist[1]

In his seminal history of social ethics in America, theologian Gary Dorrien names Martin Luther King as the most prominent figure in the story of modern Christian social ethics. "The greatest figure in the story of American Christian social ethics so vastly transcended that story that placing him in it is incongruous. The legacy of Martin Luther King, Jr. was enormous, overwhelming the boundaries and topics of a work on social ethics."[2] Such a characterization of King's place in Christian social ethics goes beyond being a mere compliment. It is yet another way of supporting his iconic status, among other things. So important was King's contribution to social ethics through his relentless organized nonviolent direct action against injustice that Dorrien lists King as one of the "three towering figures in American Christian social ethics...."[3] Walter Rauschenbusch and Reinhold Niebuhr, theologian of the social gospel, and Christian realist, respectively, are the other two.

In 2005, renowned black liberation theologian James DeOtis Roberts, published *Bonhoeffer and King: Speaking Truth to Power*.[4] Among other things, this otherwise fine book was to discuss the moral decision-making method or process of each man, noting similarities and differences, and what we might be able to appropriate from each today. When I eagerly read the book (with much anticipation that I had finally happened upon a book that deals with King's social ethics and method), I had to conclude that Roberts did a much better job of expressly addressing Bonhoeffer's method of moral decision-making than King's. More accurately, it was not that Roberts did a poor job of explicating King's method. Rather, as I read the section under the heading, "King's Ethical Method," in Chapter 14, I saw nothing that came close to actually addressing his method, even though Roberts told the reader that he would do so.[5] The ensuing discussion was actually quite good, but it was all essentially preliminary to a discussion of ethical method, which never actually occurred. All that Roberts said seemed to be building up to a discussion on Kingian moral decision-making method, but the actual discussion never happened.

Indeed, one who is familiar with the influence of personalism on King's intellectual development—as Roberts most assuredly is!—knows that he was much influence by the personalistic moral law system of moral decision-making developed by his teacher, Edgar S. Brightman. And yet, I saw no reference to this in Roberts' book. Moreover, I was surprised that Roberts, a leader in the black liberation theology movement, failed to explicitly acknowledge elements of liberation ethics in King's method of moral decision-making, although he was careful to point out that both King and Bonhoeffer "anticipated the emphasis in liberation theologies that see the focus upon dogmas and creeds as the second order of business for theologians."[6] Strangely, however, Roberts fails to cite King's emphasis on the sacredness of persons as such, and especially the oppressed. In addition, he does not focus on liberation and justice as basic to King's method of moral decision-making. Although I find these to be curious omissions, Roberts is quite helpful and suggestive in pointing out that any intelligent discussion on King's method of ethical decision-making must begin by examining the influences from his black family, church, community, and Morehouse College experiences. Roberts rightly admonishes that much of what King did and the way he did it was influenced by his black southern experience. "I would attribute much to his parents and to the Ebenezer Baptist Church in Atlanta," he said. "The seedbed of King's early intellectual preparation was Morehouse College. His encounter with leading minister-scholars at Morehouse provided a solid foundation for what he received in intellectual refinement at Crozer and Boston University."[7] In this, Roberts rightly warns that anybody who begins a discussion on King by beginning with his academic experiences in the North will end up with a truncated view of King.

Without question, one cannot adequately discuss Martin Luther King, Jr., as theological social ethicist without early acknowledging the fact that he was a *black American*, a *Christian*, and one who unashamedly adhered to *personalist* ideas and principles. Indeed, he was very much in the personalist camp, always stressing three of its basic tenets: God as personal and loving; the absolute dignity or sacredness of human beings; and freedomism (or the centrality of freedom). In King's case, these three—his race/culture, faith, and personalism—fed and mutually reinforced each other. Moreover, the texture of his Christian faith and personalism was much influenced and shaped by the fact that he was a black southerner. King loved the south, a fact that Lewis V. Baldwin, premier scholar on King, has stressed throughout his many volumes on him.[8] Since he loved and was much influenced by black southern culture, King's religious faith and his personalism were colored and much enhanced by this. In addition, the basic principles of Christianity and what I have called *homespun* or *homegrown* personalism were introduced to King in the context of his family upbringing and through the black church. Looking back, King referred to the church as his second home, since he and his siblings were there so frequently.

King's Christian faith and homespun personalism received a formal intellectual structure through his training at Morehouse College, Crozer Theological Seminary, and Boston University. Although the largest portion of his systematic formal study of personalism was at Boston University, his introductory study of it occurred at Crozer. It was here that he was introduced to Edgar S. Brigtman's philosophy of religion and doctrine of the finite–Infinite God. However, it is quite possible that King was first introduced to the term personalism and the name of its chief expositor and interpreter while at Morehouse. That man, Brightman, would be his academic advisor when he matriculated in the doctoral program at Boston University. It is at least within the realm of possibility that King had his first encounters with aspects of personalist philosophy at Morehouse, whether or not he actually heard the term personalism or Brightman's name mentioned. For it is known that two of the men at Morehouse who influenced King most—Benjamin E. Mays and George Kelsey—both espoused personalist ideas; Mays through his publications and weekly chapel talks, and Kelsey in course lectures and in periodic sermons delivered in chapel. Furthermore, Kelsey earned the Ph. D. at Yale University. For our purpose, this is significant because for more than twenty years (1881–1905) Yale had on its faculty George Trumbull Ladd (1842–1921), who contributed a number of excellent books to the literature on personalism.[9] Although Ladd was dead by the time Kelsey

(1910–1996) worked on his degree at Yale, it is highly likely that there were Ladd disciples around who continued to espouse personalist ideas in that community which may have caught Kelsey's attention. At any rate, both Kelsey and Mays talked much about a personal God and the absolute dignity of persons, for example, thus reinforcing what King had already been taught at home and at Ebenezer Baptist Church in Atlanta. The emphasis on God as personal and the inalienable dignity of persons that we find in Mays and Kelsey are also fundamental ideas in the philosophy of personalism that King would later call his own.

The fact that King was a black man who had Christian and personalist principles instilled in him as a child is significant for any who wishes to embark on a study of the civil rights icon as social ethicist. Although the more systematic look at King as social ethicist is not the purpose of this discussion, it is nevertheless important to acknowledge its importance and the need for this to eventually happen. However, mine is the more modest task of examining the meaning of theological social ethics, while also trying to get a glimpse of who King was as social ethicist, and what were elements of his process of moral deliberation. I name and discuss key elements in a working definition of social ethics, and then proceed to show that these elements were present in King's work. In doing so, I hope that my reflections will at least be suggestive of a theological social ethic that takes seriously the contributions of Martin Luther King, and that has relevance for today.

Beginnings

Martin Luther King's doctoral training was in systematic theology. From seminary through doctoral studies, he enjoyed reading and studying philosophy, social philosophy, and ethics. He read and studied these with two specific purposes in mind. He was seeking a formal theological foundation for his still developing social conscience. In addition, King was consciously seeking a viable method(s) to effect social change; a method that might lead to the establishment of justice and civil rights. His emphasis on seeking a method for social change made his social gospel qualitatively different from that of the white social gospelers, e.g., Walter Rauschenbusch and Washington Gladden. King had witnessed enough of his father's ministry and heard enough about his maternal grandfather's ministry to know that in light of the racial horrors experienced by his people, something more was required than merely preaching therapeutic and how to get happiness sermons on Sunday. Furthermore, he knew that it was not enough for one to develop a sound formal theological foundation for his social concerns, which he found in his study of Rauschenbusch. The influence of the black social gospel of his father, grandfather, other black preachers throughout the South, as well as the witness of a number of his teachers and mentors at Morehouse College made it necessary to go beyond the ascertainment of a formal theological rationale for his social conscience, to finding a reasonable method to attack and eradicate the social problems that were crushing his people.

From the time King was a little boy, influenced by the teaching and example primarily of his parents and extended church family, he had a strong desire to serve others. Initially he did not see ministry as the best means for this, despite the fact that his father was a well-respected minister with a strong social action component to his ministry, as had been the case of his maternal grandfather. In fact, King initially rebelled against the idea of going into the ministry, an action that was not at all uncommon among the children of ministers. King believed that a career in medicine or law would be the best way to serve his people in particular, and humanity in general. His grades in biology and chemistry made medicine not the best choice.

By the time King was thirteen years old, he was already rebelling against some of the fundamentalist teachings of his church and southern Baptist denomination, such as the virgin birth, the bodily resurrection of Jesus, and the infallibility of the Scriptures.[10] By the time he had completed a couple of years of college he was also rebelling against the emotionalism in the church, and in fact, later told Ralph Abernathy that he didn't understand it; was downright embarrassed by the shouting and stamping in church; as well as his father's whooping and practice of walking the pews.[11] Despite Daddy King's fundamentalist teachings and other antics that troubled King, he reports his deep admiration for his father's steadfast witness for social justice in Atlanta and other parts of the South, as well as the strong values he instilled in him and his siblings. One of these was the value of giving something back to the community through service. All in all, King credited his father's influence as a key reason for his acceptance of the call to ministry in his senior year at Morehouse College.[12]

We learn from King's wife that during one of their many premarital conversations about ministry, King made it clear that he was more concerned about what goes on this side of the grave, than knowing about "the temperature of hell or the furnishings of heaven...."[13] Although King sought to have a holistic view of the gospel's expectations, it was clear, even after he graduated from Morehouse and *before* he began studies at the predominantly white Crozer Theological Seminary in Chester, Pennsylvania, that in light of his people's struggles he needed to place more emphasis on the social aspect of the gospel. Significantly, Walter Chivers was King's academic advisor, under whom he majored in sociology at Morehouse. Chivers also taught him sociology, and introduced him to the complex relation between race and class issues. Like other social sciences, sociology stressed the importance of empirical data, fact gathering and reporting, scientific objectivity, and the importance of using such empirical data to solve social problems. We will see that gathering facts or evidence and other empirical data would be a critical aspect of King's nonviolent protest campaigns from the time he first began to be intentional about Gandhian nonviolent techniques during the Montgomery bus boycott, to the planning of the Poor Peoples Campaign, and his involvement in the sanitation workers strike in Memphis where he was assassinated. They would be important aspects of his method of doing social ethics.

In his senior year of college, King accepted the call to ministry and was ordained on February 25, 1948. He was at that time appointed associate pastor at Ebenezer Baptist Church where his father was senior pastor. By this time, it was much clearer to him that ministry would be the means through which he would fight to get the racism-classism beast off the backs of his people.

A Working Definition of Theological Social Ethics

Theological social ethics may be defined as the critical examination of *what is* in light of *what ought to be*, according to the norm of agape love.[14] That is, once one investigates and determines that racism exists in one's work place or in one's church, for example, she is then required to reflect on the meaning of agape and what it requires in the face of such a state of affairs. This is a good working definition, although it begs for further explanation. Nevertheless, it gives us a place to begin the discussion and reflections on King as social ethicist. Since King was a Christian minister it is appropriate to add that the standard or norm of theological social ethics (hereafter social ethics) is agape, which he saw as the regulating ideal in Christian ethics. We will see that he also stressed the need to be explicit about the ground of social ethics or the work of love in the world. For King, this ground is the God of the Hebrew prophets and Jesus Christ, which is why I prefer *theological* rather than *Christian* to characterize his social ethics.

Social ethics really seeks to answer two critical questions: (1) What is the actual state of affairs regarding human conduct—individually and collectively, (2) What ought the conduct to be in light of the requirements of the agape ideal? Before turning to a discussion of King as theological social ethicist, there are a number of terms and phrases that warrant clarification. These include "what is," "what ought to be," "agape," and "theological." In examining these, I want to pay close attention to what the terms seem to have meant for King, or how they were manifested in his work. Since King nowhere discusses any of these systematically, or all of them in one place, it will be necessary to appeal to a variety of his speeches, sermons, essays, interviews, and books in order to determine his view.

"WHAT IS"

The reference to *what is,* in the definition is intended to point to the importance of the social sciences and their methodology for the social ethicist. The social sciences began gaining momentum during the heyday of the Social Gospel Movement in the late 19th century and the first couple of decades of the 20th century. Regarding any given social problem the social ethicist, like the social scientist, is concerned to give an accurate reading of the actual state of affairs of that problem. Such a one desires first and foremost to determine whether there is in fact a problem. She is then bound to report as accurately as possible on that problem, being careful to also state how urgent the problem is for the community, society, nation, or world. She wants to know with a reasonable degree of certainty that racism exists or not; that poverty exists or not; that black-against-black violence and murder is a growing tragic phenomenon in the black community or not. She wants a clear reading of the actual state of affairs.

Martin Luther King gained an appreciation for social science methodology under Walter Chivers at Morehouse College where he majored in sociology.[15] In his famous "Letter from Birmingham Jail," King implied the importance of the *"what is"* component of the working definition of social ethics. He pointed specifically to the importance of investigation and fact gathering—a principle to which he was introduced in his sociology courses at Morehouse College—to determine whether a social problem or injustice actually existed in a local community. In the "Letter," King sought to assure the eight white ministers who were critical of his presence and the nonviolent demonstrations in Birmingham that no such campaign is authorized if it does not follow four steps. These steps had in fact been followed. The first step is that of fact gathering to determine whether there is in fact a problem and how severe it is.[16] This is always the first step, King said, and generally required that the Southern Christian Leadership Conference (SCLC) send a small advance contingent of persons to investigate alleged problems in a locality. Once a determination is made that a particular problem exists, meetings are then held to determine whether to implement nonviolent demonstrations. This first step, fact gathering, is absolutely critical since it can determine the success or failure of a campaign. Fact gathering must be done with care and thoroughness. It cannot be adequately done without getting to know the local community and its leaders, as well as some of the people being victimized by the alleged problem.

Evidence suggests that it was failure at this first step that had much to do with King's and SCLC's most blatant failures, namely in Albany, Georgia in 1962, and Chicago in 1966. But generally, King was meticulous regarding the fact gathering stage. This was evident in the

Birmingham campaign in 1963, for example. When it became clear early in that campaign, that their timing conflicted with the mayoralty election, King and his advisers decided to postpone the campaign. However, the work of fact gathering and getting to know the Birmingham community continued. King wrote about this in *Why We Can't Wait.*

> Meanwhile Wyatt Walker was detailed to return to Birmingham and begin work on the mechanics of the campaign. From then on, he visited Birmingham periodically, unannounced, organizing a transportation corps and laying the groundwork for an intensive boycott. He conferred with lawyers about the city code on picketing, demonstrations and so forth, gathered data on the probable bail-bond situation, and prepared for the injunction that was certain to come.
>
> In addition to scheduling workshops on nonviolence and direct-action techniques for our recruits, Wyatt familiarized himself with downtown Birmingham, not only plotting the main streets and landmarks (target stores, city hall, post office, etc.), but meticulously surveying each store's eating facilities, and sketching the entrances and possible paths of ingress and egress. In fact, Walker detailed the number of stools, tables and chairs to determine how many demonstrators should go to each store.[17]

An important point to acknowledge here is that data gathered from the fact gathering stage, as well as the course of current events, may dictate the need for changes in timing and strategy if the decision has been made to engage in a direct action campaign to address a social problem. In the present case, King found it necessary to revamp their strategy and postpone their campaign twice because of events pertaining to the mayoralty election and the need for a run-off vote. In fact, a time came during the Albany, Georgia campaign when the violent behavior of white onlookers caused King to temporarily suspend demonstrations for several days. In the interim he "visited homes, clubs, and pool rooms, urging that no retaliation be tolerated...."[18] Similarly, a time came during the St. Augustine, Florida campaign in 1964 when a concession by the Governor caused King to suspend demonstrations until a Governor appointed committee could work out a settlement.[19] For King, both the facts *and* current events may impinge on strategy and direct action. One must have the good sense to respond and make adjustments accordingly.

King had majored in sociology at Morehouse. Through course lectures, reading assignments, and outside class projects he became acquainted with key sociological principles and methods, all of which came in handy in his work in the civil rights movement. King benefited from the practical experience that other social activists had had while utilizing sociological principles and methods, but at the foundation of his own knowledge was his training in sociology. King would have learned, for example, that the two basic elements in sociological methodology are reliance on empirical data, and striving to be as objective as one can be. (He was not concerned about perfect objectivity, since he did not believe that human beings could ever be perfectly objective about anything.) Reliance on empirical data means that one who undertakes a sociological investigation will be concerned only to examine data that are detectable and observable through the five senses. This means that the findings will be capable of review, testable, measurable, and capable of duplication. Sociologist Keith Roberts illustrates the point: "If a sociologist claims that belief × causes behavior Y, empirical studies can be set up and data gathered to support or refute the hypothesis.... If members of certain religious groups or persons with particular religious beliefs are thought to be more racially prejudiced than others, only empirical investigation can establish the validity of that claim."[20] Despite a couple of significant lapses, by the time of the Birmingham campaign, King understood very well the importance of relying on empirical data, both for determining the actual state of affairs of an alleged problem in a given locality, and for what such data can contribute to actually solving a social problem.

King also understood the value of objectivity from the fact gathering stage, during the negotiating stage, and through the direct action stage. Objectivity was most crucial at the fact gathering stage. King knew that in the human condition it is generally not possible to obtain an absolutely value-neutral state of mind. One therefore tries as best as one can to prevent personal beliefs or biases from entering. And yet, King knew that the nature of the racism beast is such that it is virtually impossible for those victimized by it to be completely detached and objective, or to be detached and objective in the same sense the racist might claim to be. Furthermore, King knew that perfect objectivity escaped white racists as well. Whether admitted or not, everybody brings biases or value premises to the table. The difference is that some are willing to admit this up front. Too many others, on the other hand, pretend to be completely free of all biases.

At every point, the social ethicist should make an effort to devise the most reasonable hypothesis, based on the best, most reliable evidence and facts available at a given time. The social ethicist in the King tradition contends that truth must be defined in terms of degrees of probable truth. Such a one takes seriously the dictum of Bishop Joseph Butler (1692–1752) that, "probability is the very guide of life."[21] One who adheres to this principle expects no once-for-all, absolute truths in human experience. Rather, one must be committed to most probable truths. The latter are based on the widest variety of relevant facts and evidence and the most reasonable and coherent explanation of them. Although the social ethicist must recognize that the data and the facts of experience are never all in for finite and limited beings, one must be committed to social action that is based on the best that one knows at the time the action is initiated. It is also important to know when it may be necessary to alter one's actions based on new data, facts, or current events. We have seen that King did this a number of times in various civil rights campaigns. In a sense, what we have here is best thought out theories and best laid plans that are informed by current events and other facts. One may then need to adjust the initial plan of direct action accordingly.

"WHAT OUGHT TO BE"

As theological social ethicist, Martin Luther King was never satisfied merely to know the actual state of affairs; to only know there was a problem, and to only report the facts regarding that particular social problem. Nor was it sufficient to him to merely develop a formal theological rationale for his deepening social conscience. Instead, King was driven to bring a verified state of affairs into harmony with what ought to be in light of a religious imperative such as agape. For the Christian thinker and activist like King, then, the *what ought to be* phrase in the working definition of social ethics implies the need to consider moral imperatives and requirements based on the teachings of the Hebrew prophets and Jesus Christ. While concerned on the one hand with giving an accurate reading of what the actual state of affairs is regarding a specific social issue, e.g., racism, the social ethicist also seeks to establish a normative framework by which the empirical findings of the social sciences might be evaluated and implemented. The Christian would focus on Christian norms, the Jew on Jewish, the Muslim on Islamic norms, etc. In a nutshell, then, the social ethicist in the King tradition will primarily be concerned to focus on *what is* in light of *what ought to be*, in accordance with the highest ideals of the Christian faith. For the Christian, that ideal is agape.

Unlike many pastors and other religious leaders, King did not hesitate to state what he believed the agape ideal requires. As an ordained clergyman he believed that his divine commission was "to constantly and forever bring the ethical insights of our Judeo-Christian heritage to bear on the social evils of our day."[22] King sought from the beginning of his civil rights ministry to put agape at the center of the Movement.[23] No one who understands the meaning of Christian love, he maintained, can ever patiently and uncritically adjust to injustice. King tried to make this very point to a group of more than 200 black ministers in Birmingham in the early stages of that campaign. Many of them were afraid and were committed to ministries that focused on the individual rather than the social aspects of the gospel. "To the ministers I stressed the need for a social gospel to supplement the gospel of individual salvation," he said. "I suggested that only a 'dry as dust' religion prompts a minister to extol the glories of heaven while ignoring the social conditions that cause men an earthly hell. I pleaded for the projections of strong, firm leadership by the Negro minister, pointing out that he is freer, more independent, than any other person in the community."[24] For King, the Christian's ultimate allegiance is "to God, and if any earthly institution conflicts with God's will it is [one's] Christian duty to take a stand against it."[25]

Agape

As a member of the Christian community, it was clear to King that once a determination is made that a particular social problem exists, it then is necessary to consider what is required in light of the Christian ethical imperative of agape. The question becomes: What does agape require? So important is agape to King's thought and practice, that it will be helpful to discuss his use of the term.

King's first academic use of the term *agape* appeared in a paper written in George W. Davis's course, Christian Theology for Today. It is not clear from this paper that King actually read Anders Nygren's massive book, *Agape and Eros*. However, in the paper, he equated Nygren's concept of agape with the "eternal sacrificial love of God," and with his idea that "the divine love is purely spontaneous and unceasing...."[26] King did not quote Nygren, but these are clearly Nygren's ideas.[27] During this period of his intellectual development, King only possessed a superficial knowledge of Nygren's concept of agape. However, it would not be long before his study of the term would deepen as he read more, albeit *only* secondary sources in subsequent courses.

We next see King's consideration of Nygren's view of agape and eros in a doctoral paper written for L. Harold DeWolf at Boston University, entitled "Contemporary Continental Theology." King discusses Nygren's contrast between two kinds of love: agape and eros. Eros is equated with Platonic love, which loves in proportion to the perceived value of the object loved. Agape, on the other hand, is the spontaneous, ever flowing love of God that flows downward toward the creation but is indifferent to the value of the object. That is, agape has no concern for who the object or recipient is. It is available to every human being, just for the asking.

King's first discussion of these two forms of love is heavily dependent upon a secondary source without attribution.[28] This dependence makes it difficult to know how closely, or whether, King was actually reading Nygren at the time, although there is nothing to suggest that he read Nygren. And yet, we may surmise from the frequent discussions on agape and other forms of love in his graduate school papers and in post-graduate school sermons, speeches, and writings that King's understanding of agape deepened as he came to see it as the center or norm of the Christian ethic.

Generally, when King discussed love in post-graduate school writings, speeches, and sermons it was in the context of the three Greek terms: eros, philia, and agape. He understood eros as a kind of romantic love, perhaps between two lovers. Philia is the love that exists between friends, but clearly is not purely self-giving or unconcerned about the value of the object. According to this type of love, one loves because she is loved. However, only in agape do we find what King considered the regulating ideal of the Christian ethic. As noted before, agape is not dependent upon the value of the object loved, nor does it require love in return. In this regard, King saw agape as "disinterested love," since "the individual seeks not his own good, but the good of his neighbor (1 Cor. 10:24). *Agape* does not begin by discriminating between worthy and unworthy people, or any qualities people possess. It begins by loving others *for their sakes*. It is an entirely 'neighbor-regarding concern for others,' which discovers the neighbor in every man it meets. Therefore, *agape* makes no distinction between friends and enemies; it is directed toward both."[29] King saw "enemy-neighbor" love as the criterion of disinterested love. The latter expects nothing in return, just as one generally expects nothing good in return from one's enemy. Although King did not name either Sören Kierkegaard or Paul Ramsey, the language of enemy-neighbor love and disinterested love, respectively, belonged to them.[30]

In his deepening reflection, King also saw agape as that type of love that "springs from the *need* of the other person—his need for belonging to the best in the human family."[31] King cites the parable of the Good Samaritan as an illustration of this. He surmised that the Good Samaritan—unlike the priest and the Levite—was good precisely because he responded to the need of the man who had been beaten, robbed, and left for dead on the side of the road. King expounded further: "Saint Paul assures us that the loving act of redemption was done 'while we were yet sinners'—that is, at the point of our greatest need for love. Since the white man's personality is greatly distorted by segregation, and his soul is greatly scarred, he needs the love of the Negro. The Negro must love the white man, because the white man needs his love to remove his tensions, insecurities, and fears."[32] Unfortunately, King was not critical at this point. We may concede the lesson taught by St. Paul. However, one must question the wisdom of King placing the onus of love solely on blacks in particular, and the oppressed in general. There is no question that the white man's personality and soul are distorted and scarred by segregation, but it needs also to be said that this is a result of the white man's own choice and behavior. If his personality and soul are scarred and marred by his behavior toward blacks, what is the condition of these latter, and why is there not also emphasis on the need for whites to love them? King is wrong to put the onus to love solely on blacks.

After graduate school, King frequently defined agape as "understanding and creative, redemptive goodwill for all men."[33] This is a purely divine, spontaneous, "overflowing love which seeks nothing in return...."[34] Since God is no respecter of persons and is the fundamental source of agape, who one is or is not on some socio-cultural or economic scale, is no determinant to whether he may receive such love. He receives this love solely because God is Agape, and because he belongs to God. King said frequently that agape is, "the love of God operating in the human heart. At this level, we love men not because we like them, nor because their ways appeal to us, nor even because they possess some type of divine spark; we love every man because God loves him."[35] Agape love, then, is the regulating ideal for the actions of human beings in their individual and collective behavior. "The law of love as an imperative is the norm for all of man's actions."[36] One does not have to like the attitude and behavior of a person, but if one is in the Christian camp he is obligated to love that individual because God loves him.

King frequently discussed Nygren's view of agape and eros without offering criticism. It is important to point out, however, that (without naming him) King rejected Nygren's disavowal of self-love. In the sermon, "Three Dimensions of a Complete Life," King said: "There is such a thing as rational and healthy self-interest. Every person must have a concern for self...."[37] Although King did not here explicitly name Nygren, we know, that Nygren wrote that agape "excludes all self-love. Christianity does not recognize self-love as a legitimate form of love.... Agape recognizes no kind of self-love as legitimate."[38] This implies a negative view or estimate of the self and its importance. In fact, Nygren wrote explicitly that the difference between the eros-system and the agape-system is that the former begins by assuming the worth or value of the soul. "The soul is a pearl, which has become lost and defiled, but which returns none the less its imperishable value."[39] According to Nygren, agape is just the opposite, in that it begins with the assumption that the soul or person has no worth at all. "When man has fallen away from God, he is wholly lost and has no value at all."[40] This is an entirely anti-personalistic stance. According to King's personalism, the individual person is the moral unit and is inviolably sacred because created and loved by God. In addition, based upon who King was, what he knew about the history of oppression against his people, and his awareness of the systematic efforts of whites to deny the humanity and dignity of blacks, there was no way he could agree with Nygren's conclusion that the person has no worth. And yet, in most of his explicit discussions on Nygren's view of agape, he does not point to this negative aspect of Nygren's stance, nor does he criticize it. King only does this indirectly in "The Three Dimensions of Love."

In "The Three Dimensions of Love," King refers to self-love as the length of life. Put in the terms of the moral law system of personalism developed by King's teacher, Edgar S. Brightman,[41] self-love is equated with the Law of Individualism. As noted previously, King could not accept Nygren's view that self-love is not included in agape because he was a black personalist who believed in the absolute dignity of each human being. It would be a contradiction for such a one to deny the inclusion of self-love in agape. One cannot simultaneously confess belief in the sacredness of persons and reject self-love. King could only reject the view that the human soul has no value. In the last book that he published before his death he wrote: "Deeply woven into the fiber of our religious tradition is the conviction that men are made in the image of God, and that they are souls of infinite metaphysical value."[42] King was convinced that a person is an end in herself, because she is a child of God, imbued with the image and fragrance of God.[43]

King also stresses altruistic love, i.e., love of the other, or what is equivalent to Brightman's Law of Altruism. For King, altruistic love means concern or love for others. It broadens love beyond the mere interests of the individual. King referred to altruistic love as the breadth of life. It is important that the individual, whose nature is communal as well as personal, see herself in relation to other persons. "No man has learned to live," King held, "until he can rise above the narrow confines of his individualistic concerns to the broader concerns of all humanity."[44] King understood Christian love to require love of self, as well as love of neighbor—the length of life and the breadth of life.

But there was more. Based on his upbringing in the black church and his adoption of personalism as his basic philosophical point of departure, King also believed that God is the source of both self-regarding and other-regarding love. Therefore, in addition to stressing the length and breadth of life, one had to consider the source or ground of these. This prompted King to emphasize the love of God. The emphasis here is on the height of life, i.e., the cause and sustainer of all there is. Although there is no explicit equivalent of this in Brightman's moral law system, King was aware—having studied this system in graduate school—that Brightman only implied the need for such a law.[45] However, two of Brightman's students, L. Harold DeWolf and Walter G. Muelder, gave a name to this law (which is only implicit in Brightman's system). DeWolf called it the Metaphysical Law and defined it as follows: "All persons ought to seek to know the source and significance of the harmony and universality of these laws, i.e., of the coherence of the moral order."[46] According to King, the focus of love that is the height of life is on "that upward reach toward something distinctly greater than humanity. We must rise above earth and give our ultimate allegiance to that eternal Being who is the source and ground of all reality. When we add height to length and breadth, we have the complete life."[47]

I have often wondered whether King would have been more critical of Nygren's interpretation of agape had he actually read Nygren for himself. How might King's understanding of agape been enriched had he done a systematic biblical study of it, in addition to engaging in a historical examination of agape? Had he actually read Nygren's book on the subject he would have been subjected to at least a secondary historical examination of the term, since this is what Nygren provides in the book. Nevertheless, in the end, "King did not perceive love as an abstract concept, only tangentially related to persons in community. For him, love was concretely relevant to human social action...."[48] For King, and unlike Reinhold Niebuhr, agape was relevant not only for individuals and interpersonal relations, but for groups and nations as well. Ervin Smith makes the point very well in *The Ethics of Martin Luther King, Jr.*

> King's most enduring contribution to Christian ethics and American social progress may be the fact that he so persistently and often singularly insisted upon the relevance and applicability of love to American (and subsequently international) social problems. The persistence of this vision has brought significant social change to America and may bring greater changes yet where the courage to persist in love gains new impetus in American social action.[49]

Without question, King saw more clearly than most, that the aim of agape is the creation of the beloved community.

In addition to his emphasis on the agape imperative, King grounded his social ethics theologically. Inasmuch as he believed God to be the source of all things, God was his reason for doing social ethics; for doing all in his power to liberate the oppressed. God was the reason for King's faithfulness in the struggle from Montgomery to Memphis. This is an excellent segue to a consideration of my preference for the term *theological* in characterizing King as a social ethicist.

THEOLOGICAL

The central place of God in King's thought, ministry, and social ethics is why I characterize him as a *theological* social ethicist. God, in this case, is the ground and the reason that King devoted his life to the work of ministry. Most people would likely say that King was a *Christian* social ethicist. I hesitate to designate him this way, although I fully acknowledge that he was in the Christian community and was unashamedly Christian. I prefer *theological* because as a personalist and a man of ideas, King's thinking was so broad, and he was so open to the best ideas in all cultures, that it makes sense to put the emphasis on this more inclusive term, rather than the more narrow, *Christian*. Because King drew upon the truths of all major world religious faiths, it seems to me that *theological* is more consistent with who King really was as social ethicist.

In my view, King's is unquestionably a God-centered social ethic. Indeed, King was no less a God-intoxicated man than the philosopher Spinoza,[50] although King's was the thoroughly personal God of the Hebrew prophets, rather than Spinoza's impersonal God.

Peter J. Paris is most assuredly right in pointing to the centrality of God in King's social ethic.

In all of King's thought, speeches, and writings no other theme is more pervasive than that of God. I contend that all other important concepts pervading his works—for example, nonviolence, love, justice, human dignity, reconciliation, freedom, morality—are either explicitly or implicitly related to his understanding of God.[51]

A God-centered social ethic such as King's implies that everything that is done in the world has, in one way or another, to do with God—implicates God in some way. I like to tell my students: "It's all about God; everything you and I do implicates God in the sense that the entire world belongs to God, and God is the source and sustainer of all there is. So, what we do is about God, or, more accurately, is of concern to God." Bible man that he was, King knew full well that all lives belong to God (Eze. 18:4), as well as the cattle on a thousand hills (Ps. 50:10), and thus God is concerned about it all. This was King's stance, which is why I consider his to be a God-intoxicated social ethic. Such an ethic implies that the responsible person who knows and takes serious God's will ought to resist injustice and oppressions of all kinds, because it is the will of Agape—God.

Social Ethics as a Still Developing Interdisciplinary Field

With the publication of his massive tome, *Social Ethics in the Making*, Gary Dorrien has filled a major void in the discipline of religious social ethics. When I was a doctoral student in social ethics in the late 1970s there was no single volume that provided a systematic and historical overview of the development of social ethics in the United States. Dorren's is indeed a comprehensive treatment of social ethics from the time it was first taught as an academic discipline by Harvard ethicist Francis Greenwood Peabody in 1880, to the present. Dorrien is careful to give more than a mere passing nod to the contributions of blacks, women (black, white, and Latina), and other traditionally excluded voices, but shows how their significant contributions have vastly enriched the tradition and present status of social ethics. Indeed, one gets an immediate sense of Dorrien's sensitivity to this matter on the Dedication page of his book, which he dedicates to James Cone, "Eminent theologian and treasured friend." My sense is that for many years to come Dorrien's text will be the standard bearer of historical works on social ethics.

Martin Luther King was a theological social ethicist who was much influenced by the social gospelism of his father and maternal grandfather and other southern black preachers. He said that it was in his reading and study of Walter Rauschenbusch (especially his *Christianity and the Social Crisis*) that he found the formal theological rationale on which to ground his already strong social conscience and his advocacy of the social gospel when he arrived at Crozer Theological Seminary.[52] King was also much influenced by the social gospel witness of Boston University professors, Allan Knight Chalmers (1897–1972) and Walter G. Muelder (1907–2004), also the second, and long-time Dean of Boston University School of Theology). Before being appointed to the faculty at Boston University, Chalmers had already distinguished himself as a social gospel minister. He was appointed senior pastor of New York's Broadway Tabernacle Church in 1930, "a cauldron, a century earlier, of abolitionism and other antebellum social reform." Within a year of this appointment Chalmers, while on his way to a trustees meeting at Talladega College, was asked by a representative of the Federal Council of Churches to find out what he could about the Scottsboro case—the case of nine black males accused of raping a white woman in Alabama. Chalmers was asked to lead the Scottsboro Defense Committee. Although members of the American Communist Party were involved in the defense, Chalmers decided that he would work with anybody and any group that was interested in justice and the young men's freedom. Knowing that love is at the center of the Christian faith, Chalmers also knew that to serve justice was to serve love.[53] Chalmers was called to teach practical theology at the Boston University School of Theology the same year that King matriculated as a doctoral student in 1951. Charles Marsh writes that Chalmers was "the most tireless champion of race relations among the Boston faculty...."[54] He certainly had a history of such work, and did not back away from the challenge of race relations work as a seminary professor.

King's Boston University transcript reveals that he took no courses under Chalmers and Muelder.[55] However, he applauded both men for their "passion for social justice" and their conviction that social problems can be adequately addressed when persons join together in campaigns of cooperative endeavor with each other and God and attack the problems and their causes.[56] Muelder had taught for six years at Berea College and five at the University of Southern California prior to being called as dean at Boston University School of Theology in 1945. As a doctoral candidate in philosophy at Boston, Muelder had been one of Brightman's outstanding students and was an avid personalist who made a significant mark in the field of social ethics. Although King took no formal courses with Muelder, it is known that King much admired and respected him, and considered him to be one of his mentors. It was Muelder who helped King to solidify his understanding of Reinhold Niebuhr's social ethics, and also helped him to clarify Niebuhr's critique of Gandhi's pacifism.

The working definition of theological social ethics notwithstanding, it should be pointed out that according to the school of thought that influenced King's thinking, social ethics has not yet been adequately defined. Walter Muelder was among the first to suggest this, and characterized social ethics as an *interdisciplinary field* that has yet to achieve full maturity. In this regard, Muelder has written that social ethics is "not yet a coherent discipline," is a "young normative science," and "is a dialectical unity of theological input, history and social science, and philosophical principles."[57] Looked at this way, social ethics is eclectic in the sense that it takes seriously, and tries to appropriate, the findings of other fields of thought, such as the social sciences and their methodologies, biblical and theological studies, history, philosophy, and social philosophy. Thinking of social ethics as an interdisciplinary field is helpful because it requires that one have basic knowledge of a number of fields of thought and what they may be able to contribute toward determining the actual state of affairs relative to a specific social issue. In addition, such broad knowledge can aid us to understand the nature of that state of affairs and its underlying causes. Moreover, this interdisciplinary approach—especially the emphasis on religious and theological studies—can help us to gain clarity about what ought to be in light of a moral imperative such as agape. What is more, the interdisciplinary understanding of social ethics will assist one in determining what will need to be done in order to achieve what the imperative seems to require of us in our collective relations.

As a theological social ethicist, Martin Luther King also focused on four other things that I briefly highlight below. These include the need for specificity; presumption in favor of the poor and the oppressed; the need for self-purging; and the need to expand one's moral sphere in light of the facts and current events.

Need for Specificity

There is a growing sentiment among theological social ethicists that when it comes to matters of social justice, it is critical that one not hesitate to get right down to specifics. That is, it is important to name the specific problem(s), as well as the individuals and institutions believed to be the culprits. At this point there is no place for generalizing, or for claiming to focus on "the wider or more general social question," when the evidence suggests that it is a specific, concrete problem that warrants immediate attention.

Earlier I noted that, looking back, King himself saw that one of the critical mistakes that he made in the Albany campaign was his failure to identify a specific problem to focus on related to racial prejudice rather than try to address prejudice in general. "The mistake I made there [in Albany]," he said, "was to protest against segregation generally rather than against a single and distinct facet of it. Our protest was so vague that we got nothing, and the people were left very depressed and in despair. It would have been much better to have concentrated upon integrating the buses or the lunch counters."[58] Specificity, therefore, is important. If it is a problem of racism in a local community, then a specific manifestation(s) of racism should be the focus. "Racism in general" is too vague and too massive a problem for one group to take on. If it is a matter of gender or sexual orientation we should name and address specific manifestations of the issue. It is easier to deal with the social question if we know what the specific issues and manifestations are, as well as their causes. Not the social question in general, but a specific social problem(s) must be the target.

The theological social ethicist also insists on giving as accurate and objective an account as possible of the actual state of affairs regarding a specific social problem, drawing heavily on the findings of the social sciences. But as we saw previously, the theological social ethicist recognizes that inasmuch as every person is born into a particular family, culture, and society, it is never possible for them to be perfectly objective about anything whatever. Every person is both made by, and makes, the society in which they are born and nurtured to adulthood. In fact, one cannot even be all she can be without her relationships with others, and what she is has very much to do with those relationships or the community in which she was reared. Because the socialization process is so subtle and we internalize so many values of the group, it is virtually impossible to completely separate oneself from these values in order to make an absolutely objective assessment of anything. No matter what we do, we each bring value premises to the table, whether we are aware of them or not. It therefore behooves us to be intentional about trying to identify and ferret out our value premises when addressing issues such as racism. Indeed, from a methodological standpoint it is good to admit the value premises up front, and then proceed to be as objective as one can be in light of those value premises.

Presumption in Favor of the Oppressed

The type of theological social ethics practiced by King had a clear presumption in favor of the oppressed. King always tried to see the problem(s) through the eyes of those who are victimized by racism or poverty, for example. Because he was a dialectical thinker, King also tried to see the problem through the eyes of those who are the beneficiaries of racism. This was necessary both because of the complexity of racism, and the fact that it adversely affects not only its victims, but those who keep racism alive and well. King's fundamental conviction about the interrelated structure of reality and the world requires that one try to see the problem from all angles, since all persons are affected by it in one way or another. Any serious efforts toward the eradication of racism in its individual and systemic forms will require us to have a good sense of what whites think about their racism, how it makes them feel, what they intend to do about it, and when. This is a critical point, especially if it is the case that much of the burden of solving the problem rests with whites.

The King type of theological social ethicist will examine all social ills by trying to see through the eyes of the oppressed, as well as those of the oppressor. However, having done so, such one unashamedly privileges the experience of injustice and oppression of the victims as he seeks a solution(s) to the problem at hand. Such one is also driven by the belief that God sides with the oppressed and demands their total liberation.

Need for Self-Purging

As a personalist, Martin Luther King believed person to be the fundamental philosophical category, the basic moral unit, and the key to solving all human problems. Consequently, it made sense to him that one should always begin with what is known most immediately, namely, human experience, and proceed to the lesser known, e.g., other human beings, nature, and God. What the individual person knows most immediately is herself. Therefore, she should begin there, with self-experience, and then work her way toward the lesser known, namely other selves, God, and the world. This also applies to institutions, such as the church, such that when asked, "Where should the church begin when addressing critical social issues such as racism?," the only appropriate response that the social ethicist in the King tradition can give is that it should begin with what it knows most immediately. That is, the church should begin by examining and purging itself of the racism within itself and its members. In other words, it should begin by purging itself of the social ills it criticizes in the secular order. If racism exists in white churches, for example, well-meaning white people should begin by acknowledging this and trying to rid themselves of racism. This is not only a sound personalistic principle, but it is scriptural as well. For example, in Matthew 7:3–5 we find: "Why do you see the speck in your neighbor's eye, but do not notice the log in your own eye? Or how can you say to your neighbor, 'Let me take the speck out of your eye,' while the log is in your own eye? You hypocrite, first take the log out of your own eye, and then you will see clearly to take the speck out of your neighbor's eye." Essentially, this means that the theological social ethicist challenges the church and church sponsored institutions to clean their own house before they start giving moral counsel on such matters to other institutions.

If the churches, seminaries, and other religious institutions do not subscribe to the principle of first purging themselves of social evils that also exist in so-called secular institutions and in other parts of the world, they will be suspect in the eyes of the secular world. H. Richard Niebuhr pointed this out in 1929 when he wrote: "But a skeptic world notes with amusement where it [i.e., the church] is irreverent and with despair where it longs for a saving word, that the organization which is loudest in its praise of brotherhood and most critical of race and class discriminations in other spheres is the most disunited group of all, nurturing in its own structure that same spirit of division which it condemns in other relations."[59]

The church cannot provide moral and spiritual leadership in an area of human relations if it chooses not to acknowledge, address, and solve similar problems within its own body. The church has no credible prophetic word for the secular world and its institutions as long as racism, sexism, sexual orientation, and classism are endemic to its own structures and efforts are not being made to address and eradicate them. King was not slow to acknowledge this important point. He was among the first to say that the church must rid itself of these social evils if it expects the world to take seriously its proclamations on race, militarism, and economic injustice.

A theme that King consistently articulated in speeches, sermons, and writings throughout his civil rights ministry was that one of the best contributions the church can make is to take the moral lead by cleaning its own house and its representative institutions. He noted a number of things the church could do to achieve this. As the most segregated institution in the country, the church must first purge itself and its structures of all segregation and other manifestations of racism. "Only by doing this," King maintained, "can it be effective in its attack on outside evils."[60] The church must be willing to name these as sins against God and humanity, whether they exist in the church or in society. The church that fails to do this is marching to a beat that is not in step with the gospel. King himself criticized the contemporary church as "a weak, ineffectual voice with an uncertain sound. So often it is an arch defender of the status quo. Far from being disturbed by the presence of the church, the power structure of the average community is consoled by the church's silent—and often even vocal—sanction of things as they are."[61] King lamented the fact that historically the church has not hesitated to be the leader in conforming to the status quo and the ethic of society. In this, the church fails to be God's witness in the world. In this regard King said:

> The erstwhile sanction by the church of slavery, racial segregation, war, and economic exploitation is testimony to the fact that the church has hearkened more to the authority of the world than to the authority of God. Called to be the moral guardian of the community, the church at times has preserved that which is immoral and unethical. Called to combat social evils, it has remained silent behind stained-glass windows. Called to lead men on the highway of brotherhood and to summon them to rise above the narrow confines of race and class, it has enunciated and practiced racial exclusiveness.[62]

In order to be a faithful and effective witness in the world, King saw that the church needed to rid itself of its racism and status quo ethic.

Expanding the Racism, Economic Exploitation and Militarism Mantra

In the early 1980s, then Bishop James Armstrong of the United Methodist Church, named the "resurgence of racism" as one of the major social questions confronting the churches. This was in fact a half-truth, inasmuch as Armstrong implied that there was a period prior to the eighties when there was virtually no evidence of racism in the churches and other institutions of American society. Part of the problem here is that black Americans in particular know of no such period when there was even a moratorium on racist attitudes and behavior, whether inside or outside of churches and other institutions. Interestingly, although Armstrong named economic injustice as a major social problem in the 1980s, he did not name sexism. Of course, King did not name this as one of the critical social issues of his day either. We did not know the term *heterosexism* in King's day and into the eighties.

King began his ministry by focusing on the race issue. As a little boy he rather innocently promised to help his father to eradicate racism. Although the middle class status of the King family served as a slight buffer against racism, we know that King and his family did not completely escape the treachery of white racists. When young Martin was five or six he was told by the parents of his white friend that he could no longer play with him because he was a "Negro." Around the age of eight he became separated from his mother in a department store, accidentally stepped on the foot of a white woman, and was slapped by her. King, as well as Daddy King, reported on a number of similar racial incidents as well. Racism was an issue about which King had first hand experience. It was therefore not surprising that he began his ministry by narrowly focusing on trying to eradicate racism. However, the truth is that from the time when he was in seminary, he identified racism, economic injustice, and militarism as the trilogy of social problems he intended to address throughout his ministerial vocation. Consequently, it is not surprising that not long after beginning his ministry by focusing on racism, he recognized classism or economic exploitation as an issue that was also adversely affecting his people, as well as vast numbers of white people and others. The economic issue began to gain clarity for King during the Birmingham movement in 1963. But interestingly, even before this period—during the Montgomery bus boycott—King had expressed concern about war or militarism, and his sense that no nation could win a war. By the early to mid–1960s, he was frequently citing the racism, economic exploitation, and militarism mantra of social problems that the church should be addressing. Having begun his ministry by focusing on racism, his moral sphere had now expanded to include class issues and militarism. These were for him the three major social ills of the day, and he frequently named them in speeches, interviews, and writings. But clearly, because of who King was as Christian and personalist, and because he had established a pattern of altering his ideas and practice in light of current events, it was not far fetched to expect that his mantra trilogy would expand to include sexism. Such an expansion would have been consistent with King's personalistic method and the criterion of growing empirical coherence. But as noted above, current events also contributed to the expansion of his moral sphere. I have argued that in light of these and other reasons King, had he lived into the 1970s would have acknowledged his own sexism and would have been critical of sexism in its individual and institutional forms. For the same reasons, I would argue that his moral sphere would have expanded to include homosexuality as a justice issue to be addressed.[63] As a personalist social ethicist, Martin Luther King would have been driven to expand his trilogy mantra to include not only sexism, but homosexuality as well. This, it seems to me, is the logical conclusion of King's personalism and doctrine of human dignity, as well as his consistent openness and propensity to broaden his moral sphere in light of current events and the best available data.

Man of Ideas and Nonviolent Social Activism

There is no question that Martin Luther King thought of himself as a social ethicist who engaged in organized nonviolent social action, even though his doctoral training was in systematic theology.[64] The formal study of theology and philosophy enabled King to ground his social ethics theologically. That is, he saw God as the source or foundation of social ethics and social activism, and seldom spoke or wrote about the work of these without also making it clear that the God of his ancestors, the Hebrew prophets, and Jesus Christ is their source. Indeed, King was careful to point to the "suprarational" dimension of the Montgomery bus boycott campaign. He was adamant that the Montgomery struggle would have taken place even had he and other leaders never been born.[65] There was something beyond human beings that was the fundamental source of that movement. That "something," for King, is God. I know of few professional social ethicists who talk about God and God's expectations of persons in the world as much as King did. Indeed, the very reason that King early became increasingly more interested in social ethics than in abstract theologizing and philosophizing had much to do with how he thought about God and what God required of him and the church. King lived by the conviction that God required that he (and the church) be present in the world, i.e., that he show up and make his presence known when there was evidence of social injustice. After all, had not God so structured reality and all of life such that all life is interrelated and interdependent, so that whatever happens to anybody any place in the world affects—directly or indirectly—everybody else in the world, including the Creator-God? Since King also believed that God created persons-in-community, to live in a special type of community (the beloved community), he reasoned that persons are obligated to do all they can to create and enhance communities in which every person is respected and treated with dignity, precisely because they are beings imbued with God's image and are loved by God.

It is quite likely that had King been a different person, and had his people not been confronted with the continuing nightmare of racism and economic exploitation, he would have sought to teach in the university or theological academy, rather than return to the South to enter the pastorate and to seek means of liberating his people. But King *was* who he was, and his people knew nothing but the daily nightmare of racial injustice and economic despair. They were being crushed by these social maladies and their various manifestations. The calling to enter the ministry was strong indeed for Martin Luther King, and it did not take long for him to see that social ethics was more important to the work of the social-activist pastor than was systematic theology and philosophy.[66] In fact, King reminisced about how, as a teenager, the problem of racial injustice consumed much of his attention. Daddy King even reports that as a young boy of about six, Martin promised to "help me all he could" to eradicate racism.[67] What we see in this is the importance to the social ethicist not only what one thinks or one's theories, but what one actually does to address and eliminate injustice and oppression and to establish justice. As a social ethicist King was more than a thinker and theorizer. He was one who organized in order to do battle with social problems.

King believed that it was not sufficient for the church to remain in the arena of ideas. Important as ideas are, he was adamant about the necessity of moving into the sphere of nonviolent social action as well.[68] King was consistent in applying this principle to himself as well. He loved ideas, but these were not for him ends in themselves. As a good personalist, King insisted that ideas must be made to enhance persons and persons-in-community; must be made applicable to establishing the community of love or the beloved community. Therefore, we always see in King's social ethics a healthy and vigorous mutual interaction between ideas and social action calculated to achieve the best possible good for victims of oppression in particular, and people in general.

Martin Luther King was an excellent thinker in his own right, notwithstanding posthumous charges of plagiary. King not only loved ideas and enjoyed discussing the great Western philosophical ideas and ideals, but it is reasonable to say that he was, from seminary through doctoral studies and beyond, a man of ideas and ideals. Without question, more needs to be said about this, but for now, suffice it to say that it is never accurate to say that King was merely a social activist, although he was second to no one in this regard. The problem is that often when he is described as a social activist the tendency is to also imply that he was more of an activist or doer than a thinker or theorist. This, however, is a false dichotomy. Ideas were always important to King because he saw their potential for enhancing the well being of persons and the creation of the beloved community; of making both persons and the world better. As a personalist, King was always interested to know how ideas could contribute toward making better persons and communities.

Martin Luther King did not engage in social action willy-nilly. Any action in which he engaged was based on sound thinking, reflection, discussion, and analysis, and was calculated to liberate his oppressed people. Ideas and social action must mutually inform and sharpen each other. King had this in mind when he wrote: "Education without social action is a one-sided value because it has no true power potential. Social action without education is a weak expression of pure energy. Deeds uninformed by educated thought can take false directions. When we go into action and confront our adversaries, we must be as armed with knowledge as they. Our policies should have the strength of deep analysis beneath them to be able to challenge the clever sophistries of our opponents."[69]

Social Ethics and Social Gadflies

In the late 1970s, Nelle Slater, then Associate Dean of Boston University School of Theology, asked a group of Ph.D. candidates in a teaching colloquium what they intended to do once they completed their requirements for the degree. I responded, saying that I wanted to be remembered as having been a social gadfly in and out of the churches, especially regarding issues of race prejudice in its many forms, until the problem has been solved. I had been reading the dialogues of Plato at the time and recalled that in the *Apology*, Socrates had characterized himself that way in the presence of the powers, i.e., as one who "clings to the state as a sort of gadfly to a horse that is large and well-bred but rather sluggish because of its size, so that it needs to be aroused. It seems to me that the god has attached me like that to the state, for I am constantly alighting upon you at every point to arouse, persuade, and reproach each of you all day long."[70] Moreover, I knew this to be consistent with the prophetic tradition of the Jewish and Christian faiths, as well as the long protest tradition of black Americans.

The dictionary tells us that a gadfly is a persistent, annoying social critic. The gadfly in the King tradition of theological social ethics is required to be vigilant in reminding the forces of injustice of what the Source of their being requires of them in the area of human relations. The social gadfly in this tradition *never* lets up; never lets the powers and the oppressors off the moral hook. She is to them a constant annoyance.

Theological social ethicists in the tradition of Martin Luther King understand themselves to be nuisances to the powers and the privileged. Even those Kingian social ethicists in the academy are not merely interested in teaching their students the basic principles of social ethics, or about the need to do social ethics *out there*, i.e., outside the walls of the academic institution where the teaching is occurring. Convinced of the imperative to purge from within, i.e., to clean one's own house of social injustice first, such persons do not hesitate to challenge institutional policies and practices that are thought to undermine the dignity of persons affiliated with those institutions. Because the social ethicist influenced by King believes that the church has a mandate to stress the need for ethical prophecy,[71] i.e., prophecy in the tradition of the eighth century Hebrew prophets and Jesus Christ, they are always poised to challenge even top administrators when the situation seems to require it. The personality, class, and socio-cultural background of each of these persons will be different. But this only means that each must find the best way(s) to challenge powers that are thought to be unjust. What is important is not so much *how* they challenge the powers, but *that* they challenge them. When injustice is present, every social ethicist in the King tradition is obligated to declare, in the words of the Hebrew prophets, "What thus says the Lord God."

The theological social ethicist is mandated to do all in his power to make it virtually impossible for human beings to forget that all persons are imbued with the image of God, and that because all persons derive from a common source, all are one in the eyes of the God of the Hebrew prophets and Jesus Christ. This means that all must necessarily be treated with dignity and respect. The social ethicist in the King tradition will want nothing more than to do the work of justice, which is to him the work of love.

King's aim was not to be a nuisance or pest, as such. Rather, his sole desire was to be faithful to the God of his faith; faithful to God's expectation that justice be done in the world, and that the beloved community be actualized. And yet, he knew from experience—his own and that of others—and history that one who strives to be faithful to God's requirement that justice be done in righteous ways will suffer the consequences at the hands of racists, the powers, etc. The price of doing social ethics based on Kingian principles, of being faithful to the requirements of the gospel, will indeed be costly. King had this in mind when, early in the civil rights movement he said: "Christianity has always insisted that the cross we bear precedes the crown we wear. To be a Christian, one must take up his cross, with all of its difficulties and agonizing and tragedy-packed content, and carry it until that very cross leaves its marks upon us and redeems us to that more excellent way...."[72] Throughout the movement King did not hesitate to make known his awareness of the costliness of real Christian ministry. Months before he was assassinated he was compelled to say: "When I took up the cross, I recognized its meaning.... The cross is something that you bear and ultimately that you die on. The cross may mean the death of your popularity. It may mean the death of a foundation grant. It may cut down your budget a little, but take up your cross, and just bear it. And that's the way I've decided to go."[73] Martin Luther King, in fact, suffered all of these things as a result of his decision to break silence on the war in Vietnam.

PART II

PURSUING THE DREAM

7

The Humanity of King and the Continued Vigilance in Pursuing His Dream[1]

The advent of King Day as a federal holiday on the third Monday in January 1986 was a reminder of Martin Luther King, Jr.'s symbolic force as a national and international leader in the movement toward human rights, peace, justice, and what he called the beloved community. The realization of this national holiday was spearheaded by celebrity figures such as Coretta Scott King, R&B singer Stevie Wonder, and former Indiana Congresswoman Katie Hall.[2]

Martin Luther King, Jr., Day is a day to remember whence we have come and the price paid to get here. It is also the occasion to believe that we humans need not accept the world as it was when we were born into it. The world can be a better place for all, if we are willing to make the sacrifices that King and many others, locally, nationally, and globally were willing to make. King Day, the Rev. Betty Gilbert of Indianapolis, Indiana reminds us, is not intended to be "a day off, but a day on." That is, it is to be a day for reading, study, reflection, and celebration. It is a day for discussing with others best means for achieving that gentler, sweeter day when all of God's people the world over will commit to being what God intends them to be, as well as establishing the community of love.

Lewis V. Baldwin, recently retired preeminent King scholar at Vanderbilt University, has written of the significance of King Day, noting that it confirms four important points: (1) It is a reminder to all persons that a black person, one from a traditionally oppressed community, "deserves the highest measure of recognition and respect." (2) It supports "the prevailing definition of King as a symbol of American values and ideas." (3) It supports the claim that King represents "the best and the brightest" in the American tradition of organized mass nonviolent civil dissent. 4) It means that King's celebrated dream must become for persons everywhere "a sustaining vision" of what can be and what persons and communities can achieve when they exhibit commitment, determination, and a willingness to work together cooperatively. In this way, all that we do is somehow driven by the vision of a gentler, sweeter world.

There are two points of emphasis in this presentation. First, I focus on the humanity of Martin Luther King, and why it is absolutely critical that adherents of his basic ideas remember at all times that he was, first and last, a human being. To be sure, he was a human being who did some very extraordinary things in the world. But at the end of the day he was, like you and me, a human being, with all of the possibilities and limitations of every other human being.

The second point to be emphasized is the need for all of us to be vigilant throughout the year in our endeavors to actualize King's dream of the beloved community, rather than merely congregate at King Day and Black History month celebrations to listen to speeches, sing, pray, and return to business as usual for another year. The question is: What will we need to do daily in order to keep the dream alive? Before addressing this question, let's consider the importance of remembering the humanity of Martin Luther King.

The Humanity of King

Martin Luther King was, pure and simple, a human being. His only sister, Christine King Farris, sought to highlight this point not long after he was assassinated.[3] Farris reminds us that her brother did not just appear on the scene one day, fully formed and developed, as if he had always been the extraordinary person he was without ever having been tried and tested in the fires of life. "They think he simply happened," Farris writes, "that he appeared fully formed, without context, ready to change the world. Take it from his big sister, that's simply not the case."[4] King knew that he was not perfect. Nor would he want to be an icon, or be placed on a pedestal. He was a human being. He made mistakes, some of which suggest that his character was flawed.

It is unquestionably the case that since his assassination in 1968 many attempts have been made to tarnish King's image and even destroy the image of him as a national and international symbol of humanity and community, love and justice. Such attempts were particularly noticeable in the 1980s, especially as efforts were being made to gain approval to make his birthday a federal holiday.[5]

The war against Martin Luther King's symbolic image was waged fervently by politicians such as Jesse Helms and governors of eight states (most especially Arizona), as well as conservative religious leaders such as Patrick Buchanan. Moreover, intended or not, efforts to undermine King's image were reinforced by various segments of the academic community. The challenge from that sector began in earnest with the publication of two Pulitzer Prize winning books: David Garrow's *Bearing the Cross: Martin Luther King, Jr. and the Southern Christian Leadership Conference* (1986), and the first volume of Taylor Branch's trilogy on King, *Parting the Waters: America in the King Years, 1954–63* (1988). Garrow painted a picture of a womanizing King who was asked by a friend about "his compulsive sexual athleticism."[6] Since there is no evidence that the friend actually used these words, I cannot help wondering what drove Garrow to use such language regarding King, and why, in any case, he has such an image of King. In addition, Garrow seems to accept, uncritically, FBI Director J. Edgar Hoover's characterization of King as "a 'tom cat' with obsessive degenerate sexual urges."[7] This is at best an odd move by Garrow, considering Hoover's racism and his unabashed and glaring efforts to destroy King psychologically, emotionally, socially, and politically. In any case, Garrow claims that King had numerous extra-marital affairs; that he saw one of the women "almost daily"; and that, "That relationship, rather than his marriage, increasingly became the emotional centerpiece of King's life, but it did not eliminate the incidental couplings that were a commonplace of King's travels."[8] Garrow also claims that because King's professed views on sexual ethics were different from his actual behavior he was frequently overcome with deep-seated guilt and depression. Furthermore, Garrow would have us believe that on the question of sex, King was generally morally off balance.[9]

Branch's book (*Parting the Waters*), as well as Ralph Abernathy's, *And the Walls Came*

Tumbling Down: An Autobiography (1989), essentially added fuel to the flames ignited by Garrow.[10] In his book, *I May Not Get There With You: The True Martin Luther King, Jr.* (2000), Michael Eric Dyson writes of what he considers to be similarities between King and the late rap artist Tupac Shakur.

> Although it may seem blasphemous to say so, there is a great deal of similarity between Martin Luther King, Jr., and a figure like Tupac Shakur. They both smoked and drank, worked hard, and with their insomnia waged a "war on sleep." King and Shakur cursed, told lewd jokes, affectionately referred to at least some of their friends as "nigger," had fierce rivals, grew up in public at the height of their fame, shared women with their friends, were sexually reckless, wanted to be number one in their fields, occasionally hung out with women of ill repute, as youth liked nice clothes and cars, were obsessed with their own deaths, made a living with words, lived under intense scrutiny, allegedly got physical with at least one woman, had their last work published posthumously, and died before reaching their full potential.[11]

Now, by his own admission, it was not Dyson's intention to place Shakur and other rap artists like him on the same level as King, or to suggest that they, like King, were on a mission to radically transform the United States and the world and establish the beloved community. What Dyson does do, albeit in a rather crude way, is to remind us of King's humanity and consequent shortcomings—shortcomings that we also find in many rap artists. But despite Dyson's claim, it cannot be denied that his discussion fanned the flames ignited by Garrow and others, thereby unwittingly contributing to efforts to undermine King's powerful symbolic image.

I frankly wonder about the motives of those who have been so eager to focus on King's personal moral lapses. I agree wholeheartedly with black women religious scholars, such as Cheryl A. Kirk-Duggan, who argue that we should not become defensive or pretend that King was not guilty of such lapses when so much evidence suggests that he was.[12] Nevertheless, when I think about what appears to have been an overwhelming attempt to discredit King by focusing so heavily on his moral lapses, I am reminded of something that philosopher Bertrand Russell once wrote about St. Jerome, St. Augustine, and Pope Gregory the Great. He said that at a time when the Roman Empire was deteriorating internally and crumbling all around them, they devoted vast amounts of energy and ink to condemning infant baptism and the decision between consenting adults to engage each other sexually. Russell put it this way.

> It is strange that the last men of intellectual eminence before the dark ages were concerned, not with saving civilization or expelling the barbarians or reforming the abuses of the administration, but with preaching the merit of virginity and the damnation of unbaptized infants. Seeing that these were the preoccupations that the Church handed on to the converted barbarians, it is no wonder that the succeeding age surpassed almost all other fully historical periods in cruelty and superstition.[13]

It cannot be denied that Martin Luther King had personal moral lapses, since he himself confirmed the fact.[14] Nor can it be denied that in a way and to an extent that most of his white male critics have not been, King was faithful to God's call that he do justice and be the voice of the voiceless. He literally gave his life to the establishment of the community of love.

The discovery of King's plagiarism also contributed to the undermining of his reputation. Charges of plagiarism against King surfaced in the 1990s when Professor Clayborne Carson and his team of research assistants at Stanford University began editing the voluminous King papers.[15] The discovery was made that King plagiarized large sections of his doctoral dissertation, and that the plagiary was evident in many of his papers written in seminary and during doctoral studies. Without making excuses, I would say that King's womanizing and plagiary are but reminders that he was a human being, susceptible to the same shortcomings as *any* human being. In a word, King was an ordinary human being with all of the potentials and limitations of other human beings. And yet, he was a human being who did some very extraordinary things regarding the enhancement of both persons and community in this country and throughout the world. None expressed the powerful vision of the beloved community more forcefully and consistently, for example, as did King. He was finite and limited, a sinner missing the mark, just like the rest of us, and yet he was faithful to God's call. He will have to answer to God for his failings, but I hardly think he has to answer to you and me. We did not walk in his shoes, nor do we know fully enough what that might mean.

Was Martin Luther King a womanizer? The smoke around this matter is too thick. My own experience tells me that frequently when there is the presence of such dense smoke there is likely a fire somewhere, or we would be wise to at least do some investigating. The truth is that King loved women, and indicators are that his otherwise indomitable will was not always up to the challenge of saying NO to his extra-marital sexual desires. Did King plagiarize significant portions of his doctoral dissertation, as well as some of his papers written in seminary and during doctoral studies, in addition to post-doctoral writings, speeches, and sermons? In light of criteria established by the academy, the evidence that he did so is overwhelming.

Martin Luther King made no claims to possessing a flawless character and personality. He was not perfect; he was not sinless. He was the first to admit it. This is not to make light of any of the behaviors that made King as human as you and me. It is to say, however, that it is simply amazing that the God of the Hebrew prophets and Jesus Christ could use such an imperfect earthen vessel like Martin Luther King to contribute so significantly towards the achievement of God's purposes in the world. God uses in amazing ways what is available. This is a clue to what God can do through any person who opens self to God's will and who strives to be faithful to God's expectation that we do justice and stand with the least of these. No matter what else Martin Luther King did or failed to do, he did this better than most, during or since his time.

King liked to say that more than anything else, he was a Baptist preacher.[16] Unlike many who masquerade as ministers of Jesus Christ, King actually loved the ministry, and viewed his own call as "a vocation of agony."[17] He insisted that God's call was not to be taken lightly. But as a call or vocation, King knew that he had to live his commitment to ministry every single day. He was in solidarity with those he sought to serve, and was deeply touched by the condition and plight of the poor. His humanity was frequently revealed as he worked among those in the margin, and who had no voice. In a little known conversation with Jewish Rabbis just ten days before he was assassinated, King shared an experience he had in Mississippi. In his recounting of the experience, one can sense his agony and pain. He told of being in Marks, Mississippi where he found himself among some of the most impoverished people he had ever met. He met children who had inadequate clothing, and many of them had no shoes to wear. He saw the distended bellies of little crying children with runny noses who were clearly undernourished. He told of parents who were unemployed and had no hope of ever being employed. Many of these had no income at all, and were receiving no welfare benefits. King told the Rabbis that the experience caused him to "literally" cry.[18] On another occasion, King told of losing his appetite as he sat at a table in a restaurant in Jamaica in 1966, picked up a copy of *Ramparts* magazine, and saw pictures of Vietnamese children who had been badly burned and killed by napalm bombs.[19] Having been silent on the Vietnam War for nearly two years, King said that when he read that article, "The Children of Vietnam," he said to himself: "Never again will I be silent on an issue that is destroying the soul of our nation and destroying thousands and thousands of little children in Vietnam."[20] He decided at that moment that there comes a time when one has to speak up in light of one's highest ideals, no matter the social, personal, political, and economic consequences. Surely we can sense the humanity of Martin Luther King, an imperfect, earthen vessel, who heard and responded affirmatively to the divine call to serve God and the least of the sisters of brothers; and to serve them to the very end of his days.

When all is said and done, then, I think the most significant issue will be whether Martin Luther King was faithful to God's call to the very end. Faithfulness to God was important to King. We get a clear sense of this when, one year before he was assassinated, he deviated from the text of a sermon he was preaching at a friend's church in Chicago and said that when he died he did not want either a long funeral or a long eulogy. Instead, he wanted somebody to be able to say that he was faithful to his call, and to his God. He wanted to be remembered as one who did all he could to serve others.[21] King wanted to be remembered as having been faithful to God's call. The divine call or commission to ministry was important to Martin Luther King in a way it was not, and is not, to very many pastors and other religious leaders today.

The question for us is simple. Are we—seminary administrators and professors, ministers, students, and others—being faithful, indeed, do we want to be faithful to the God of Micah, who requires that we do justice, love mercy and kindness, and walk humbly with God? Who among us desires to be faithful to God, not only when it is convenient or politically correct, but even when our very reputations and lives are at stake? Who among us would be faithful to God to the end? Where is the evidence of our faithfulness? I frequently wonder how many of King's critics can claim such faithfulness to God and to those with their backs pressed against the wall (to use a favorite phrase of Howard Thurman), until such time that they too become the target and victim of a 30.06 slug which ended King's life this side of the grave.

To Keep the Dream Alive

Martin Luther King's dream for America and the world was of a thoroughly integrated society in which power and privilege would be shared equitably throughout, and in which the humanity and dignity of every person, regardless of sexual orientation,[22] race, gender, or class will be acknowledged and respected. King characterized such a society as the beloved community, a nomenclature that can be traced to the philosophical writings of Josiah Royce in *The Problem of Christianity* (1913).[23] The beloved community is one that acknowledges, affirms, and celebrates the values and contributions of both individuals and the community. It is a community in which *every* person is valued and respected just because they are persons, in whom the image of the divine is imprinted. In this yet to be realized community, there will be no such thing—as in today's communities—as a selection committee to determine who is a person and who not; who deserves to be treated humanely, justly, and with dignity, and who not; who is a member of the community and who not. The God of the universe established from the foundation of the world that every person possesses infinite, inviolable worth, is absolutely precious to God, and should be treated accordingly. Human beings have merely to accept this fact, not debate it.

In order to keep this dream alive, we have to live each and every day *as if* the dream were already a reality. This means that everything I do, everything that you do, interpersonally and communally, should be consistent with the values of the beloved community. The beloved community ideal is the principle of principles, the chief criterion through which we judge our own, and the behavior of others, including the powers and principalities. This means, among other things, that we have to be intentional about behaving in ways that honor the humanity and dignity of every human being—those who look and act like us, and those who don't. I can think of no better way for Christians, Jews, Muslims, and representatives of other religious faiths to both keep King's dream for America and the world alive, and to pursue it, than to live lives that exemplify faithfulness to God's expectation that justice be done in righteous ways, i.e., ways that respect the dignity of every person, in the world.

Year after year, Martin Luther King's dream is presented in celebration after celebration as a mere memory of the great speech he delivered in the sweltering heat in the shadows of the Lincoln Memorial on August 28, 1963. King Day celebrations frequently depict King as a man who gave what was arguably the greatest speech of the twentieth century, and at the conclusion of the speech remained at the Lincoln Memorial, frozen in time and place. It is as if King's civil rights ministry ended when he uttered the final words of his famous speech: "Free at last, free at last, thank God Almighty we're free at last." Those who take King's dream seriously will need to liberate both he and the dream from the steps of the Lincoln Memorial. Yes, it was there that King told America about a dream that he had had which, essentially encompassed his vision of the beloved community. But we have to remember that not long after delivering the "I Have A Dream" speech, King sadly proclaimed that he saw his dream turn to a nightmare in Birmingham, Alabama, and other places throughout the Deep South. Indeed, barely four months before he was assassinated, King reflected more explicitly about his sense of the dream turning to a nightmare. In "A Christmas Sermon on Peace" (December 1967) he said that the first time he witnessed the dream turn to a nightmare was when white racists bombed the Sixteenth Street Baptist Church in Birmingham, Alabama during the Sunday school hour on September 15, 1963, less than one month after the "I Have A Dream" speech. Four black children were killed that morning: eleven year old Denise McNair, and three fourteen year olds: Cynthia Wesley, Addie Mae Collins, and Carol Robertson. Two other black children were killed in Birmingham that day. One was killed by a group of white supremacist thugs as he rode his bicycle. The other was killed by Birmingham police.

King said further that he watched the dream turn into a nightmare as he saw his people in the ghettos of the North "perishing on a lonely island of poverty in the midst of a vast ocean of material prosperity,"[24] while the nation did nothing to rescue them. Moreover, King watched the dream turn to a nightmare as he observed his people "in the midst of anger and understandable outrage, in the midst of their hurt, in the midst of their disappointment, turn to misguided riots to try to solve that problem."[25] Finally, King saw his dream turn to a nightmare as he watched the escalation of the war in Vietnam,[26] where the war on poverty was shot down on every battlefield.[27]

The Martin Luther King that we should pay more attention to today is not the King who delivered that famous "I Have a Dream" speech on that hot day in August 1963. Rather, we need to focus on the King who had to figure out how to remain faithful to God's call in the face of the myriad ways that his dream for America and the world had turned to a nightmare. It is this King that I have in mind; the hardheaded realist whose faith in God was such that he refused to be a pessimist and defeatist, even though he was "not totally optimistic." This King lamented the prospect of not being able to "turn the Negro's disillusionment and bitterness into hope and faith in the essential goodness of the American system,"[28] knowing that if this did not happen, it could mean the demise of the nation. This King, the post-"I Have a Dream" speech, King, was totally realistic in his depiction of white America's treatment of blacks. "This is not a nation of venal people," he said in "A Testament of Hope." "It is a land of individuals who, in the majority, have not cared, who have been heartless about their black neighbors because their ears are blocked and their eyes are blinded by the tragic myth that Negroes endure abuse without pain or complaint."[29]

The dream of the beloved community will become a reality only as persons, churches, synagogues, mosques, civic organizations, and government at all levels (city, state, and federal) work toward its realization on a daily basis; only if they realize each and every day that in order for this to happen in God's world *it will be necessary to give up something.* I have met many otherwise well-meaning white people throughout the course of my academic career who are the recipients of unearned privilege and power. Many of these have spoken of their desire that things change for the better for blacks and others who have been historically, systematically deprived economically, politically, and socially. The problem is that such well-meaning people have resisted the idea of having to give up something of substantive value to them in order to contribute to the actualization of the stated desired change.

In the last three years of his life, Martin Luther King devoted vast amounts of time and energy to the question of where the nation and the world should be going and how best to get there. Although he continued to the very end to dream of the establishment of the beloved community, there is overwhelming evidence that he was not so foolish or naïve as to think that it would happen willy-nilly, or that it would even happen in his lifetime. However, it is quite conceivable that you and I can determine today whether it will happen in our lifetime. And if not this, we can at least choose to lay the foundation for it to happen in our children's or grandchildren's lifetime.

If we are to have a chance at all to actualize King's dream of the beloved community, it will be critical for members of the white community to name, acknowledge, and own their racism, not in some abstract way, or in some distant tomorrow, but today. This means they have to somehow discover the courage and find in their religious and other values the means to fess up, i.e., to acknowledge both their racism and their *unearned privilege* and position. Any whites who may wonder whether this really applies to them should read the 8th edition of *From Slavery to Freedom: A History of African Americans* (2000) by John Hope Franklin and Alfred A. Moss, Jr., or *Two Nations: Black and White, Separate, Hostile, Unequal* (1992, 1995), by Andrew Hacker. There is also the excellent book by Joe R. Feagin, *Racist America: Roots, Current Realities, and Future Reparations* (2000). The collection edited by Paula Rothenberg, *White Privilege: Essential Readings on the Other Side of Racism* (2002) is excellent. Or, whites may ask blacks or Latinas/os who have enough integrity and courage to tell the truth about the matter of race. In any case, it is absolutely crucial that whites get in touch with their own racism and figure out how, in their daily activities, they are complicit in racial discriminatory practices, how this makes them feel, what they intend to do about it, and when. Ultimately both whites and blacks will have to be brutally honest with each other about race relations and what they intend to do about it. Not until this happens, i.e., not until both are willing to tell the truth about racism, can we genuinely hope for meaningful solution and progress toward realizing King's dream.

Although King was not one to play the blaming and finger pointing game, he placed the responsibility for racism squarely on white America. In a taped interview in London, England in 1968, King said: "I think we have to honestly admit that the problems in the world today, as they relate to the question of race, must be blamed on the whole doctrine of white supremacy, the whole doctrine of racism, and these doctrines came into being through the white race and the exploitation of the colored peoples of the world."[30] In the same interview, King noted that to a large extent the eradication of racism in its individual and systemic forms depends on the will and moral resolve of the white community. Whites the world over will have to take racism and unearned privilege seriously, and stop minimizing it or pretending that it does not exist. Failure in this regard could very well lead to a global race war. King expressed the point as follows.

> I think ultimately this is going to depend to a large extent on the white peoples of the world. The fact is that the colored races have been terribly exploited, and trampled over with the iron feet of oppression, and this exploitation is not going to exist any longer. The cup of endurance has run over, and there is a deep determination on the part of people of color to be freed from all of the shackles that they faced in the past. Now if the white world does not recognize this and does not adjust to what has to be, then we can end up in the world with a kind of race war. So it depends on the spirit and the readjusting qualities of the white peoples of the world, and this will avoid the kind of violent confrontation between the races if it is done properly by the white peoples.[31]

King insisted on the need for whites to confess their own racism and deal with it. Historically, white men, especially those who possess massive power and privilege, seem to find it very difficult to confess their wrongdoing, whatever it may be. When it comes to racism this seems all the more difficult, or they seem all the more unwilling to confess that they have done anything wrong. At any rate, King was certain that a first step toward solving the race problem is that of confession and thorough self-examination. This should be followed by taking immediate steps to eradicate one's own racism, as well as that which is endemic to every major American institution, i.e., family, education, politics, economy, religion. One is responsible for addressing both individual and institutional racism. Further emphasizing his point, in the same London interview, King said that it "is very important for every white person to search his own soul and seek to remove all of the vestiges of racism and white supremacy. But along with this must be concrete justice that the white person and the white power structure will go out to establish.... As long as there is discrimination on any level the Negro is not free."[32] King concluded that racism is one of the four greatest threats to establishing the beloved community, locally, nationally, and internationally (the other three are global poverty, sexism, and war).[33]

Very many whites, and strangely, some blacks as well, have been deluded into thinking that racism was somehow eradicated during the civil rights movement. The claim was even made in the early and mid–1990s by members of the academic community.[34] Dinesh D'Sousa even declared the end of racism in his book by that title (1995).[35] Racism is, in his judgment, at best a figment of certain Americans' imagination.

What most *thinking* black Americans know, and what is confirmed by their day to day experience, is that racism is still alive and well in white churches, seminaries, and other religious establishments, including schools, places of employment, government, social welfare agencies, police departments, courtrooms, and legislative bodies. In a word, racism is still deeply embedded in the structures of this society.

Until white people acknowledge their own racism and unearned privilege and how they benefit from it; until they are willing to talk about how their racism really makes them feel, how they feel about that, what they intend to do about it, and when, I would say that it is ludicrous for any honest and reasonable person to believe that whites are serious when they talk about resuming the movement toward the beloved community, or when they speak of pursuing and keeping the dream alive.

Because of Martin Luther King's faith about the interrelated structure of reality and the relational nature of creation, the challenge for us all is that we come to see that no one group among us can do it all; can solve the race problem alone. If there is any hope at all that the dream of the beloved community will be a reality, all must work together cooperatively and relentlessly, to make it happen. This is the only way. Merely criticizing, denouncing, praying, and separating oneself from the world, rather than taking steps wherever one happens to be located, to change it, will not do. King's relational view of the universe and reality means that what affects any one of us, any group of us, affects the rest of us—directly or indirectly—including God. We are all affected because we are, whether we like it or not, a part of each other, a part of the interrelated structure of reality. I am a part of you, and you are a part of me, whether you like it, or I like it, or not. Neither of us can do anything about it. The better part of wisdom suggests that we thank God for giving us each other, and that we consciously and relentlessly seek ways to actualize the dream of the beloved community.

In a convocation speech given at Sarah Lawrence College in 1972, literary artist Alice Walker told her audience that their job, upon graduating, was the same as the women who preceded them—"to change the world.... For the world is not good enough; we must make it better."[36] Similarly, Martin Luther King held that young people, both in and out of the university, have a significant role to play, not only in eradicating racism,[37] but in making the world better than it is in other ways as well. Indeed, in the posthumously published, *The Trumpet of Conscience* (1968), King wrote of the role of university and non-university students of all races in establishing a more humane, justice oriented world house.[38]

Social evil exists because good people say and do nothing, or remain silent for too long. King had this in mind when, in his famous "Letter from Birmingham Jail," he declared that it will be necessary for Americans to repent not only for the hateful words and deeds of the bad people, "but for the appalling silence of the good people."[39] The ultimate tragedy is the silence and nonchalance of the good people.[40] W. E. B. DuBois had something like this in mind in 1957 when he wrote about the cause of the continuing race problem in the South. He said: "But I am inclined to place the chief blame for race friction in the South on the respectable white Southerners of impeccable morals, education and high social position, who for a hundred years have been silent or tacitly consenting to beliefs and measures which they knew were wrong and destructive."[41] Tragically, what DuBois said next remains true, even today: "While the world was beginning to realize that in all essentials, black folk were equal to white, in our South, the leaders of public opinion, supinely or openly in sermon and lecture, in book and paper, in home and school let two generations of young whites grow up to believe that white people were so inherently and eternally superior to blacks, that to eat, sit, live or learn beside them was absolute degradation."[42] We can be sure that such behavior detracts from, rather than contributes to, the realization of King's dream of the beloved community.

We are, all of us, imperfect, finite, and limited beings, on whom God has emblazoned the seal of preciousness. In this regard, Martin Luther King was no different. It is important that we always keep before us King's humanity, even as we remember, praise, and celebrate his many contributions to the wellbeing of persons-in-community. By remembering that he was as thoroughly human as any other human being we may be less tempted to condemn him and his accomplishments when word comes that his character was flawed. We need to remember that as a human being, Martin Luther King had weaknesses, even as he exhibited extraordinary faithfulness to God's expectation that he be the voice of those who have no voice.

8

Josiah Royce and the Beloved Community[1]

On April 29, 2005, I responded to two excellent papers on the concept of the beloved community in the writings of Josiah Royce and Martin Luther King, Jr., absolutistic and theistic idealistic philosophical personalists, respectively. The occasion was the spring meeting of the American Philosophical Association (Midwest Division, Personalistic Discussion Group) in Chicago.[2] Professor Randy Auxier of the University of Southern Illinois at Carbondale was the convener. The papers were presented by men who were writing their doctoral dissertations in philosophy under Auxier: Dwayne Tunstall,[3] and Gary Herstein,[4] and both have since earned their doctorates. Herstein and Tunstall studied—among other things—the philosophy of personalism under Auxier and had read extensively in the literature—particularly but not exclusively—that of personalists who taught and published from Boston University. In addition, the two men were quite familiar with the writings and social activism of the best known social activist personalist in the twentieth century, Martin Luther King, Jr., a Boston University alumnus. That Tunstall and Herstein both studied the philosophy of personalism is critical since both Royce and King were personalists, although I know of no place where Royce declared himself to be such. However, in a letter written to Edgar S. Brightman (a former student of Bowne's) in 1913, Royce said: "I wish that somebody would tell me what my precise relation to Bowne is."[5] Royce was clearly familiar with Bowne and his work. Unlike Royce, King, on the other hand, was quite clear in naming personalism as his basic philosophical point of departure.[6] Without question, Royce conceives of both God and human beings as personal.[7] He also stresses the dignity of persons. These two foci place him squarely in the personalist camp, though not a thoroughgoing personalist.

I was impressed by the sharpness of thought in the work of Herstein and Tunstall, as well as their eagerness to grapple with ideas and their implications for actual living in the world and making it a better place for all. For this is fundamental to personalism, and most especially that type which was developed at Boston University and lived and practiced through the civil and human rights ministry of Martin Luther King, unquestionably the quintessential social personalist of his day. King was nothing if not a man of ideas and ideals who was adamant about applying these ideas to life and efforts to attain the beloved community; that community in which every person is treated with dignity and respect, and whose basic human needs are provided for just because they are persons. King's was a *practiced* or *applied* personalism, which is to say that he was less concerned about theoretical personalism than what personalist ideas means for human beings in their daily living and relating in the world.

As implied before, at this writing Martin Luther King is still the most distinguished member of the Boston University personalist tradition. Indeed, while still a student at Crozer Theological Seminary in Chester, Pennsylvania, King made the decision to attend Boston University Graduate School precisely because of his desire to study personalism under the premier personalist, Edgar S. Brightman. When Brightman died suddenly during King's second year of studies, L. Harold DeWolf, a Brightman protégée became his academic and dissertation advisor. Under DeWolf's guidance King studied personalism in depth. He exhibited his mastery of personalist ideas by writing papers and taking examinations on it.[8] He then further sharpened his understanding of this philosophy and the doctrine of God by writing his doctoral dissertation on Paul Tillich and Henry Nelson Wieman, using their thought as foils to hone his essentially personalist conception of God.[9] In what follows I react to the papers presented by Tunstall and Herstein, "Royce and King on *Agape* and the Beloved Community," and "The Roycean Roots of the Beloved Community," respectively.

"Royce and King on Agape *and the Beloved Community"*

Early on, Dwayne Tunstall pointed to the significance of the black Baptist church tradition for King's intellectual development. He was careful to note that long before King was introduced to the term "personalism," he had already developed two chief personalist convictions: (1) that God is personal, and (2) because persons are created by God, and imbued with the image of God, they necessarily should be treated with dignity and respect. King was taught these principles by his parents and maternal grandmother at home, and got reinforcement in Sunday school and church at the Ebenezer Baptist Church, where his father was pastor. Tunstall was right to argue that these two convictions were instilled in King by his family and the black church tradition. His conviction about these was only strengthened as he formally studied the white social gospel tradition, and was introduced to the philosophy of personalism at Crozer Theological Seminary. King's formal and systematic study of personalism occurred at Boston University. This gave him a language and a philosophical framework through which to think about the implications of these (and other personalist) convictions for ministry.

Admittedly, I hoped that Tunstall would have placed even more emphasis on the importance and place of the less formal influences on King's thought development, e.g., his family upbringing and the black church tradition. Instead, he said that it was not his intention to write yet another paper chronicling the influence of the various schools of thought on King's philosophical development, including the black Baptist tradition. And yet, it was precisely the church and other less formal influences, such as in-home teachings, that I wish Tunstall had said more about. For despite some very good work that has been done on black American cultural, family, and religious influences on King by the likes of James Cone, William Watley, Garth Baker-Fletcher, and most especially the two premier King scholars, Lewis Velvet Baldwin (recently retired Professor of Religious Studies at Vanderbilt University), and Clayborne Carson (Director of the King Papers Project, and Professor of History at Stanford University), much remains to be done. For example, we do not know nearly enough about the extent to which King was influenced by Delia King (King's paternal grandmother), A. D. Williams (King's maternal grandfather), Daddy King, Benjamin E. Mays, George Kelsey (who earned his Ph. D. degree at Yale, where the personalist George T. Ladd taught for many years), William

Holmes Borders, and Howard Thurman. To what extent did these influence King's under-standing of agape and the beloved community? We know, however, that Howard Thurman wrote an article on the beloved community,[10] although it is not known whether he and King actually had conversations about that subject.

Furthermore, the very good work that has been done by the leader of the black cultural studies genre in King Studies, Lewis Baldwin, is frequently not taken as serious by some white males who write on King. For example, I wrote reviews on two otherwise very good books on King: Stewart Burns, *To the Mountaintop: Martin Luther King, Jr.'s Sacred Mission to Save America 1955–1968* (2004), and Peter J. Ling, *Martin Luther King, Jr.* (2002). Generally, I concluded that of the biography genre, these were two of the best works on King at the time of their publication. And yet, both texts are limited by their failure to take seriously enough black cultural studies on King that we find in the work of Baldwin. If one does not have a clear sense of the black cultural, family, and church influences on King, it would be easy to conclude with Stewart Burns that the pressure on King during the last two years of his life was such that he was nearly incapacitated a number of times during that period because of severe depression.[11] And yet, when one has a sense of the real strength and encouragement that King drew from family, including his extended church family, the sense of relaxation that came from hearty conversation as he consumed his favorite soul food meals, the sense of calm that came from boyish horseplay with close friends (as occurred just hours before he was assassinated), the use that King made of humor and jokes, etc., one might well conclude that like any human being a person under such pressures would most assuredly experience moments of depression and despondency. However, this alone does not necessarily mean that King was incapacitated. Fur-thermore, humor and jokes played such a central role in King's daily life that, more often than not, he was able to cope with whatever was thrown at him.[12]

On the other hand, had one read Baldwin's book, *Toward the Beloved Community: Martin Luther King, Jr. and South Africa,*[13] one could not claim, as Peter Ling does, that by 1956 King had little awareness of the struggle against apartheid in South Africa.[14] If white (and other) scholars will not take the work of black scholars on King seriously, black scholars should. In the case of Baldwin's work, it is quite possible that by virtue of his own love for the Deep South (a sentiment shared by King), he brings something of great value to the interpretation of the cultural and black family influences on King that might not be available to white scholars, or even black scholars who do not share Baldwin's love for the south.

Good work has been done on the less formal cultural, family, and church influences on King's intellectual development, but more needs to be done. In the mean time, we need to continue to challenge white scholars on the importance of reflecting these influences in their writing, teaching, and lecturing on King. This means that black scholars will need to be inten-tional about doing the same thing in our own work on King. The argument here is not that *either* the less formal *or* the more formal influences on King's development is more important, but that both are important for one who seeks a fuller, more thorough understanding of King and his work. Neglecting either of these necessarily leaves one with a truncated understanding of the life, work, and contributions of King. This suggests the need to examine not one, but both sets of influences, and to take them both seriously.

King expressed the need for his people to take more seriously the African aspects of their culture and to stop being ashamed of that part of their heritage. Part of this has to do with the need to uncover the cultural contributions of blacks, naming them, and boldly declaring them in the most public ways.[15] King referred to this phenomenon as "the dilemma of being a Negro in America," another way of characterizing what W. E. B. DuBois described as the "double consciousness" or "sense of twoness" of black Americans.[16] "In physical as well as cultural terms," King said, "every Negro is a little bit colored and a little bit white.... The Negro is the child of two cultures—Africa and America."[17] Too frequently, he went on to say, too many blacks are inclined to embrace only one side of their double nature and culture. Frequently it is the American or white side that is embraced. Just as blacks must be more intentional about embracing both sides of their heritage, white scholars who write on King must allow their work to be informed by the African side of who he was. At the bare minimum, this means that they will have to take more seriously the work of black scholars on King who have stressed the black cultural, family, and church influences on his ideas and practice. For King reminds us: "The American Negro is neither totally African nor totally Western. He is Afro-American, a true hybrid, a combination of two cultures."[18] Blacks are an admixture of Africa and America, black and white. In order to understand blacks, in order to understand and appreciate King, one must carefully examine both sets of influences.

I therefore challenge scholars, regardless of racial-ethnicity, to delve into black cultural, family, and church studies as they seek deeper understandings of King and his contributions. And we need not be pretentious about this. As a matter of course, from elementary school to graduate school, students of all races and ethnicities in the United States are given very little exposure to Africana studies in the educational system.

Tunstall rightly contends that while one can separate and analyze King's doctrines of agape and the beloved community, one cannot hope to glean the fullest understanding of his thought if these are not ultimately kept together. The beloved community, in King's thought, means nothing apart from agape. By definition agape—the spontaneous, unmotivated, over-flowing love of God operating in the human heart—must necessarily point to the beloved community. The beloved community is the agape community, i.e., the community of love.

Tunstall was also right to describe King as civil rights leader, social critic, *and* "public intellectual." I underscore "intellectual" because despite the well-documented charges of plagiarism against King in the 1990s,[19] he was always very much a man of ideas and ideals and an excellent thinker in his own right, a truth for which an earlier generation of King scholars (prior to the 1980s) gave him little credit. One should not ignore or soft-peddle his plagiarism; nor should one downplay or ignore the fact that Martin Luther King was, nevertheless, a great thinker—a man of ideas. Tunstall was careful to remind us of this important point.

In addition, and fundamentally, King understood himself to be a Baptist preacher, which means that virtually everything he did must be seen in light of this. Consequently, the work that he did as civil and human rights leader, social critic, and public intellectual, was for him less a result of a chosen career than a chosen *vocation*. The difference here is that while one may easily or conveniently switch professions, one cannot do so quite as easily if she understands hers to be a vocation or calling from God. In such a case one is devoted to a calling, not a 40 hour per week job.

Without question, Martin Luther King believed that he was called by God. His was not the dramatic, seemingly supernatural type of call experience reported by the Apostle Paul and Protestant reformer, Martin Luther. King's was a more gradual call experience; one that led him, over time, to accept ministry as his life's vocation.[20] Furthermore, King understood that when God calls, and one acknowledges and accepts that call, he has to stay the course, no matter what; that even when one is being lambasted by the State Department and the President of the United States, by major news media outlets, other civil rights leaders, and even close friends and members of his own organization because he criticized the war in Vietnam, he has to stay on task, always remembering who *called* and *calls* him to it.

King understood that one's calling from God is essentially one's life, and that all life comes from, and ultimately returns to, the God who calls. In this, I am in agreement with Conley Hughes that, "essential to any study of King's thought and action is a clear understanding that King was a Christian *thinker and practitioner*. That is to say, the whole of King's life was centered around a Christian understanding of the world. This fact cannot be overemphasized, for it is the essential link to also understanding the interconnection between his deep rooted heritage in the black religious experience and his serious study of philosophy and theology."[21] It is absolutely critical that we remember that *King was a man of Christian faith who believed that he was called by God to his ministerial vocation.* This helps to explain, at least in part, why he took the Movement north to Chicago in 1966, even though he was strongly advised by close advisors Stanley Levison and Bayard Rustin, that it was politically and economically unwise to do so. King did not disagree with this advice. He just knew that he had to answer to a different, more compelling voice, i.e., the One who called him. Consequently, in King's mind, it was the morally right thing to do, both because injustice existed in Chicago, and because there were cries from there for help. This was his rationale for implementing the Birmingham campaign in 1963.[22] Therefore, King was less concerned about political astuteness and correctness, than about being morally right. Politically, it was not feasible for him to go to Chicago, or to criticize the Johnson administration's foreign policy. But to King's way of thinking, he was morally correct in his decision to go to Chicago, and to publicly criticize the war in Vietnam.

In a helpful way, Tunstall pointed to what he perceived as "a problem" in King's doctrine of the beloved community. He asserted that on the one hand, King suggests that the beloved community is an ideal that is "partially" achievable in history, while at other times he contends that the beloved community is that which can be fully achieved in history. For a long time, scholars on King have argued—rightly in my judgment—that the concept of the beloved community is the chief regulating principle in King's theological social ethics. This is the view of Lewis Baldwin, Ira Zepp, Jr., and Kenneth Smith, for example. Since I share this view, I often find myself asking my students what this or that belief, idea, or action has to do with King's doctrine of the beloved community. What does it contribute toward establishing the beloved community? What place does racism, heterosexism, sexism, classism, or ableism have when we invoke the beloved community ideal? Do any one or more of these have a place at all in such a community? Aren't these contradictions when seen in relation to the beloved community ethic?

Martin Luther King speaks and writes about the beloved community as if it was something that is not only partially achievable in history, but that which may, at some point, be fully achievable. There is evidence for both of these positions in King's writings and thought. However, I would caution us to remember that King was more of a theological realist than some are aware. That is, despite the strong personalist influence, that of theological liberalism, and also social gospel ideas, King had a keen awareness of the prevalence and depth of human sin on the individual and group levels. Interestingly, King had this awareness long before he read Reinhold Niebuhr's *Moral Man and Immoral Society*, and *The Nature and Destiny of Man* in seminary and graduate school. He had seen racism at work when he was a youngster and knew even then that it was contrary to the best in the Jewish and Christian traditions. He knew that racist behavior was a result of human sin, and that it displeased God. Therefore, King refused to pretend that racism was acceptable. In light of his awareness in this regard, we should remember King's theological realism, i.e., his understanding of the depth of human sin on every level of human achievement in the world. This sense came from the influence of his own first hand boyhood and adolescent experiences with social evils such as racism, as well as the influence and awareness of the experiences of his father and maternal grandfather. King was also much influenced in this regard by his Morehouse College mentors and professors, including Benjamin E. Mays, George Kelsey, Samuel Williams, and Walter Chivers (his academic advisor).

Furthermore, when we remember that Martin Luther King lived by the faith that the universe hinges on morality, or is fused with value, it must be the case that for him the beloved community is at least partially achievable, and that through the relentless cooperative endeavor between human beings and God, it is possible to achieve ever higher forms of this community, or to more nearly approximate it. King clearly believed that if persons, in conjunction with God, commit their best efforts to establishing the community of love, it is possible to more nearly approximate its actualization.

What is not as obvious to me is that King really believed that the beloved community is achievable in the fullest sense in history, despite the fact that he himself declared in a number of speeches, not least his last speech at Mason Temple the night before he was assassinated, that blacks would get to the promised land (or beloved community). And yet, I believe that this was, for King, at least a very real hope. Anybody who really believes as King did, that "the arc of the moral universe is long but it bends toward justice,"[23] would very likely believe in the possibility of the full actualization of the beloved community.

The beloved community concept was for King more than an operative or regulative ideal, although it was also this. He believed that as long as human beings put forth the effort we can more nearly approximate the requirements of such a community. I am certain that King was not naïve enough to believe that his generation and that of his children would live to see the full actualization of the beloved community.

Increasingly, I like to talk about the beloved community in language that Reinhold Niebuhr once attributed to Christian love, namely as the "impossible possibility."[24] Because of individual and group interest, and the occurrence of sin on virtually every level of human achievement, it is impossible, according to Niebuhr, to achieve all that Christian love (or agape) requires. And yet, because of what goodness there is in human beings, it is possible to achieve ever higher degrees of justice, although we must recognize that this is still less than what agape requires. I think that Martin Luther King had something like this in mind when he spoke and wrote about the beloved community. Because of his awareness of the depth of human sin, selfishness, and pride he recognized that we would not likely achieve all that the beloved community ideal requires. However, because he also saw a fundamental goodness in human beings, he was convinced beyond doubt that through mutual cooperative endeavor persons and God can achieve infinitely higher degrees of what the beloved community ethic requires. We can be sure of King's rejection of any notion of *inevitable progress* toward the beloved community. Any progress, he concluded, will be the result of intensive, relentless effort and struggle. Progress, he liked to say, does not roll in on the wheels of inevitability.[25]

In what I take to be a position shared with Gary Herstein, Tunstall made the claim that all of the most important aspects of King's beloved community ideal were already present in Josiah Royce.[26] I gather that he meant that most of the *philosophical* aspects of King's beloved community ethic already existed in Royce. I am in general agreement with this point. However, I also think that King went well beyond Royce in characterizing the actual concrete nature of such a community, as well as proposing and consistently applying a method—nonviolent direct action—for achieving it. Royce did none of this.

However, it is not at all clear to me that inherent in Royce's doctrine of the beloved community is a vision of the social, economic, and political *equality* of black Americans and their white counterparts. While this was absolutely the case regarding Martin Luther King, I know of no definitive evidence that Royce did not believe whites to be the superiors of blacks, even though he might have been more advanced in his thinking about race than many of his white contemporaries. Moreover, to his credit, and unlike his philosophical colleague across the Charles River at Boston University, namely the personalist Borden P. Bowne, Royce at least published essays on the race question and various prejudices attributed to it in 1905 and 1908. Although he appeared to have a sense that his own race was superior to blacks in the United States, Royce seemed convinced that this was not due to any inherent fundamental differences in mental and other capacities, but was tied more to socio-historical conditions.[27] Royce's views on the matter were not as enlightened as one might wish, but he did not seem to adhere to the elitist racial views of most whites of his day.

And yet, it is also known that Royce occasionally used the term "nigger."[28] Was Royce's (at best) what David Levering Lewis characterized as a "vague concern about race relations?"[29] That is a question the answer to which I personally would like to know. DuBois was convinced that Royce did not understand "the Negro problem."[30] During his junior at Harvard, DuBois took an English course with Royce entitled "Forensics." He later took a philosophy course under Royce and was impressed with his keen philosophic analysis.[31] That DuBois announced Royce's death in the November 1916 issue of *The Crisis* does, nevertheless, say something about his respect for this teacher of philosophy.[32]

Martin Luther King clearly had no problem thinking of whites and blacks as equals, and from the beginning to the end of his ministry he insisted that the beloved community is one in which persons as such have inherent dignity and worth and must—every one of them—be respected and treated accordingly. However, I am not unmindful that it can be argued that while Royce's concept of the beloved community was limited relative to the issues of race and gender, King's was limited relative to the issue of gender. This, I have argued elsewhere, is a major contradiction or limitation of his personalism and doctrine of human dignity.[33]

I agree with Tunstall that we find in King's ethic of the beloved community most of the same ideas already present in Royce, e.g., a commitment to love, justice, and acknowledgement of the inalienable dignity of persons, although it is not clear to me that King himself gleaned these ideas from an actual reading and study of Royce. It is more likely that his knowledge of Royce's beloved community ideal was derivative, i.e., a result of what he heard in course lectures given by Edgar S. Brightman and L. Harold DeWolf at Boston University. He might also have seen the reference to Royce's concept of the beloved community in Brightman's book, *Religious Values*.[34] King cited this book in a paper in Brightman's course on Philosophy of Religion.[35] Subsequently, I return to the matter of how and where King may have gained knowledge about the beloved community.

I cannot help but wonder whether King, who surely was familiar with Kingdom of God ideas long before he went to seminary, actually heard these characterized in ways similar to descriptions of the beloved community. When it is remembered that Benjamin E. Mays and George Kelsey were recipients of the Ph. D. from the University of Chicago and Yale University, respectively, and thus were both much influenced by liberal social gospel teachings about the Kingdom of God as well as their own convictions about the importance of social gospel Christianity in the black religious tradition, I can easily imagine King having heard things about the Kingdom of God that he would later hear said about the beloved community. Furthermore, when we remember that as a student at Morehouse College, King was required to attend chapel on Tuesdays, when Mays frequently preached or lectured, this even increases the likelihood that he heard about the Kingdom of God in language that was essentially beloved community language. Consider the following passage regarding the nature of the Kingdom of God on earth from a sermon by a black pastor that Mays and co-author Joseph William Nicholson quoted in the *Negro's Church* (1933).

> If I understand what is meant by the Kingdom, it means the existence of that state of society in which human values are the supreme values. It means the creation of a world in which every individual born into it would be given an opportunity to grow physically, to develop mentally and progress spiritually without the imposition of artificial obstructions from without. Everything in the environment would be conducive to developing to the nth degree the individual's innate powers. At the center of our social, religious, political and economic life would be not a selfish profit motive, not a prostituted conception of nationalism, not a distorted notion of race superiority; but at the center of our lives would be the sacredness of human personality; and whatever we did, the chief aim would be to protect life and improve it.[36]

This sounds very much like language that King later used to describe the beloved community and its emphasis on the sacredness of persons and how they should be treated. And how would the United States and other areas of the world be transformed if the type of Kingdom preached about in the above passage actually existed? The minister went on to say:

> As an individual, I would not wish any good thing for myself that I would not wish for every other man on God's earth. And if the thing I want, though beneficial to me, would be damaging to my neighbor of whatever color or class, I would not want that thing. I would not and I could not pile up my millions if I had to do it at the expense of long hours and low wages on the part of those who produce the wealth.
>
> Our government with such a Kingdom as this could not spend 78 per cent of its national income on past and future wars. The nations of the world would not spend their billions in preparation for human slaughter. It would not be a question of the reduction of armaments but the abolition of armaments....
>
> If this kind of Kingdom should come to the world, there would not be a mad rush to control and dominate the economic resources of the earth; but a passion to share all the goods of God's world with all of God's people....
>
> If this kind of Kingdom should come to the earth, no race would want to keep another race down.[37]

Although Mays and Nicholson recorded this sermon in 1933, it was preached in 1914. Moreover, King would likely have heard such ideas expressed in the Tuesday sermons and talks given by Mays.

In his second year of seminary, King wrote an essay in which he said: "The Kingdom of God will be a society in which men and women live as children of God should live. It will be a kingdom controlled by the law of love."[38] He said further: "God, the great architect, chose this world as a site on which to build a wonderful structure; a global union of real brothers sharing in his good gifts, and offering all achievement as a form of worship to him."[39] Of course, by 1957 it was clear to King that the end of all nonviolent struggle against social injustice is "the creation of the beloved community,"[40] which was for him the chief aim of the Southern Christian Leadership Conference.[41] The aim is reconciliation between the races, integration with power, "a new relationship ... between the oppressed and the oppressor."[42] Any real hope of achieving even partial realizations of the beloved community, according to King, will require a "revolution of values," or what Friedrich Nietzsche referred to as a "transvaluation of all ancient values."[43] This means, in part, that there is need to "rapidly begin the shift from a 'thing'-oriented society to a 'person'-oriented society."[44] Only when this happens in earnest, will persons and groups begin to seriously challenge and resist unjust social policies and practices in light of the principles of love, fairness, and justice. This is consistent with Royce's insistence that such policies and practices be judged by the standards of the beloved community ideal.[45] Without such resistance, without a revolution of values, *some* poverty, *some* unemployment and underemployment, *some* racism, *some* heterosexism, *some* sexism, *some* classism, *some* urban communities that are little more than urban battle zones, will continue to be deemed by many to be tolerable and acceptable. The transvaluation of values, King maintained, means that no level of poverty, unemployment/underemployment, racism, militarism, etc., will be deemed tolerable. It means that our outlook must not be just local and national, but global.[46]

I wonder if the beloved community ideal, rightly understood, whether in the thinking of Royce or King, permits oppression of any kind. Ideally, I think it does not, although I also understand Tunstall's concern that some thinkers may worry that this Ideal may be misappropriated in such ways, as in the totalitarian regime, thus confusing "their human-constructed ideals for the ideal of the beloved community and oppress their fellow persons in its name." But I dare say that these two terms, "beloved community" and "oppression," are oxymoronic at best.

What Dwayne Tunstall proposed in terms of "easing the tension" in King's doctrine of the beloved community, viz., his tendency to speak of it as a partially realizable and regulating ideal, and also as a fully achievable ideal in history, convinces me of my own need to return to a much closer reading of Royce's discussions on the beloved community in *The Problem of Christianity* (1913). For, admittedly, to this point in my work on King, I have not paid as much attention to Roycean ideas on the beloved community. Although I have found no evidence that King actually read and studied Royce, I can now see the wisdom of studying his contributions to the beloved community ideal, and how this may impact the Kingian version of the beloved community. I have Tunstall to thank for this insight.

I have no doubt of the veracity of two of Tunstall's three claims: First, that Royce's metaphysics of community adequately supports King's claim that the beloved community is to some extent, achievable in history; second, that the God of the Hebrew prophets and Jesus Christ desires that such a community be achieved as far as possible in every era of history. Tunstall's third claim, "that it is likely that we would actualize more and more of it *once more and more persons truly live their lives by that ideal,*" is a bit too individualistic for me, as I suspect it would be for King. For, a disturbing implication is that if only enough individuals would live by the love ideal, there would be no social problems. Considering the prevalence and depth of human sin, pride, and selfishness in human beings, and especially in privileged and powerful groups and nations, I hardly think the key to achieving the beloved community is to be found in more and more individuals who seek to live their lives by its chief ideals. The problem with this idea is that it does not address the institutional or systemic nature of social problems. To be sure, the hearts and minds of individuals must be influenced by love, but this alone will not solve the problems. A more realistic view is that we must come to real terms with the idea that notwithstanding the level of morality among individuals in powerful and privileged groups, such groups themselves will fight fiercely and relentlessly, often to the death, to maintain their level of privilege and power. Even when individuals are changed by the power of love, the structures from which they and their groups benefit must be dismantled and rebuilt on the basis of justice and equality for all.

On a different note, Tunstall rightly suggests that Martin Luther King's insistence that means and ends must cohere,[47] could strengthen "a conceptual weakness" in Royce's doctrine of the beloved community. More specifically, Tunstall wonders how it is possible for one to proclaim a beloved community ethic, as Royce clearly did, while simultaneously advocating war against Germany in World War I. Such a stance is, according to Tunstall, a clear contradiction of the beloved community ideal, particularly as advocated by King. King was, after all, committed absolutely to the principle of nonviolence as a way of life, and thus rejected war.

What is evident in Dwayne Tunstall's discussion on Royce's pro-war stance is that Royce was much more Niebuhrian in outlook than was King regarding such matters. Royce—who died in 1913—did not know about Niebuhr who began his Detroit pastorate in 1915 and left in 1928 to join the faculty at Union Theological Seminary in New York City. Nevertheless, any student of Niebuhr knows that he did not rule out the ethical validity of war if it could be shown that there was reason to believe that degrees of justice could be the end result. In fact, as noted earlier, Niebuhr was emphatic that it is not possible to achieve all that the agape ethic requires, especially in relations between groups and nations. The most we can hope for, according to Niebuhr, is the achievement of higher and higher degrees of justice (not love). It appears that Royce had no illusions about the complete actualization of the beloved community in history. Nevertheless, he insisted on the need to strive continuously to achieve higher degrees of the ideal community, a point to which King would be in agreement.

While I agree with Tunstall that violent means will never lead to the full requirements of the Christian love ideal, I think that such means may sometimes lead to higher levels of justice, if only temporarily. And justice, King himself acknowledged, is the instrument of love (which is not to say that King would have agreed with Royce's stance regarding war). However, it is important to remember that King did not hesitate to utilize, and indeed expected the support of, law enforcement during civil rights campaigns. He had an appreciation for what he described as the "intelligent" use of police force.[48] Consequently, King must have known that this would sometimes mean that local law enforcement officers would have to use physical force to restrain those who attacked the nonviolent demonstrators. In my heart of hearts, I wonder whether King's was not a kind of back door appeal to physical force to protect those seeking the noble end of civil rights, freedom, and justice. I now turn to reflections on the paper presented by Gary Herstein.

"The Roycean Roots of the Beloved Community"

As I read the papers by Tunstall and Herstein, I was reminded that black Americans have been longing for the actualization of the beloved community since they were first violently torn from the womb of the African continent and forced into what was arguably the most dehumanizing form of enslavement in all the annals of history.[49] Gary Herstein's paper, "The Roycean Roots of the Beloved Community," seeks to uncover Roycean contributions to the development of King's beloved community ethic. Herstein maintained that these roots go much deeper than heretofore acknowledged. In addition, he believes that King actually read Royce and borrowed from him, although he was careful to note that there is no hard evidence for this belief, and thus it is not possible to demonstrate it. Nevertheless, he contends that there is sufficient circumstantial evidence to suggest the plausibility that King read Royce (most likely under Brightman and DeWolf) and appropriated some of his ideas on the beloved community. "My hope," Herstein argued, "is that the plausibility will become so overwhelming, as the details of the similarities are brought out, that in the absence of any evidence to the contrary, the claim for the depth of the connection may be accepted as reasonably established." Although Herstein clearly produced sufficient evidence to show the similarities between Royce and King's understandings of the beloved community ethic, it does not seem to me that he sufficiently supported his belief that King himself actually read Royce. That John Ansbro suggests that Royce's text *The Problem of Christianity* was on the "recommended" reading list of L. Harold DeWolf's graduate students should not be taken to mean that King in fact read Royce.[50] In addition, there is no evidence to this point, that DeWolf actually *required* his students to read Royce's book. My own experience of three decades in the theological academy convinces me that the fulltime student who reads "recommended readings" in a course is a very rare bird indeed. Students complain enough about the amount of *required* readings in courses. It is a special, most outstanding, student who diligently reads both required and recommended or collateral readings for a course. I do not doubt that DeWolf "recommended" the reading of Royce's book. I just know that at this writing there is no evidence that King read *The Problem of Christianity*.

In reading the papers by Herstein and Tunstall, I found that Royce's conception of the beloved community may not be as abstract as Ira Zepp believed.[51] Therefore, I agree with Herstein that such a stance falls short of what was the actual position of Royce regarding the beloved community. The papers convince me that there is more concreteness in Royce's conception, as well as more similarity to the biblical ideal of the Kingdom of God on earth. However, I remain convinced that, inasmuch as Royce was not explicit about the inclusion of blacks and other people of color in his beloved community ideal, his view was to this extent less concrete and inclusive than King's. It will be recalled, however, that I also maintain that while by definition King's doctrine of the beloved community points to an inclusive community, from the standpoint of actual practice, he himself fell short in this regard. For example, by definition, women would be included in the beloved community with the same absolute dignity, as well as full rights and privileges of all others. In actual practice, however, it is known that King was sexist. Nevertheless, he was on target in both theory and practice regarding racism, economic injustice, and militarism. Moreover, there is clear evidence that had he lived, King would most likely have turned the corner on sexism and become a chief advocate against it.

I heartily applaud Herstein's effort to determine whether King actually read Royce. However, I do not believe he convincingly makes the case for any direct Roycean influence on King's beloved community ethic. I direct most of my comments to this part of Herstein's paper, primarily because I think that what he tried to do was important work, and a real contribution to King Studies. Since the beloved community nomenclature is traceable to Royce, and was later picked up by King and essentially made the chief regulative principle of his theological social ethics, it makes sense that we should know better than we have previously known, just how King came to know and appropriate the term.

Herstein essentially proposed and tried to support the hypothesis that King had direct knowledge of Royce's doctrine of the beloved community. Although he added the important caveat that he could not "prove" this, I want to propose yet another hypothesis that, although also is indemonstrable, may be a more reasonable way of thinking about the matter. Unquestionably, both hypotheses offer the correct assumption that King was very likely first introduced to the beloved community terminology during his studies at Boston University. One difference is that, unlike Herstein, I also contend that even before his arrival at Crozer Theological Seminary and later at Boston University, King was already quite familiar with the idea expressed by the beloved community, even if he did not then know the term. We have seen that what he did know was the term "Kingdom of God" and the effect it would have on the world; an effect that is not different from that of the beloved community. At any rate, what follows is a brief discussion of how I think King came to know the term beloved community.

Herstein was right to suspect that the location of King's introduction to the beloved community terminology was Boston University. In his 1977 essay, "Foundations of the Beloved

Community," John Cartwright wrote: "Although King does not specifically account for his use of the expression, 'Beloved Community,' it is known by some that the term was a part of the popular theological vocabulary of the Boston University School of Theology during the period when he was in attendance there as a doctoral student (1951–1955)."[52] Cartwright goes on to tell us that the term is traceable in philosophical literature to the absolutistic personalist Josiah Royce. He then proceeds to make the unsubstantiated claim that, "King would have been well acquainted with Royce...," since he studied under Brightman, DeWolf, and Peter A. Bertocci.[53] Cartwright was confident that the basic ideas of the beloved community ideal for King were already present in Royce. He was concerned that King, unaware of Royce's influence on social gospeler Walter Rauschenbusch,[54] credited the latter with the Kingdom of God ideal and its emphasis on individual self-sacrifice in the interest of an inclusive human community. In *A Theology for the Social Gospel* (1917), Rauschenbusch pointed to the significance of Royce's book, *The Problem of Christianity*, while characterizing him as "one of the ablest philosophical thinkers" produced in this country.[55] Rauschenbusch had little appreciation for Royce's view that Jesus defined the ideas of Christianity inadequately, and "the Church was the most important event in the history of Christianity. Not Christ but the Church is the central idea of Christianity."[56] Rauschenbusch concluded that this was one of the most unsatisfactory ideas in Royce's book.

The truth in Cartwright's claim is just what I found in Herstein's essay, namely, that there are Roycean roots in King's doctrine of the beloved community. However, Cartwright does not make the case for his claim that King would have been well acquainted with Royce. The claim is confusing at best, because one does not know whether he means that King actually read *The Problem of Christianity*, or whether he means that having studied under Brightman and DeWolf, King would likely have heard much about Royce and his doctrine of the beloved community. In light of my own research, the latter is much more plausible than the first. To this point I have seen no conclusive evidence that King actually read Royce. Having read dozens of King's published and unpublished papers, and having examined "King's Personal Library: Selected Works,"[57] I have yet to see a reference to Royce, or to *The Problem of Christianity*. Nevertheless, we can make a stronger case for the claim that the beloved community terminology was so popular in the Boston University School of Theology community during King's student days that he very likely heard it both in the hallways as well as the classroom. One of the ways to substantiate this is to consider: 1) Whether Royce influenced Brightman (King's teacher and academic advisor), and 2) What King actually read under Brightman.

ROYCEAN INFLUENCE ON BRIGHTMAN

We know from Brightman's own autobiographical writings that while he came under the influence of a number of philosophers as an undergraduate student, he was for a number of years most influenced by the absolute idealism of Royce, until as a graduate student William James's *Pragmatism* appeared and swept him off his feet.[58] Although Brightman later became committed to the personalism of Borden P. Bowne, the Roycean influence on him continued. We find multiple references to Royce in Brightman's books, e.g., *An Introduction to Philosophy* (1925, 1951, 1963), *Religious Values* (1925), *The Problem of God* (1930), *Moral Laws* (1933), and *A Philosophy of Religion* (1940).[59] It is significant to note that these are books that King read while in seminary or during doctoral studies at Boston University. I return to this point momentarily.

From 1912–1915, Brightman taught philosophy at Nebraska Wesleyan. According to Jannette Newhall, during the 1914 school year, he taught a course on Royce. Since *The Problem of Christianity* was published the year before, it was quite likely one of the required texts in that course.[60] Indeed, it is known that Brightman's letter to Royce (July 13, 1913) was occasioned by his reading of *The Problem of Christianity*.[61] Royce was clearly important to Brightman, and I simply cannot imagine this not being the case when he returned to Boston University to teach philosophy.

There are many Roycean citations in the aforementioned books by Brightman. Our concern is whether there is explicit reference in any of those books to Royce's doctrine of the beloved community. One looks in vain for such a reference in *Moral Laws* and *A Philosophy of Religion*. However, in *Religious Values*, we find just such a reference. Here Brightman writes that "the supreme consummation of worship..., the very goal and purpose of the universe" is "the Community of Love, or, as Royce called it, *the Beloved Community*."[62] To this point, then, we know that Brightman was much influenced by Royce. This lends credence to Cartwright's claim that the beloved community was a popular term in the Boston University School of Theology community. What more can we say about King's introduction to Royce and his beloved community nomenclature?

WHAT KING READ UNDER BRIGHTMAN

Previously, I observed that it is known that King was familiar with five of Brightman's books. In four of these (*An Introduction to Philosophy*, *The Problem of God*, *Moral Laws*, and *A Philosophy of Religion*) King would have seen multiple references to Royce, although not specifically to his concept of the beloved community. Only in *Religious Values* would he have seen an explicit reference to Royce's beloved community terminology, as well as Brightman's preferred phrase, *community of love*. King included a paraphrase from *Religious Values* in a paper written in Brightman's course on philosophy of religion,[63] so we know that he was acquainted with this book.

There is presently no evidence that Brightman required that King and his classmates read Royce, specifically *The Problem of Christianity*. The best available evidence suggests that King knew Royce's work only indirectly, i.e., through what he heard Brightman or DeWolf say in class or private conversation. More so, nowhere in intellectual autobiographical statements in "Pilgrimage to Nonviolence," do we find him even citing Royce's name, let alone referring to Roycean ideas that may have influenced him.

Did Roycean ideas influence King's doctrine of the beloved community? Yes. Is there evidence that King actually read Royce's work? No. Were Brightman and DeWolf influenced by Royce to the point that each likely espoused Roycean ideas in the classroom? Yes. Is it more reasonable to believe that King heard *about* Royce and the beloved community nomenclature through course lectures under Brightman and DeWolf? I think it is. Herstein was therefore right when he said that "there is at least an indirect influence of Royce on King." At this point, I do not think we can say much more than this about the Royce-King connection.

I now comment briefly on a few other matters in Herstein's paper. First, King was indeed influenced by Brightman's moral law system, especially when making difficult moral decisions, e.g., King's decision to finally break silence on the war in Vietnam on April 4, 1967. Herstein rightly asserted that Brightman did not "invent or discover" the moral laws. However, Brightman both named the moral laws and formulated them into a *system* for helping to make responsible moral judgments. Furthermore, I have shown elsewhere that the idea behind each of

Brightman's moral laws, as well as the communitarian laws in Walter Muelder's social ethics, may be found in Bowne's 1892 publication, *The Principles of Ethics*.[64]

Second, Herstein contends that Royce's doctrine of loyalty points to the most inclusive community, i.e., one in which no person is left behind or excluded. However, I wish that Royce had been explicit about *who* he took to be "mankind" or "humanity." For during his day, and in some circles even today, when whites referenced "men," "women," and "humanity," the intention was not to include persons of black African descent who, in the minds of too many, are little more than sub-humans. Here I am reminded of the likes of Thomas Jefferson who argued in his *Notes on the State of Virginia* that blacks are the inferiors to whites[65]; to the observations of Alexis de Tocqueville in *Democracy in America*, where he argues that white Americans essentially detested blacks and thought of them as less than human[66]; and to the more contemporary ruminations of Andrew Hacker in his provocative book, *Two Nations: Black and White, Separate, Hostile, Unequal* (1992), in which he suggests that many whites still hold views about blacks similar to those of Jefferson.[67] Although Royce grappled with the race question to an extent in his publications that not even the personalist Bowne did, I have seen no evidence that his doctrine of an ideal and inclusive community was in fact intended to include blacks. Royce would have done well to state explicitly that such a community must be inclusive of blacks, especially since he knew well the status of race relations in the country during his day. To be sure, even if it could be argued that Royce's doctrine was intended to be inclusive of blacks, indicators are that he considered whites to be their superiors in matters of intellect and culture. This raises the question of the place of the equality of the races, and the inherent dignity of the person, in his beloved community ideal.

We cannot let Royce off the moral hook in this regard, any more than we should let Bowne off the hook for his utter silence regarding the race question in his published writings.[68] Notwithstanding his failure to acknowledge his own sexism and to work toward dismantling sexist structures, we know that when Martin Luther King talked about the beloved community he unquestionably believed that the principle of equality applies to persons as such, and that no group is inferior or superior to any other. In addition, in principle, King held that persons as such possess inherent dignity because all are called into existence, loved, and sustained by God.

Finally, both Martin Luther King and Josiah Royce believed suffering to be redemptive in some way. King's personalist teachers also articulated this view. Frequently when people cite King's oft-quoted words, "unearned suffering is redemptive," they mistakenly conclude that for King this meant that suffering as such is redemptive. Nothing could be further from the truth. According to King, unearned suffering must be made to be redemptive by sustained and determined nonviolent struggle against it. The oppressed must struggle to eliminate the causes of their suffering with the intention of moving in a more determined way toward the beloved community. Royce advocated the need for action to address unearned suffering, but he proposed no method for doing so. Martin Luther King advocated a method, i.e., nonviolent resistance, for addressing injustice and suffering, and showed by his own consistent practice that progress could be made toward the attainment of the community of love, but only when people are vigilant and cooperatively working toward it.

9

Call to Establish the Beloved Community[1]

Generally, when I have given public lectures on Martin Luther King, I have done so with a sense that most of those in the listening audience know very little about the man and his civil rights ministry. I know of no instance in which I have been wrong about this. Consequently, my tendency is to share as much detailed information about King as I can get away with in the time allotted for the lecture. This was the case when I presented an earlier, briefer version of this chapter at Messiah College in Grantham, Pennsylvania on January 17, 2006. The occasion was the celebration of King Day. Although the address focused on King's understanding of the beloved community and the responsibility of every intelligent person to contribute to its actualization, I also talked briefly about the emergence of King Day, the fact that King was an imperfect earthen vessel who chose to be faithful to God's call and what it meant for him to be both called and faithful. I also named and briefly discussed a number of things that we all can do in efforts to establish the beloved community.

It is indisputable that the keystone of Martin Luther King's theological ethics was his *beloved community* ideal. The philosophical roots of this term can be traced to the work of the absolutistic personalist, Josiah Royce (1855–1916).[2] Royce viewed the beloved community as the criterion of all morality, and all morality is to be judged by its standards. Accordingly, every action is to be tested by whether it contributes to actualizing such a community.[3] Indeed, the "principle of principles" in Christian ethics, according to Royce, is that one does whatever she can to contribute to the establishment of the beloved community.[4] There is no question that in King's work (as in Royce's) the beloved community is synonymous with the Kingdom of God ideal. This ideal dates back to the time of Jesus. Social gospel leader Walter Rauschenbusch argued that the Kingdom ideal was "the last social ideal of Christendom" and that it was at the center of Jesus's teachings.[5] King credited Rauschenbusch with providing him with a sound theological foundation for his strong passion to eradicate the social ills that adversely affected black people.[6]

In a seminal essay, "Black Christians in Antebellum America: In Quest of the Beloved Community," Lawrence N. Jones has argued that blacks have been searching for the beloved community for as long as they have been in this country.[7] He further maintains that during slavery, blacks primarily appealed to the Declaration of Independence and the Bible as they sought to ground their desire for the actualization of the beloved community.[8] These documents were their primary sources of authority on the matter. Jones's point is not that the term "beloved community" was known during the antebellum period. Instead, he sought to show that from the time of American slavery blacks have always sought inclusion in the type of society represented by what came to be known as the "beloved community"—a society based on justice, respect for self and others, and equality of opportunity to be the best that one can be.

Martin Luther King was utterly captivated by the beloved community ideal and how best to actualize it in the world, notwithstanding the fact that he nowhere writes systematically about it. One has to read the corpus of his published and unpublished writings, sermons and speeches in order to piece together his philosophy, theology, or ethics of the beloved community. But important as this idea was for King, I have been wondering about the significance of some of his basic personalistic doctrines, their ethical implications for personal-communal living today, and how or whether they undergird the keystone of his theological social ethics, i.e., the beloved community ideal.

For many years, I have argued that the Martin Luther King to whom we should pay more attention is not the King who delivered the famous "I Have A Dream" speech on a hot, humid day in August 1963 in the shadow of the Lincoln Memorial. Rather, we should focus on the King who had to figure out how to remain faithful to God's call in the face of the dynamite bombing murders at the Sixteenth Street Baptist Church in Birmingham, Alabama, barely two weeks after the March on Washington for Jobs and Freedom. The bomb killed four beautiful black girls that Sunday morning, September 15, 1963. Later that day, two black boys were killed by white racists; one while he was riding his bicycle minding his own business; the other was killed by the police. In addition, King had to assess his dream in light of massive numbers of black and other poor people who saw no way out of their poverty. And then, there was the matter of unemployment and underemployment, which guaranteed the have-nots that they would never have the material things needed to insure that they would have a life worth living. But this was not all. There was the Vietnam War, which King considered to be totally unjust. King knew that the condition of his people and the poor, of all races, was nightmarish even before the March, and that it was no less so in its immediate aftermath. It is this King—the King who left the steps of the Lincoln Memorial to confront directly the system and racist attitudes that created the opening for the bombing of the Sixteenth Street Baptist Church; the King who sought to address economic problems that led to mass impoverishment and joblessness—that I have in mind. This King is the hardheaded realist who, against the advice of some of his key advisors, would take the movement North to Chicago in 1966, only to discover that racism there and other places in the North was even more vicious than what he had experienced in Mississippi and Alabama.[9] And yet, this is the same Martin Luther King who said to his staff in a retreat at Frogmore, South Carolina in 1967, that he was "not totally optimistic," but neither was he a defeatist.[10] His faith in God was such that he could not resort to pessimism. This is the Martin Luther King who would say to us today: "Stop appealing to the 'I Have a Dream' speech as if that alone is the extent of your witness, and make your own contributions to establishing the beloved community; a community where *every* person will be honored and respected just because she is a child of God, and is loved by God. Stop appealing to the 'I Have a Dream' speech, and do what you can right now—where you are—to make the dream a reality." This same Martin Luther King would admonish us to stop the foolhardy practice of devoting but one day a year, i.e., King Day, to demonstrating our hope, faith, and commitment to achieving the community of love.

King would say that the dream of the beloved community stands a greater chance of becoming a reality only as persons, churches, synagogues, mosques, and yes, religious and non-religious institutions of higher learning work toward its realization on a daily basis; only if they understand that in order for this to happen in God's world *it will be necessary to give up or sacrifice something.* We can be certain that on the surface, many white people who are the recipients of unearned privilege and power want things to change for the better for others, but they do not want to sacrifice anything of substantive value in order to support such change.

Isn't this really the question for all of us today, especially those who claim to be among the committed? What are we, and the communities to which we belong, willing to give up, in order to significantly contribute toward the actualization of the beloved community? More concretely, what are we willing to do, and sacrifice, for the establishment of the beloved community within the context of the places in which we live, work, and worship? What are we willing to do on the corners on which we happen to occupy on any given day? I can think of no better way to honor and show real appreciation for the life and ministry of one who gave his adult life to the cause of actualizing the beloved community. How colorful and otherwise diverse could our communities, places of employment, education, and worship be if we were willing to strive and sacrifice for the realization of the beloved community? What are we willing to do, in concrete, substantive ways, to create and sustain the beloved community?

Martin Luther King, Jr., Day

On October 19, 1983, the United States Senate posthumously honored Dr. Martin Luther King, Jr., by voting to designate the third Monday in January, beginning in 1986, as a national holiday in his honor. The fight for this national holiday was led by Coretta Scott King, R&B superstar Stevie Wonder, and former Indiana Congresswoman Katie Hall.[11] This honor is clearly symbolic of King's importance as a national and international leader in the struggle for civil and human rights, peace with justice, and the creation of the community of love. Although Josiah Royce introduced the beloved community nomenclature in 1913, the concept enjoyed a great deal of popularity among King's teachers at Boston University, e.g., Edgar S. Brightman and L. Harold DeWolf. King most likely first heard or read about the term during doctoral studies at Boston University.

Martin Luther King, Jr., Day; a day to remember; a day to serve; a day to be reminded anew, that we humans can be better than we are in the matter of our treatment of self, others, our communities, the environment, and the plant and animal kingdoms. We can be better than we are, and we can make the world better than it is, but only if we are willing to do the things necessary to make this happen. Martin Luther King, Jr., Day is not—nor should it be—"a day off, but a day on." That is, it should be a day for serving one's community through volunteer work. Or, it can be a day for reading, study, reflection, celebration, and discussing with others the best means to achieve that gentler, sweeter community where all of God's people throughout the world will work hard to be and do what God intends. And make no mistake about it. *All* people are God's people, and are loved equally by God. This was one of King's most fundamental beliefs.

Martin Luther King, Jr., Day is a reminder to all persons that a black American, one from a historically oppressed community, "deserves the highest measure of recognition and respect." Moreover, it is a reminder that King is a symbol of the best of American values and ideas. In addition, this national holiday supports the claim that King represents "the best and the brightest" in the tradition of organized mass nonviolent civil dissent. Furthermore, King Day means that if we humans are to be all that we can be in community, King's dream must be seen as more than a dream; it must become what Lewis Baldwin refers to as "a sustaining vision" of what individuals and communities can accomplish through determined cooperative endeavor with each other and the Creator of this vast, wide universe.[12] In this way, all that we do may be viewed as being driven by the vision and hope of a gentler, sweeter world.

An Imperfect but Faithful Vessel

It is important to remember that as a person Martin Luther King was not flawless—morally or otherwise. Nor can it be said truthfully that any person is perfect and sinless, or should ever expect to be. In fact, King himself acknowledged his own sinfulness. One month before he was assassinated—dreadfully tired, emotionally depleted, and trying to come to terms with some personal moral indiscretions—he told the members of Ebenezer Baptist Church where he was co-pastor: "You don't need to go out this morning saying that Martin Luther King is a saint.... I want you to know this morning that I'm a sinner like all of God's children. But I want to be a good man. And I want to hear a voice saying to me one day, 'I take you in and I bless you, because you try. It is well that it was within thine heart.'"[13] King knew that he was finite and limited, and was susceptible to moral failures like everybody else. However, it is most assuredly true that he wanted more than anything to be faithful to the God of Abraham, Hagar, and the Hebrew prophets; to the God of his own parents and grandparents. Indeed, he desperately wanted to be faithful to the God he discovered late one night during the Montgomery bus boycott after receiving a telephone call from one of the local racists who threatened to blow up his house if he did not leave town. Not able to get to sleep after the call, King paced the floor for a while, and then made a pot of coffee. As he sat at the kitchen table all alone, trying to figure out how he could remove himself from the boycott without appearing to be a coward, King finally decided to turn it all over to God. He lowered his head and prayed, vowing to depend fully and solely on God from that point forward. King said that after his prayer he experienced a sense of calm, the likes of which he had not experienced before. He was certain that the God that he *rediscovered* at the kitchen table that night had promised to be with him always if he remained faithful to God's expectations. That is the God to whom he wanted to remain faithful.

Martin Luther King knew that the Christian journey is a process, and that mistakes will inevitably be made along life's journey. However, he was convinced that, "God does not judge us by the separate incidents or the separate mistakes that we make, but by the total bent of our lives."[14] This is not to make light of any of the specific morel missteps that made King as human as you and me, such as plagiarism and philandering. It is to say, however, that it is absolutely awesome that the God of the Hebrew prophets and Jesus Christ could use an imperfect earthen vessel like Martin Luther King to contribute so significantly towards the achievement of the beloved community. This itself is a clue to what God can do through any person who opens self to God's will and who strives to be faithful to God's requirement that we do justice, love mercy, walk humbly with God, and stand in the margins with those counted among the least of these. No matter what else Martin Luther King did or failed to do, he remained faithful to God's call that he speak truth to the powers, and that he stand up for justice for those forced into the gutters of society. There is no question that, notwithstanding King's human weaknesses, the depth of his faith and the drift or "total bent" of his life pointed toward divine approval and acceptance.

Both Called and Faithful

Martin Luther King liked to say that more than anything else, he was a Baptist preacher.[15] Before he was a civil rights leader, before he was recipient of the Nobel Peace Prize and dozens of other honors and awards, he was a preacher of the Christian gospel. All that he did as a civil rights leader he did because he believed it to be part of his ministry; part of what his call from God required of him. In 1967, King declared that ministry was his first calling, and then emphatically declared, "it still remains my greatest commitment." He went on to say: "I have no greater ambitions in life but to achieve excellence in Christian ministry.... I don't plan to do anything but remain a preacher."[16] Unlike many in ministry, King actually loved the ministry, and viewed his own call as "a vocation of agony."[17] God's call was not to be taken lightly. Because he believed ministry was his calling, King knew that he had to live his commitment to ministry every single day. In part, this meant that he needed to be in solidarity with those he sought to serve.

King was deeply touched by the condition and suffering of the poor. His level of sensitivity and his humanity were frequently revealed as he worked among impoverished people, whether in the Deep South or in the north. In a little known conversation with Jewish Rabbis ten days before he was assassinated, Martin Luther King shared a deeply troubling experience he had in Mississippi. Through his words one can sense his agony, pain, and depth of concern.

> I was in Marks, Mississippi the other day and I found myself weeping before I knew it. I met boys and girls by the hundreds who didn't have any shoes to wear, who didn't have any food to eat in terms of three square meals a day, and I met their parents, many of whom don't even have jobs. But not only do they not have jobs, they are not even getting an income. Some of them aren't on any kind of welfare, and I literally cried when I heard men and women saying that they were unable to get any food to feed their children.[18]

This says much about King's sense of humanity and concern for the neighbor. This is also evident when one considers his loss of appetite and his overwhelming sense of anguish when he picked up a copy of *Ramparts* magazine in 1966 and saw pictures of Vietnamese children who had been severely burned or killed by napalm bombs.[19] He had been silent on the Vietnam War for nearly two years, but after reading that article, he said that he could not, under any circumstance, remain silent in the face of such devastating destruction of massive numbers of innocent children in Vietnam.[20] He therefore decided that moment that there comes a time when one has to speak up in light of his highest ideals, no matter the personal, social, political, and economic consequences. King was an imperfect earthen vessel, but his sense of humanity, of the inviolable dignity of every person, and his sense of the love of God was such that he heard and responded affirmatively to the divine call to serve God and the least of the sisters of brothers; and to serve them to the very end of his days.

Theologically, to be faithful is to exhibit utter and relentless trust in, and reliance on, God. This does not mean that one will lead a flawless life, for no human being is able to do this. It means, rather, that one will commit his entire life to the One who called him into existence and placed the burden of a call on his life. When the day is done, then, the most significant issue will be whether Martin Luther King was faithful to the very end, to God's call. Faithfulness to God was more important to King than most people were aware. We get a clear sense of the significance of this to King when, one year before he was assassinated, he deviated from the text of a sermon he was preaching at a friend's church in Chicago and said:

> And John [Thurston], if you and Bernard [Lee] happen to be around when I come to the latter day and that moment to cross the Jordan, I want you to tell them that I made a request. I don't want a long funeral. In fact, I don't even need a eulogy of more than one or two minutes.
> I hope that I will live so well the rest of the days. I don't know how long I'll live, and I'm not concerned about that. But I hope I can live so well that the preacher can get up and say *he was faithful*. That's all, that's enough. That's the sermon I'd like to hear. "*Well done thy good and faithful servant*. You've been faithful; you've been concerned about others."
> That's where I want to go from this point on, the rest of my days. "He who is greatest among

you shall be your servant." I want to be a servant. I want to be a witness for my Lord, do something for others.[21]

Martin Luther King wanted to be remembered, not as a "saint," but as having been faithful to God's call on his life. The divine call or commission to ministry was important to King in a way and to an extent that it was not, and is not, to very many pastors and other religious leaders. Therefore, in the final analysis, when the most authoritative biography of King is written, the author will have to conclude that whatever else King was or was not, *he was faithful to God to the end.* According to King, one does not have to actually reach the goal, but one has to be vigilant and faithful in trying, regardless of the cost.

Dream of the Beloved Community

For America and the world Martin Luther King dreamed of a thoroughly integrated society wherein power, privilege, and the world's material goods will be shared equitably by all people. In such a society, the humanity and dignity of every person will be acknowledged and respected in the most concrete sense. As noted previously, King characterized this society as the beloved community; a community that acknowledges, affirms, and celebrates the values and contributions of both individuals and the community. It is a community in which *every* person is valued and respected just because they are persons. The theologically inclined person makes the additional claim, consistent with the best in all theistic religions, that every person is precious and sacred because they are loved by God, and bears the image of God. Human beings are sacred because they are created and loved by God. Consequently, in the yet to be realized beloved community, there will be no such thing—as is too often the case today—as the need for a selection committee to determine who is a person and who is not; who deserves to be treated humanely, justly, and with dignity, and who does not; who is a member of the community and who is not. Martin Luther King lived by the conviction that the God of the universe established from the foundation of the world that every person possesses infinite inviolable worth and should be treated accordingly. Human beings have merely to accept this fact, not debate it. Simply put, the beloved community is a community, even more intimately a family of insiders,[22] which is another way of saying: Everybody belongs, because every person belongs to, and is loved and revered by, God.

In order to keep the dream of the beloved community alive, we have to live each and every day *as if* it were already a reality. This means that everything I do, everything that you do, interpersonally and communally, should be consistent with the values of the beloved community. It means that we have to be intentional about behaving in ways that honor the humanity and dignity of every person—those who look and act like us, and those who don't. I can think of no other way for Christians, Jews, Muslims, and representatives of other religious faiths to keep King's dream of the actualization of the beloved community alive, than to live lives each and every day that exemplify faithfulness to what God and such a community requires.

Frequently I hear King's dream about the establishment of the beloved community depicted as a mere memory of the great speech he delivered in the sweltering heat in Washington, D.C. on August 28, 1963. Those who take King's dream seriously will need to liberate that dream from the steps of the Lincoln Memorial. It is true that on that day, King told America about a dream that he had had which, essentially encompassed his vision of the beloved community. But we have to remember that not long after delivering that speech, King said that he saw his dream turn to a nightmare. He reflected on this in, "A Christmas Sermon on Peace" in 1967, saying that the first time he witnessed the dream turn to a nightmare was when white racists bombed the Sixteenth Street Baptist Church in Birmingham. Four black girl children were killed in the bombing: eleven year old Denise McNair, and three fourteen year olds: Cynthia Wesley, Addie Mae Collins, and Carol Robertson. It is important that we call their names as often as we can, lest they remain forgotten, or as little more than a statistic in the minds of many. But for the Rev. Joseph Ellwanger, pastor of the all-black Lutheran church in Birmingham,[23] no other member of Birmingham's white community attended the funeral services of those children.[24] In his eulogy of the four girls, King characterized them as "the martyred heroines of a holy crusade for freedom and human dignity."[25] They did not live long, "but they lived meaningful lives."[26] They were, for King—and must be for us today—"sweet princesses."[27]

Martin Luther King also said that he watched the dream degenerate into a nightmare as he saw his people in the ghettos of the North "perishing on a lonely island of poverty in the midst of a vast ocean of material prosperity,"[28] while the nation—frightfully similar to its response to the cries of the poor of all races in hurricane Katrina ravaged New Orleans—was very slow to address their needs. Furthermore, King said he watched the dream turn to a nightmare as he observed his people "in the midst of anger and understandable outrage, in the midst of their hurt, in the midst of their disappointment, turn to misguided riots to try to solve that problem."[29]

In the last three years of his life, Martin Luther King devoted large amounts of time and energy to the question of where the nation and the world should be going and how best to get there. Although he continued to the very end to hope for the establishment of the beloved community (even when he did not use the beloved community nomenclature,[30] and even though he had good reason to believe that he himself would not live to see its actualization), there is overwhelming evidence that King was not so naïve as to think that it would roll in on the wheels of inevitability. However, it is quite possible that you and I can determine whether, or to what extent, the beloved community will emerge in our lifetime. Or, we can at least lay the foundation for it to materialize for our posterity.

King left significant clues as to where we should be going, and what we can do to get there. Based on this, I want first to suggest three ideas that are fundamental to the process of establishing the beloved community. The first is a theological assumption about the universe and what this must mean for our relating to each other, to God, and other living and non-living life forms. The second goes to the issue of leadership and what it means to be a true leader in church and world. The third idea points to the importance of education and the responsibility of educators in the establishment of the beloved community.

Universe Based on Morality

Martin Luther King lived by the belief that the universe is situated on a moral foundation. In other words, he believed that the universe is fundamentally good, no matter what happens in any moment on any given day. This clearly did not mean for King that the world is free of social and other sins. Rather, it meant that the foundation of the world is good, in as much as it hinges on morality. The world is fundamentally good, even when we humans choose to sin. Such a conviction led King to believe in the existence of an objective moral order. King shared this belief with family members, as well as teacher-mentors at Morehouse College, Crozer Theological Seminary, and Boston University.

I have argued persistently in my writing and teaching on King, that if one fails to acknowledge and understand his faith that there is an objective moral order and moral laws that ought to be obeyed, there is little chance that such one will be able to fully understand the foundations of his theological social ethics, his commitment to nonviolence as a way of life, and why he remained faithful to God's call to the end of his life. King's deepest faith was not in human beings as such, but in the source of the objective moral order and moral laws. That is, his deepest faith was in God's faithfulness and reliability. This was the source of King's optimism, even during that most turbulent last year of his life.

Martin Luther King's family and religious upbringing convinced him of the fundamental goodness of the universe.[31] As a child, King saw concrete signs of this in the way his parents expressed their love toward each other and their children, which made it easy for him to think of the universe as fundamentally good.[32] This is essentially what we see in the creation story in the Book of Genesis, where we find God looking out over all that was created and saying that it was all very good indeed. King was convinced that the universe is fused or thoroughly charged with value, which in turn means that everything that we humans do has value implications. If the universe rests on a moral foundation and thus is fundamentally good as King believed, it is reasonable to conclude that the mistreatment of any person, for whatever reason, goes against the grain of the universe; against the expectations of God, who is the source of all being, goodness, justice, and love. Every human being, according to King, has been stamped with intrinsic value, and thus should be respected and treated as such through socio-economic, legal, educational, and political policies and practices.

If King was right, it is both possible and reasonable to conclude that human beings always have cosmic and divine companionship along the way, even when we are not aware of it; even when we arrogantly think we can manage alone. The fact that there was some positive advancement during the civil rights movement, for example, convinced King that there is "something about the core and heartbeat" of the universe that reminds us that it is value-fused, and on the side of good and justice. This was, for him, clear evidence that those who engage in the struggle for the establishment of justice do not struggle alone, but have companionship among cosmic and divine forces. King knew, as we must learn, that as finite and limited beings we humans simply cannot, on our own, establish the beloved community.[33]

If it is true that the universe rests on a moral foundation, as King so thoroughly believed, then injustice, untruths, and abusive behavior toward human beings and other areas of creation cannot endure forever. In such a universe justice, truth, and respect for persons will ultimately win the day, even if not in my lifetime or yours. Martin Luther King was certain that, come what may, injustice cannot and will not have the last word in a moral universe. In any case, this faith in the basic goodness of the universe and in cosmic companionship should provide consolation during the more difficult moments in the struggle to establish the beloved community.

People in positions of power and leadership in church and society, including educators and school administrators, should remember this critical point about the basic morality of the universe when they seek only to instruct students to conform to the way things are, rather than teach them to think their own thoughts and to be critical of ideas, policies, and practices that demean and dehumanize human beings, individually and collectively. King believed the universe is friendly or moral, and therefore it is reasonable to conclude that no lie can live forever. The conviction that the universe is built on morality bring to mind the words of the old gospel hymn, "you can't do wrong and get by, no matter how hard you may try."[34] Reflecting on the old apartheid regime in South Africa, and reminiscent of Martin Luther King, Archbishop Desmond Tutu said that his "confidence was not in the present circumstances but in the laws of God's universe." He went on to say: "This is a *moral* universe, which means that, despite all the evidence that seems to be to the contrary, there is no way that evil and injustice and oppression and lies can have the last word. God is a God who cares about right and wrong. God cares about justice and injustice. God is in charge."[35] Consequently, the Church, the Synagogue, the Mosque, and the educational establishment must be the moral-spiritual leaders, not followers of the example of politically correct politicians and chief executive officers like the late Kenneth Lay of the Enron Corporation, and top executives of Worldcom. This brings us to the issue of leadership.

Leadership and the Beloved Community

In his address to the First Annual Institute on Non-Violence and Social Change in 1956, Martin Luther King reflected on the need to face the challenges of a new age, and the importance of organizing in order to actualize it as quickly as possible. After the Montgomery bus boycott, King believed that the opening had been created for the establishment of the beloved community. He was convinced of the need for this to occur immediately, and not in some distant tomorrow. King was confident both that the God of his faith is always present and working in history to influence the emergence of the new age, and that one of the crucial ingredients in the process is a certain type of leadership, whether in religion, politics, education, or business.

Like his good friend, Rabbi Abraham Joshua Heschel, King was convinced that one of the most pressing needs was for intelligent, committed, and most especially *morally* courageous leaders in the religious, educational, and civic communities. Interestingly, neither King nor Heschel used the term "politician" when discussing the need for sound leadership. In fact, Heschel rejected the word politician when discussing leadership, but said that he had "great respect for the word statesman."[36] The statesman is one who is skilled at managing the sociopolitical and economic affairs of the city, state, or nation; one who is adept at managing the common good. But in the spirit of Martin Luther King and Rabbi Heschel, I want to add something to this description. The statesman is one who is staunchly committed to enhancing the dignity, worth, and wellbeing of *every* person, without exception or qualification, and regardless of racial-ethnicity, gender, age, sexual orientation, class, and ability. The statesman, therefore, promotes and fights for the good of all citizens, not for a favored or select group, as is generally the practice of politicians at all levels of government in the U.S. and other nations.

Experience frequently reveals politicians to be people who generally lack moral integrity, and do not have the best interests of the most deprived citizens at the top of their agenda. Even if we had a kind of magical roadmap to the future, it wouldn't matter if there were no leaders with integrity who take seriously the well being of those counted among the least of these in society. Martin Luther King would say that we need, not politicians, but statesmen, for by definition the task of such persons is to be sound leaders with integrity. But in addition, such persons seek to educate their colleagues, as well as those they represent. Indeed, when it is evident that the people themselves seem to desire what is not in their best interest or the best interest of a thoroughly diverse and inclusive community, the statesman takes the high road and endeavors to educate and prod them in that direction.[37]

It is important that those in leadership positions assume the leadership role; that they stop trying to master the art of compromise solely in the best interest of the privileged; and that they come to see that it is of utmost importance to the statesman to *be in the margins with the masses of the people.* For it is here, in the margins, that they will also find the one called Christ. It is here, in the margins, that they will discover what it truly means to be a human being. If we would keep alive the dream of establishing the beloved community, it will be necessary to demand and expect leaders of integrity and courage. In this regard, King paraphrased Josiah Gilbert Holland's poem, "Wanted" (1872):

> God give us leaders! A time like this demands strong minds, great hearts, true faith and ready hands; Leaders whom the lust of office does not kill; Leaders whom the spoils of life cannot buy; Leaders who possess opinions and a will; Leaders who have honor; leaders who will not lie; Leaders who can stand before a demagogue and damn his treacherous flatteries without winking! Tall leaders, sun crowned, who live above the fog in public duty and private thinking.[38]

At this time in history, church, nation, and world are starving for statesmen, not politicians. We will make little progress toward the beloved community as long as our leaders prefer to be politicians rather than statesmen; as long as they are more inclined to take the low, rather than the high road. Something as noble as the beloved community will require virtuousness of character in those who pursue it and wish to live in it. For, reminiscent of Ralph Waldo Emerson, we are reminded that the man of character is the conscience of his society.[39]

Education for the Beloved Community

Few people understood as well as Martin Luther King the importance of formal education, at all levels, on the road to the beloved community. He believed that education which focuses on helping students learn how to think for themselves, that helps them understand the importance of questioning everything and everybody—including the God of the universe—plays a critical role in the pursuit, establishment, and sustaining of the beloved community. Even during his junior year at Morehouse College in 1947, King wrote of the connection between education, the development of intelligence, character, and concern for the least of these. His essay, "The Purpose of Education," was published in the campus newspaper, *The Maroon Tiger.* Therein he argued that education alone is not sufficient. "Intelligence plus character—that is the true goal of education," he wrote. "The complete education gives one not only power of concentration, but worthy objectives upon which to concentrate."[40] King believed that the right education could take us a long way toward changing attitudes about people and groups different from us. It can also help "to break down the spiritual barriers to integration...."[41] Education at its absolute best must also be supplemented with social action, i.e., with concrete steps toward the realization of the beloved community. "Education without social action," said King, "is a one-sided value because it has no true power potential. Social action without education is a weak expression of pure energy. Deeds uninformed by educated thought can take false directions."[42] Clearly, in the Kingian view, one is not truly educated, regardless of where she has acquired her degrees and academic honors, if her character and sense of responsibility to beloved community-making are underdeveloped or nonexistent.

Indoctrinating students to believe and think a certain way was not, for King, the goal of authentic education. Rather, education for establishing the beloved community requires that students from junior high school onward be taught to be reflective and to question anything, everything, and everybody. King would have agreed with what James Baldwin told a group of teachers in 1963.

> The purpose of education, finally, is to create in a person the ability to look at the world for himself, to make his own decisions, to say to himself this is black or this is white, to decide for

himself whether there is a God in heaven or not. To ask questions of the universe, and then learn to live with those questions, is the way he achieves his own identity.... What societies really, ideally, want is a citizenry which will simply obey the rules of society. If a society succeeds in this, that society is about to perish.[43]

Baldwin knew, as King did, that the mark of the truly educated person is extreme uneasiness with things as they are for the vast majority of people in society.

The educated person acknowledges her own conscience, and thus finds herself almost constantly "at war" with her society. She realizes, as others do not, that if she thinks of herself as truly educated, she is morally obligated to change her society[44]; to make the world better than it is. Such a one knows that she must examine everything and everybody; that she must accept nothing uncritically, or without thought. In this regard, education itself becomes an effective instrument in the establishment of the beloved community. This is most especially the case when, in formal educational settings, there is intention and vigilance in teaching students about the vision of the beloved community and what concrete steps can be taken to actualize it. How may blacks, whites, and the wider community contribute toward establishing the community of love?

What Blacks Can Do

It is important to understand that blacks are not guilty of causing the conditions that have led to the tragic phenomenon of black-against-black violence and murder in urban centers all over the nation. At this writing, no place has worse statistics regarding this phenomenon than the Southside of Chicago. Not only did blacks not create the socio-economic and political conditions for this tragedy to proliferate, neither did they create the conditions that led to the exorbitantly high number of black men incarcerated and on death row. These are the unfortunate by-products of generations of racism, economic injustice, and undeserved, and frequently unacknowledged, white privilege.

I think it is fair to say that blacks are not guilty of the causes of many of the social ills that threaten their communities and their existence. In his sermon, "The Meaning of Hope," Martin Luther King declared: "Considering what our forebears went through, it is a miracle that the black man still survives."[45] However, believing that all persons are autonomous moral beings, King was just as adamant that, similar to all persons, blacks are *responsible for the way they respond* to the violence, murders, and crimes in their community that lead to incarceration and death row. So the question is: Will blacks—individually and collectively—merely continue taking it on the chin, or will they be intentional about finding ways to remove the hand that tries to blemish the image of God in them? One way to resist such attempts to mar the image of God in blacks is to teach every black child to love their heritage and themselves, especially their bodies.

Black Americans, and they only, can teach their children—while they are very young— the importance of loving themselves whole; of loving their bodies so much that they will resist with every ounce of their will and humanity any easy tendency to violate or take the life of another black child. Because of the deleterious consequences of American slavery on his people, King wrote of their need to "assert for all to hear and see a majestic sense of [self] worth."[46] That is, blacks need to affirm their sense of "somebodyness," i.e., their refusal to hate or be ashamed of themselves, even as they teach black children "to stand tall with their heads proudly lifted."[47] King wrote further: "Life's piano can only produce the melodies of brotherhood when it is recognized that the black keys are as basic, necessary and beautiful as the white keys."[48] In addition to developing a "rugged sense of somebodyness,"[49] King said that blacks need to "work passionately for group identity,... in order to participate more meaningfully at all levels of the life of our nation."[50] If blacks will begin to do these things and do them faithfully, then and only then, will they be positioned to work effectively toward establishing the beloved community.

What Whites Can Do

The white community can take a huge step toward the actualization of the beloved community by naming, acknowledging, and owning their racism, not tomorrow, but today. This means that whites have to somehow summon the courage and find in their religious and other values the means to fess up, i.e., to acknowledge their racism, and their *unearned privilege*. It is absolutely critical that whites get in touch with their own racism and figure out how—in their daily activities—they are complicit in racial discriminatory practices, how this makes them feel, what they intend to do about it, and when. This is what white feminist Naomi Wolf expressed with clarity and eloquence in her essay, "The Racism of Well-Meaning White People." Because of the significance of what she said and the absolute necessity for well-meaning white people to understand their own racism and unearned privilege if they are to position themselves to contribute to establishing the beloved community, I want to share an extended passage from Wolf's instructive essay. She critically examines her own racism and finds that:

> This is what a white person hears about race when she travels in educated, overwhelmingly white, *very well-meaning* circles. First of all, she almost never hears overtly racist language, which is grounds for social ostracism (such language is rightly considered reprehensible; but, too, it is considered vulgar—literally low-class). What she does hear is white people talking at length about black people who are talking about racism. Or else she hears white people talking about the racism of institutions—such as the police department, or the FBI, or political parties whose views are unpopular in those enlightened circles.
>
> In these conversations, the white people tend to assume a highly conventionalized facial expression—lots of shaking of heads, furrowing of brows, even a tsk-tsk or two. It is a little body-language set piece, stylized as the attitudes on a Greek urn, and meant to convey, "Isn't it awful? We're all in this together." More loudly it conveys, "I am a good, concerned, altruistic citizen." The tone is that of conscientious neighbors shaking their heads over the rubble left from an earthquake or a landslide—that is, a mindless, impersonal force of nature that is nothing to do with who they are. Finally, periodically and usually only when there is a black person present, she will hear a kind of equally stylized "personal" (but actually quite impersonal) breast-beating: "I was so *hurt* and *troubled* when I began to understand that our black sisters feel marginalized in this organization." What is odd about these moments is how rigid and unspontaneous they are, how repetitive. *There is a safe groove somewhere in this dangerous field*, the impulse seems to suggest; *Lord, let me find it; let me stay there; let me stray from the path*. What one doesn't hear—what I've never read, for instance, despite the formal "we are all racists" mantra on the white left—is an anti-racist white person talking honestly about what their own racism looks like, sounds like, feels like.[51]

All well-meaning white people should read and ponder Naomi Wolf's instructive essay. In truth, after thirty years in the theological academy, I have yet to hear a white colleague talk openly and honestly about *his* unearned privilege, what it looks like, what he intends to do about it, and when. What is most troubling about this is that these are among the most progressive, presumably anti-racist, pro-reconciliation white people. *They* are not the problem, they seem to say. "It's those other white people."

Martin Luther King placed the responsibility for enduring racism squarely on the shoulders of white America. White people introduced and maintain the doctrine of white supremacy. According to King, "The concept of supremacy is so embedded in the white society that it will take many years to cease to be a judgmental factor."[52] King noted further, that to a large extent, the eradication of racism in its individual and systemic forms depends on the will and moral resolve of the white community. Whites in the United States and the rest of the world will have to take racism and unearned privilege seriously, stop minimizing it, pretending that it does not exist, or that it is no more serious than any other social problem. King believed that failure in this regard could very well destroy Western civilization.[53] He insisted on the need for whites to confess their own racism, confront it head on, and then immediately take steps to eradicate it. In a taped interview in London in 1968, King said that it "is very important for every white person to search his own soul and seek to remove all of the vestiges of racism and white supremacy. But along with this must be concrete justice, that the white person and the white power structure will go out to establish.... As long as there is discrimination on any level the Negro is not free."[54] According to King, racism is one of the three greatest threats to establishing the beloved community, locally, nationally, and internationally. King was certain that "racism is still that hound of hell which dogs the tracks of our civilization."[55]

Numerous whites, and some blacks, have been deluded into thinking that racism was somehow eradicated during the civil and human rights movement. The claim was even made in the early and mid–1990s by members of the academic community.[56] Dinesh D'Souza even declared the end of racism in his book by that title (1995).[57] D'Souza argues, quite fantastically, really, that at best racism is a figment of our imagination.

It is a popular myth in some circles that Martin Luther King believed that most white people were not racist. The truth is that near the end of his life, King was compelled to say that, "the largest portion of white America is still poisoned by racism, which is as native to our soil as pine trees, sagebrush and buffalo grass."[58] This same Martin Luther King declared that the United States "is deeply racist and its democracy is flawed both economically and socially."[59] Moreover, he said that, "the concept of supremacy is so imbedded in the white society that it will take many years for color to cease to be a judgmental factor."[60] King even charged that racism was running amuck in the U.S. Congress. His hope was that the people of the nation would vote the racists out of office.[61]

In 1967 King said: "Among the moral imperatives of our time, we are challenged to work all over the world with unshakable determination to wipe out the last vestiges of racism."[62] He argued that it would be a grave mistake to build a world house on a racist foundation. "Racism can well be that corrosive evil that will bring down the curtain on Western civilization."[63] Failure to grapple creatively and relentlessly with racism will only prompt future historians "to say that a great civilization died because it lacked the soul and commitment to make justice a reality for all...."[64]

It is important to remember that racism is still alive and well in white churches, schools, seminaries, and other religious institutions, government and legislative bodies at all levels, social welfare agencies, police departments, and courtrooms. Racism is still deeply embedded in the structures of this society and continues to be America's most despicable shame.

What We All Can Do

As for what we all can do to contribute toward the establishment of the beloved community, it is important that we see that no one group can do it all. Moreover, if there is any hope at all that some semblance of the beloved community will be achieved in our lifetime *it must be an all-out inter-racial, inter-ethnic, inter-religious, inter-sexual, multicultural cooperative endeavor.* What affects any one of us, or any group of us, affects the rest of us, including God. We are all affected because we are, whether we like it or not, a part of each other, a part of the interrelated structure of reality. James Baldwin made the point in a way that King would have approved, saying:

> But we are all androgynous, not only because we are all born of a woman impregnated by the seed of a man, but because each of us, helplessly and forever, contains the other—male in female, female in male, white in black and black in white. We are a part of each other. Many of my countrymen appear to find this fact exceedingly inconvenient and even unfair, and so, very often, do I. But none of us can do anything about it.[65]

This means that I am a part of you and you are a part of me, and there is nothing that you or I can do about it, except to do what so many proponents of Christianity fail to do, namely to thank God for giving us each other: female in male, male in female, and all the races. Think about that! The blood of virtually every person on earth flows in the veins of every other. This is the case historically and sociologically because of the intermixing of the races, voluntarily, and involuntarily as in the case of the rapes of African women by their white captors during American slavery. Arguably, the blood of every person flows in the veins of every other person.

Whether we like it or not—and very many clearly do not like it, if we are to judge by their behavior toward those who are different from themselves—we are a part of each other. Looking to the Bible, Martin Luther King reminds us time and again that out of one blood God created all persons.[66] Philosophically and theologically, King held that we are made to live together because of the interrelated structure of reality. It is a historical, sociological, and theological fact, then, that black, white, red, brown, and gold people in this country—indeed throughout the world—are inescapably a part of each other.[67] We are left only with futile attempts of denial.

We are, whether we like it or not, members of a universal or global community. It matters not what is our religious affiliation (or whether we have one); matters not what is our race, class, gender, sexual orientation, age, or health. Important as these characteristics are, Martin Luther King knew that something more was needed and required, especially by those who are proponents of the Christian faith. The universal community must be *made* to take on the characteristics of the beloved community. That is, it must be made to be a community in which love-justice prevails, and the dignity and worth of every person is acknowledged and respected just because they are created in the image of God and are loved by God. Josiah Royce left an instructive word in this regard. "One is to love one's neighbor because God himself, as Father, divinely loves and prizes each individual man. Hence the individual man has an essentially infinite value, although he has this value only in and through his relation to God, and because of God's love for him."[68] This, in part, depicts the genius of Christian love, in as much as its chief attribute is not the elevation of the needs and interests of others above those of one's self. It does not require the total denial or abandonment of one's self and one's interests. Rather, every person is to "delight" in self *and* the neighbor since each is God's beloved.[69]

It is absolutely the case that both whites and blacks will have to be honest and straightforward, and put the race cards on the table—which has never happened in most places in this country, including religious institutions of all kinds that otherwise claim to be among the most progressive. In addition, it is imperative that blacks not allow themselves to be pulled so low as to do to white people what they have done to them. James Baldwin aptly reminds us of the self-destructiveness of blacks doing to whites what they have done to them. "Whoever debases another," said Baldwin, "is debasing himself."[70] This is consistent with King's conviction about the interdependency or interrelatedness of all life under God. He spoke eloquently to this point in "A Christmas Sermon on Peace," in 1967. Borrowing from Benjamin E. Mays (but without attribution), King said: "We are all caught in an inescapable network of mutuality, tied into a single garment of destiny. Whatever affects one directly, affects all indirectly. We are made to live together because of the interrelated structure of reality."[71]

Conclusion

Although we, like Martin Luther King are but imperfect earthen vessels, we do not have to leave this world the way it was when we entered it. It is up to you; it is up to me; it is up to ecclesial, political and civic organizations to decide whether we will be the type of community that God desires us to be, or whether we will continue doing all we can to discourage the establishment of the beloved community. But we need to remember that if we choose to go the way God would have us go, we will have to be willing to give up something along the way, whether power and privilege, or something else. But we can be sure that we will not know that gentler, sweeter community unless we are—all of us—willing to work and sacrifice for it. King admonished that the beloved community will not roll into existence on the wheels of inevitability.[72] It will take constant vigilance, hard work, human and divine cooperation, and sacrifice. King frequently spoke about this ongoing need for a divine-human partnership or what he referred to as cooperative endeavor between God and human beings in the struggle to actualize the beloved community. Indeed, Archbishop Tutu had this in mind when he admonished:

> God calls on us to be his partners to work for a new kind of society where people count; where people matter more than things, more than possessions; where human life is not just respected but positively revered; where people will be secure and not suffer from the fear of hunger, from ignorance, from disease; where there will be more gentleness, more caring, more sharing, more compassion, more laughter; where there is peace and not war.[73]

Young people, both in and out of academic institutions, have a significant role to play in the eradication of racism and other forms of injustice, and establishing a racism-free society based on justice and equality for all. Lewis V. Baldwin has written that present day antiracism coalitions on college and university campuses, for example, is "consistent with King's prediction, made in the early 1960s, that college and university students will be 'a part of a worldwide thrust in the future' to end racism."[74] Indeed, in the posthumously published *The Trumpet of Conscience* (1968), King wrote of the role of university and non-university students of all races in establishing a gentler, sweeter world house.[75]

During and beyond King Day celebrations, the genuinely serious celebrant will be diligent in seeking to know the true meaning and requirements of the beloved community, as well as identifying those places where signs of the community of love already exist, and how best to build on and expand it. Martin Luther King would have agreed with Josiah Royce that if we cannot find the beloved community in the schools, places of employment, and churches, we must devote our energies, resources, and talents to creating it. Royce admonished: "Do whatever you can to take a step towards it, or to assist anybody,—your brother, your friend, your neighbor, your country,—mankind,—to take steps towards the organization of that coming community."[76] Royce knew, as did Martin Luther King, that any possibility of establishing the beloved community depends on cooperative endeavor between God and human beings as they try to do all in our power to create and sustain it as best we can. Accordingly, "the principle of principles" in Christian morality is that if we cannot find the beloved community we are obligated to do all in our power to create it, and to do so not "with all deliberate speed," but with a sense of utmost urgency.[77]

Finally, we are, all of us, imperfect and limited beings, in whom God has emblazoned the seal of preciousness. In this regard, Martin Luther King was no different. It is important that we always keep before us the idea of King's humanity, even as we remember, praise, and celebrate his many contributions toward establishing the beloved community. By remembering King's humanity we may be less tempted to condemn him and his accomplishments when word comes that he was not perfect in character. We need to remember that, as a human being, Martin Luther King was neither perfect, nor pretended to be, even as he exhibited extraordinary faithfulness to God's expectation that he be the voice of the voiceless masses as he did all he could to establish the beloved community. He was, after all, *called* to the vocation of establishing the community of love. Precisely this, i.e., his deep sense of call, and faithfulness to his God, is the best explanation for why, in the face of impending death virtually every day of the last year of his life, King stayed the course until a 150-grain slug from a 30.06 Remington Gamemaster tore away the right side of his jaw, ending his life and work that was devoted to making the world better than it was when he entered it. The only question that remains for you and me is: What are we willing to do to contribute toward creating the beloved community where we live, work, attend school, worship, and play? That is the question we need to answer today.

10

When a King Dreamed in Public[1]

The March on Washington for Jobs and Freedom and the dream articulated by Martin Luther King was primarily about a radical reordering of values; of viewing every U.S. citizen as a full-fledged human being with all of the rights, privileges, and opportunities thereto pertaining; of moving from a thing-oriented nation to a person-oriented nation. In addition, the dream was about a fundamental restructuring of U.S. society such that the basic needs of every individual and group will be met. At this moment in history, all indications are that King's dream remains at best "a dream unfulfilled."

The famous March on Washington on August 28, 1963, where upwards of 200,000 people—mostly blacks—attended, was not the first time that American citizens marched (or planned to march) on Washington. We can be certain that in no case were the marchers welcomed with open arms by the respective presidential administrations and congressional members.

> Leaders of Corey's Army of the jobless in 1894 were arrested and jailed upon arrival. In 1932, thousands of World War I veterans in the Bonus Army were teargassed and driven out of town by U.S. soldiers under the command of General Douglas MacArthur. A decade later, black labor leader Asa Philip Randolph, founder of the Brotherhood of Sleeping Car Porters, was angry enough to ignore the precedents. In the summer of 1941, as a surge in military spending began to lift white America out of the Depression, the needs of the black unemployed were being ignored. Randolph threatened President Franklin Roosevelt with a mass march by 100,000 Negro citizens.[2]

Randolph organized the March on Washington Movement. The goals were equal employment opportunity for blacks in the defense industry, and the desegregation of the armed forces. It looked as if Roosevelt was not going to meet the July 1 deadline. As it turned out, with just one week to spare, a bargain was struck in which the President issued an executive order establishing the first national Fair Employment Practices Commission. The Commission itself had no power to enforce its will. It had only moral authority, but it at least gave willing employers the opportunity to say that by hiring blacks they were in compliance with federal government policy.[3] With this and the improvements that followed, Randolph postponed the march. He was too politically savvy and too much of a political realist to outright cancel the march and uncritically trust the powers that be. So the better part of wisdom led Randolph to postpone rather than cancel the planned March on Washington in 1941. Although it might not have occurred to Washington politicians, the possibility of a future March surely remained a viable option for A. Philip Randolph.

For twenty years the idea of the March on Washington remained dormant. By the beginning of the 1960s, however, it was becoming increasingly clear that things were getting progressively worse, not better, for blacks. The unemployment rate for blacks was double that of whites. In addition, little progress had been made in the attainment of civil rights, despite the success of the bus boycott in Montgomery, Alabama from late in 1955 through most of 1956 when the Supreme Court ruled against that city and state's segregation ordinance.

The spring and summer of 1963 were utterly devastating months for black people in Deep South places such as Birmingham and Gadsen, Alabama; Savannah, Georgia; and the Mississippi Delta. Civil rights demonstrators were the victims of vicious police dog attacks, and high-powered fire hoses that emitted cannon-like bursts of water that could peel the bark off trees. Dozens were wounded in racial disturbances in Americus, Georgia, and one black man was killed. The extent of police brutality was almost unprecedented in some of these cities. Local police and state troopers used electric cattle prods and blackjacks on nonviolent demonstrators. The governor of Maryland called in the National Guard to bring some semblance of order in Cambridge, Maryland. The violence and anger were unprecedented, and it all seemed to be coming to a head during the spring and summer of 1963.

When word got to Washington that A. Philip Randolph wanted to make real his promise to march on Washington—with an emphasis on jobs and freedom—and that other big name civil rights leaders such as Martin Luther King, Jr., Whitney Young, and Roy Wilkins were supportive of a march, President John F. Kennedy—who had actually barely won the election as a result of the black vote, but made the mistake of not making civil rights a priority in his administration—summoned about thirty civil rights leaders to the White House in the hope of talking them into calling off the march. Perhaps had the Kennedy administration been supportive of blacks' struggle for civil rights the President might have been able to convince civil rights leaders to at least consider a postponement. But the President's administration had not been supportive of the civil rights struggle, and therefore had no credibility with black leaders, and no bargaining chips. "Unlike 1941, this was not a quid pro quo situation. Blacks were not asking Kennedy for an executive order. They were instead offering their support for legislation the President had already proposed to Congress. And whether Kennedy liked it or not [and we can be assured that he did not like it], they were going to bring their bodies to Washington to make their witness in August."[4]

Although many in 1963, and subsequently, assumed that the March on Washington for jobs and freedom was Martin Luther King's idea, it is important that we know that this was not the case. A. Philip Randolph renewed his call for the march, and invited his protégée, the controversial but excellent strategist and organizer, Bayard Rustin, to be the deputy director, responsible for planning and logistics. King, whose major civil rights activity had been in Birmingham throughout much of 1963, was one of the major leaders who answered Randolph's call to join the March. King was also invited to be one of the chief planners in a group pejoratively referred to by outsiders (not least Malcolm X) as the "Big Six." In addition to King (SCLC), these included Randolph (Brotherhood of Sleeping Car Porters), Roy Wilkins (NAACP), Whitney Young (National Urban League), James Farmer (CORE), and John Lewis (SNCC). Anna Hedgeman was the only woman member of the planning committee. Hedgeman found herself standing alone when she tried, unsuccessfully, to get the otherwise all-male group to agree to the inclusion of even one woman among the speakers on March day. It was but one instance of male chauvinism in the raw.

I want to reflect on the following topics related to King's "I Have a Dream" speech: (1) The charge that King stole the Dream speech; (2) The source of the "I have a dream" refrain;

(3) The claim that King was prompted by someone on the speakers platform to tell about his dream; (4) The aftermath of the speech; and (5) Celebrating the dream.

Did King Steal the Dream Speech?

On January 20, 2008, Jim Hoft posted a blog titled, "Bummer ... Martin Luther King, Jr. Stole 'I Have a Dream' Speech."[5] Hoft misleadingly claims that King stole the speech from black republican the Rev. Archibald Carey, Jr., who presumably gave the speech at the 1952 Republican National Convention. Of Hoft's and other glory seeking, poorly informed, would-be historians' *fantastical* claim (to use actor Denzel Washington's term), I want to make just a couple of comments.

First, Martin Luther King did not steal the "I Have a Dream" speech as such from Archibald Carey, or anybody else for that matter. It is true that King appropriated and adapted two paragraphs from Carey's speech that figured prominently in what came to be the famous "I Have a Dream" speech. The lines from Carey that King appropriated and adapted to his own oratorical style and rhythm are these:

> We, Negro Americans, sing with all loyal Americans:
> My country 'tis of thee,
> Sweet land of liberty,
> Of thee I sing.
> Land where my fathers died,
> Land of the Pilgrim's pride
> From every mountainside
> Let Freedom ring!
> That's exactly what we mean—
> from every mountain side, let freedom ring.
> Not only from the Green Mountains and White Mountains
> of Vermont and New Hampshire;
> not only from the Catskills of New York;
> but from the Ozarks in Arkansas,
> from the Stone Mountain in Georgia,
> from the Blue Ridge Mountains of Virginia
> —let it ring not only for the minorities of the United States,
> but for the disinherited of all the earth—
> may the Republican Party, under God, from every mountainside,
> LET FREEDOM RING![6]

In the "I Have a Dream" speech, Martin Luther King introduced the patriotic song with the phrase: "This will be the day when all of God's children will be able to sing with a new meaning: 'My country 'tis of thee....'" After the words of the song he goes into his version of the "Let freedom ring" refrain:

> And if America is to be a great nation, this must become true.
> And so let freedom ring from the prodigious hilltops of New Hampshire.
> Let freedom ring from the mighty mountains of New York.
> Let freedom ring from the heightening Alleghenies of Pennsylvania.
> Let freedom ring from the snowcapped Rockies of Colorado.
> Let freedom ring from the curvaceous slopes of California.
> But not only that: Let freedom ring from Stone Mountain of Georgia.
> Let freedom ring from Lookout Mountain of Tennessee.

Let freedom ring from every hill and molehill of Mississippi.
From every mountainside, let freedom ring.[7]

See the difference? Yes, Martin Luther King appropriated and adapted for his purpose lines from Carey's speech. Did he "steal" the "I Have a Dream" speech from Carey? How does one steal what is not there to be stolen? One cannot, and this is the second thing I want to say about Hoft's claim that King stole the Dream speech from Carey. The "I Have a Dream" refrain is not even in the Carey speech, nor is he known ever to have uttered those words in a speech or penned them onto paper.

In speeches on December 3 and 15, 1956, and January 1 and April 10, 1957, we do find King using his own refined versions of Carey's "let freedom ring" refrain. In the 1957 versions, King introduced the refrain with words that clearly inform the reader that the idea was not his own, saying on January 1: "*As I heard a great orator say some time ago*, that must become literally true. Freedom must ring from every mountain side."[8] It will also be seen that King's wording in each of those first four usages are different from each other and from what appeared in the 1963 Dream speech.

Archibald Carey, Jr., was senior minister of Chicago's Quinn Chapel AME Church, and was a good friend of King's. Indeed, as early as December 27, 1955, approximately three weeks after the start of the Montgomery bus boycott, King wrote to Carey and other black religious and civic leaders in Chicago on behalf of the Montgomery Improvement Association (MIA) to ask that they lobby the National City Lines in that city. National City Lines owned the Montgomery city bus line.[9] Without Carey's prior knowledge, King and the MIA named him chairman of the Chicago committee to lobby National City. Others named to the committee included J.H. Jackson, J.W. Eichelberger, William L. Dawson, and Earl Dickerson.[10] When King heard little from the Chicago committee after nearly a month, he expressed disappointment that black religious and civic leaders did not seem to be concerned about blacks' plight in Montgomery. When Carey finally wrote to King on February 24, 1956, he asked what Northerners like him could do to support the struggle in Montgomery, and to do so in ways that would not indicate that they were meddlesome outside instigators. Carey's letter gave no hint of awareness that he had been selected as chairman of the group to make the grievances of the MIA known to the National City Lines. After asking King what he and others could do to support the work in Montgomery, Carey then offered to take up a collection from his congregation and send it.[11] As further evidence of the close acquaintance between King and Carey, on December 20, 1957, King wrote Carey to thank him for his "dynamic and inspiring address" at the Second Annual Institute on Non-Violent Social Change in Montgomery on December 8.[12]

King had a penchant—might I say a gift—for borrowing the words and ideas of others and making them sound better, as well as provide a clearer meaning than that given by the original author. He refined, sharpened, and improved those words and ideas such that his adaptation of them was sweeter to the ears, truer to the experiences of his audience, and more consistent with the flow of his oratory. In a word, King had a gift for saying an author's words better than the author himself. Is this ever an excuse or even reason for plagiarism of any kind? NO! Nor is it excusable because King and the author knew each other well, as in the case of he and Carey. But this does not undermine the fact that Martin Luther King was—in the idiom of the black preaching tradition—a "bad boy" preacher-orator reared in the powerful rhetorical tradition of the southern black Baptist preacher. That is, he could just flat out tell the gospel story, and tell it in a way that held his audience captive until the last word was spoken. Congressman John Lewis, who as a SNCC student leader marched with King many times and was also a speaker at the March on Washington reflected on the power and sweetness of King's oratory.

> When he spoke, the masses knew from his words that they were somebody.... No matter where he spoke, an electricity filled the air. After listening to Dr. King we were so inspired and so moved, we were prepared to march into Hell's fires. Like all great orators, Dr. King was keenly aware of the audience. His dramatic cadence and voice was like a baby's lullaby; you could not resist his call to your conscience.[13]

Looking back after thirty years, Myrna Carter, who was twelve years old when she participated in the Children's Crusade in Birmingham in 1963, also remarked about the power of King's oratory. "The drawing power of Dr. King's voice," she told Ellen Levine, "was like that of no one else who was connected with the struggle. ... [H]e had that power that could make you actually leap and you didn't realize you were leaping."[14] Indeed, Septima Clark, a grassroots organizer during the 1950s and 1960s also recalled how powerful and alluring was King's voice and his ability to articulate well in getting people on board and believing that they could make a difference in the struggle for freedom and civil rights. "As he talked about Moses," she said, "and leading the people out, and getting the people into the place where the Red Sea would cover them, he would just make you see them. You believed it."[15] King had a way of saying it such that listeners actually believed that if they but made the sustained effort they themselves could cause justice to roll down like waters, and righteousness like a mighty stream.[16]

King was a "bad boy" preacher who could just say it better, more powerfully, and convincingly than most people, including the author of words or phrases that he appropriated without attribution. For the record, to date the Martin Luther King, Jr. Papers Project under the direction of Professor Clayborne Carson at Stanford University has uncovered no evidence of King ever having copied entire texts without attribution, or as if they were his own. Instead, King's habit was that of "weaving together his words with those of others to express his views."[17]

Without question, Martin Luther King understood the potential power of the spoken word. Civil rights sociologist Aldon D. Morris makes the point well. "His gift for oratory was nurtured by some of the greatest black orators of the twentieth century. The oratorical tradition runs deep in the black community and is riveted into the culture through the church. King clearly understood the social power of oratory and used it as a tool for agitating, organizing, fundraising, and articulating the desires of the black masses."[18] Because King was always aware of his audience his speech was generally tailored to that audience. He knew instinctively that he could not effectively communicate with every audience in the same way. He would have to tailor his language. "To church people he would preach protest by citing relevant scriptures from the Bible. To a highly learned audience he would preach protest by engaging in precise historical and philosophical discourses."[19] King was simply masterful and creative in weaving together his ideas with those of others (even when failing to credit those others) in ways that captured his audience and communicated to listeners what others failed to communicate. Morris provides yet another instructive comment on the matter.

> He coherently wove together the profound utterances of ditch-diggers, great philosophers, college professors, and floor-scrubbing domestics with ease. To inspire the poor black masses and the educated through oratory King would tell the street sweeper to go out and sweep streets the way Michelangelo painted pictures or Beethoven composed music or Shakespeare wrote poetry. Moreover, King had the ability to convey in folksy language the commonalities that the contemporary black movement shared with great liberation movements of biblical times.[20]

Martin Luther King did not steal the Dream speech from Archibald Carey. In fact, the Dream speech is actually a compilation of parts of King's speeches that are not included in the Carey speech at all. Unknown to him at the time, King actually began working out the Dream speech in various speeches, addresses, and sermons from the mid–1950s right up to what is thought to be the first or earliest known transcription of "I Have a Dream" on November 27, 1962 during a night speech in Rocky Mount, North Carolina.[21] The speech that night was titled, "Facing the Challenge of a New Age."[22] In the "I have a dream" section of that speech King states several times: "I have a dream tonight,"[23] the clearest indication that it was a night speech.

In any case, it is as if unknown to him at the time, Martin Luther King was actually rehearsing for he knew not what. The second time he gave a version of the Dream speech was at the Freedom Rally in Detroit's Cobo Hall on June 23, 1963, where 150,000 people attended. King called it the largest and the greatest demonstration for freedom in the history of the United States to that point.[24] The Cobo Hall rally occurred approximately two months before the March on Washington. The address at Cobo Hall was by far the best dress rehearsal for the subsequent Dream speech in Washington. But the Cobo Hall address did not top what would happen two months later.

From Whence Came the "I Have a Dream" Refrain?

As noted before, Martin Luther King had already been telling America about his dream for the nation since the mid to late 1950s. In his Address at the Religious Leaders Conference under the aegis of the President's Committee on Government Contracts in Washington, D.C. on May 11, 1959, King told those gathered that the dream of American democracy is "a dream yet unfulfilled." He went on to characterize the dream saying:

> A dream of equality of opportunity, of privilege and property widely distributed; a dream of a land where men will not take necessities from the many to give luxuries to the few; a dream of a land where men do not argue that the color of a man's skin determines the content of his character, where they recognize that the basic thing about a man is not his specificity but his fundamendum; a dream of a place where all our gifts and resources are held, not for ourselves alone, but as instruments of service for the rest of humanity; the dream of a country where every man will respect the dignity and worth of all human personality, and men will dare to live together as brothers—*that* is the dream. Wherever it is fulfilled we will emerge from the bleak and desolate midnight of man's inhumanity to man into the bright and glowing daybreak of freedom and justice for all of God's children.[25]

Nearly a year and a half later, on September 5, 1960, King delivered the address, "The Negro and the American Dream" at the Annual Freedom Mass Meeting of the North Carolina State Conference of Branches of the NAACP. In words that also anticipated the Dream speech, King said:

> It is the dream of a land where men of all races, colors and creeds will live together as brothers. The substance of the dream is expressed in these sublime words: "We hold these truths to be self-evident, that all men are created equal, that they are endowed by their creator with certain unalienable rights, that among these are life, liberty and the pursuit of happiness." This is the dream. It is a profound, eloquent and unequivocal expression of the dignity and worth of all human personality.[26]

And yet, although Martin Luther King was speaking fairly regularly about his dream for the United States between the late 1950s and most of 1962, we know of no place where he expressly used the phrase, "I have a dream," before that November night in Rocky Mount, North Carolina. He had not used the phrase because it had not occurred to him to do so. Or, he had not heard the phrase used, or heard of it being used. So from whence came the phrase?

In 1961, King and SCLC were invited by Dr. William G. Anderson, president of the Albany (Georgia) Movement to lend support to the Albany campaign for civil rights. By all accounts Albany was a failed campaign for King and SCLC, although they learned important lessons for subsequent nonviolent direct action campaigns, beginning with Birmingham, Alabama. King and SCLC left Albany some time in August of 1962. However, it is known that the mass prayer meetings and protest demonstrations continued long afterward under the leadership of the Student Nonviolent Coordinating Committee (SNCC) and some local black churches. Because of the ongoing activity of demonstrations and mass prayer meetings SNCC, unlike SCLC, did not consider the Albany movement to be a failure.

I mention the Albany movement because there is evidence that the "I have a dream" phrase was first uttered at a mass prayer meeting near Albany barely two weeks after King left the city. It is believed that SNCC activist Prathia Hall uttered the phrase at a mass prayer meeting around September 14, 1962. Drew Hansen, author of *The Dream: Martin Luther King, Jr. and the Speech that Inspired a Nation* (2003), contends that when he interviewed Hall on November 15, 2001, she recalled using the phrase, "I have a dream," at the prayer service at the remains of the Mount Olive Baptist Church in Sasser, Georgia (after segregationists burned it to the ground). Hall remembered telling those present about her dream of freedom, namely: "Being free from the bullets and the burnings, being free to worship and free to learn."[27] Some thought they remembered King being present at that prayer meeting, in which case he would have heard Hall use the "I have a dream" phrase. However, others remember differently, and Hall herself had no recollection of King being present. The most important thing that Hall told Hansen was that whether King was or was not present, she had no desire to take credit for his use of the "I have a dream" phrase. King, she said, had done much more with it than she ever could have done.[28] Remember, the prayer meeting occurred around September 14, 1962. Even if King was not present, it is quite possible that someone in attendance told him about the use of the phrase.

SCLC staff member and director of the Citizenship Education Program, Dorothy F. Cotton has written of yet another possible source of the "I Have a Dream" refrain. According to Cotton, she first heard it used in a speech to elderly blacks at a wooden rural church, given by a white co-ed from Vassar College in August or September of 1962. The young woman told those present about a vision she had had. Cotton recalled hearing her say: "All I want is a better America. I have a dream that one day my little children can hold hands with your little children and grandchildren and play together. I have a dream that they can study and learn together without it seeming strange or unusual."[29] The young woman got in a rhythm, according to Cotton, and went on with the dream refrain for a while. When Cotton picked up King at the airport in Charleston, South Carolina, the next day for the SCLC staff retreat, she told him what she had heard at the old wooden church. She recalled King's excitement as she told him about the "I Have a Dream" refrain. "Martin listened intently. I could see both the preacher and the poet working inside him," Cotton recalled.[30] The fact that King later used the dream refrain, especially at the March on Washington, led her to believe that he was much "inspired by that White girl's vision."[31]

As previously observed, the earliest known transcription of King's use of the "I have a dream" refrain occurred on November 27, 1962. This would have been a little over two months *after* Hall reportedly uttered the phrase, and not long after Cotton heard the Vassar co-ed tell about her vision. In his address that night King told his Rocky Mount, North Carolina, audience:

> And so, my friends of Rocky Mount, I have a dream tonight.
> It is a dream deeply rooted in the American dream.
> I have a dream that one day down in Sumter County, Georgia,
> where they burned two churches down a few days ago because
> Negroes wanted to register and vote....
>
> I have a dream tonight. One day my little daughter and two sons [Bernice
> Albertine was not yet born] will grow up in a world
> not conscious of the color of their skin but only conscious of the
> fact that they are members of the human race.
> I have a dream tonight. Some day we will be free.[32]

I think we can be reasonably assured that SNCC activist and late Boston University School of Theology professor Prathia Hall, along with the white co-ed, were among the first to utter the "I have a dream" phrase.

It is important to remember that Martin Luther King emerged from a long tradition of black preachers who took the art of preaching serious and therefore worked very hard and deliberately at delivering the spoken word and holding their audience. Preaching was thought to be an art, which meant that one had to work unrelentingly at both content and oratorical flair. Because of this, King "could preach the phone book," declared Cotton.[33] But it also meant (and means!) being attentive to the preaching of others and what comes out of their mouths: words, phrases, and ideas. Indeed, those striving to be great preachers, to be in a class virtually by themselves, also take mental and written notes that go in the special category: "This will preach." Cotton implied that King was doing something of this nature as she told him about the use of the dream refrain used by the Vassar co-ed.

In any event, to hear such words ordinarily means that at some point in the not too distant future they will be heard anew in a sermon or speech with some creative and rhetorical additives. For the object is to take what was heard said by the Reverend Whatshisname to a much more meaningful level or place, such that while one recognizes the idea as belonging to Whatshisname, she is left with the sense that the Reverend Whatshisname said it, but the Reverend Whatshername *preached* it. And the truth is that nobody did this kind of thing better than Martin Luther King. Indeed, had not King's seminary professor, Morton Scott Enslin said of him in his confidential evaluation: "All is grist that comes to his mill," and he "rarely misses anything which he can subsequently use?"[34] I can just imagine that having told various audiences different versions of his dream for America over several years, when he first heard the phrase "I have a dream" (from whatever quarter he heard it), King immediately thought to himself: "*This* will preach." So he soon began preaching "I have a dream," and preaching it in ways that it had literally never been preached before, or since.

"Tell 'em about your dream, Martin"

In Clarence B. Jones's book, *Behind the Dream* (2011), the reader gets a good sense of what went into the making of the famous speech that Martin Luther King gave on March day. We learn that King selected a small group of people, including Jones, his confidant, attorney, fundraiser, and sometime speechwriter, to meet with him the night before the March from whom he solicited ideas for his speech.[35] We learn that King asked Jones to take notes and try to capture the most important ideas and themes offered. We learn further that the group engaged King for several spirited hours. In addition, we learn that the phrase about coming to the nation's capital to redeem a promissory note was offered by Jones.[36] There is no evidence that references were made to the "I have a dream" refrain during the group discussion, nor that a specific title was given the speech to be developed from the ideas offered.

We learn a number of other important things from Jones's book, but none more consequential than a matter that was not addressed, namely the exclusion of women from the group of speech advisors. This omission was all the more glaring because while only one woman, Anna Hedgeman, was on the March planning committee, it was she and she alone who expressed dismay to her male colleagues (the "Big Six") that no woman was invited to speak on the day of the march. It was Hedgeman who stood bravely and alone before her male colleagues and read a strong letter of protest, of which she received no support from even a single member.[37] A number of black women, not least Septima Clark, Dorothy Height, and Pauli Murray, expressed their complete dismay over the treatment of black women regarding the famous March. What Murray said about the matter is consistent with the position of many black women of that period. I quote liberally from the speech that she gave at the Leadership Conference of the National Council of Negro Women in Washington, D.C., nearly one month after the March.

> What emerges most clearly from events of the past several months is the tendency to assign women to a secondary, ornamental or "honoree" role instead of the partnership role in the civil rights movement which they have earned by their courage, intelligence and dedication. It was bitterly humiliating for Negro women on August 28 to see themselves accorded little more than token recognition in the historic March on Washington. Not a single woman was invited to make one of the major speeches or to be part of the delegation of leaders who went to the White House. This omission was deliberate. Representations for recognition of women were made to the policy-making body sufficiently in advance of the August 28 arrangements to have permitted the necessary adjustments of the program. What the Negro women leaders were told is revealing: that no representation was given to them because they would not be able to agree on a delegate. How familiar was this excuse! It is a typical response from an entrenched power group.
>
> Significantly, two days before the March, A. Philip Randolph ... accepted an invitation to be guest speaker at a luncheon given by the National Press Club in Washington in the face of strong protest by organized newspaper women that the National Press Club excludes qualified newspaper women from membership and sends women reporters who cover its luncheons to the balcony. Mr. Randolph apparently saw no relationship between being sent to the balcony and being sent to the back of the bus.[38]

Dorothy Height reflected that all kinds of lame excuses were given to why it was not necessary to include women speakers at the March. She recalled it being "unnerving to be given the argument that women were members of the National Urban League and of the other organizations, and so, they were represented."[39] According to Height, even those men, e.g., King, Whitney Young, and James Farmer, who showed some sensitivity to the women's demands, failed to take action.[40]

In any event, the exclusion of women from the speech advisory group was even more glaring because later in his book Clarence Jones claims to have been deeply troubled that women were not invited as speakers on March day, but that he did not verbalize his resentment or discomfort.[41] Jones himself was not a member of the planning committee, and may not have known until March day that women would not be among the speakers. As such, I think that Jones was not morally culpable in that particular situation. However, he was indeed morally blameworthy in the matter of the all-male speech advisory group since he was a member of that group, was aware that no women were members, and in the end said and did nothing to challenge his male colleagues, including King, to include women. This is why I take with a grain of salt Jones's claim to have been disturbed that no woman was invited to be a speaker on March day. It is always easier to be righteously indignant when one is on the outside and in no position to even express his discontent about matters of injustice, than when one is actually on the inside and can—if one has the courage—make or at least try to make a difference (even if one makes enemies in the process).

At any rate, once Martin Luther King listened to the many suggestions that might be included in his speech, Jones had the task of going off to write a summary capturing the major themes and offering any other suggestions he might have. Once King received Jones's summary and notes he went to his room where he reportedly worked until around 3:00 a.m. before he had a draft of the speech he thought he would deliver. The "I have a dream" refrain was not in the written speech that King took to the podium on March day, a fact that both Jones and King later confirmed.

It was agreed that by virtue of the sheer power and eloquence of his oratory, King would be the last speaker on March day. It is likely that any speech following his would have been anti-climactic at best. At least this was the sentiment of the planners. While SNCC leader John Lewis's was by far the most radical speech of the day, 200,000 and more people that day had—unknown to them at the time—come to hear the speech delivered by Martin Luther King.

For just over half of what we know as the "I Have a Dream" speech, King spoke from a written manuscript. King biographer Taylor Branch observes that a few lines in the first half of the written speech were completely omitted by King, perhaps because he sensed during the delivery that they would not flow smoothly with the rhythm and meter of his oratory.[42] All that he had said to that point had gotten the crowd worked up to a level of excitement that he had not experienced before, even at the Cobo Hall rally two months earlier. The mark of a superior orator in touch with his audience, King seemed to sense that the moment, the spirit, the people were clamoring for something even deeper, something more, than what was in the remainder of his written text.

Moreover, reportedly at least one person seated on the speaker's dais near King seems to have sensed this as well. For she, and perhaps many others like her in the huge and thunderous crowd, were now feeling that they were in a church-like atmosphere. So, this woman gospel singer and dear friend of King's, Mahalia Jackson, who had heard King speak about his dream at the Cobo Hall rally—is said to have shouted: "Tell 'em about your dream, Martin. Tell 'em about your dream." This writer has seen photos of Jackson on the speaker's platform. She was clearly seated near enough to King for him to have heard her voice. Taylor Branch reports that Cleveland Robinson (one of the speech advisors on the platform near King and Jackson) told him in an October 28, 1983 interview that seated behind King on the platform, Mahalia Jackson shouted to King: "Tell 'em about the dream, Martin."[43] Actually, Jackson is pictured as just a few feet to the left and just adjacent to the lectern.[44] Robinson made no claim that Jackson's words were actually heard by King; only that she spoke them. From where Jackson was seated there is no question that if she in fact urged King to tell the crowd about his dream, he would have heard her, even had he not recognized the voice.

Let's think about the speech for a moment. After King tells the people to go back to Mississippi, Alabama, South Carolina, Georgia, Louisiana, and the slums and ghettos of the North, and that they are not to "wallow in the valley of despair," something happens at just that moment that seems to disrupt the rhythm of the speech. Reportedly, it was just at this point that King seemed to be reacting to what could have been a distraction of some kind, whether real or imagined. Had he actually heard a voice urging him to speak about his dream, even though he might not have recognized the voice itself in that moment? Had he sensed from the overwhelming thunderous response from the crowd that something quite different from what was in the remainder of the written text was now needed?

The late Senator Edward Kennedy wrote in *True Compass: A Memoir* (2009), of having gone to his office on March day to listen to King's speech. "I listened to those remarks and watched as Dr. King finished and turned to sit down and then abruptly turned back to the crowd. Although I could not distinguish her, and her voice was not picked up by the microphones," Kennedy said, "the great gospel singer Mahalia Jackson had blurted out to Dr. King from behind him, 'Tell them about your dream, Martin! Tell them about the dream!' And Martin Luther King did. In a decade in which cataclysmic events inspired lasting oratory, the Georgian-born minister spontaneously delivered the great aria of the civil rights movement."[45] Having watched televised delivery of King's speech many times, I have seen no evidence of him turning to sit down, and then abruptly turning back to the crowd and going into the "I have a dream" speech. Since Kennedy was not in the huge crowd that day, let alone seated on the speakers dais near Mahalia Jackson, and since the microphones did not pick up her voice, if in fact she told King to tell the crowd about his dream, Kennedy could only know after the fact, what he reports in his memoir. That is, he very likely was remembering what was reported to him after King's speech, or what he read in the *Washington Post* or any number of other media that reported on the March and the Dream speech. What is important for our purpose is that whether lore or fact, Ted Kennedy, like a number of others, remembered (from whatever might have been the source) and reported *a Mahalia Jackson connection* to the "I have a dream" portion of King's speech. It is not yet known whether Jackson addressed this point in her papers, although we do know that she is silent on the matter in her autobiography, *Movin' On Up* (1966).[46]

Clarence Jones claims to have heard Mahalia Jackson urge King to tell the crowd about his dream. He also claims that, years later, he discovered that Ted Kennedy also heard her. (Of course, we saw above that Kennedy could not have heard her, since he was not even present at the March.) Jones contends that not many people actually heard her. "But I did," he declares.[47] Commenting on when King's speech seemed to be disrupted and he moved from the written manuscript to extemporizing, Jones goes on to say:

> Yet in this split second of silence something historic and unexpected happened. ... [Mahalia Jackson beckoned him to tell about his dream.] ...
>
> I had an instant to wonder what was about to take place. Then I watched Martin push the text of his prepared remarks to one side of the lectern. He shifted gears in a heartbeat, abandoning whatever final version of the balance of the text he'd prepared late the previous night, turning away from whatever notes he'd scrawled in the margins. Observing this from my perch, I knew he'd just put himself in Mahalia's hands, given himself over to the spirit of the moment. ...
>
> I leaned over and said to the person standing next to me, "These people out there today don't know it yet, but they're about ready to go to church." From his body language and the tone in his voice, I knew Martin was about to transform into the superb Baptist preacher he was; like the three generations of Baptist preachers before him in his family.
>
> Then, honoring Mahalia's request, Martin spoke those words that in retrospect feel destined to ring out that day: "*I have a dream...*"[48]

As we can see, Jones is convinced that King actually heard Jackson's voice and request. Although Jones claims that years after the Dream speech was given he found that Kennedy "heard

Mahalia as well,"[49] this statement has already been disproven by Kennedy's own words in his Memoir.

Although it may not be as clear to others that King appeared to be distracted, and because of this the rhythm of his speech was momentarily disrupted after telling the people to go back to their respective homes in the South and the ghettos and slums of the North, I am convinced that this was the case; that having strayed from the written text, for whatever reason(s), King was searching for a way to end his speech on the highest positive note. I am inclined to believe the story about Mahalia Jackson urging him to tell the audience about his dream, and thus agree with Clarence Jones on this point at least, whether or not King could distinguish her voice. It seems reasonable that what he heard and resonated to, was the call to tell about the dream, which of course was still fresh in his mind after the Cobo Hall rally. Otherwise, I don't know how one can explain King's injection of the phrase: "I say to you today, my friends, so even though we face the difficulties of today and tomorrow...."[50] From this it is clear in my mind both that King was not certain what he would say next, and that whatever it was, it would be a significant transition or deviation from the prepared text. If he in fact heard a voice beckoning him to tell the crowd about his dream, this would have been as good a place as any to do what he in fact did, namely to shift to the "I have a dream" refrain. "[S]o even though we face the difficulties of today and tomorrow," he had said, "I still have a dream. It is a dream deeply rooted in the American dream."[51] For King, unlike many, then and now, the best in the American dream had nothing to do with the United States playing big brother to, and going to war against weaker, less powerful nations. Rather, the best in the American dream had to do with respecting and acknowledging the dignity of all persons and guaranteeing liberty and justice for all.

When an interviewer asked King about the speech he replied that he had used the "I have a dream" phrase in the Cobo Hall address. Clayborne Carson records that King said: "I had used it [the "I have a dream" refrain] many times before, and I just felt that I wanted to use it here. I don't know why. I hadn't thought about it before the speech. I used the phrase, and at that point I just turned aside from the manuscript altogether and didn't come back to it."[52] King told Donald H. Smith in an interview on November 29, 1963, that the idea to transition to the "I have a dream" material just "came to me."[53]

King surely believed what he told Donald Smith in the interview. But it is just as likely that the "I have a dream" refrain just came to him because he had heard a voice—Mahalia Jackson's voice—prompting him to tell about his dream. King said that he had wanted to use the phrase, but did not know why. Evidence suggests that the answer to the "why" is, at least in part, found in the voice prompting him to tell about his dream. Because he had the crowd at such a high pitch of emotionalism and enthusiasm his keen sense of where his audience was at that moment convinced him in a matter of a few seconds that it was time for a shift in speech, and it is quite likely that a woman helped him to get there, even if he could not recall actually hearing her voice. The message delivered by the voice is what was most important. Even if King had no recollection of hearing the voice, what is important is that he told America and the world about a dream he had had.

The Aftermath of the "I Have a Dream" Speech

While I am happy to be around to participate in the celebration of the fiftieth anniversary of the March on Washington for Jobs and Freedom and the famous "I Have a Dream" speech,

I would be remiss if I did not comment on ensuing problems or issues associated with that historic moment and King's dream for the nation. I cite two issues here.

First, in a *Washington Post* article titled "Triumphal March Silences Scoffers," published two days after the march, Marquis Childs said that it was difficult to know what—if anything—the great march and the events of the day would mean for President Kennedy's civil rights legislation.[54] Somewhere in the minds of the planners of the march was surely the *hope* that the march would influence lawmakers to stop playing political football with civil rights and pass a bill that had real substance. As the elder statesman who had threatened a March on Washington twenty years previous, this was most important to A. Philip Randolph who was concerned about employment discrimination against blacks and the absence of civil rights. It was a real disappointment that in the immediate aftermath of the march, and for months and months thereafter, little progress was made toward passage of the civil rights bill that Kennedy sent to Congress. Only after the President was assassinated did the executive branch push through the Civil Rights Bill in 1964.

Not long after the March, Bayard Rustin reportedly said that Malcolm x told him: "You know, this dream of King's is going to be a nightmare before it's over."[55] What a fortuitous comment! Indeed, looking back, Martin Luther King declared that, "not long after talking about that dream I started seeing it turn into a nightmare,"[56] manifesting itself in various ways, not least through some horrific acts of racist violence. King did not mean to imply that blacks and the nation were not already living in the nightmare, as Walter Brueggemann rightly put it.[57] King meant that the dream he shared with the nation was stained by unprecedented acts of violence and a failure of that dream to have a substantive impact upon the impending civil rights bill and the struggle for civil rights and freedom. In any event, the violent backlash is the second major issue in the aftermath of the March and the Dream speech. Barely two weeks after the Dream speech was delivered, a powerful bomb detonated at the end of the Sunday school hour at the Sixteenth Street Baptist Church in Birmingham, Alabama on September 15. Just weeks before, that church was a key rallying point for adults and thousands of black children who faced Bull Connor's police attack dogs and high-powered fire hoses. A number of people were injured in the bombing. Four girl children: Addie Mae Collins, Carol Denise McNair, Cynthia Diane Wesley, and Carole Robertson (names that we do not recite nearly enough) were killed as they were leaving Sunday school and preparing to attend worship service. They were eulogized by King as "the martyred heroines of a holy crusade for freedom and human dignity."[58] Two other black children were killed that day, one by white racists as he was riding his bicycle and the other by the police.

Indeed, having faced vicious racists in Montgomery, Albany, and most recently, in Birmingham; having seen the brutal violence to which student sit-in activists and Freedom Riders were subjected, Martin Luther King was possibly surprised only by the enormity of the violent racist backlash against the March on Washington, as evidenced by the dynamite murders of Carol Denise McNair, Carole Robertson, Addie Mae Collins, Cynthia Wesley, and the murders of two young black males. King was not surprised that there would be a violent backlash. He had no idea, however, that racists (who most likely considered themselves to be good upstanding born again Christians) would bomb a church just before the worship hour on a Sunday morning. There had been numerous bombings of churches and other establishments in black communities throughout the Deep South, and no place more so than Birmingham, which had earned the nickname: "Bombingham," so frequently were residences in the black community dynamited.

Birmingham's WENN black deejay "Tall" Paul White was one of those who was questioned at length by the FBI regarding what he might have seen from the radio station, located near the Sixteenth Street Baptist Church, prior to the bombing. White reported that in the early morning hours of the day of the bombing, he had seen "a suspicious-looking blue and white car containing several white men in the vicinity of the church."[59] He also reported that he believed he saw the same car on several earlier occasions, cruising near the church. "On one such occasion he had even jotted down the license number and given it to Ernest Gibson, the manager of the Gaston Motel, who passed it on to the FBI."[60] The latter did nothing with this information, until five weeks after the bombing, when White and Gibson again reported seeing the same car cruising near what remained of the church.

Although the FBI knew that Klansman Robert Edward Chambliss (aka "Dynamite Bob") was responsible for the bombing of the Sixteenth Street Baptist Church, they never presented the Justice Department with evidence to prosecute the case. They even claimed that "they had lost all of their records, and most of the physical evidence that [they] collected at the scene that day was nowhere to be found."[61] Because of the cooperation of White and Gibson, Chambliss was eventually prosecuted and convicted of first-degree murder by the state of Alabama on November 18, 1977, which brings to mind the words of the nineteenth-century Unitarian preacher-abolitionist Theodore Parker—who King frequently quoted: "The arc of the moral universe is long, but it bends toward justice."[62] I may not live to see it. You may not live to see it. But in a universe that hinges on a moral foundation, as King liked to say, *justice will have the last word.*

Then there was the matter of the Freedom Summer Project in the Mississippi Delta in 1964, involving more than 600 mostly white college student volunteers primarily from the north, but also from the south. Much of their intensive one-week training in nonviolence took place on the campus of Western College for Women in Oxford, Ohio in June. When CORE workers Michael Schwerner (from Brooklyn) and James Chaney (a lifetime resident of Meridian, Mississippi), and CORE volunteer Andrew Goodman (a college volunteer from Queens College in New York City) left on June 21 to investigate a church bombing in Neshoba County near Philadelphia, Mississippi, they disappeared. Immediately, veteran SNCC and CORE activists feared the worst, for they knew that if you disappear in Mississippi, you're dead. Such was the fate of the two Jewish activists Schwerner and Goodman, and the black, Chaney. The bodies of the three civil rights activists were found buried in an earthen dam on a farm near Philadelphia, Mississippi, on August 4. All three had been shot, and Chaney had clearly been subjected to indescribable torture, as evidenced by the multiple broken *and* crushed bones throughout his body. As true to form in that part of the country, in those days, arrests were made in connection with the murders, including the sheriff and two of his deputies, but the charges were subsequently dropped. However, seven of the men were later convicted of violating federal civil rights laws and sentenced to periods ranging from a measly three to ten years. On June 12, 2005, Edgar Ray Killen (known as the "preacher"), long suspected to be the one who orchestrated the murders, was put on trial for the reduced charge of manslaughter. He was convicted and incarcerated, where he remains.[63]

A third indicator to King that the dream had turned into a nightmare was the escalation of the war in Vietnam. This would continue into the Johnson administration, proliferating to crisis proportion from the mid–1960s onward. A fourth indicator was the fact that the dream speech had no immediate positive effect on the swelling unemployment and underemployment rates among blacks and the poor. The numbers continued to go up.

King pointed to a fifth indicator that the dream had become a nightmare. He had not yet begun to make the connection between the Vietnam War and massive poverty in the United

States, but he was very much aware of deepening, entrenched poverty among people of all races. This too was a nightmare, and a contradiction of the dream.

Yet another sign that the dream had turned into a nightmare was the assassination of President Kennedy three months after the March. It was further indication of the depth of hatred and violence in this country. King was deeply affected by the President's assassination, and told his wife that because of the mean, violent spirit in the country, his too would likely be a violent end.[64]

The Dream speech had no immediate positive impact on the impending civil rights legislation. If anything, the opposition in Congress and much of the country stiffened. This, and King's sense that the dream had turned into a nightmare, are but two of the problems associated with the aftermath of the dream speech. The March and the speech itself aroused unprecedented excitement among people who were demonstrating for jobs and civil rights, but this led to no positive, constructive change; did not result in a viable action plan to achieve the goals that King articulated in his speech. Ivanhoe Donaldson, a student at Michigan State University and a SNCC activist captured this sentiment when he said: "I think that a lot of people felt, because of the drama [surrounding the march and the speeches] and the vast greatness of it all, that somehow we had turned the mystical corner, that a new era of humanity and social consciousness and social justice was now on the table. That didn't happen."[65] Nothing in the form of a policy change and practice occurred as a result of the March and the dream speech. Similarly, theologian and pastor, Reinhold Niebuhr, applauded the march and the Dream speech, but declared that they would not likely have any meaningful, positive impact on hardcore racists and the powers that be at any level of government. He did seem to think, however, that the event and speech would have some influence in the nation generally.[66] Generally, people, especially the very powerful, wealthy, and privileged are not good enough that their behavior will be positively altered by a great mass march and a great speech. This pertains even more so to groups. This is why, upon leaving Washington, King was more determined than ever to apply sustained organized nonviolent direct action resistance to the ongoing struggle for freedom and civil rights.

Martin Luther King was surely hopeful that the great march and the events of the day would at least arouse the conscience of the nation and show the President and the Congress the true face of poverty, of people who were unemployed (due to no fault of their own), and who were also determined to have a better life in the United States of America. Surely if the politicians saw the massive numbers of people at the foot of the Lincoln Memorial who had come from all over the nation to show a force of unity and determination in the struggle for jobs and civil rights, this might spur some politicians to at least see the problem in a new light. To his credit, Martin Luther King was too much of a realist to expect much more than this. He remained convinced that only the pressure from mass nonviolent direct action campaigns in the streets would force politicians into liberating action.

Celebrating the Dream?

Years ago, I began paying attention to how individuals and organizations celebrate the anniversary of the March on Washington, and later, Martin Luther King, Jr. Day. I became convinced that most people are virtually ignorant about who Martin Luther King was, and what he sought to do. I was also convinced that most of those who either hosted or attended such celebrations were not in the least committed to the achievement of the ideals espoused in King's famous speech. I have seen too many times—even in theological schools, where one would least expect to see—leaders who essentially misuse or misappropriate the language and ideas of King to support their own selfish projects that effectively undermine the dignity of the laborers in their institutions. They even host programs that intend, ostensibly, to honor King and his contributions, but in their daily operations it is not unusual to see injustice at work. In any case, celebrations pertaining to the great March and King Day were (indeed are!) generally limited to poor, uninformed speeches (often given by celebrities or big name preachers or politicians); the linking of hands and singing "We Shall Overcome"; and listening to "I Have a Dream." I concluded that it is as if King gave only one speech during his entire thirteen-year civil rights ministry; as if he is frozen at the dais on the Lincoln Memorial, if not on the steps. It is as if the Dream speech was the pinnacle or climax of King's ministry, and after its delivery there was nothing more that he did, or that needed to be done. So people left King frozen right there at the Lincoln Memorial, as they strolled off to celebrate that day and that speech, as if that was the totality of the contributions and legacy of the Dreamer who was also the King of love.

Because of this *convenient* tendency of people to freeze Martin Luther King on the steps of the Lincoln Memorial, there was a long period of time when I refused to listen to the "I Have a Dream" speech, especially on King Day, and on the anniversary of the March on Washington. I knew that for King, the March on Washington was little more than a beginning; that it was only the prelude to the massive amount of work still needing to be done. I have known for a long time that there are less popular, but inestimably great speeches and addresses that King gave *after* the famous Dream speech. While that speech had prophetic elements in it (not least the words of the prophet Amos to, "Let justice roll down like waters, and righteousness like a mighty stream"), it was an essentially palatable speech, easy on the ears and minds of those listening on August 28, 1963. The Dream speech sought to unify a nation, and thus was more pacific than many of King's post–Dream speeches, when it had become clear that the dream had degenerated into a nightmare.

Arguably, the most provocative, prophetic public speech that Martin Luther King gave in the post–Dream speech years was his address at Riverside Church in New York City, precisely one year to the day before he was assassinated. A speech that was enthusiastically applauded by most of those in attendance, such as Union Theological Seminary president John C. Bennett, and King's good friend Rabbi Abraham J. Heschel of the Jewish Theological Seminary, King was lambasted by many people around the country, including the White House, the State Department, Congress, as well as major civil rights organizations such as the NAACP and the National Urban League. He was even roundly criticized by some of those affiliated with his own organization, the SCLC. This is all the more interesting considering that among whites it was primarily the most diehard racists who criticized the Dream speech, while white moderates, liberals, and even some blacks criticized the Riverside speech.

Those who freeze Martin Luther King on the steps of the Lincoln Memorial know little or nothing about the King whose moral outlook focused on problems of racism, economic injustice, and war. When he began his civil rights ministry in Montgomery his primary focus was on racism. But King had already determined, even before he entered Crozer Theological Seminary in the fall of 1948, and even before he was introduced to the social gospel writings of Walter Rauschenbusch, that there was in fact a trilogy of social problems to which his ensuing ministry must address. Racism was one of these. Economic deprivation and war (with their related problems) were the others. From the beginning, all three of these social problems were on King's mind and he frequently referenced them, both during and after the Montgomery bus boycott. Economic injustice gained increasing attention from King from the Birmingham campaign in 1963 through the Chicago campaign of 1966, to the planning of the Poor People's campaign in late 1967. In addition, as early as 1956 King made it unequivocally clear, that he wanted nothing to do with the war business. By 1965 he began explicitly speaking out against the war in Vietnam. He became silent when he was subjected to brutal criticism from the powers. In the Riverside address he broke silence on Vietnam once and for all.

By all accounts, the Dream speech was an almost unmatchable piece of oratory, and even more than the Birmingham campaign, it gave King national and international standing in the fight for justice and civil rights. But as we have seen, the oratory had no substantive effect on the lives of his people, the privileged, or the powers that be. With the escalation of the war in Vietnam, and King's recognition of its adverse effects on the condition of the poor, he felt compelled to speak against the war even if it meant that he would have to endure the vitriol of most segments of society. Unlike most ministers of his day and now, Martin Luther King figured out early that ministry is not about being popular. Or, as I like to tell my students: "Ministry ain't no popularity contest, and anybody interested in it as such, don't have the slightest clue what Christian ministry is about." Based on sermons I have heard, and ministries I have observed, I would say that this includes a substantial number of ministers and would-be ministers even today.

Conclusion

I submit that the most relevant Martin Luther King for us today is not the King of "I Have a Dream" fame who, from all indication, remains frozen on the steps of the Lincoln Memorial. This is the King of those on the religious and secular right who, more than most, misuse and misappropriate King's dream, a point that is thoroughly scrutinized in the collection edited by me and Lewis V. Baldwin, *The Domestication of Martin Luther King, Jr.* (2013). Conservative right wing people conveniently believe that King's reference in the Dream speech to his children being judged by the content of their character had nothing to do with his equally strong contention that deeply entrenched racism is the reason that blacks generally are judged by white America only on the basis of their black skin. In reality, King's dream was that white people would root out their own individual racism, as well as institutional racism, so that the King children and every other child would not be judged by the color of their skin, but by the content of their character. King knew that until white people address their own and the racism of the structures from which they benefit mightily, any talk about judging blacks by the content of their character—of which we hear so much from those on the religious and secular right—is little more than a smoke screen to conceal white racism. As long as blacks are victims of racism and economic deprivation—which they did not do to themselves, but had it done to them—it is unreasonable for even otherwise well-meaning white people to talk of blacks being judged by the content of their character, as if we already live in a racism-free society. Let's be clear. It is important that people be judged by the content of their character. It is just as important that the racial field of play be level, a point that King stressed right up to the end.

The Martin Luther King spirit that is most relevant for us today is not that of the King who told America about a dream that he had had, or even the King who so often sang, "We Shall Overcome." The King spirit needed today is that which declares: "Enough of dreaming! I told you about my dream fifty years ago. It's time to stop dreaming—*if* that is all you intend to do—and start *doing* and *sacrificing* in order to actualize that dream before the light of your life goes out." The King spirit that is most relevant to us today is that which holds out the faith that King himself expressed in 1967 when he declared that, "we will be able to sing in some not too distant tomorrow, with a cosmic past tense: 'We *have* overcome! We *have* overcome!' Deep in my heart, I *did* believe we would overcome."[67]

11

Contributions of Children
and Young People[1]

Addressing students, faculty, and administrators at Manchester College in Indiana on February 1, 1968 (barely two months before he was assassinated), King made it clear that despite the difficulties and frustrations he and the movement encountered, the one thing that lifted his spirit and gave him a new sense of hope was any opportunity he had to engage and talk with students. He believed that students, regardless of race and ethnicity, brought something to the table that adults did not. They were not only courageous, but were not afraid to see with new eyes and to imagine a fundamentally different social order. Moreover, unlike their parents, King said, white university students often declared that they were finished with both racism and militarism.[2] One can only hope that King would be as optimistic about the present generation of college, university, and seminary students across the nation were he alive today, although the evidence is not strong that he would be.

Although we do not often read or hear it said, Martin Luther King loved, adored, and respected children and young people, both because he saw them as persons, and because he realized that they have a stake in how things are done in this nation and the world. Indeed, King envisioned a world in which children and young people would have all of the things that are necessary for a life that is truly worth living, such as the best formal education, the best healthcare, decent and relatively safe housing and neighborhoods to live in, etc. Children and young people, he believed, could make constructive contributions toward achieving freedom and liberation, and that strategically there could even be times when they can energize campaigns for freedom and democracy.

After this brief introduction to Martin Luther King, I now focus on a topic that has received far too little attention in King Studies to this point, namely the role of children and young people in the civil rights movement, the mutual influence between them and King, and the legacy they left for us.[3] In this chapter I discuss—all too briefly—some of the contributions of children and young people in King's civil rights ministry as he sought to establish what he called the beloved community—a community in which *every* person will be treated like a being of infinite, inviolable worth. In virtually every campaign for freedom, from Montgomery, Alabama, to Memphis, Tennessee, young people were involved. In some instances, e.g., the Montgomery bus boycott, their participation was not formally planned by the Montgomery Improvement Association (MIA), the organization providing leadership for the boycott. In other instances, e.g., the Children's Campaign in Birmingham, Alabama, children and young people actually led the way, though they were organized and supervised by SCLC. Then there were instances, such as the sit-in movement in 1960, and the Freedom Rides in 1961, when young people acted on their own, thus leading the charge for freedom and civil rights. Regarding the latter, it was not a case of the adults taking the children by the hand and leading them into the struggle. Rather, it was the children who led the adults and the nation in those nonviolent direct action campaigns for freedom and human dignity.

About Martin Luther King, Jr.

On the third Monday of January 1986, Martin Luther King, Jr., Day was first celebrated as a federal holiday. It was the least that the nation could do to honor the quintessential civil rights leader of the twentieth century. A self-declared "drum major" for peace, justice, and righteousness, Martin Luther King, at age thirty-nine, was assassinated as he stood on the balcony outside his room at the Lorraine Motel in Memphis, Tennessee, in the early evening of April 4, 1968.

Martin Luther King was a man of ideas and ideals, civil and human rights warrior, author, orator, father of Yolanda, Martin III, Dexter, and Bernice, husband of Coretta Scott King, *Time* magazine's "Man of the Year," recipient of numerous honorary degrees and other awards from around the world, recipient of the Nobel Prize for peace in December 1964, and much more. By his own admission, however, he was first and foremost a minister of the gospel of Jesus Christ, and he never grew weary of reminding people of this all-important point. In fact, King unashamedly declared that long before he received awards and accolades from around the nation and the world he was an ordained preacher of the Christian faith. He took his ministerial calling to mean that he was charged with the responsibility of declaring and fighting for the left outs and those forced into the margins. He understood that his call to ministry meant that he was to be the voice of the voiceless, and those forced to live in the gutters of this society and the world, and whose dignity as human beings was routinely and systematically undermined. "I was a clergyman before I was a civil rights leader," he said in a "Face to Face" television interview in 1967, "and when I was ordained to the Christian ministry, I accepted that as a commission to constantly and forever bring the ethical insights of our Judeo-Christian heritage to bear on the social evils of our day."[4] This declaration placed King squarely in the best of the social gospel tradition in black and white. In this, he understood Christianity and ethics to be integrally connected and not to be separated one from the other. King held that one could not be genuinely Christian without also understanding that Christianity requires that she live in ways that honor and respect the dignity or sacredness of every human being, which means that such a one must also be a champion of justice since the God of the Jewish and Christian faiths requires that justice and righteousness be done. This, King maintained, says something about the utter seriousness of being a Christian.[5] Consequently, Christians must decide whether to obey God or the powers.[6] The racist who is converted to the Christian faith cannot persist in being a racist, and persist in participating in racist behavior of any kind. Instead, such a one is required to work diligently to extricate herself from racism. Martin Luther King was absolutely clear that one could not continue to be a racist and Christian at the same time, for example.[7] Anyone who thinks to the contrary has, at best, a poor understanding of the Christian faith.

Although he was honest enough to confess that everybody likes to be praised even when they don't deserve it, and even when they know they don't deserve it,[8] Martin Luther King had no real interest in all of the honors and awards that came his way; no interest in professional politics or lucrative careers in business and other professions. This is accented by the fact that money from his speaking engagements and publications went to the Movement, rather than in his pockets. He was one of those rare individuals who believed he was *called* by God to his task, and unlike many, he understood what that required of him. Sometimes it would mean having to stand alone when an unpopular decision had to be made, such as the decision to take the movement north to Chicago, to publicly criticize the war in Vietnam,[9] or to undertake the Poor People's Campaign (which he did not live to lead). He also understood that being called by God meant that he must be willing to pay the ultimate price as he sought to be faithful, not so much to human beings, but to the One who called and sustained him. For by being faithful to God he could not be unfaithful to those to whom justice was being denied. Conversely, by being faithful to those whose humanity and dignity were being crushed, he was also being faithful to the One who called him to ministry.

All of this is to say that Martin Luther King was fundamentally a Christian minister, and he was most proud of this fact. Indeed, in the waning months of his life he declared: "This was my first calling, and it still remains my greatest commitment."[10] He went on to say, "all that I do in civil rights I do because I consider it a part of my ministry. I have no other ambitions in life but to achieve *excellence in the Christian ministry*. I don't plan to run for any political office. I don't plan to do anything but remain a preacher."[11] Having felt the urge to consider ministry while in high school, King was finally able to accept the call to ministry in his senior year at Morehouse College.

Martin Luther King was, pure and simple, a man of ideas. This is my way of acknowledging that he was a theologian in the best sense, albeit not a formal academic theologian who wrote, read, and published abstruse and abstract papers in the theological academy. Referring to King as a man of ideas is also a way of acknowledging that he was an excellent thinker who not only loved ideas from the time he was a boy, but more than most women and men of ideas, his deepest desire was to make ideas relevant to eradicating social problems and establishing justice. Indeed, from the time he entered seminary in 1948, he expressed a desire to address a trilogy of social problems throughout his ministry: racism, economic exploitation, and war. Unlike most long time ministers who fail to make the discovery, King knew even before his formal theological education began that these and related social evils were inconsistent with God's will for human beings and the world. It was therefore the responsibility of the Christian minister to consistently and forthrightly preach, teach, and stand against injustice of all types. This effectively meant that such a one is morally obligated to resist social evils with all her might.

I have consistently argued in my work on King that had he lived into the 1970s he would have been so influenced and moved by the emerging women's movement of that period that his basic philosophical and ethical stance about the absolute dignity of persons as such would have logically and morally led him to be a staunch supporter, advocate, and activist for women's rights. I also believe that King would have been a strong advocate for the Lesbian Gay Bi-Sexual and Trans-Gendered Movement for equal rights. Let's be clear. I concede that we cannot know any of this with absolute certainty since King is no longer living,[12] and he had not turned the corner on this matter before he was assassinated. However, I base my strong belief on the fact that King was a personalist theologian, and thus emphasized the sacredness of persons because each is imbued with the image of God, and is of infinite value to God. In addition, throughout his civil rights ministry, there is clear and solid evidence that King's moral trajectory and thought processes was constantly expanding, which meant that he was both willing and felt compelled to include more and more of those people who had previously been left out, e.g., women and gay, lesbian, bi-sexual, and transgendered people. Based on the trajectory of his growth in both thought and practice, it seems reasonable to posit that one can make a good case for what King's stance most likely would be regarding such matters were he alive today.

Although King knew in seminary that his ministry would focus on racism, economic exploitation, and war, he began his work in Montgomery by focusing on racism. The early emphasis was on racism did not mean that he was not concerned about the other two issues. The immediate context in Montgomery required the focus and attention given to racism. But even then, King saw the economic implications of the segregation ordinance in the state of Alabama and what its eradication could mean for employment possibilities for blacks. The segregation ordinance meant, for example, that blacks were not hired as bus drivers, or as policemen. King early saw the connection between racism and economic deprivation, but circumstances in Montgomery in late December of 1955 required that the issue of racism be addressed first. However, it was not long before the movement was addressing the issue of economic injustice in the Albany, Georgia and Birmingham, Alabama campaigns in 1961 and 1963, respectively. By 1965, King and others in the movement were already speaking out publicly against the war in Vietnam. Not long thereafter, the issue of poverty was a major related concern. There was a clear expansion of King's moral sphere from Montgomery to Memphis. Because of the kind of person he was and the way his moral trajectory was expanding, it seems reasonable to surmise that had King lived he would have championed women's rights, as well as gay rights; would have seen both as justice issues.

I have seen no evidence—but would be happy to entertain it if it existed—to suggest that the expansion of King's moral field would not have continued had he lived longer. In addition, there is the Coretta Scott King factor that must be considered. King fed off his wife as she did him. Mrs. King actually joined her voice of protest with the Peace Movement before her husband. She strongly encouraged him to join this effort. In addition, she was later a strong supporter of women's rights, and then a staunch advocate for the LGBT Movement for equal rights. I simply cannot imagine that as personalist theologian and man of ideas King would not have been influenced by his wife to advocate for the rights of women as well as Lesbian Gay Bi-Sexual and Trans-Gendered people. This means, of course, that he would have been supportive of the stance of his sons and late wife and daughter, and against his youngest daughter, Bernice, who was appointed president of the SCLC in Atlanta in 2009, and was a staunch activist against the LGBT movement.

One of Martin Luther King's basic theological convictions is that the universe is fused throughout with value, and thus hinges on a moral foundation.[13] In addition, King was certain that reality is communal or relational and that human beings and the world are interdependent, such that whatever happens to one affects all others, directly or indirectly. The destiny of each is inextricably linked with that of the other. This is what it means to say that reality is relational, and that human beings are social or they are nothing. These are both metaphysical claims, i.e., statements about the nature of reality itself. They are meant to convey the idea that what is most fundamental about human beings is not our individuality, important as that is. What is even more fundamental is our *individual-communal* nature. We are created as individuals— yes—but more fundamentally, we are created as individuals-in-community, *for* community. Therefore, human beings function best, not in isolation or as individuals, but in relationship. One is most fully human or personal in community, which leads to King's basic insight that: "Whatever affects one directly, affects all indirectly. We are made to live together because of the interrelated structure of reality."[14] What King's principle implies, but does not expressly say, is that whatever affects human beings also affects—on some level—the One who is their source and sustainer.

The quintessential man of ideas and of social activism, Martin Luther King believed wholeheartedly in the absolute dignity of every person. This explains his insistence that everything humanly possible should be done to honor and respect life in general, and human life in particular. As we saw earlier, he was most especially concerned about the plight of those who were among the historically, and systematically left outs; those he often referred to as "the least of these."

King, Young People and Self-Determination

I have long been fascinated with the idea of what children and young could contribute toward the struggle for justice. Moreover, in light of a particularly tragic phenomenon that has plagued urban centers, many middle class suburbs, and even some rural areas of this country at least since the 1980s, I have often wondered about the relevance of the legacy of Martin Luther King for black youths. What has this legacy to say about the phenomenon to which I refer, namely, black-against-black violence and homicide among young black males between 15–25 years of age? In 1985 the Centers for Disease Control declared that the leading cause of death among young black males in this category is not diabetes or heart disease, but homicide. Little has happened in ensuing years to cause a significant drop in the numbers. Indeed, in places like the Southside of Chicago, the numbers have risen to epidemic proportion.

When I think of the contributions of King and black youths from the mid–1950s through the 1960s, I can see the possibilities for young people today, despite the exorbitantly high incidence of black-on-black violence and homicide. I realize that there are underlying systemic problems, not least racism, economic injustice, poverty, and militarism, that contribute greatly to the cause of the tragic phenomenon of intra-community violence and homicide among young black males. I am also aware of the difficulty involved in trying to eradicate this tragedy. But I have long wondered about the role of individual self-determination and moral agency in addressing this problem. That is, I have pondered what individuals can do, in spite of the structural causes of the problem that support this tragic phenomenon, and the need to address the systemic causes as well.

What can individual residents do in a neighborhood being torn apart by intra-community violence and homicide? For at the end of the day, it is absolutely necessary to address the structural issues involved, e.g., substandard housing and education, poor to non-existent health care, no job training, no living wage jobs, a racist and classist police force and judicial system, etc. And yet, it is just as necessary to address the role that individuals can play in efforts to resolve this problem. For the systemic problems cannot be addressed and solved without individuals, and individuals will not be around long enough to challenge the structural problems if *decided* steps are not taken by them to put an end to a tragedy such as that under discussion. Do individual members of communities have a role to play in stemming the tide of violence in the face of systemic changes that occur at a snail's pace, if at all?

Generally, when the subject of self-determination arises among black Americans in such conversations there are loud cries of "foul play," and the charge that the victim is being blamed. It is neither my intention nor my desire to blame the victim. As a theological social ethicist trained in the tradition of personalist social ethicists such as Walter G. Muelder and Martin Luther King, I understand that social problems will more likely be adequately addressed and solved when strategies focus on both systemic causes as well as choices made by individuals. Moreover, it is important to remember that Martin Luther King criticized not only the unjust structures of this society and called for a *revolution of values*, but he was also very careful to criticize the lack of self-determination on the part of many oppressed people, including his own.

For example, King was critical of any tendency of blacks to shirk their duty to be responsible citizens in black communities and throughout the nation. Even though they were victimized by systemic problems, King saw this as no excuse for not doing all in one's power to decide and act against such things as crime, including the practice of too often inflicting violence and homicide on each other.[15] In this regard he said: "We must not let the fact that we are the victims of injustice lull us into abrogating responsibility for our own lives."[16] Acknowledging that systemic "external factors" such as racial discrimination and economic injustice make life miserable for blacks, and insisting that these must be eradicated, King nevertheless demanded that blacks "must work within the community to solve the problem while the external cause factors are being removed."[17] He recognized that the battle was on both fronts—the point of individual decision as well as the structural causes of the problem. He was adamant that blacks had to work simultaneously and relentlessly on two fronts. "On the one hand," he said, "we must work to remove this system which is the causal basis for our ills.... But we have another job. And that is to work to improve these standards that have been pushed back because of the system of segregation."[18] As a moral agent, each individual is responsible for doing his part to make low-income black communities decent and civilized places to live. King would not let either individuals or unjust social systems and their chief benefactors off the moral hook, nor should we.

For Martin Luther King, young people, like adults, are self-determining, autonomous beings, capable of choosing or deciding for themselves how to respond to the injustice and racism that they experienced everyday right along with their parents and other black adults. Even during the Montgomery bus boycott—his first major civil rights campaign—King sensed that children and young people understood that their freedom was being denied solely because of their race. It was therefore reasonable to him that they should be allowed to participate in demonstrations to attain their civil rights and freedom although the SCLC's first organized effort to allow such participation would not occur until the Birmingham campaign in 1963.

What roles did the children and young people play during the movement years, and what are some implications for youths today?[19] For our purpose, I want to focus briefly on student activists' contributions to the sit-in movement in early 1960, the Freedom Rides in the summer of 1961, and the Birmingham campaign of 1963. In each case, we will meet young people— black and white—who were self-determined and committed to making their society better than it was. They were willing to sacrifice everything, including potential careers and their lives, toward this end. They made the all-important individual decision to resist injustices and to press for the establishment of justice and equality for all.

They Sat Down for Freedom

Martin Luther King and SCLC were essentially between civil rights campaigns when the decade of the 1960s began. This is not to say that King and his organization were not busy trying to determine next steps. At the same time, he was still honing his theoretical knowledge of the Gandhian type of nonviolence and how best to apply it in the Deep South context amid some of the most brutal racial assaults in the nation. During this period, however, King had no way of knowing about the wildfire that was about to erupt in early February 1960. By the time the fire erupted and he found out about it, it was already sweeping across college campuses, including some white ones, and he knew that he and other adult civil rights leaders could at best play the role of supporting cast.

In Greensboro, North Carolina, four black college freshmen at North Carolina A & T College, Joseph McNeil, Franklin McCain, Ezell Blair, Jr. (now Jibreel Khazan), and David Richmond had been discussing among themselves and with a white clothing store owner, Ralph Johns, what to do about the segregated lunch counters at white department stores such as the local Woolworth. Frequently meeting in the back of Johns' store, the owner encouraged them to take some kind of direct action against the segregated lunch counters. Johns, who had been in business for a long time, had also encouraged various groups of A & T students—over several years—to take such action.[20] On February 1, 1960 McNeil, McCain, Blair, and Richmond went to the local Woolworth store, purchased a few items, took seats at the lunch counter, and ordered food. When told by the waitress that they could not be served, they decided not to leave until they were. When closing time came they decided to leave, but with the intention of returning the following day, and each day thereafter, until served. As soon as word got out about the sit-in, other students from A & T, as well as white women students from a local college, joined them. It didn't take long for the number of students sitting-in to grow very large, ultimately causing management to close down the lunch counter. Nor did it take long for the sit-in idea to catch on among other black and well-meaning white students on college campuses across the South, and in some places in the North. The phenomenon grew like wildfire. "By the end of the month, sit-ins had taken place at more than 30 locations in 7 states, and by the end of April over 50,000 students had participated."[21] Reportedly, by the end of 1960 approximately 70,000 students had either sat-in or participated in marches in support of the sit-in campaign.[22] The students themselves understood that they were essentially sitting-in in order to be able to stand up for their dignity and freedom, as well as that of others who would come after them. In a sense, then, they sat down and refused to move (much like Rosa Parks did on that bus in Montgomery), in order to be able to stand up with dignity.

Unknown to the four initiators of the sit-in movement, James Lawson, then a student at Vanderbilt University Divinity School in Nashville, was training and holding workshops in Gandhian nonviolence for student activists who would themselves become key players in the movement. These included Diane Nash, John Lewis, Marion Barry, and others. Part of their training involved direct action demonstrations in downtown Nashville. Unaware of discussions and plans being made by their Greensboro brothers, the Nashville students had already planned to begin sit-in demonstrations in the early days of 1960. As it turned out, the Greensboro students actually started the movement, thus causing the wave of sit-ins across the South primarily, but also in the North.

The Nashville student activists had the advantage of being thoroughly trained in the theory and techniques of Gandhian nonviolence. All of the students had the advantage of being able to engage in direct action campaigns without the supervision of adults. The students did in fact reach out to adult leaders for consultation, although they were not asking for adult leadership as such. What they needed and wanted more than anything was advice and resources. It became clear that they did not want to be led by or answer to adults when student representatives from across the country met at Shaw University during Easter weekend of 1960. Ella Josephine Baker, then executive director of SCLC played a leading role in organizing the Shaw meeting, and strongly encouraged the students—much to the chagrin of King, but more especially some SCLC board members, e.g., Wyatt Walker—to remain autonomous if some kind of organization came out of the meeting.

Having been invited by the students to deliver a keynote address, King had in fact recommended in his speech the need for some type of organization, although he believed the better part of wisdom was that they be under the supervision of SCLC. The students followed only a part of his advice. They formed the Temporary Student Nonviolent Coordinating Committee, later dropping "Temporary" from the name. The organization would be completely autonomous and the members would answer to its own leaders, not those of SCLC and other traditional civil rights organizations. King also suggested that the students should take the struggle for civil rights into every Deep South community. In this regard, they followed King's advice more closely. In many of the toughest, most dangerous southern communities where blacks were denied civil rights and the right to vote, it was the student activists in SNCC who were the first to courageously go into those areas to do the difficult and dangerous groundbreaking work to prepare rural black residents (in many cases) to be organized and to participate in voter registration campaigns. Not only were they frequently the first to go in, they were generally among the last to leave the communities in which they engaged in direct action and voter registration-education projects.

The lives of many of these student activists were not only threatened by the Klan, White Citizens Councils, and other local white hate groups, many were also beaten severely, and some were even killed. In addition, they saw local black residents who were brave enough to join the struggle, beaten and killed as well. The student activists paid dues that no young people should have to pay for that which is actually God-given. Quite legitimately, the students often complained that after they had done such dangerous and painful groundbreaking work, SCLC would come in and—intended or not—get all of the media exposure and the lion's share of any financial resources that might be made available through various channels. It is not clear that this was intentionally done by King and SCLC, but it is the way it worked out in some instances, beginning with the Albany, Georgia campaign in 1961.

To his credit, Martin Luther King did everything in his power to avoid upstaging the student activists. Not only did he deliver the keynote address at what turned out to be the founding meeting of SNCC, he did everything he could to support the sit-ins, voter registration-education projects, and other student-led direct action campaigns. He praised the students for their courage and determination and for their many contributions. He defended the sit-ins and freedom rides to white liberals in the interracial Fellowship of the Concerned, for as James M. Washington rightly asserted, King and SCLC knew that the criticisms of those direct action efforts of student activists actually came from the liberals in the group, who, not at all surprisingly, felt that they needed to slow up.[23]

Defending nonviolence even against some within the ranks of the civil rights movement, King used as an illustration the fact that it was modeled very well by student activists in the sit-ins. King told of the effects of the students' nonviolent sit-in protests at segregated lunch counters—how it affected their parents, causing them to get angry and close their charge accounts at such stores; how the demonstrations embarrassed city and state officials; how they frightened off many potential white shoppers; and how they eventually led to such an economic threat to local business interests that management was compelled to change their policy and practice. All of this and more, King declared, was a result of the nonviolent sit-in demonstrations of the students.[24]

King characterized the sit-ins and their effect on college campuses as "electrifying" and as shattering "the placid surface of campuses and communities across the South. Though confronted in many places by hoodlums, police guns, tear gas, arrests, and jail sentences, the students tenaciously continue to sit down and demand equal service at variety store lunch counters, and extend their protest from city to city."[25] What the students did in such cases was without question historic, King said. "Never before in the United States has so large a body of students spread a struggle over so great an area in pursuit of a goal of human dignity and freedom."[26] King knew that black youths were not merely acting willy-nilly. They had some sense that what they were doing was not unique to them; that they were not the first of their race to resist injustice by demonstrating for freedom. They knew enough about their nation's history to know that many of their enslaved foreparents resisted enslavement every way they could. They knew about what King called "the incomplete revolution of the Civil War."[27] They were aware of the struggles for freedom among people of color in Asia and Africa. Praising the youthful activists further, King said: "They are an integral part of the history which is reshaping the world, replacing a dying order with modern democracy. They are doing this in a nation whose own birth spread new principles and shattered a medieval social society then dominating most of the globe."[28] More than any other single international influence on the students' stride toward freedom and their impatience with the slowness of change in the United States, King held, was the part played by students in freedom struggles on the African continent.[29] Unlike the criticisms of white moderates and some liberals as well, student activists, King knew, were not interested in piecemeal and token changes. Instead, they were revolting against an entire unjust system. They were revolting against a system that historically left out, and otherwise crushed, people of color. The students were prepared, King said "to sit-in, kneel-in, wade-in and stand-in until every waiting room, rest room, theatre and other facility throughout the nation that is supposedly open to the public is in fact open to Negroes, Mexicans, Indians, Jews or what have you. And for this achievement they are prepared to pay the costs—whatever they are—in suffering and hardship as long as may be necessary."[30] There was no question in King's mind that the student movement and its many contributions would someday be deemed by historians to be among the most significant periods in American history.

It is important to observe that King himself participated in at least one sit-in. This was at Rich's Department Store in his hometown of Atlanta. This occurred in October of 1960 when student activists convinced King to join them in the sit-in. King and several hundred students were arrested. The students were later released, but King was detained under suspicion by authorities that his involvement in the sit-in was a violation of his probation. After relocating to Atlanta from Montgomery he was arrested for driving without a Georgia state license and sentenced to probation. King's probation was revoked when he was arrested during the sit-in at Rich's. He was sentenced to six month's hard labor at the Georgia State Prison at Reidsville, about 200 miles from Atlanta. King's release was procured as a result of an intervention on the part of presidential hopeful Senator John F. Kennedy and his brother and campaign manager, Robert F. Kennedy. The revocation of King's probation and his sentencing to hard labor in the state prison should be kept in mind when we come to the matter of King's refusal to join the Freedom Rides at the request of Diane Nash and other SNCC activists.

Young people did not only take the lead in the sit-ins. When it seemed that the Freedom Rides were going to be called off by the Congress of Racial Equality (CORE) after riders were brutally beaten and had their bus bombed just outside Anniston, Alabama, in the summer of 1961, young student activists again stepped up to the plate. In this case, it was Nashville student activist Diane Nash who insisted to CORE director James Farmer that it would be a dreadful and costly mistake to call off the rides because of the violence done by racist thugs. To call off the rides, Nash argued, would send the message that anybody who desired to put a stop to a civil rights campaign needed only to subject participants to violence. Her biggest fear was not over what could happen should the rides resume. Rather, her greatest fear was over what would happen should they not continue. Almost defiantly, Nash told New York Times reporter David Halberstam over the telephone: "We aren't going to stop, not now. Why, those people in Alabama think they can ignore the president of the United States, that they can still win by beating us Negroes over the head. They beat us, and we're stronger than ever."[31] Nash was convinced that there could only be "one outcome."[32] Nash and her youthful cohorts were adamant. "If the signal was given to the opposition that violence could stop us ... if we let the Freedom Ride stop then, whenever we tried to do anything in the Movement in the future, we were going to meet with a lot of violence. And we would probably have to get a number of people killed before we could reverse that message."[33] Trained in Gandhian nonviolence ideas and techniques, Nash argued that the rides must be allowed to continue, and that SNCC student activists were ready to replace CORE riders.

They Took a Ride for Freedom

The youthful activists had a good sense of what they were up against. After all, the last group of Freedom Riders had been brutally bludgeoned and one of their buses was bombed. This is precisely what caused Martin Luther King and other adult leaders such concern when the Nashville student activists insisted on continuing the rides. And yet, any who had been trained in Gandhian ideas and techniques had to agree with Nash and the students. Gandhi argued that it was better to be the recipient of violence than to retaliate violently against one's opponent. Nash interpreted this principle, saying: "The students have chosen non-violence as a technique; there is no reason why they couldn't have taken up guns. It was a responsible choice, I think. We have decided that if there is to be suffering in this revolution (which is really what the movement is—a revolution), we will take the suffering upon ourselves and never inflict it upon our fellow man, because we respect him and recognize the God within him."[34] In addition, the Nashville student activists trained under Lawson had bought into the idea that unmerited suffering is redemptive.

Among those who would continue the freedom ride from Montgomery to Jackson Mississippi, was SNCC activist Hank Thomas, who had been bludgeoned in Anniston. Unlike the Nashville student activists, Thomas was actually a student at Howard University, but somehow through the trials and tests with the former, became a lifelong friend with them. Many of the students who agreed to continue the ride wrote out their will and left it in a sealed envelope for their parents or other relatives in the event they did not return. They knew Mississippi's reputation regarding blacks; knew that it was a state known for its utter intimidation of blacks; known for lynching and otherwise brutally murdering blacks and dumping their bodies in rivers, such as what happened to young fourteen year old Emmett Till in 1955 when he left Chicago to visit his uncle, Mose Wright, in Money, Mississippi. In Mississippi, especially, blacks were the "strange fruit"(to use singer Billy Holiday's term) that could on any day or night be seen hanging from a tree with a rope around her or his neck. Blacks were frequently made to disappear in that state. For to disappear in Mississippi, black residents knew, and student activists soon found out, meant that one was dead. Blacks had no rights whatever that white people in the state of Mississippi was bound by law to respect. And yet, this was the state to which the SNCC student activists determined to continue a ride for freedom. This was the state that SNCC activists such as Bob Moses, and later Diane Nash Bevel, Jim Bevel and others, bravely went to organize blacks for voter registration in the Delta region and other places in the state. Of all the Deep South states there were activists, such as James Lawson, who believed that Mississippi had to be cracked if there was to be hope of a forward moving civil rights movement. David Halberstam said that Lawson believed that "they could not win in the South ... without coming to Mississippi, and they could not come to Mississippi without risking their lives."[35] The riders made it to Jackson, and all twenty-seven were arrested when they entered the segregated waiting room at the bus terminal. Unknown to the riders, Attorney General Robert Kennedy had made a deal with local and state officials that federal authorities would essentially turn a blind eye if the riders were allowed safe passage to the bus terminal in Jackson. The notorious white supremacist Dixiecrat Senator James Eastland, Chairman of the Senate Judiciary Committee, guaranteed the safety of the riders to the terminal. "During the Freedom Rides, Kennedy conferred with Eastland no fewer than thirty times."[36] Kennedy was less concerned about the safety of the riders, than the nation's image on the international scene. Thus he wanted to avoid at all costs another tragedy such as that which occurred outside Anniston. Escorted to the Mississippi state line by Alabama National Guardsmen, the Freedom Riders were met by Mississippi National Guardsmen and escorted safely to Jackson.[37] Upon arrival at the terminal, local officials promptly arrested the riders when they left the bus and entered the all-white waiting room.

Earlier, I intimated that King would be asked to join the Freedom Ride, but declined. Diane Nash and other SNCC activists believed his participation was crucial to gaining national media attention, and possibly federal intervention. King declined the invitation for security reasons. Furthermore, because he was on probation he did not feel that he could stand another arrest at that time. We saw earlier what could happen when he was found to be in violation of his probation after the arrest following the sit-in at Rich's Department Store in Atlanta. It should not be hard to understand why this would be fresh in King's mind, but even so the students concluded that his response was a cop-out. I am not so sure that this was in fact the case. Considering the experience after the Rich's department store sit-in, it seems reasonable that King would be concerned about violating his probation again. The students may have reasoned that some of them were on probation for their movement participation as well, and that violation would also place them in jeopardy of being arrested and sent to jail. And yet, they were willing to risk it by participating in the Freedom Rides. What the students were not seeing as clearly was that for the white authorities King was the big and most significant fish in the pond, which meant that whatever punishment might be meted out to them would be meted out to King fourfold or more, with every means of intimidation applied as well. When the judge revoked his probation after the sit-in at Rich's, and ordered him to six months hard labor at Reidville prison, guards were sent to his county jail cell in the middle of the night to transport him. He was shackled hands and feet and was not told where he was being taken or why. This was nothing but an intimidation tactic intended to frighten and throw King off balance. King himself later said that he believed that this was the end of him; that he would never see his wife and children again. Once he got to the prison, he was held incommunicado. Without question, any of the youthful activists who violated their probation would have been incarcerated for being in violation. However, it is hard to imagine that the authorities would have—in the case of the youthful activists—gone to such lengths as in King's case. It is equally hard to imagine that the authorities would be less brutal and intimidating should King violate his probation a second time.

Although there is the matter of the security issue, i.e., that it would have been easy for racist thugs to get at King were he on one of the Freedom buses, I don't see that fear was as big an issue for King as the SNCC activists seemed to think. For by the time of the Freedom Ride invitation, his life had already been threatened more times than he could remember or number. He surely had reason to believe that some of the threats were credible, and yet he continued civil rights work. Moreover, he knew and accepted the fact that one engaged in civil rights ministry in the Deep South could be physically brutalized and even killed on any given day. What King probably did not consider at the time that he declined the invitation to participate in the rides was that this would be the occasion for tension and division between he and student activists all the way to Memphis. Nevertheless, such dissension, conflict, and rifts between King and the youths did not cause him to be any less supportive of their contributions. Instead, King remained their number one cheerleader.

In a letter to the Rev. Kelly Miller Smith, King praised the Nashville students for being the best trained, best organized, and best disciplined of the student activists.[38] He referenced the "heroic southern students" who "have injected their very bodies into the non-violent struggle for freedom and have declared undying battle against Jim Crow."[39] He also praised black and white students for demanding an end to gradualism in the battle for freedom and civil rights.[40] Aware that white students joined with black students in the sit-ins and in many instances suffered worse name calling and physical violence than their black counterparts; aware that some white youths had suffered brutality on the Freedom Rides, e.g., Bob Zellner and James Zwerg, King spoke strongly of the importance of white student allies.[41] He told white students at Cornell University that the best way they could be supportive of the movement in the South was to do all they could to eradicate racism in the north.[42]

The SNCC student activists took King's recommendation seriously about taking their civil rights activity into all southern communities that their resources would allow. While they did their groundbreaking voter rights education-registration and organizing in Albany, Georgia, the Mississippi Delta, and elsewhere in the Deep South, King and SCLC were testing the legitimacy of nonviolence as more than a technique or strategy for social change. SCLC followed SNCC youths into Albany in 1961, but poor planning and a goal of addressing racism in general, led to what can only be described as a failed campaign. King was determined to learn from the mistakes in Albany. He was convinced that nonviolence was on trial and he essentially went looking for the next place to test it. Based on the strong urging of SCLC board member the Rev. Fred Shuttlesworth, a founding member of the Alabama Christian Movement for Human Rights (ACMHR) in Birmingham, the decision was made to draw up plans for a campaign there.[43] They gave it the name "Project C" ("for Birmingham's Confrontation with the fight for justice and morality in race relations"). This would also be the first time that black students would play prominent roles in King-SCLC led civil rights campaigns. Young people played significant roles during the Montgomery bus boycott, but there was not a planned strategy for utilizing them. Initially this was not the case in Birmingham either, but that all changed when the campaign stagnated early on. In Birmingham we see the use of thousands of black children and young people in what came to be known as the Children's Crusade.

The Children of Birmingham

In his famous "Letter from Birmingham Jail," Martin Luther King described Birmingham as the most thoroughly segregated city in America, a place unlike any other in the country.[44] He said that, "It was a community in which human rights had been trampled for so long that fear and oppression were as thick in its atmosphere as the smog from its factories."[45] King said that one found in Birmingham "the most powerful, the most experienced and the most implacable segregationists in the country."[46] The Birmingham campaign was launched on April 3, 1963, with students from the all-black Miles College staging sit-ins at five downtown department stores.[47]

When King decided to violate a temporary state court injunction[48] against demonstrations in Birmingham, fourteen-year-old Bernita Roberson made the decision to disobey her parents and to march with him and other demonstrators.[49] Roberson and many other young people were arrested. Once at the county jail the children were removed to the Juvenile holding area where King greeted and hugged each as they walked by. Each felt a heightened sense of dignity, for even at their young age they believed their actions made a difference, or would. "If you had gone to jail," said Myrna Carter looking back years later, "you were somebody."[50] The very next day eight white Birmingham clergymen published an open letter to King in a Birmingham newspaper, calling his demonstrations "unwise" and "untimely," and accusing him of being an outsider. This prompted the writing of King's famous literary and theological classic, "Letter from Birmingham Jail," initially etched on scraps of newspaper, toilet paper, paper smuggled in to his jail cell by his attorney, and anything else King found to write on.

From the beginning of the Birmingham campaign, King pondered the viability and the wisdom of using students in the demonstrations. Although he believed that their involvement would be necessary if they were to succeed,[51] he was slow to call on them at first because he knew that it was an idea that would not be well received by black parents, other adults in the black community, and other civil rights leaders. By the third week of the demonstrations, however, the campaign had stalled, and it appeared that defeat was inevitable if a solution was not found.

King met with the SCLC staff about their predicament. It was the youthful, passionate, somewhat eccentric, James Bevel who proposed what King himself had been thinking about, but had not yet offered up. Indeed, Bevel not only proposed the use of massive numbers of young people in the demonstrations, but the use of schoolchildren—from elementary to high school.

In Bevel's thinking, the situation was simple. Most of the black adult residents involved in the demonstrations were already in jail, and there were few left to carry on the mass demonstrations and the goal of over-filling the jails. However, Bevel knew that there were vast numbers of elementary, secondary, and college students, including an already "well defined, strong community" of young people in the high schools. Furthermore, Bevel argued, black children in the Deep South considered themselves to be "at least partially free," unlike many black adults. This was a lesson that he and his wife, Diane Nash Bevel, learned during their efforts to recruit and organize black youths in Mississippi. Experience told Bevel that it was black youth, more than their parents and other adults, who were willing and courageous enough to take real risks for freedom, even if their parents were unwilling to support them or give permission for their involvement. But when parents and teachers forbade their participation, the children and youths defied them and went to the mass meetings and demonstrations anyway.

After an impassioned debate with Bevel and other SCLC staff members about the minimum age for youth involvement, King agreed to use only high school students, declaring that the minimum age should be fourteen. But Bevel was not to be denied. He strongly objected to the minimum age limit, arguing that the black Baptist church had never raised a concern over the fact that many children join church and make a faith commitment at age five or six, and no adult member contests it. Their silence, Bevel said, implies their belief that children at this age are old enough to have a sense of what they are doing in this regard. If the children were not too young to choose Christ, Bevel's argued ran, they were not too young to choose to live out their faith by bravely participating in demonstrations for their freedom from racism and segregation. It was therefore agreed that the children who had a sense of what was going on—regardless of age—should be allowed to *live* their faith, even to the point of participating in the dangerous demonstrations. Once that decision was made, the Birmingham campaign became *a children's crusade for freedom.*

When some of the first waves of children were arrested for violating the injunction against demonstrations and were transported to the county jail, King sought to ease the anxiety that some of them experienced. Before long, however, the children came to see going to jail for freedom as a badge of honor.[52] They became, King said later, "jailbirds and troublemakers" for freedom (which is far different from the youthful jailbirds and troublemakers in black communities across the nation today). Black youths of Birmingham were seeking a new way of living and relating in these United States of America.[53]

Martin Luther King was also well aware that many of the young, would-be demonstrators, volunteered against the wishes of their parents. He recalled one such situation in which a father, initially in favor of SCLC's involvement in Birmingham, turned a cold shoulder when his own teenage son vowed to participate. Although his father forbade him to participate, King recalled the boy saying: "Daddy, I don't want to disobey you, but I have made my pledge. If you try to keep me home, I will sneak off. If you think I deserve to be punished for that, I'll just have to take the punishment. For, you see, I'm not doing this only because I want to be free. I'm doing it also because I want freedom for you and Mama, and I want it to come before you die."[54] This was not the case of a young man who was disobeying his father in a disrespectful manner. Rather, it was an example of one who vowed to disobey his parent if he were not allowed to participate in organized efforts to obtain something quite noble, namely, freedom and civil rights. Such conviction and actions on the part of young people convinced King that they had a real sense of what was at stake, and were willing to sacrifice for it.

Later in the campaign, King proudly recalled that when an eight-year-old demonstrator was asked by an amused police officer, who did not think the children knew what they wanted and what they were doing, she eyeballed him and said: "F'eedom." Indeed, another demonstrator, a young boy, was all of four years old. His mother had the wisdom and foresight to see that because the demonstrations were about the quality of his future he too should participate along with the wave of young marchers that she led. Refusing to comply with police orders to disperse, the woman reportedly declared: "This baby is mine and he's in it too!"[55]

The children and young people brought energy, they brought life and hope to the stalled Birmingham campaign. They were the reason their parents and many other black adults finally got behind the movement.[56] Frequently the adults joined in because the lives of black children had been threatened by racist onlookers, including the police. It was a case of the children leading the way.

Although wealthy black businessman A. G. Gaston was initially critical of King's decision to involve the children, this all changed in an instant. Gaston was sitting in his office talking on the telephone and telling a white attorney, David Vann, that he wished King would leave and give the new city administration a chance. At about that time, looking out the window, Gaston saw a small black girl being rolled down the street by high powered fire hoses. At that moment he said: "Lawyer Vann, I can't talk to you now or ever. My people are out there fighting for their lives and my freedom. I have to go help them."[57] David Vann himself later reflected: "And there in a twinkling of an eye, the whole black community was instantaneously consolidated behind King."[58] Fred Powledge is most assuredly right when he says that, "hell hath no determination like mothers and fathers concerned about the welfare of their children."[59] This was the case with many black adults in Birmingham (and in Selma two years later).

At any rate, the point to be made in all this is that children and young people led the way in Birmingham, a fact that gives lie to the claim that children don't really know what is going on in the society around them, and that they have nothing positive to contribute to the struggle for justice and human rights. What was proven in many of the civil rights campaigns is that children and young people possess substantial untapped power to influence current events when that power is harnessed and channeled toward creative ends.

James Bevel had convinced black youths that it was up to them to free their parents, teachers, themselves, and the country.[60] (One wonders whether we are at this point today, when the children must lead us to equality and a racism free nation.) In any event, Bevel, Dorothy Cotton, Andrew Young, and Bernard Lee initially worked the black schools in the Birmingham area, focusing on identifying leaders among prom queens, cheerleaders, and athletes. Representatives of these groups were invited to nonviolent training sessions and mass meetings. Bevel and his colleagues believed that if they could convince these young people to get involved, they, in turn, would be able to convince many of their peers to join them. The strategy worked better than they imagined.

Interestingly, but not altogether surprising, Bevel recalled that it was actually young black female students who led the way, thus making it easier to recruit the males. Bevel reasoned that: "They're probably more responsive in terms of courage, confidence, and the ability to follow reasoning and logic. Nonviolence to them is logical: 'You should love people, you shouldn't violate property. There's a way to solve all problems without violating. It's uncomfortable, it's inconvenient to have an immediate threat upon you; however, if you maintain your position, the threat goes away.'"[61] Elementary school kids had already agreed to participate when the high school males finally committed themselves. Their initial hesitation might have been due to the fact that most—but not all—racial violence in the South was committed against black males. Consequently, theirs was a natural, understandable initial fear.

On May 6, 1963, Bevel and other SCLC staffers launched what they called D-Day. Because they did not want to alert the authorities ahead of time of the precise day, time, and place of the first children's demonstration, the youths took their cues from two local well known disc jockeys, Shelley "the playboy" Stewart, and "Tall" Paul White, who were also recruited by Bevel, who immediately understood that black-oriented radio stations and deejays were ideal vehicles for inspiring and organizing Birmingham's black youth."[62] Stewart and White spoke to the youths over the air in coded language that only they understood. This way, they knew exactly when to leave school and where to meet up. Brian Ward describes how the deejays contributed to the Birmingham campaign, especially the Children's Crusade.

> ... Stewart on WJLD and White on WENN played an important part. Early on Thursday, May 2, they directed their young fans to the mass meetings and demonstrations by broadcasting coded announcements concerning a "big party" to be held in the city's downtown Kelly Ingram Park, or at one of the local churches. "We good old Baptists knew there wasn't going to be any dance," recalled Larry Russell, a high school participant in the demonstrations. Like most black kids in Birmingham, Russell knew precisely what the deejays meant. Eight hundred of them were absent from school that day. They even knew what to make of Shelly Stewart's curious instruction "Bring your toothbrushes, because lunch will be served." Toothbrushes were in short supply in Birmingham jails, and the children needed reminding that prison was where most of them were headed. Around one in the afternoon, Tall Paul suddenly started audibly shivering on air at WENN. "It's cold," he declared. The temperature outside was in the eighties. This was the secret

signal for the first wave of students to leave the Sixteenth Street Baptist Church and begin their march.[63]

As it turned out about six hundred black children and youths left the Sixteenth Street Baptist Church that day as they gave the campaign the pure shot of adrenalin it needed, "helping to intensify the pressure on the city jails and propel the Birmingham crisis toward its climax."[64] In the next days there were thousands more youths demonstrating.

There can be no doubt that the massive number of students, from kindergarten to college, caught Birmingham authorities completely off guard. Wave after wave of young people left various church locations to march to undisclosed locations downtown. They quickly filled all available paddy wagons. Bull Connor, the racist Commissioner of Public Safety, had to use police cars and (ironically) even school buses to transport the still growing numbers of youths to jail. When there was no more available jail space, the children were transported to the state fairgrounds as a temporary prison.

David Halberstam contends that by the time the Children's Crusade ended, an estimated ten thousand children had been jailed in Birmingham.[65] They had been eager to get involved, and exhibited no fear for their own lives. Already painfully aware of what it meant to be black in the Deep South, many of the children seemed to have a sense of destiny, and sensed that they stood to lose more if they did not get involved. Furthermore, black youth from surrounding towns walked as much as eighteen miles just to get to Birmingham in order to participate in D-Day.

In some instances, third graders were in jail as long as a full week. Audrey Faye Hendricks was one of these. Looking back she said: "I was about seven.... The night before at a meeting, they told us we'd be arrested.... We started from Sixteenth Street Church. We always sang when we left the church. The singing was like a jubilance. It was a release. And it also gave you calmness and reassurance. I was in jail seven days."[66] Children who did not participate in the first march felt ashamed, and many rallied to participate the second day (called "Double D-Day"); the day when Bull Connor unleashed the fire hoses and dogs on them.

The Children and Bull Connor

Unlike Sheriff Laurie Pritchett of Albany, Georgia, Birmingham's Bull Connor was so blatantly racist and hated blacks so much that he was absolutely committed to using violent force to discourage and stop the demonstrations. Sheriff Pritchett was also blatantly racist and hated blacks, but he knew enough about King's method of nonviolence and the fact that its potential "success" in a campaign depended to a large extent on the prompting of a violent crisis or confrontation by the authorities or white onlookers. Pritchett knew that were King successful in this regard, the news media would soon appear in large numbers. He also knew that the one thing that would attract large numbers of media people to Albany was violence perpetrated against the nonviolent demonstrators. Pritchett wisely ordered his men not to resort to violence against King, the demonstrators, and media representatives. This way, he rightly surmised, efforts to launch a movement for civil rights would fail, and consequently few if any media people would show up.

In this regard, Laurie Pritchett was more successful in Albany than King and SCLC. Bull Connor, on the other hand, was both a diehard racist and bull headed, refusing to learn from Pritchett's experience or to take his paid advice seriously enough to act on it.[67] (Connor had hired Pritchett as a consultant.) Consequently, when Connor ordered his men to unleash attack dogs and high powered fire hoses on children, youths, and adults who were marching for the right to be treated humanely and with dignity in what had been touted as the most civilized and democratic nation in the world, it was all captured on film and was the leading story on the evening national and world news.

Through his vicious actions against the nonviolent demonstrators, Bull Connor had essentially made Birmingham the perfect test case for King's philosophy of nonviolence. People throughout the nation and the world were horrified at the pictures of children and adults being pummeled by high powered fire hoses and bitten by vicious German shepherd attack dogs. President John F. Kennedy said that the pictures made him "sick," but it is not clear that he meant this because of a genuine concern for blacks' struggle and their safety, or whether "he meant this in the spirit of 'this is going to make America look bad in Russia, Nigeria, etc.'"[68] For the nation's international image had been a huge concern for the Kennedy administration up to that time.

Nevertheless, the brutal images coming out of Birmingham in May of 1963, and the federal government's showdown with Governor George Wallace barely a month later over the admission of Vivian Malone and James Hood at the all-white University of Alabama in Tuscaloosa, pushed the President to give his most serious and provocative speech on institutional racism on June 11, 1963, in which he declared that racism was much deeper than a mere political issue. It was a moral issue. The speech was the clearest sign that the Birmingham campaign was now at the top of the Kennedy administration's agenda. In part, the President said:

> We are confronted primarily with a moral issue. It is as old as the scriptures and is as clear as the American Constitution.... If an American, because his skin is dark, cannot eat lunch in a restaurant open to the public, if he cannot send his children to the best public school available, if he cannot vote for the public officials who will represent him, if, in short, he cannot enjoy the full and free life which all of us want, who among us would be content to have the color of his skin changed and stand in his place? Who among us would then be content with the counsels of patience and delay?
>
> We preach freedom around the world, and we mean it, and we cherish our freedom at home, but are we to say to the world, and much more importantly, to each other that this is the land of the free except for the Negroes; that we have no second-class citizens except Negroes; that we have no class or caste system, no ghettoes, no master race except with respect to Negroes? Now the time has come for this Nation to fulfill its promise.[69]

Tragically, the very next night, the response of a segment of white America was to ambush and assassinate NAACP field director Medgar Evers in the driveway of his home in Jackson, Mississippi.

At any rate, by all accounts the barbaric tactics of Bull Connor contributed significantly to what "success" King and SCLC had in Birmingham. "The ball game was over," said Attorney David Vann, "once the hoses and the dogs were brought on."[70] Historian Lerone Bennett, Jr., declared even more poignantly: "Connor blundered into the hands of Negro demonstrators by using tactics (fire hoses and police dogs) that went beyond the 'polite repression' America had become accustomed to."[71] Bennett was convinced that many whites—including moderate and liberal ones—were not opposed to blacks being treated inhumanely. What they opposed was the very public way that Bull Connor did it.

Reflecting on the Birmingham campaign, Martin Luther King recalled that when an elderly black woman during the Montgomery bus boycott was asked why she chose to walk rather than accept a ride from one of the designated Montgomery Improvement Association drivers, she responded that she was walking not for herself, but for her children and grandchildren.

But in Birmingham, King observed, the children and grandchildren were demonstrating for themselves, for their parents and grandparents, and for those who would come after them. Indeed, they were doing it, he said, to save the soul of the nation. Young people were leading the adults to higher moral ground. The Children's Crusade had broken the back of white Birmingham, according to Wyatt Walker. They were the unsung "sheroes"[72] and heroes. In a real sense, then, Bull Connor was actually beaten by the children. What then, may be lessons we can take from King and the children's crusade in Birmingham? There are many, but I propose seven.

Lessons to Be Learned from Movement Children and Youth

First, people in my generation, the generation ahead of mine, and quite possibly the generation immediately behind mine cannot be counted on to make the necessary changes that will lead to a more inclusive and multi-cultural society in which the basic civil and human rights of every person will be both acknowledged and respected, and where basic human needs will be met as a matter of principle. The apathy, fear, negligence, and me-first individualism of people in the aforementioned generations is, pure and simple, off the chart. In addition, and understandably to a degree, many are both tired and burned out from the struggles of an earlier period of their lives. So they also lack the energy needed to initiate and sustain the social struggle on the way to the beloved community.

The first lesson necessarily implies the second, namely that young people step up, and as far as possible, assume responsibility for their own future. Because black youths in Birmingham and other southern cities knew without question that frequently the adults were simply afraid, whether of losing jobs, the lives of their children, or their own, they knew they had to take charge. The older generation was moving too slowly or not at all, and too many who were moving at all seemed to subscribe to gradualism. Young people instinctively felt that they and the nation were on the verge of something new and good for everybody, but they also knew that the breakthrough would not roll in on the wheels of inevitability, as King liked to remind people. They would have to work daily and relentlessly to make it a reality. In fact, in December of 1959, King told delegates of the Eighteenth Ecumenical Student Conference at Ohio University that the new order "is a crusade of the young ... for the old will not change.... We must be patient with them but strive ever onward in this great cause."[73] Young people must carry the torch themselves.

Interestingly, by taking the initiative, children and young people in the South unexpectedly discovered that stepping up had the effect of drawing in many parents, teachers, and other adults who were previously complacent and fearful. The children were leading the way, and when their safety was threatened, black parents and other adults also stepped up to the plate by joining the demonstrations. Parents who love their children will not likely stand idly by while they are being abused for engaging in nonviolent demonstrations to insure a better life for themselves and those who will follow after them.

Third, should today's young people have the good sense to step up, a Kingian ethic would challenge them to seek excellence in all that they do that is worth doing, rather than continuing to show the world that mediocrity, and doing just enough to get by, is sufficient. Young people must find their calling, and then seek to do their life's work so well that no one—the living, the dead, the unborn—could do better.

Generally, my experience has been that from the university, to government offices, businesses and factories of all kinds, and to the city public works office, the American worker is committed to anything but excellence. And if you think this claim is too harsh, just pay attention some time to how people do their work—whether in school or on the job—and their attitude towards it. Nothing makes me angrier than to see city sanitation workers in middle and low income neighborhoods spill trash on the street on collection day, and leave it; to empty trash containers and violently throw them on their side rather than return them to the upright position they found them. Watching such people work, one can only conclude that they take no pride in the work they do, or in the neighborhoods in which they do the work. They have no sense of the dignity in honest work, even if their wages are not what they ought to be. As King so often declared, "All labor (All labor) has dignity."[74] Barely two weeks before he was assassinated, King told the American Federation of State, County and Municipal Employees (AFSCME) in Memphis, Tennessee that "whenever you are engaged in work that serves humanity and is for the building of humanity, it has dignity, and it has worth."[75] This does not mean, of course, that such labor should not be rewarded with a living wage. Young people must bring an entirely new attitude to what they do that is worth doing, whether it be study, work, or both. The point here is not that they should compete with others, but that they should commit themselves to doing the absolute best they can do. What young people do affects not only themselves, but their respective communities, and this they need to be aware of at all times.

A fourth lesson is that by getting involved constructively, black children and young people during the Movement learned important things about themselves, not least the importance of acknowledging their own dignity and self-respect, as well as that of other human beings. In addition, many of them, King said, "learned that in opposing the tyrannical forces that were crushing them they added stature and meaning to their lives."[76] They learned that it is not only important to declare one's dignity and self-respect. One must also assert her dignity with all her might, especially when it is being trampled upon by forces internal or external to her community. So, by getting involved in constructive and creative ways black youths, and well meaning white youths, acknowledged their awareness that human and racial relations could be better than they were, and that they themselves had important roles to play to achieve it.

The fifth lesson, the one thing that no one could deny regarding the sit-ins, Freedom Rides, and the Children's Crusade (in Birmingham), is that the children and young people were fearless. Reflecting on the role of young people in the struggle King said: "The blanket of fear was lifted by Negro youth. When they took their struggle to the streets, a new spirit of resistance was born."[77] They knew that they could be pummeled by high-powered fire hoses and bitten by ferocious attack dogs. And yet, they kept before them the goal of freedom and were determined to press ahead, regardless. They would not be deterred, no matter what. This is one of the great lessons for young people today. They must be determined to the point of not giving up, despite the obstacles they surely will face.

A sixth lesson is that young people who are influenced by the teachings and example of Martin Luther King must learn and be disciplined by the principles and practice of nonviolence. It cannot be expected that the vast majority of them will be committed to nonviolence as a philosophy and way of life. Neither King nor Gandhi believed that this would be a possibility even for most adults, let alone young people. Rather, they believed that only a small "creative minority" will be committed to nonviolence as a way of living in the world. In virtually every community, King said, there will be a few individuals who are "unswervingly committed to the nonviolent way," and these "can persuade hundreds of others at least to use nonviolence as a technique and serve as the moral force to awaken the slumbering national conscience."[78] Vast numbers of people of good will in every community are capable of learning the principles of nonviolence and being trained to discipline themselves to abide by them. Such training and discipline might well cause a change in the hearts of participants, as well as create openings for change in the mind and behavior of oppressors.

Finally, we learn from Movement children and young people that there is no time in the future for our salvation. There is only today, so that *now*—this very moment—is the time to take *decided* steps to eradicate all forms of injustice, thus clearing the way for the righteous reign of God. The God of the Hebrew prophets and of Martin Luther King does not require of us that justice and righteousness be done when local, national, and international leaders believe it is politically viable or expedient. Rather, this God expects and requires that justice and righteousness be done right now—today! Martin Luther King himself emphasized the need to get busy and expressed it most poignantly and poetically in his provocative speech against the war in Vietnam at Riverside Church in New York City on April 4, 1967, precisely one year before he was assassinated. King put it this way:

> We are now faced with the fact that tomorrow is today. We are confronted with the fierce urgency of now. In this unfolding conundrum of life and history there is such a thing as being too late. Procrastination is still the thief of time. Life often leaves us standing bare, naked, and dejected with a lost opportunity. The "tide in the affairs of men" does not remain at the flood; it ebbs. We may cry out desperately for time to pause in her passage, but time is deaf to every plea and rushes on. Over the bleached bones and jumbled residue of numerous civilizations are written the pathetic words: "Too late." There is an invisible book of life that faithfully records our vigilance or our neglect. "The moving finger writes, and having writ moves on...."[79]

12

Not All Suffering Is Redemptive[1]

Feminist and womanist theologians have tried to help us to understand that it is preposterous to hold that suffering itself is redemptive.[2] Redemptive suffering implies that God wills human suffering, or that there is nothing inherently wrong with one group suffering at the hands of another. It would be a contradiction to say that God is love and requires that love-justice be done in the world, while at the same time maintaining that God also wills the suffering of particular groups; or even that God willed the death of Jesus Christ, God's own son, for human beings' sins. This highlights the surrogacy motif regarding the relationship between God and Jesus, which is problematic for feminists and womanists. The idea is that human beings have been redeemed because Jesus died on the cross in their place.

Martin Luther King, Jr., was a theologian-social activist who frequently appealed to the doctrine that unearned suffering is redemptive. Did this mean, for King, that suffering is necessarily redemptive, or did he believe that something else needed to happen besides the suffering in order to give it redemptive value? Might there be a sense in which King's real view—notwithstanding his frequent claim that unearned suffering is redemptive—is closer to a womanist theology of suffering? Some proponents of womanist theology claim that suffering, especially for black women, must be both *redemptive* and *resistant*.[3] That is, suffering must be *made* to be redemptive, and a significant way this can happen is through acts of resistance against it. It is unquestionably the case that some who have written on King, seem to think that he believed, pure and simple, and without the need for interpretation, that unearned suffering is redemptive. Because of the way King sometimes spoke and wrote about redemptive suffering he left himself open to the criticism of feminists, womanists, and other critics. Reflecting on nonviolence, King argues, for example, that "suffering can be a most creative and powerful social force. Suffering has certain moral attributes involved, but it can be a powerful and creative social force."[4] One not fully familiar with King's personalism and doctrine of human dignity will read his statement and likely conclude that there is something redemptive in passively accepting suffering inflicted on one. King's personalism and doctrine of human dignity stresses the inherent, inviolable sacredness of every human being, and requires that this be acknowledged by every person. If one acknowledges and accepts her own self-worth it would be a contradiction for such a one to passively accept suffering—that which violates her personhood. Instead, she would be expected to determine best ways of resisting suffering inflicted on her by another. I think this idea is implicit in King's doctrine of human dignity. Moreover, when we read carefully what King said in the previous quote about suffering, we will see that he did not say that suffering *is* "a powerful and creative social force." Rather, he said that it "can be." This suggests that what remains to be determined is the "how." I know of no place where King says that unearned suffering *will* transform a social situation, or those individuals who inflict suffering on others. But he does say that it *may* serve such a purpose. Clearly, for King, this does not happen by merely passively receiving suffering caused by others. This is what I think most critics fail to see when they read King's statements on redemptive suffering. Had King had the leisure time and peace of mind, he could have developed his use of redemptive suffering more fully by thinking through the implications of his view in relation to traditional atonement theories, and how he believed his idea went beyond such theories. Unfortunately, he did not have the luxury of doing this.

Martin Luther King frequently counseled that God will not do for human beings what we are capable of doing for ourselves in cooperation with each other and with God. In addition, King lived by the conviction that human beings are morally autonomous beings who can, if they will, quarantine suffering—when it seems that is all that can be done—and force it to produce best possible good. I have no illusions about the complexity and potential problematic of King's oft heard claim that unearned suffering is redemptive. Although not intended by King, many have interpreted the doctrine to mean that in order to be worthy of God's love or acceptance they must first "go through something." Even some women who are victims of domestic and other forms of abuse sometimes see their suffering as a means to their own, as well as the salvation or redemption of their abuser. Indeed, far too many Christian ministers preach sermons week after week that seem to make a virtue of any suffering that congregants may be experiencing. It seems to me that the effect of such sermons is to cause people to be resigned to their suffering, including that caused by the evils of racism, sexism, heterosexism, ageism, and classism. Without question, none of this is consistent with what Martin Luther King meant by the doctrine that unearned suffering is redemptive. Notwithstanding this, I am not unmindful of womanist theologian Cheryl Kirk-Duggan's important reminder and challenge that: "Given the strong connections between suffering, blood sacrifice, and atonement, preached by many, the language [of redemptive suffering] could still be misleading to the general reader, and needs much more nuancing to avoid re-victimizing the victim, and providing a 'get out of jail card' for the perpetrator."[5] Delores Williams, another womanist theologian, holds out the assumption "that African American Christian women can, through their religion and its leaders, be led passively to accept their own oppression and suffering—if the women are taught that suffering is redemptive."[6] But this latter, in my view, is precisely the difference between King's real view and what his critics think is his position, namely that suffering is redemptive, and may transform evildoers. Women are undoubtedly taught that suffering is redemptive, and when this is the case the results are often what Williams, Kirk-Duggan, and others say—*if* they are taught that suffering is redemptive. The criticism and caution raised by womanists and feminists is both valid and important, and one that I hope to give adequate response to at some point. Presently, however, I want to respond—all too briefly—to what one particular writer has said about King's conception of God and unearned suffering. Because his understanding of King's doctrine is similar to that of womanists and feminists, my response to him serves also as a preliminary response to them. Because of the value of the womanist and feminist critique of King's stance, I realize that this challenge will have to be met.

It is indisputable that Martin Luther King's doctrine of God was influenced by his study of personalism in general, and more particularly, the writings and lectures of his teacher-advisor-mentor at Boston University, L. Harold DeWolf (1905–1986). However, one goes too far when suggesting that King's conception of God and evil is solely, or even most significantly, dependent on the work of DeWolf or some other Euro-American theologian. Brian Kane makes this mistake. He writes, for example: "It is evident, then, that Martin Luther King, Jr.'s doctrine of evil was largely inherited from L. Harold DeWolf. A belief in an omnipotent God, the redemptive power of unearned suffering, and the ideal of a developing community are all facts of King's thought that reflect DeWolf's position."[7] It cannot be denied that such facts "reflect DeWolf's position." However, Kane is misleading, inasmuch as he fails to also acknowledge that King possessed these same ideas about God, evil, and redemptive suffering even before entering seminary. There is no denying that DeWolf would later help King to sharpen each of these ideas, but he did not introduce them to him. One sees evidence of each of these ideas in the literature—including sermons—of blacks from slavery to the present. In addition, King heard his father and other black preachers preach about these from childhood onward. In any case, let us look briefly at one of the three ideas in DeWolf's thought which, according to Kane, strongly influenced King's concept of God: Unearned suffering is redemptive. What did King mean to convey when he uttered these words?

Unearned Suffering Is Redemptive

Kane contends that for King, suffering as such is redemptive. He arrived at this conclusion through discussion of the six characteristics of nonviolence that King listed in *Stride Toward Freedom*.[8] Two of these are pertinent for the discussion here. The first is that there must be absolute commitment to *ahimsa* or non-injury to life. Since King was a personalist he believed that human life has the right of way, and thus focused on non-injury to human beings. This is not to say that his personalism did not stress the dignity of all life, human and non-human. It did. Indeed, King himself expressed his deep appreciation for nature; how, as a seminary student he often communed with nature, and saw God in that experience.[9] This clearly implied his appreciation and respect for non-human life forms. His primary reason for focusing on non-injury to human life had much to do with the long history of the denial of the humanity and dignity of his people as a result of enslavement and racial discrimination. King's insistence on non-injury to human life was a way of affirming the humanity and worth of people in general, and his own people in particular.

The proponent of the King and Gandhi type of nonviolence is willing to endure suffering and violence without inflicting it on her opponent.[10] King's justification for this stance was his conviction that "unearned suffering is redemptive." Those who adhere to this type of nonviolence contend that suffering "has tremendous educational and transforming possibilities."[11] King quoted Gandhi approvingly in this regard: "'Things of fundamental importance to people are not secured by reason alone, but have to be purchased with their suffering,' said Gandhi. He continues: 'Suffering is infinitely more powerful than the law of the jungle for converting the opponent and opening his ears which are otherwise shut to the voice of reason.'"[12] Here one can see why some have been critical of the doctrine of redemptive suffering, with its emphasis on educating and transforming the opponent. In this regard, King often said that the aim of nonviolence, of receiving blows in a loving spirit and without retaliating, was not to defeat or humiliate the opponent, but to win his friendship.[13] One can see how the woman who is the long time victim of domestic violence, and who is aware of such a doctrine, may easily conclude that it is somehow her responsibility to endure such abuse in the hope of redeeming or transforming her abuser, rather than doing all in her power to remove herself from such abuse.

Although redemptive suffering language can be perceived as problematic, it is an important idea in the King type of nonviolence. It is significant that King was a thoroughgoing theist who believed that it is impossible for a person to continue to receive blows without retaliating in kind, *unless* she possesses deep faith in God, regardless of how she defines and understands God. In this regard Gandhi wrote, and King would concur: "To bear all kinds of tortures without a murmur of resentment is impossible for a human being without the strength that comes from God. Only in His strength we are strong. And only those who can cast their cares and their fears on that immeasurable Power have faith in God."[14] Accordingly, the proponent of nonviolence depends first and last on God, "his only Rock."[15] Consequently, to accept nonviolence as one's creed or one's way of life requires absolute dependence on, and faith in, God. According to Gandhi: "A non-violent man can do nothing save by the power and grace of God. Without it he won't have the courage to die without anger, without fear and without retaliation. Such courage comes from the belief that God sits in the hearts of all and that there should be no fear in the presence of God."[16]

According to Kane, the second characteristic of King's nonviolence that points to the idea that suffering in itself is redemptive is the conviction that the universe is on the side of justice, and is friendly to the achievement, conservation, and enhancement of value.[17] King dates his commitment to this idea to his childhood experience of growing up in a strong black family that was permeated with the love of parents, grandmother, and siblings. This made it easy for him to be optimistic and to think of the universe as essentially friendly. "It is quite easy for me to think of the universe as basically friendly mainly because of my uplifting hereditary and environmental circumstances,"[18] he wrote in a first year paper in seminary. Accordingly, King believed that the universe is built on a moral foundation, which means that all of creation, and most especially human beings, have intrinsic value. It means, further, that goodness is the heartbeat of the universe. It is important to understand that this is a metaphysical claim (applying to the nature of reality itself), and thus does not mean that everything that happens in day to day living in the world is good. It does mean, however, that evil and suffering in such a world cannot have the last word. Even though I may not, and you may not live to see good triumph over evil and suffering, the universe itself is constructed such that this will eventually happen. To say that goodness is at the foundation of the universe is another way of saying that reality is thoroughly fused with value. In other words, all of creation has intrinsic value because created, sustained, and loved by the God who is Love. God is the source (*axiogenesis*), sustainer and continuer (*axiosoteria*) of value or good.[19] To say that the universe rests on a moral foundation is also to say that it is friendly to, and sides with, social justice and those who consciously strive to achieve and sustain it, particularly through the method of nonviolence. Indeed, this very conviction—that the universe hinges on morality—is, according to King, the best argument and foundation for absolute nonviolence in the social struggle. The nonviolent resister has good reason to be optimistic about the future, since she lives by the conviction that justice and goodness will win out. She can have such confidence because God is the source and continuer of good, and therefore in the struggle for social justice she need never feel that she is alone, but rather has cosmic companionship.[20]

Kane concludes from his study on King that, "Persons choose to suffer in order to act according to God's will. *Suffering in and of itself is redemptive because of the purposes of God.*"[21] Concretely, what does such a claim really mean? Is this what King himself meant to convey?

What Did King Mean?

A person might well "*choose* to suffer in order to act according to God's will," but this is quite different from being forced to suffer by a power that disregards one's humanity and dignity. Moreover, suffering may not necessarily be the best teacher, or, I might add, the best means to redemption or moral transformation of an individual perpetrator or a group. For example, what is the redemptive or transformative element in systemic race discrimination for blacks? Why is it that vast numbers of whites are not transformed by this, such that they take aggressive and radical steps to dismantle the structures of racism? Where is the evidence that the racist Birmingham, Alabama police commissioner Eugene "Bull" Connor was transformed by the nonviolent suffering of black demonstrators? I have no doubt that a white person here and there might have been redeemed by this, but considering the amount and longevity of black suffering, I would say that in the short term this is negligible; that the price for such redemption was too high.

The Author of justice, righteousness, and goodness would surely will that persons respect human life, internalize the principle of ahimsa (non-injury), and live and behave accordingly. But to say as Kane does, that suffering as such is redemptive, is problematic and borders on the insane and unethical. I say this particularly in light of native peoples' and black Americans' long history of unearned suffering and oppression at the hands of people of European descent. This may also be said in light of the numerous cases of domestic abuse, particularly the abuse of women by male companions. However, we will see below that King himself may have unwittingly contributed to the conclusion drawn by Kane and others.

Long before beginning seminary, and then doctoral studies, Martin Luther King had a sense that unearned suffering could be redemptive. He had witnessed this phenomenon at work in his father's ministerial leadership. In addition, he had read about unearned suffering in the experience of enslaved ancestors. He read of how they resisted the dehumanizing treatment of the white enslaver through deception, attempts to run away, and other means at their disposal, while managing to retain their dignity and determination to keep pressing for freedom.

M. Shawn Copeland has shown that black women frequently resisted their captivity during slavery through the use of language, usually "sass." This was frequently the only way they could defend themselves against the sexual and physical assault of white men, as well as the dehumanizing treatment of white women. Sassy language is "impudent" or "disrespectful" language, and thus is not intended to please the one toward whom it is directed. It is an instrument of resistance. In her commentary on the use of sass, Copeland writes: "Enslaved Black women use sass to guard, regain, and secure self-esteem; to obtain and hold psychological distance; to speak truth; to challenge 'the atmosphere of moral ambiguity that surrounds them,' and, sometimes, to protect against sexual assault."[22] Copeland found that sass is of West African derivation, and that it "comes from the bark of the poisonous West African sassy tree. Deconcocted and mixed with certain other barks, sass was used in ritual ordeals to detect witches. If the accused survives the potion, she is absolved; if not, the sass poisons, it kills. For the enslaved women, sass is a ready weapon; it allows them to 'return a portion of the poison the master has offered.'"[23] So, as we can see, sass is not intended to make one feel good. Rather, it is a way of asserting one's agency, as well as one's displeasure with being mistreated or disrespected by one who holds power over her.

In any event, the doctrine that unearned suffering is redemptive was stressed in courses that King took under George W. Davis at Crozer Theological Seminary, and L. Harold DeWolf and Edgar S. Brightman at Boston University. DeWolf wrote about the possibility of suffering being transmuted into good. He argued that no matter how grave the evils inflicted upon a person, his attitude and response to them could have redeeming value. "All natural evil, when confronted with faith, prayer and courage," he writes, "can become a means to good."[24] It is important to observe that DeWolf did not add a note of necessity here. That is, he did not say that suffering (of any kind) is necessarily redemptive or capable of leading to good, and he surely did not contend that suffering or evil is good. Instead, he maintained that suffering *can* lead to good *if* one has the faith, character, and the courage to face it in a certain way. It is also of interest to note that his reference was not to moral evil, although I think he meant to include it. Evil, whether natural or moral, is evil, and thus is not itself a good.

The doctrine that unearned suffering is redemptive made sense to Martin Luther King precisely because of the way he thought about God and the universe. In his view, and in agreement with DeWolf, nothing distressful or evil that happens to a person may be considered final. "Because God lives evil never has the last word."[25] If, as King maintains, God is essentially love, and the universe is anchored to a moral foundation and thus is fused with value, it must be the case that evil and suffering cannot have the last word.

Although King vacillated regarding Brightman's doctrine of the finite-infinite God,[26] at one time expressing his criticism,[27] and later seeming to be in agreement with it,[28] he likely saw Brightman's explanation of God's control of the non-rational Given to be support for the conviction that because of who God is, evil and suffering will never have the last word. King was encouraged by what Brightman said about God's control of the non-rational Given. According to Brightman:

> God's will is eternally seeking new forms of embodiment of the good. God may be compared to a creative artist eternally painting new pictures, composing new dramas and new symphonies. In this process, God, finding The Given as an inevitable ingredient, seeks to impose ever new combinations of given rational form on the given nonrational content. Thus The Given is, on the one hand, God's instrument for the expression of his aesthetic and moral purposes, and, on the other, an obstacle to their complete and perfect expression. God's control of The Given means that he never allows The Given to run wild, that he always subjects it to law and uses it, as far as possible, as an instrument for realizing the ideal good. Yet the divine control does not mean complete determination; for in some situations The Given, with its purposeless processes, constitutes so great an obstacle to divine willing that the utmost endeavors of God lead to a blind alley and temporary defeat. At this point, God's control means that no defeat or frustration is final; that the will of God, partially thwarted by obstacles in the chaotic Given, finds new avenues of advance, and forever moves on in the cosmic creation of new values.[29]

It is important to see that, according to Brightman, God eternally and persuasively resists the nonrational Given through reason and will, thereby creating openings for the achievement of good in the world. God does not passively accept this aspect of the divine nature. Rather, God chooses to resist. King surely saw in this the need for oppressed people to resist the suffering imposed on them by oppressors. This brings us to an important point in King's doctrine of nonviolence.

People may *choose* to suffer, such as to suffer violence in nonviolent campaigns against injustice. Proponents engage in nonviolent campaigns in order to comply with what they understand to be God's will that all people be free and able to live with dignity. But let's be clear. In such cases it is not that redemption is in the suffering itself. When, however, an oppressed people choose to intentionally and methodically engage in nonviolent resistance to end injustice and oppression, they are, by virtue of their choice to resist, *making their suffering redemptive*; adding the redemptive element to their suffering. Walter Wink provides an instructive comment when he writes: "To *have* to suffer is different from *choosing* to suffer. The latter can be powerfully redemptive for some people. Such martyrdom comes out of abundance. This suffering is not necessary but chosen."[30] This is quite different from saying, as Brian Kane does, that the suffering itself is redemptive. While Martin Luther King would prefer that the oppressed resist nonviolently, for the moment it is important to grasp the significance of the need for them to resist the oppression by whatever means available to them. Previously we saw that during the period of American enslavement black women often resisted their oppressive condition through sass. This did not eradicate their suffering, but it allowed them to retain their sense of dignity, knowing that they were not passively accepting the injustice and suffering heaped upon them. As human beings, there was something in their nature that caused them to push back against inhumane treatment by whatever means available to them. In this case, it was sass. I cannot say strongly enough that it is in the resisting that the suffering is made to have redemptive value. M. Shawn Copeland stressed this as an important point in any reasonable womanist theology of suffering. Faith, prayer, and courage are all important, but their importance is enhanced when an individual or group also acts to resist, eradicate, or to transform the suffering such that as much meaning as possible can be gleaned from it.

The claim that suffering as such has redemptive value is incomprehensible to many oppressed people. If suffering itself has redemptive value, why resist oppression and injustice, for it would seem that to suffer is itself a virtue. All one need do is passively accept his suffering, for great will be his reward in some distant future and place beyond this world. If suffering as such is redemptive, it would be reasonable for oppressed people to simply accept all that is done to demean and undermine their humanity and dignity. Therefore, an important question is: Who benefits most from the idea of redemptive suffering? It is most assuredly not the oppressed.

There is no moral value in suffering as such. Indeed, it is immoral to tell those who live under a constant state of systematic injustice and oppression that somehow their suffering is ordained by God, and that by passively enduring, they, their oppressors, or both, will experience redemption. Suffering itself is not redemptive, at least not in any way that makes sense to one who possesses a mature moral sensibility.

If suffering itself is redemptive, it might be possible to even say that God *wills* suffering, especially the suffering of select groups of people. But by definition it must be a contradiction to say this, inasmuch as God is thought to be Agape, and no matter how we cut it, Agape does not will human suffering. However, it does seem reasonable to say that such love seeks to eliminate or at least find meaning in the suffering once it occurs. This is not to say that suffering is actually willed by God, or by any moral being. And yet, by resisting suffering and oppression persons or groups *cause* these to have redemptive value.

Martin Luther King himself sometimes wrote and spoke of the necessity of suffering and its redemptive value. Such a view clearly lends itself to misinterpretation. Looking back on his early struggles in the civil rights movement, King wrote that he had had many trials and tribulations. His home had been bombed twice, he had been jailed five times, and seldom a day passed without he and his family being threatened with violence by white racists. In addition, he was nearly stabbed to death by a crazed black woman as he was autographing his first book in Harlem. These and related trials, King said, taught him the value of "unmerited suffering." He learned early in the movement that one can respond to such suffering through retaliatory anger and bitterness, or one can work cooperatively and nonviolently with others and with God to eliminate or transform the suffering into that which is conducive to beloved community-making.

In an article written for *The Christian Century* in 1960, King wrote: "*Recognizing the necessity for suffering I have tried to make of it a virtue.* If only to save myself from bitterness, I have attempted to see my personal ordeals as an opportunity to transform myself and heal the people involved in the tragic situation which now obtains. I have lived these last few years with the conviction that unearned suffering in redemptive."[31] For King, unearned suffering is "an opportunity" for the suffering to be made redemptive. Suffering is necessary only in the sense that human beings possess freedom and may choose to make others (or themselves) suffer. Those who are victimized in this way soon discover that added suffering may be the price of freedom and justice. It is not passive suffering, but the suffering that is sure to come when one finally decides to resist with all her might those forces that oppress and demean her humanity and dignity. This is what King meant when he said that "those who dare to take a stand for justice must be willing to suffer and to sacrifice."[32]

In the racially unjust situation it can be said that suffering is necessary in the sense that the victims suffer physical and other forms of oppression, while even the oppressor suffers a kind of spiritual oppression. The suffering itself, in either case, is not transformative. However, it can be made to be transformative if the oppressed choose to struggle against it as nobly and determinedly as they can. The same can happen for oppressors who come to see the evil of their behavior and choose to stop it. If former oppressors now suffer because others in their group are against their new stance, their suffering may, to that extent, become redemptive.

Conclusion

My own resistance to the concept of unearned suffering—whatever validity it may have, or was intended to have—is that it is frequently seen as a necessity for only select groups of people, and more often for those who are victims of domestic abuse and systemic oppression. In concrete existential terms (which is different from the metaphysical claim that because of the nature of the world we live in suffering is inevitable), I would say that preventable evil and suffering is necessary only in the sense that people are created in freedom and therefore have the power to decide whether to make others suffer needlessly. To speak of the metaphysical necessity of suffering for a particular group of persons only, such as women, blacks, homosexuals, and the poor must say something about how one understands God. Martin Luther King's God is creator, personal, love, and the source and sustainer of the objective moral order. God is therefore the God of all people, or of no people. If this is true, then it must be the case that it is no more necessary that one group suffer injustice, abuse, and oppression than any other.

I began this discussion by saying that feminist and womanist theologians have been adamant that suffering as such is not redemptive. This is clearly a point stressed in an essay by Joanne Carlson Brown and Rebecca Parker. These authors are critical of classical theories of atonement, such as "the moral influence" theory. This theory, they maintain, suggests that by passively taking unearned suffering upon themselves, victims are somehow able to appeal to the conscience and reason of oppressors that they will set their captives free. This theory seems to assume something about oppressors that may be—indeed often is—utterly false. Just because oppressors are human beings does not mean that the moral sense of every oppressor is developed to the point that they will necessarily be affected by the suffering of the oppressed such that they will willingly put an end to the cause of their suffering, or that they themselves will be transformed. "The problem with this theology," Brown and Parker write, "is that it asks people to suffer for the sake of helping evildoers see their evil ways. It puts concern for the evildoer ahead of concern for the victim of evil. It makes victims the servants of the evildoers' salvation."[33] Too much of the onus is put on the sufferer, the victim. Not only does such a one suffer at the hands of the oppressor, but she is then asked to bear the burden of changing or redeeming the oppressor by her willingness to bear—nobly!—unearned suffering. She is thus the victim of double jeopardy. Already suffering from domestic abuse, for example, she is then essentially asked to be the savior of her attacker, rather than focus on her own deliverance by whatever means are available to her. Surely we can see at least one of the major problems with moral influence theories which are little more than theologies of martyrdom. Thus, the critique of Brown and Parker, as well as the earlier criticism cited from womanist theologians Cheryl Kirk-Duggan and Delores Williams must be seen as a serious challenge to the doctrine that unearned suffering is redemptive. And yet, I agree with Lewis Baldwin that Martin Luther King—right or wrong—was an advocate of restoring the church's image as sacrificial servant, "the chief symbol of redemptive suffering," and as "perhaps the most powerful way for that institution to take King's values into the twenty-first century."[34] Right or wrong, King believed that Christian social witness was directly related to the cross.[35] Nevertheless, as noted above, I am also of the view that King's stance warrants more attention than heretofore has been the case among King scholars.

I remain convinced that Martin Luther King did not adhere to a theology of martyrdom. It is not clear that King had occasion to think deeply enough about the possible implications that his conviction that unearned suffering is redemptive may have for those who are already made to suffer at the hands of others. It is known, however, that because of his total commitment to leading nonviolent direct action campaigns against injustice, and because he lived under the constant threat of death, King did not have either ample time or peace of mind to compose a systematic theology of suffering. I offer this not as an excuse for his failure in this regard, but as a fact to remember, as we try to determine what he meant when he said that unearned suffering is redemptive, and what might be implications of this for both the victims and their oppressors. Because King was a man of ideas who was thoroughly devoted to using those ideas to make better persons and a better world, I am convinced that he would have welcomed the criticism raised by feminist, womanist, and other thinkers regarding his stance on redemptive suffering. Moreover, because of his deep conviction that human beings as such possess absolute, inviolable dignity, King, after dialog with such critics, would have been intentional about further explaining what he meant to convey by his doctrine.

I have tried to show that Martin Luther King did not believe that suffering as such is redemptive, or has redemptive value. Those, like Brian Kane, who contend that King believed that suffering itself is redemptive, misinterpret what he really intended to convey. In addition to his claim that unmerited suffering has redemptive value, there is also King's staunch insistence that the oppressed should not, under any circumstance, passively accept oppressive, unjust treatment. As (fundamentally) self-determined autonomous beings, oppressed people are obligated to resist evil done to them, although for King such resistance must be of the militant nonviolent type. Therefore, it was never, for King, a matter of requiring that the oppressed passively suffer in the hope that by doing so their witness and courage would somehow redeem oppressors. King was unquestionably an idealist, but his idealism was tempered with the realism of his experience with racism while growing up in the Deep South, and the militant realism of Reinhold Niebuhr. Looking back on his introduction to Niebuhr's thought in seminary, King wrote of the powerful impact it had on him and his prior uncritical commitment to liberal theology's overly optimistic view of the goodness of human nature.[36] King was also much influenced by Niebuhr's analysis of the relation between morality and power, and his insistence that sin is present on every level of human achievement.[37] Therefore, King was enough of a realist to know that just as those who possess massive, unchecked power and privilege do not generally cease their wrongdoing just because the socio-ethical and political theories that justified their policies and practices had been discredited, he also knew that there are certain personality types, such as the Adolf Hitlers, Benito Mussolinis, Bull Connors, Jim Clarks, Roy Bryants, C.W. Milams, and Cecil Prices of the world, who are not redeemed by the unearned suffering of nonviolent demonstrators for freedom and civil rights. Such people do not cease their inhumane, unjust practices merely because their victims exhibit their capacity to endure the unmerited suffering caused by them, or because they have shown them the immorality of their ways. People of this sort need to be *made* to change their behavior, if not at first, their thinking.

For Martin Luther King, suffering which also resists "*can* be a most creative and powerful social force." Passive suffering insures only sustained and even more, suffering. Therefore, King was not naïve, but realistic, when he proclaims that "suffering *may* serve to transform the social situation."[38] Suffering *may* redeem or teach oppressors the more humane way of relating in the world. Furthermore, we should remember King's experience when he took the movement north to Chicago in 1966. After leading what was essentially an unsuccessful march through white neighborhoods near Marquette Park, King said: "I've never seen anything like it. I've been in many demonstrations all across the south, but I can say that I have never seen—even in Mississippi and Alabama—mobs as hostile and as hate-filled as I've seen in Chicago."[39] Before Chicago, King had believed that the moral sense of most whites was such that they too wanted integration between the races, and social justice for blacks. But in Chicago he experienced a level of white hatred that he had not known before, which caused him to remark that Chicago whites could teach Mississippi and Alabama whites much about race hatred.[40] King was also troubled by the virtual silence of white liberals throughout the nation. (Most of these were at best, "fair-weather liberals," and therefore were not the thoroughly committed, courageous liberals like the white college student volunteers who participated in the Freedom Summer Project in the Mississippi Delta in 1964, and in the Summer Community Organization and Political Education (SCOPE) Project in 1965.) The Chicago campaign forced King to be more realistic when considering the level of development of the moral sense of most whites. King knew that one with an adequately developed moral sense and awareness of the basic humanity and sacredness of blacks, would not have responded as Chicago whites. After Chicago, King knew that it was unreasonable, and at best naïve, to assume that most whites could be easily loved into doing the right thing in the area or race, or that they would easily be moved to change their behavior because demonstrators exhibited a willingness to endure unearned suffering.

Martin Luther King reportedly told reporter David Halberstam that after Chicago he was convinced that only a small percentage of whites, mostly young college students, were genuinely committed to freedom and racial equality.[41] He got this sense by having witnessed the courageous struggles of such students during the Freedom Summer and SCOPE projects for voting rights. King had never asked his people to suffer—primarily or solely—for the sake of helping racist whites to see their evil ways, in the hope that this alone would cause them to change their behavior. *If* he had ever had doubts before, after the Chicago experience, King knew without question that it made no sense to ask any people, let alone his own, to bear suffering solely for the purpose of redeeming their oppressors. King's purpose was to nonviolently resist suffering in the interest of establishing justice for his people. Of course, he also wanted reconciliation between the races, but he knew that the very painful work of resisting oppression and establishing justice needed to happen first. There is nothing good about suffering itself. I agree with Edgar S. Brightman, King's teacher, that, "an experience which in itself is meaningless or evil may be transformed to meaning and good when the right attitude is taken toward it.

Suffering is evil, but courage and patience, sympathy and hope, may make it a constituent of a larger good."[42] To be sure, this and other positive outcomes *might* be a byproduct of unearned suffering, but this is different from *expecting* or *requiring* people to suffer for this reason.

Although King's experience in Chicago did not cause a shift in his absolute commitment to nonviolence as a way of life, he was left with a much better sense of the need for a fully developed moral sense in white racists if nonviolence as a strategy was to be successful. The Chicago campaign, and King's sense of realism, helped him to see that if the opponent has an underdeveloped moral sense, the achievements of nonviolent demonstrators will not be what they otherwise might. Depending on the level of moral sensibility possessed by opponents, they may not be capable of being transformed morally by the prolonged unmerited suffering of their victims.

Martin Luther King did not derive pleasure or satisfaction of any kind from suffering itself. In addition, there is no evidence that he ever expected this of his people. Rather, for King, suffering has a moral quality only to the extent that—if removable—the sufferer has done all in her power to remove it, as well as its cause(s). Suffering has a moral quality only when it is the suffering of one who has relentlessly—and for King nonviolently—struggled against it. Only this type of suffering can be deemed redemptive or to have a redemptive quality. It might well be the case that in the end only God, the Great Companion and Fellow Sufferer, can bring redemption out of unmerited suffering. This is one reason why I believe that one's conception of God will have much to do with how she interprets the idea of redemptive suffering. I think this is no less the case for Martin Luther King, and if we are to truly make sense of the idea in the way he seemed to have used it, it will be necessary to critically examine his conception of God. King believed that unearned suffering is redemptive because of something he believed even more deeply about God, namely, that God will not allow evil to have the last word; will not allow evil and injustice to be victorious over good and justice. In the sermon, "Questions that Easter Answers," King told the congregation that Easter gives an affirmative answer to the question of whether the universe is on the side of justice and goodness. In this regard, he said that Christianity teaches that:

> Good Friday may occupy the throne for a day; but ultimately it must give way to the triumphant beat of the drums of Easter. It says to us that somehow nagging tares may come in to stand in the way of stately wheat but one day the tares must pass away and the wheat will grow on. It says to us sometimes a vicious mob may take possession and crucify the most meaningful and sublime and noble character of human history. It says to us that one day that same Jesus will rise up and split history into AD and BC so that history takes on new meaning.[43]

Accordingly, King held that Easter reminds us that at the end of the day, the forces of evil and injustice must give way to good and justice. That Easter comes after Good Friday, was proof enough for Martin Luther King, that good and justice will ultimately triumph in God's world—a moral universe—whether you and I live to see it or not.

PART III

WHERE DO WE GO FROM HERE?

13

Sexism as Contradiction to King's Personalism[1]

As a Christian and champion of the philosophy of personalism which stresses the conviction of God as personal, and the infinite, inviolable worth of persons as such, Martin Luther King possessed an unusual capacity for personal development and change of practice. I particularly have in mind King's stance on women in the public sphere. More explicitly, I have in mind King's sexism. The thesis here is that, because of King's personalism and his devotion to personalistic ethics and methodology, his adherence to basic Christian principles, and his uncanny ability *and* willingness to alter his views and practice in the light of the evidence, facts, and current events, King would have entered the ranks of *recovering sexists*[2] had he lived into the 1970s to experience the height of the woman's movement during that period. Although there were surely rumblings regarding women's rights among various feminist groups in the mid-to late 1960s, this was somewhat peripheral to a Martin Luther King, who, by that time, had expanded his battle for human rights to include public and passionate resistance to militarism. It will be recalled that King began his civil rights ministry in Montgomery, Alabama, by focusing primarily on racism and its various manifestations. In the first year of seminary he had already decided that he would address a trilogy of social evils (racism, economic injustice/poverty, and war) throughout his ministry. Consequently, it should not be surprising that before too long, it was clear to King that integrally related to the problem of racism was the issue of economic equality and classism. By the early 1960s, then, he was focusing on both racism and economic exploitation. As the war in Vietnam escalated and he could see not only that very many of those being sent to fight what he considered an unjust war were young men of color and the poor, and that expending such massive human and economic resources toward the war was severely undermining the war on poverty in this country, King slowly became a staunch, and very public opponent of that war. Indeed, even before this, he was a longtime opponent of war in general. As far back as 1949, while still in seminary, he prayed that human beings "work with renewed vigor for a warless world, a better distribution of wealth, and a brotherhood that transcends race or color."[3] King stressed this trilogy of social problems (race, economic injustice, and war) from seminary throughout his civil rights ministry. By 1957, he declared that he would never adjust to "the madness of militarism."[4]

I disagree with the tendency of some King scholars and media people to say that King's call for a "phase two" of the Movement meant that he moved "beyond civil rights and voting rights to 'economic equality,'" and that this meant that he essentially "shifted from attaining

199

civil rights to creating a basis for 'economic equality.'"[5] Terms such as "moved beyond" and "shifted" imply that King began focusing his energies, time, attention, and other resources on some other issue, thereby leaving behind others, e.g., racism. Even when King told the members of the American Federation of State, County and Municipal Employees (AFSCME) on March 18, 1968, in Memphis that: "You are going beyond purely civil rights to questions of human rights,"[6] he did not mean that he himself would no longer focus on issues of race. Rather, it was an acknowledgement that other social ills needed to be addressed too; issues that were directly related to the race problem. Besides, King saw race, economic exploitation, and war issues as interconnected and feeding on each other. Moreover, in a 1967 "Face to Face" television news interview, King told those who thought that his focus on the war in Vietnam meant that he was no longer focused on racism, that 95 percent of his time was still spent in the civil rights struggle.[7] That he now championed the campaign against the Vietnam War did not mean that he was leaving the issues of racism and economic inequality beyond. Therefore, it seems more reasonable to say that King's agenda *expanded* to include creating a foundation for economic equality. The same should be said regarding his focus on the Vietnam War.

At any rate, the important point is that we endeavor to see King as a man who possessed an amazing capacity to change when his ideas, the evidence, and current events suggested the need for it. In light of what I suggest is a clearly established pattern, in addition to his fundamental conviction that every person is sacred because endowed with the image of God and loved and cared for by God, the only thing that prevented what I think was King's imminent confession of his own sexism, and acknowledgement of the structural sexism which is embedded in the fabric of this nation, was the 30.06 slug that ended his life on April 4, 1968.

I concede at the outset that much of my argument that King would have championed women's rights had he lived, hinges on circumstantial evidence, considering that we cannot really know for certain that such a change would in fact have occurred in King. However, I try to show that much of my argument actually goes to the issue of King's commitment to personalistic method and principles, and to basic Christian convictions, e.g., that all persons are sacred and equal before God, and that God loves all persons equally. In addition, from Montgomery to Memphis, King showed an amazing capacity to change when current events of which he was aware indicated the need for such change. One who understands the method of personalism and its requirement to consider all relevant evidence and be willing to adjust one's stance and behavior accordingly, knows that one committed to such a method, as King most assuredly was, will feel compelled to do what it requires in terms of one's beliefs and practices. My claim is that such a view has important implications for the issue of King's sexism, and my belief that he would have confessed his sexism had he lived longer, and had he the opportunity to have ongoing direct—rather than peripheral—exposure to basic concerns raised by women during the late 1960s. King surely knew that historically, white women had taken up the struggle for the right for (white) women to vote. Indeed, he applauded "the glorious fight for women's suffrage."[8] Stewart Burns has rightly argued in his otherwise excellent book on King, that although he was aware of the founding of the National Organization for Women (NOW) in 1966, King was not on record as a supporter of their protests against gender discrimination.[9] However, I am not entirely on board with Burns' critique, since it is not clear to me at this writing, what King actually knew about NOW and its platform. To what extent was he in serious, ongoing conversation with members—especially black members, e.g., Pauli Murray—of that organization? Furthermore, we will see that sexist though King certainly was, he was not as rigid in some of his thinking about women as is frequently believed.

To those who quickly assert that my argument is based on pure speculation, I say only that my research on the death penalty in the United States reveals that more men of color have been sentenced to capital punishment and executed on the basis of speculation and circumstantial evidence than we will ever know. The argument presented in this chapter contends that if we follow closely King's commitment to personalistic ideas and method and to basic Christian principles, as well as the development and expansion of his moral outlook on social problems, the circumstantial evidence supporting the thesis here presented would seem to be more solid than the death penalty cases of many black men.

For one such as Martin Luther King, for whom the dignity of persons as such was a fundamental philosophical-theological-biblical principle, it may, on the surface, seem ludicrous for me to claim to reflect on his sexism. How can the charge of sexism be lodged against one whose doctrine of human dignity was as thoroughgoing as King's? Indeed, how is it possible that there can be even a modicum of truth in the charge that he was sexist? And yet, a number of King scholars, not least James H. Cone[10] and Lewis V. Baldwin,[11] have argued persuasively that this was the most glaring limitation or contradiction in King's liberation project. It is also the severest challenge to his personalism and doctrine of human dignity. In addition, other scholars familiar with King's work, e.g., Paula Giddings[12] and Cheryl A. Kirk-Duggan,[13] also name and critique King's sexism. Although there are scholars, e.g., Andrew Billingsley,[14] who try to minimize the significance of King's practice relative to black women's public role, my own research reveals that the preponderance of the evidence supports claims that King was both chauvinistic and sexist.

In light of King's personalism and its method, his doctrine of human dignity, and his conviction that the image of God exists equally in all persons, one can only conclude that *in principle*, he believed there to be a fundamental equality between the sexes. However, in his actual practice there was much to be desired in this regard. How comes it that King had the principle right, but not the practice regarding the equal treatment of women in general, and black women in particular? This is the overriding question that prompted me to share some of my reflections on sexism as contradiction to King's personalism. While I concede that the most one can do is speculate whether King would have eventually renounced sexism had he lived longer, it seems reasonable to me that one muse about this, both in light of his personalistic method, and his clear-cut overwhelming capacity to grow and change in the face of evidence and events that seem to warrant it.

Since in principle sexism is a contradiction of basic personalistic tenets, one wonders whether there might have been such anomalies among the founders and early developers of philosophical personalism. Perhaps a brief consideration of the progenitor of systematic personalism in the United States will shed some light. Toward this end, a look at his stance on racism may be instructive.

Borden P. Bowne: Systematizer of Personalism

As a doctoral student at Boston University, Martin Luther King was no stranger to the work of Borden P. Bowne (1847–1910), who systematized and developed personalism into a philosophical method.[15] This prompted his student, Albert C. Knudson, to characterize it as "systematic methodological personalism."[16] From the time that Bowne—long time professor of philosophy and dean of the graduate school at Boston University—developed personalism into a philosophical method, from the latter part of the nineteenth to the first decade of the twentieth century, its proponents have, in principle, exhibited a deep respect and reverence for both human and nonhuman life forms. In other words, Bowne advocated respect for all life, which means that from its inception there was inherent in the philosophy of personalism the outline for developing a doctrine of the dignity of human *and* non-human beings. The person, however, is thought to be the highest intrinsic value in this philosophy.

We not only see evidence of attention to the dignity of all being in the metaphysics of personalism, but in its ethics as well, a point borne out by Bowne's *Metaphysics* (1882, rev. 1898) and *The Principles of Ethics* (1892). In the latter text, we see the outline of what may be characterized as Bowne's *developmental ethic*. The importance of this ethic for our purpose is that it lays the foundation for the important *need to expand the moral field* to include those entities and issues that were previously left out. This idea is based, in part, on the personalist view that human beings are not just isolated individuals, but are, in fact, persons-in-community. The person is fundamentally a *socius*. This places the emphasis on the fact that the person does not exist in solitariness, and cannot be all she can be in isolation. This is not unlike the African traditional view: "I am, because we are; and since we are, therefore I am."[17] According to personalism, to characterize the person as a *socius* means that such one "is in its very nature relatedness, and yet, uniqueness."[18] There is to be not only respect for the autonomous individual, but for the community, as well as for persons in their myriad relations with each other and other areas of the creation. The significance of this idea for ethics is at least twofold. First, it means that the ethicist must always be intentional about bringing an increased number of human acts under the heading of morality and duty. Bowne considered (white[19]) women's suffrage to be one such act, for example. Women are both individuals and also in relationship with the wider society or human family. Consequently, Bowne argued, the moral sphere should be expanded to the point of taking seriously their claim to socio-political and voting rights. Second, the expansion or broadening of the moral field means that persons owe duties to beings—both human and nonhuman—who in times past were not included within their moral sphere, e.g., women and their political rights, the plant and animal kingdoms. Sadly, Bowne did not—as he did with white women's rights, child labor laws, and non-human life forms—push this form of expanding the moral sphere as he should have regarding racism and racial discrimination.

Like many early white social gospel advocates of the first two decades of the twentieth century, such as Walter Rauschenbusch, Bowne was more silent than vocal about the race question. In principle his personalism was unquestionably against racism—anything that alienates human beings from each other and from God. The problem is that he did not address this in any of his published writings,[20] including his excellent book on ethics. For now, suffice it to say that he at least provided the theoretical framework and created the opening for such expansion and consideration to occur. In principle, at least, Bowne's personalism requires that the existence of racism and sexism be acknowledged, criticized, and eradicated. Curiously, but not completely surprising, Bowne devoted considerable energy to addressing the issue of the political and human rights of white women,[21] but his published writings reveal no sustained attention to the racism of his day. One wonders how this was possible, considering that all kinds of abolitionist activity occurred in the city of Boston prior to and after Bowne's arrival there to teach at Boston University in 1876. What is more, The First National Conference of Colored Women was held in Boston in 1895,[22] after Bowne had been teaching for two decades. Bowne was both a brilliant teacher and was generally well informed regarding civic events. Notwithstanding this, it was as if Bowne was completely blind to racism. What may have accounted for this blindness?

I suggested earlier that the most glaring breakdown in Martin Luther King's personalism, or more specifically, his doctrine of human dignity, was his view of the public role of women, most particularly in the context of the black church and community. That such a break-down could creep in to a philosophy such as personalism has more to do with environmental factors than the philosophy itself. If one has been thoroughly socialized to possess a chauvinistic view of women long before he is formally introduced to the philosophy of personalism and takes it as his fundamental philosophical point of departure, there is a strong likelihood that such factors will tarnish his actual practice of that philosophy relative to women, unless he has undergone radical conversion. Indeed, without such conversion one's spoken and written language regarding the dignity of women may be consistent with all of the chief tenets of personalism, but he will likely find it difficult to be as consistent in his actual behavior toward women.

Bowne illustrated this very point quite well in his ethics. He argued that it matters little how much one writes and speaks about the dignity of being as such, or more specifically about persons and non-human life forms, if such a one does not also possess the highest possible esti-mate of their worth. Without this, the tendency—almost always—is to engage in the mal-treatment of such beings. In other words, our conception of the worth of human and non-human beings affects the way we actually apply moral principles. Bowne put it this way:

> Our conceptions of the worth and significance of humanity, and our general theory of things must have a profound influence upon our theory of conduct. The formal principles of action may remain unchanged, but the outcome will be very different. Thus, a low conception of the sacredness of personality or the meaning of human life will result in corresponding action. If it does not produce inhumanity, it will certainly tend to indifference. We may not inflict needless pain upon the animals, but, except in this respect, we regard them as having no rights. We enslave them, or exterminate them, at our pleasure; and any effort for their development we make rests mainly on self-interest. This action on our part rests upon an implicit assumption concerning the relative insignificance of animal life. Or, rather, it should be said that only such an assumption can justify our action; in practice no justification has ever been thought of or desired.[23]

Bowne essentially argued that it matters not that one claims to adhere to the principles of agape and justice, for example, if she does not possess a corresponding and deeply ingrained high conception of the worth of a particular group of persons. It matters little how eloquently a white man speaks or writes about love-justice for blacks, if he considers them to be at best sub-humans, and thus of less value than whites. In such a case, blacks will generally be treated as persons who are not deserving of equality and just treatment. The ethical principle of love-justice must be bonded to the highest possible conception of the worth of blacks. In an earlier book, Bowne further developed the idea expressed here. He sought to show that both Plato and Aristotle espoused worthwhile ethical theories, but each came up short because of their low estimate of the value of persons.

> Only a high conception of humanity gives sacredness to human rights and incites to strenuous effort in its behalf. The golden rule, also, must be conditioned by some conception of the true order and dignity of life; otherwise it might be perfectly obeyed in a world of sots and gluttons. With Plato's conception of the relation of the individual to society, Plato's doctrine of infanti-cide seems correct enough. With Aristotle's theory of man and his destiny, Aristotle's theory of slavery is altogether defensible. From the standpoint of the ancient ethnic conceptions, the accompanying ethnic morality was entirely allowable. Apart from some conception of the sacredness of personality, it is far from sure that the redemption of society could not be more readily reached by killing off the idle and mischievous classes than by philanthropic effort for their improvement.[24]

Indeed, as a dedicated Christian and a philosopher, Bowne did what few professional philosophers of his day dared. He introduced faith convictions to support his stance. He went on to argue, for example that while Christianity did not introduce new moral principles as such, what it did do was to introduce a new conception of God and persons and their mutual relations. That is, Christianity made all persons daughters and sons of a common Parent, thus undermining "the earlier ethnic conceptions and the barbarous morality based upon them."[25] If every person is a child of God and is heir to eternal life, each possesses an incontrovertible and inviolable sacredness. Bowne's point in all this is simple. With the appearance of Christianity, "*Moral principles may be what they were before, but moral practice is forever different.*"[26] At least it ought to be.

Personalism acknowledges the absolute and inherent dignity of all persons because each is created, loved, and sustained by the one God of the universe. Every person has infinite, inviolable worth because each is infinitely valued by the Creator-God. This notwithstanding, we can see that some early personalists were in fact racists,[27] or at best racially and culturally insensitive. Not only was this the case of Bowne, whose racial and cultural insensitivity was revealed when he implied that one with a strong aesthetic sense would surely know that the Venus of Milo (white) is necessarily a fairer work of art than the Hottentot Venus (black).[28] Bowne's disciple, Albert C. Knudson, long time dean of Boston University School of Theology, who, more than any other personalist, systematically developed personalism's theological implications,[29] expressed blatantly racist views. S. Paul Schilling, a third generation personalist, has pointed to "some regrettable gaps in Knudson's treatment of Christian social ethics," for example. Schilling observes rightly that Knudson was quite realistic in listing attitudes of racial superiority among the major causes of war, but he made no mention of racial segregation and other forms of injustice to so-called minorities within nations like the United States.[30]

In any event, the point is not that Bowne was a blatant racist who openly exhibited hatred toward blacks and people native to this country, anymore than King was a blatant sexist who exhibited hatred toward women. Although Bowne's student, Francis J. McConnell, maintained that his teacher championed the rights of oppressed races,[31] we see nowhere in Bowne's published writings where he lodged protests against racism or wrote of its utter incongruity with personalism. The most we can say, then, is that in principle, Bowne would have favored the rights and better treatment of blacks, but he was guilty of benign neglect regarding the issue of race. We are therefore left with trying to explain the presence of racism and sexism among personalists, persons who are advocates of the fundamental dignity of persons as such.

King's Homegrown and Academic Personalism

Martin Luther King's parents, other adult relatives, and extended family members at Ebenezer Baptist Church modeled for him and his siblings the importance of respect for self and others, the inherent dignity in self and others; the high value on community or social solidarity; and the importance of belief in a supremely personal and loving Creator-God. In addition, there was an emphasis on living one's life such that these values were highlighted in all that one did. In this regard, we can say that King's first introduction to the basic tenets of personalism was not in a formal classroom setting, but within the context of his family and church. His was a kind of homegrown personalism, although neither the boy King, nor those who influenced him in his home and church settings, knew the term "personalism." It should come as no surprise that he easily resonated to philosophical personalism in seminary and during doctoral studies, so familiar was he with its basic ideas as he was growing up.

During his last year in seminary, King applied for graduate studies at Edinburgh University, Boston University and Yale University, claiming parenthetically that Yale was his preference.[32] He was not admitted to Yale because he failed to submit his Graduate Records Examination scores. David Garrow erroneously claims that King was accepted at Yale.[33] At any rate, King said that one of the two reasons he wanted to do graduate work at Boston University was because of his interest in studying under the premier personalist at that time, Edgar S. Brightman (1884–1953).[34] In addition, he had received a strong recommendation from one of his Crozer professors, Raymond J. Bean, a Boston University alumnus. During his seminary years at Crozer, King received more explicit exposure to Brightman's work under his academic advisor and mentor, George W. Davis.

By his own admission, King was a thoroughgoing philosophical personalist. Personalism gave him philosophical and metaphysical grounding for two of his most fundamental convictions: (1) God is Personal and (2) The preciousness of persons.[35]

As thoroughgoing a personalist as King was, however, his practice of personalism was marred primarily by his socialized view of the public role of women. King was in fact sexist, and it serves no good purpose to pretend otherwise, or to try to soften this fact by claiming that, "he was a man of his times." There is no question that sexism, like racism, is both inconsistent and incompatible with personalism. So, how do we account for King's sexism? Was there something endemic to personalistic method that would have eventually driven him to acknowledge and address his sexism? If King exhibited the propensity to change from the very beginning of his public career, i.e., to broaden his own moral sphere to include that which he previously left out, is it reasonable to claim that had he lived longer he would have confessed his own sexism and male privilege, especially in the black church and community, and committed himself to becoming a recovering sexist? Is it conceivable that King would have acknowledged and worked to eradicate his sexism, as well as institutional forms of it? In other words, would King have expanded his moral sphere to include sexism and sexual discrimination, especially if enlightened and educated by the voices of emerging feminists of that period? Indeed, in the famous speech at Riverside Church on April 4, 1967, when he broke silence on the war in Vietnam, King himself spoke of the need to expand the moral sphere to include those social issues heretofore excluded, e.g., the war.[36] I return to this important point subsequently.

"Men" Must Lead in the Public Sphere

The "presupposition of male dominance" in King's thought and his failure to acknowledge it is the most obvious place we encounter a serious flaw in his doctrine of human dignity,[37] and thus in his personalism. Although there is no question that, in general King fought for the dignity of all his people, he was also quite traditionalist in his thinking about the public and private roles of women in the black community. Indeed, had not his own father modeled this for him? As the head of the household it was the man's responsibility to earn a living for his wife and children, with the wife primarily operating on the home front.[38] Indeed, as far back as 1952, while still a doctoral student, King wrote to Coretta Scott to express his loneliness for her and how frustrated he would be if he in his "little kinghood could not reign at the throne of Coretta."[39] Whether he intended it or not this conveyed the traditionalist view of the male in a dominant position over the woman. Looking back many years later, Coretta Scott

King wrote that while her husband was more liberated than most men, he made it clear even before they married that he intended to be the bread winner and that he expected his wife to be home to greet him at the end of the work day.[40]

We know that even in the organization of which King was president, i.e., the Southern Christian Leadership Conference (SCLC), there were numerous significant contributions made by black women. However, these women were not allowed to be in leadership positions, nor were their contributions always fully acknowledged. James Cone has addressed this issue in *Martin & Malcolm & America* (1991). Reporting on what King included in an Albany, Georgia "jailhouse diary" (July 27-August 10, 1962), Cone wrote:

> Identities, with names and titles, were given to the men, but the women were rendered invisible even though their number was larger. "One can find scant indication that Dr. King recognized the indispensable work of black women within the Civil Rights Movement," June Jordan has correctly written. "There is no record of his gratitude for Ella Baker's intellectual leadership. There is no record of his seeking to shake the hand of Mrs. Fannie Lou Hamer." King also failed to acknowledge properly the major role that Jo Ann Robinson, Mary Fair Burks, and other women of the Women's Political Council played in the success of the Montgomery bus boycott.[41]

King's diary tells us that ten persons were arrested along with he and Ralph Abernathy. The diary names the three men (Dr. W. G. Anderson, Slater King, and the Rev. Ben Gay), but not the seven women.[42]

In fairness to King, he did acknowledge elsewhere that the Montgomery bus boycott was first conceived by Jo Ann Robinson and the Women's Political Council (WPC).[43] In addition, he expressed appreciation for Robinson's courage to challenge Montgomery city officials, and the leadership she and Mary Fair Burks provided in the WPC.[44] Lewis V. Baldwin contends that King acknowledged Robinson and Rosa Parks as "unknown heroes" and forerunners of the Montgomery bus boycott.[45] However, although King publicly acknowledged some of the contributions of black women in the civil rights struggle from Montgomery to Memphis,[46] there is no question that his chauvinism prevented him from encouraging their involvement at the level of leadership, especially in his organization. As difficult as it might have been for King, there is clear evidence that he spoke highly of the black woman who, with the most meager financial and human resources at her disposal, set up the SCLC office and got the organization up and running. In a letter to Mrs. Katie E. Whickam, dated July 7, 1958, King referred to Ella Baker as "our associate director" who "is a very able person and a stimulating speaker."[47] Commenting further on the latest potential contributions of women to the movement, King said—although it is surely a moot point—that his awareness of this potential had much to do with his selection of a woman as associate director of SCLC. There is much more to the King-Ella Baker relationship than I can discuss here.[48] At any rate, King's comments about Baker in the letter to Whickam take a bit of the sting out of June Jordan's claim that there is no evidence of his gratitude for Baker's leadership. More than black men in Montgomery, it was black women who initiated the bus boycott, agreed to be plaintiffs in the federal case against the city segregation ordinance, and consistently turned out in the greatest numbers at the numerous mass church rallies that kept things going. And yet, the women were conspicuously absent from the planning and strategy sessions held by black male leadership,[49] just as they were similarly absent from the brainstorming session that focused on ideas for King's speech for the March on Washington for jobs and freedom on August 28, 1963.[50]

Pauli Murray (1910–1985), the first black woman to be ordained as an Episcopalian priest, expressed her strong devotion to King's leadership and witness. However, she had less admiration for King as a person, because she believed "he had not recognized the role of women in the civil rights movement (Rosa Parks was not even invited to join Dr. King's party when he went abroad to receive the Nobel Peace Prize)...."[51] Murray, like many black women, appreciated what King sought to do for his race and the many sacrifices he made, but believed he fell short of properly acknowledging the contributions of black women. More than this, Murray was aware that King, despite grudgingly appointing Ella Baker as associate director of SCLC, had done virtually little to include women in leadership positions in that organization. However, it was not just Murray and other black women who were critical of King in this regard. Although envy or jealousy may have been behind his criticisms, E. D. Nixon, long time community activist in Montgomery, accused King and his supporters of using Rosa Parks for their own ends, and then refused to hire her for a paid Montgomery Improvement Association position when she desperately needed a job. Virginia Durr, a close (white) friend, reportedly said that Parks was "very disgruntled with MLK...."[52] In addition, at the first mass rally that was held at the Holt Street Baptist Church during the early days of the Montgomery bus boycott, Rosa Parks was introduced after King spoke. When she asked black ministers if they wanted her to speak they said: "You have had enough and you have said enough and you don't have to speak."[53] Looking back, Parks said she did not think very much of it at the time. She simply accepted what the ministers said. She recalled: "The other people spoke. I didn't feel any particular need to speak. I enjoyed listening to the others and seeing the enthusiasm of the audience."[54] The "other people" who spoke that evening were all males. And yet, one must find it interesting that the person whose arrest ultimately sparked the boycott was not encouraged to speak at that first rally. Lynn Olson puts it more bluntly when she writes that the black community of Montgomery had made it clear at the Holt Street Baptist Church rally that they had had enough, "*but the woman who had shown them the way was denied a voice of her own.*"[55] Admittedly, it was not King who denied Parks' voice that night, but he was present and near by when she asked the other ministers whether they wanted her to speak. King could have intervened to express his own preference. As if this slight was not enough, Parks was not even invited to ride the desegregated buses with King and Abernathy the day after the Supreme Court ruled against Montgomery's and the state of Alabama's segregation ordinance on November 13, 1956. The failure of King and Abernathy to include Parks in this profoundly symbolic gesture spoke volumes about their attitudes toward key women in the boycott in particular, and in the public sphere in general. In addition, Parks and other female civil rights leaders, e.g., Ella Baker, Septima Clark, Diane Nash Bevel, and Daisy Bates were not allowed to march alongside male leaders in the March on Washington. Nor were any of them asked to speak that day.[56] "'All I remember Rosa saying,' [Daisy] Bates recalled, 'is that our time will someday come.'"[57] Recalling that the women's rights movement was not up to full steam in those days, Parks was pleased, a few years later, that women did not tolerate being kept in the background as she and others were from the mid–1950s through the 1960s.[58]

Honest and courageous black women did not hesitate to point to the contradictions in King's liberation project relative to the place of women in general, and black women in particular. One of these, as noted above was Ella Baker. She was among the first to suggest to King the need for an organization (like SCLC) to try to link all of the civil rights efforts throughout the South.[59] Neither King nor the all male ministerial led board of the fledgling SCLC really wanted Baker as director. She was too sassy, headstrong, self-determined, and did her own thinking and decision-making. And as if this was not enough, she refused to kowtow to men.[60] It was just not in her nature to do so. Such traits offended and made many of Baker's male colleagues uncomfortable and thus unwilling to support her.[61] Much to her chagrin, Baker discovered that King and his all male board possessed little actual organizing experience. She was also deeply distressed that they preferred an individual charismatic model of leadership, rather than investing the power of leadership in the people themselves. We can be certain that there were frequent clashes between Baker, King, and various members of the SCLC board. Although Baker had invested several years into getting SCLC off the ground, when the time came to hire a permanent executive director, she was passed over for Wyatt Tee Walker, a black Baptist preacher. She was therefore rightly, and quite naturally, angry and disappointed. Coretta Scott King confirmed this point saying:

> Ella eventually separated herself from Martin, and that was a breach that even he could not heal.... Later on she was upset that she did not get the job as executive director of SCLC—Wyatt Walker was chosen instead in 1960. *She always felt persecuted as a woman and I cannot say that she was not justified. I am sure there were a lot of slights to her.* She was a very intelligent woman. Often she was the only woman in the councils of men. She used to say to me, "Coretta, you need to be among the councils of the men. You have a lot to say."[62]

I find it rather telling that Mrs. King was sympathetic and agreed with Baker's claim that she was mistreated by the leadership of SCLC because she was a woman.

In any event, it is significant that by the end of the Montgomery bus boycott, Martin Luther King possessed a clearly developed ethic of the dignity of all persons. When one considers this, along with his desire to forge SCLC into a powerful and influential southern organization, it should not be difficult to fathom the idea that he would urge the board of directors to call Baker as executive director. Nevertheless, this was not to be, which must leave us wondering why. There are no easy answers.

Because of King's stature by the end of the bus boycott, we must wonder whether other factors were involved in his failure to name and support Baker as executive director of SCLC. By then, he was totally committed to the doctrine of the absolute dignity of persons as such. This was more than just an abstract philosophical stance for King. The idea of the dignity of persons had been battle tested; forged and given a more earthy texture than that of the purely philosophical personalists that King studied. Why, then, was King not willing to support Ella Baker, the person who, by all honest accounts, was the most qualified among women *and* men to be executive director of SCLC?

Like many other things, one can be a theoretical personalist, but fail to live this out in all areas of one's day-to-day living, as we saw in the case of Bowne and racism. And yet, the type of personalism that King forged, and to which he adhered—especially in its ethical form— places more emphasis on what one does, than what she thinks. In principle, the thoroughgoing personalist is obligated to reject sexism in all of its forms. This notwithstanding, however, we found that King's behavior toward Ella Baker meets the definition of sexism, i.e., the prejudicial behavior against women plus the power to effect that behavior and to know that the perpetrator(s) will be insulated or protected from prosecution, or at least coddled if prosecution occurs. How is it that Martin Luther King, Jr., the personalist, is open to the charge of sexism? The point here is not that King was misogynistic, as Malcolm × had been during an earlier period of his ministry.[63] Nor is there evidence that King was intentionally abusive, verbally or physically, toward women.[64] And yet, there is convincing evidence that he had difficulty with the so-called strong, sassy, confident woman in the public sphere, a point that Andrew Young corroborates.[65]

I am not here arguing that Martin Luther King was a misogynist. Nor am I arguing that he went out of his way to abuse and mistreat women whenever the opportunity presented itself. The type of family and religious values that were instilled in King as a child, as well as his adoption of personalism as his basic philosophical framework, required that he respect, in theory *and* behavior, the dignity of all women; not just women in general, or an abstract universal woman, but concrete individual blood and guts women. This notwithstanding, we need to also remember that King grew up in a household in which his father was considered the head of the family. Considering the systematic attempts of white enslavers to break up black families during American slavery, it is understandable that black couples in many instances agreed among themselves that as long as the family could be kept in tact, it was important that the husband be the head of the household. At least in the context of the black family, then, the idea of male headship is not in itself entirely problematic. What did come to be problematic, however, was the way headship often got interpreted, and more importantly, how it got lived out, by many black men. Many came to think of it as their inherent right to rule over women and children, while they in turn had no right to question male decisions or actions. Consequently, the practice of male headship went much further than was initially intended in the quarters of the enslaved.

Therefore, our problem is not even with King's notion of headship, and his firm belief that the black male's "manhood" had been taken from him and there was need to restore it. King had seen headship modeled by his own father, and maintained that it worked well between his parents. Indeed, as noted earlier, King and Coretta Scott had long discussions about the type of family arrangement they each desired. Consequently, after they were married, Mrs. King was well aware of her husband's more traditional views about husband-wife relations and parenting. She essentially conceded this to him, although she herself had always been a very strong, independent woman. Especially after they began to have children, it seemed to her that the more traditional family arrangement—with the husband providing a living and the wife essentially managing the family—worked fairly well. Therefore, while there were issues with King's sexism, even in the private sphere of the home, the problem was exacerbated regarding his stance and behavior in the public arena of women in leadership positions.

King's Sexism and Personalistic Method

Having studied the philosophy of personalism, its method, and criterion of truth, and taken them as his own, Martin Luther King understood the importance of identifying his own, as well as the strengths and limitations in the thought *and* practice of others. He knew that this critical outlook is necessary if one is truly interested in ascertaining truth. He heartily concurred with Hegel's adage that the true is the whole.[66] Among other things, this meant that no idea, no person, no group, is exempt from criticism, including the personalists who made this an integral part of their philosophical method. This is consistent with the logic of personalistic method, which requires that one be willing to examine all relevant facts and evidence, and be critical of inconsistencies. For example, one cannot claim to take seriously the idea that the true is the whole, while simultaneously refusing to take seriously that which was previously left out, whether human or non-human beings, or ideas. If I accept the idea that the true is the whole, and I become aware that women are accusing individuals and the structures of society of sexual discrimination, I must be willing to truly hear and respond appropriately to those accusations. Moreover, my responsibility does not end once I have heard the concerns and criticisms. As one in the personalist camp, I must then become a champion of equality between the sexes. Not even Martin Luther King is exempt from criticism when limitations or contradictions are identified in his thought and practice. Regarding the issue of sexism and the women's movement in the 1960s, we have to try to determine what King did and did not know about this. But suffice it to say that as one who adhered to personalist method, he surely would have been open to women's stories and criticisms had they approached him. My sense is that King had some awareness of the emerging women's movement, but because of his focus on the war in Vietnam and the Poor People's Campaign it was at best a peripheral awareness. Indeed, Coretta Scott King implied as much in an interview with Alice Walker.[67]

Nevertheless, notwithstanding his failure to acknowledge and address his own sexism and that of SCLC, King would be the first to acknowledge the ongoing need for criticism, correction, and development of his views and practice. This, for example, is why he agonized over the war in Vietnam and whether he should speak against it publicly. The facts and events surrounding this tragedy were too blatant and loud for him to ignore them.

As one who considered himself a thoroughgoing personalist, King's method was synopsis, and his criterion of truth was *growing empirical coherence*.[68] This was his means of testing all truth-claims and all relevant facts and evidence on the way to truth or most reasonable hypotheses. In a nutshell, the coherence criterion maintains that because persons are finite and limited and are capable of only knowing in part, the facts of experience are always forthcoming. Since we have no way of knowing all there is to know in any given moment, we are limited to hypotheses or claims to truth that must be based on the largest amount of available data and evidence relative to the particular issue in question. These data and evidence should be rationally interpreted and orchestrated into the most reasonable, creative, and coherent hypothesis, but with the understanding that as long as there is more living to be done and more evidence and facts unknown to us, any hypothesis we arrive at today must have a dynamic or tentative character about it. That is, we must be willing to alter that hypothesis in light of new evidence or facts that may appear later.

King himself was a quick study and clearly exhibited the capacity, willingness, and courage to change in the face of new evidence and compelling social events. In this regard, we need only remember the internal struggle that ultimately led him to break silence on the war in Vietnam. He had to come to terms with his own conviction about the interrelated structure of reality and what this must mean in the most concrete terms regarding the war. As he told the eight white clergymen in his famous "Letter from Birmingham Jail," he had done the same thing before agreeing to come to Birmingham. He said that it would have been unethical and unchristian for him to sit by silently in Atlanta and not be concerned about what was happening in Birmingham or any other city in the United States. At this point (1963), King had broadened his moral field to include ethical problems beyond the local community, to any place in the United States. "Injustice anywhere is a threat to justice everywhere," he said to the white clergy in Birmingham. "We are caught in an inescapable network of mutuality, tied in a single garment of destiny. Whatever affects one directly, affects all indirectly.... Anyone who lives inside the United States can never be considered an outsider anywhere within its bounds."[69] King adamantly espoused the doctrine of the interrelated structure of reality. After being awarded the Nobel Peace Prize on December 10, 1964, it was clear in King's mind that this principle needed to be expanded to include the whole world,[70] which supports Lewis Baldwin's description of him as an internationalist.[71]

What we need to remember is that Martin Luther King began his ministry by focusing on the problems of a particular local community. The most immediate problem for him was racial segregation, especially as manifested in the public transportation system in Montgomery. His awareness of facts and events would cause his views and practices to evolve and expand significantly during ensuing months and years. Increasingly, he could see how social problems on the local, national, and international levels were interrelated. This served to contextualize and give texture to his basic conviction about the interrelated structure of reality and the fundamental interdependence of persons throughout the world. Consequently, we can easily trace his development from concern about the race problem in Montgomery, and then throughout the South; his decision in the mid–1960s to take the Movement North to Chicago; his concern about crushing social problems in India, South Africa, and Latin America; his sense that the "second phase" of the civil rights movement should focus on economic inequality; and his stance against the Vietnam war. In all of this, King was only behaving in accordance with what I earlier referred to as personalism's developmental ethic, which is to say that over time he expanded his moral sphere to include more and more things that had previously been left out; things that he previously knew little about. In light of this pattern of expansion and development, there is no reason to assume that had King lived longer, this would not have affected his stance on the role of women in public leadership. Stated differently, there is no reason to believe that one with such an enormous capacity to change and who in fact consistently revealed his ability to do so, would not have come to the point of acknowledging his male privilege, subject it to radical critique, and be intentional about expanding his moral sphere to include the equality of women in the public arena.

In light of the person King was coming to be, especially in the last three years of his life, it is difficult to imagine that he would not have cleanly turned the corner on sexism had he lived into the 1970s and witnessed and experienced the women's movement. Had this been the case, the best circumstantial evidence suggests that he very likely would have confessed his own sexism, followed by rejection of it in its individual and systemic forms. Considering his fundamentalist upbringing, and the preference for headship practices in his own and most families with which he was familiar, it is an understatement to say that it would not have been easy for King to undergo this conversion. But just as he heard the loud protests against the war in Vietnam, was deeply affected by the pictures of children who had been badly burned by napalm,[72] and had frequently reminded himself of the interrelated structure of reality, there is no reason to think that he would not have heard and responded similarly to the loud protests of women during the 1970s, particularly as more and more black and other women of color joined the chorus of women's voices. Remember, King had already made the connection between racism, economic exploitation, and militarism. But by 1968, he had not yet heard clearly enough the voices of women who were seeking political and other rights in the public domain. The contemporary women's movement was not yet in full bloom near the end of King's life, although his own human rights efforts served as an impetus for the emergence of that movement. Moreover, King had not been exposed to large numbers of black women's criticisms, and no evidence has yet been uncovered to suggest that he explicitly engaged in dialog with such persons regarding their experience of sexual exploitation and the role that he and other prominent male leaders played in it. It is also the case that most black women of that period saw the women's movement as a middle class white woman affair that had little or nothing to do with the problems of the black community. This might well have been the voice that King heard and reacted to, thus prompting his silence. My hope is that King scholars will pursue this matter much further than we have to date.

As a thoroughgoing personalist, Martin Luther King would have responded appropriately to women's protests about not being acknowledged as full-fledged human beings with all the rights thereto pertaining, had such protests actually been in his line of sight during what was an unstable and turbulent period for him in the civil rights movement from the mid to late 1960s. For we must not forget that even before King ever heard the term "personalism," he believed firmly that the image of God was etched into the soul of every person, which meant for him that *every* person is infinitely valuable to God. Although like most people of his day he used the generic "man" to refer to persons in general, nothing in his speeches and writings suggests that he believed women to be less human than men or to possess less of the divine image, and thus to have less worth than men. King attributed to the Christian tradition "the conviction that every man is an heir to a legacy of dignity and worth." Theologically, this means that every person is stamped with the image of God. From this, he concluded that every person should be respected and revered precisely because of her relatedness to God and the conviction that God loves her. "An individual has value," said King, "because he has value to God. Whenever this is recognized, 'whiteness' and 'blackness' pass away as determinants in a relationship and 'son' and 'brother' are substituted."[73] I have seen nothing in the published and unpublished writings of King to suggest that he believed women to be of less value to God than men.

Although much of the focus here was on race relations, I am suggesting that had King lived into the 1970s *and* retained his personalist stance and commitment to personalist method, he would have broadened his theological and moral perspective—which already included an adamant rejection of racism, economic inequality, and militarism—to include sexual analysis and the need to eradicate sexism. Such a change would have been consistent and compatible with how King's thought and practice evolved from a primary focus on racial discrimination to include economic exploitation, international liberation struggles, and militarism. Because of the person he was, there can be little doubt that King would have begun by confessing his own sexism, and subsequently, calling for other men to do similarly, had he lived into the decade of the 1970s.

Influenced by the existentialist theologian Paul Tillich, Martin Luther King held that freedom constituted the essence of personhood,[74] and that to be a person is to be free, and vice versa. Although reared in a male chauvinist and sexist culture, King was enough of a personalist to not make the mistake of considering women to be less human than men. And yet, he was very much influenced by his environment and culture, and therefore failed, in practice, to acknowledge fully the humanity and dignity of women, especially in the public arena. However, we need to remember his pattern of including more and more of what he previously did not focus on. There is no reason to believe, then, that he would not have been just as supportive of women's rights had he actually heard their voices of protest. Furthermore, when King declared throughout his civil rights ministry that God's image inheres in all persons, an idea that was not new by any means, but had been present in much of black religious history,[75] he meant *all* persons. But this also meant for him that God loves all persons equally. God loves no individual or race of people more than any other. This must also mean that God does not love men more than women. God loves all persons equally. Theologically, King was certain of this fact. Practically, however, he fell short regarding women. Nevertheless, the logic of personalistic method, and King's conviction that every person has etched into her being the image of God, can only mean that there would have been a reversal of his sexism had he lived longer.

Conclusion

Martin Luther King was, by and large, without peer in his application of personalistic principles to the social ills of his day. This point looms large when considering the subject of his sexism. His staunch conviction that a person cannot be all that she can be in isolation was consistent with both the personalistic principle of the unity of humanity, as well as the African traditional view of the primacy of community. We are not persons in isolation. Human beings are, rather, persons-in-community. In this regard, King said: "At the heart of all that civilization has meant and developed is 'community'—the mutually cooperative and voluntary venture of man to assume a semblance of responsibility for his brother."[76] According to this view, a person cannot even be a person without interaction with other persons. As we saw earlier, personalism holds that the person is fundamentally a *socius*.

King always held in tension the value of the autonomous individual and that of the community. Ultimately he sought the establishment of the beloved community, a thoroughly inclusive community based on the principle of equality and respect for the humanity and dignity of every person. There is no question that King included women in his vision of the community of love. His was the problem of uncritically accepting the gender practices of his day, practices, I maintain, that he did not have to accept, even though the women's movement was not in full swing during his life time. For he had as models the likes of Frederick Douglass and W.E.B. DuBois, men that he respected greatly, and were considered the quintessential male supporters of women's rights during their day. King also had the strong, firm, critical voice of Ella Baker to challenge him to face up to his chauvinism. Once the papers of Coretta King are available we may know more definitively the nature of her challenges to her husband regarding the role of women in the public arena. It is also important to note that many of King's closest male companions were either young Baptist preachers or black males affiliated with other denominations, many of whom were conservative in theological outlook regarding gender relations. This would have made it very difficult for King to be challenged on his own position regarding women, or even to be self-critical. For, those who were around him most frequently saw no problem with the way black women were treated when it came to the matter of leadership and authority. King himself saw no problem with it, as his social reality relative to women was little different from theirs. The blind do not do the best job of leading the blind.

Earlier in this chapter I said that there is evidence that near the beginning of King's civil rights ministry he was more liberated in some of his views on women and male-female relations than most men of his day. What King said in a Mother's Day sermon at Dexter Avenue Baptist Church on May 8, 1955, must lead us to believe that his stance on women was complex, or at least conflicted; that he was at least troubled about the more traditional view of male headship, even though, like many things, he left no carefully worked out position on the matter. In "The Crisis in the Modern Family," he told the congregation:

> Men must accept the fact that the day has passed when the man can stand over the wife with an iron rod asserting his authority as "boss" ... the day has passed when women will be trampled over and treated as some slave subject to the dictates of a despotic husband. One of the great contributions that Christianity has made to the world is that of lifting the status of womanhood from that of an insignificant child-bearer to a position of dignity and honor and respect. Women must be respected as human beings and not be treated as mere means. Strictly speaking, there is no boss in the home; it is no lord-servant relationship.[77]

Although King credited Christianity for lifting the status of woman to one of dignity, he would have done well to have softened this claim. There is no evidence that Christianity as such did this. It is truer to say with social gospel advocate, Walter Rauschenbusch, that the real source was a small or minority segment of Christianity, mostly the voices of women, not "by any direct championship of the organized Church."[78] The 19th century abolitionist and "radical woman suffrage man," Frederick Douglass, argued similarly and most convincingly:

> We have heard a great deal of late as to what Christianity has done for woman. We have a right to call upon these Christian ministers to show that what has been done, has not been done in spite of the church, but in accordance with its teachings. One thing is certain, when the chains

of woman shall be broken, when she shall become the recognized equal of man, and is put into the full enjoyment of all the rights of an American citizen, as she will be, church and ministry will be the first to claim the honor of the victory, and to say, "We did it!"[79]

Unquestionably, the status of woman changed significantly for the best as a result of the influence of the church, but this is not the same as saying with King, that the church as church, changed it.

King's statement to the church in that Mother's Day sermon was that of a man who appeared to be more liberated in his views on relations between man and woman. And yet by December of 1961, we find him making very traditional claims about the nature of man and that of woman. Although he still argued against the idea of man ruling over woman, he scribbled the following words in outline form on a scrap of paper:

> A man's wold [sic] is largely one of action. He is never happy unless he can measure his success or failure in terms of conquest in the exterior world. On the other hand, despite all her success in the exterior word [sic], a woman is never happy outside an emotional world. She is most at home in the world of love and maternity.
>
> Woman is subjective, realistic concrete
>
> Man is objective abstract and general
>
> Every woman has her world of love, devotion and sympathy, and wise is the man who understands and appreciates it. Man has his world of action and creativity and wise is the wife who understands it.[80]

Clearly, King was not settled in his views about the place of woman. Although he at times made statements that gave the appearance that he was more liberated, the evidence suggests that although he had a more liberated stance on the status of woman in the home, he was much more traditional regarding their place in the public domain.

Finally, King's behavior toward Ella Baker and other women in the Movement is evidence of a significant contradiction in his theory of human dignity, but it is a point from which persons who survived him can learn much. This, in the end, is the point. Those who survived King can learn from what is an obvious major contradiction in his personalism. The chances of learning from this may be vastly increased if we first name the problem for what it is. Indeed, King himself cited this as the first step in his method of nonviolent resistance to evil, viz., to get the relevant facts, identify, and name the problem.[81] Once we know the problem and put a name to it, we can then begin the work of determining how best to address and eradicate it. That Martin Luther King did not live long enough to be transformed regarding gender discrimination is no reason or excuse for us to fail in this regard today.

14

King and Intra-Community Black Violence[1]

This chapter addresses Martin Luther King, Jr.'s meaning and message for us today. More especially, I am concerned with his meaning for the black community in light of the tragic phenomenon of black-on-black violence and homicide among young black males, particularly, but not exclusively, in inner city urban areas. Indeed, the "new" element in this unprecedented phenomenon is the fact that it now rears its ugly face in suburban and other areas. From about the 1970s through much of the 1990s, the increasingly high incidence of intra-community homicides among young black males was generally isolated in inner city areas. Only within the last two decades have there been signs of the tragedy showing signs of proliferation in outlying areas of the inner city. The only "good" news about the latter—if one can say anything truly "good" about this tragedy—is that the numbers are much lower than what we see in inner cities such as the Southside of Chicago, and Indianapolis, Indiana, (where I live). It does seem, however, that the perpetrators, by which I mean the young men (many just boys, really) who actually pull the trigger of the guns that maim and mortally wound, are getting increasingly bolder regarding the locations of the violence and homicides they commit. There still seems to be much apprehension among many in the wider society to name the perpetrators who are the fundamental cause of the tragedy that has manifested itself as intra-community violence and homicide among young black males. I return to this important point momentarily.

Throughout this book we have seen that Martin Luther King had much to say, not only about the dignity of persons as such,[2] but about the dignity of his own people. A first rate personalist theologian and social ethicist who stressed the inviolable sacredness of all persons, King encountered the eroding sense of self-worth and self-esteem among young black males in a big way when he took the Movement north to Chicago in 1966. There is no question that his message about black dignity in the 1960s is relevant to the black community today. Before examining this, and what King had to say about black-against-black violence and homicide, I want to briefly consider the philosophy of personalism and its importance for King as he sought to liberate his people's thinking about themselves as human beings.

That King was at bottom a Christian pastor who loved the church and saw both its possibilities and its weaknesses; that he was often known as a "trouble-maker" and agitator, is important for what follows. But it is also important to point out that King's familial background and his training in the Ebenezer Baptist Church in Atlanta, Georgia instilled in him three personalistic ideas that he would later study formally when he was introduced to the philosophy of personalism at Crozer Theological Seminary and studied it in depth at Boston University: God as personal and loving; the sacredness of persons; and the importance of freedom.

King and Personalism

Although Martin Luther King's is the name usually associated with the philosophy of personalism, he was not the first black person to be formally trained in that philosophy at Boston University, then the key center for personalistic studies in the United States. John Wesley Edward Bowen (1855–1933) was the first black person to be trained in personalist philosophy,[3] and in 1887 was the first black to earn the Ph.D. at Boston University. Inasmuch as he studied under Borden P. Bowne (1847–1910), who developed that philosophy systematically, and is considered to be the father of American personalism, we may think of Bowen as the first black academic personalist.

Without question, Bowen was influenced by Bowne's insistence that persons have the right of way and that in all things their innate sense of dignity should be acknowledged in the way they are treated. Bowen was easily drawn to Bowne's emphasis on the centrality and dignity of persons. However, he went well beyond his teacher in this regard. Aware of his people's daily experience of racism, Bowen was adamant and forthright in lifting up the significance of their selfhood and sense of dignity. Like Martin Luther King nearly seventy years later, Bowen did not need the personalism of Bowne to create in him his already long held belief in the inherent sacredness of his people and his conviction that God is personal and loving. Instead, Bowen quickly and easily took to personalist philosophy because it provided philosophical grounding for his two basic faith claims: that God is personal, and the inalienable dignity of all persons. Much like King would do later, Bowen assumed the humanity and preciousness of his people. This assumption was of particular importance since during Bowen's day, and King's (and since!), for vast numbers of white people assumed that blacks were not as fully human as they, and moreover, that they had no rights that whites were bound by civil law to acknowledge and respect (to echo the words of Chief Justice Roger B. Taney in the famous case of Dred Scott vs. Sanford in 1857). Bowen, of course, rejected this idea, arguing instead, that because blacks have the same basic humanity and dignity as all other persons, they have the same civil and human rights that ought to be acknowledged and respected. What warrants respect, he reasoned, is not the color of one's skin as such, but one's humanity. Bowen was adamant in his claim that, "The Negro is a human personality,"[4] and should be respected and treated as such. Regarding the matter of race, Bowen said explicitly—quite unlike his teacher, Bowne—that "we belong to each other."[5] This was Bowen's way of saying that because God is personal and creator of all, and has created all for the love and glory of God, all races and ethnic groups are inextricably related, such that none can be all they can be, if others do not have the same advantages and opportunities to be all they can be. Although at this writing, I have seen nothing in the corpus of published and unpublished King papers to indicate that King was aware of Bowen, we can be certain that he adhered to the idea of the interrelatedness of all human beings, united under the One God of the universe.

We have seen that King's greatest contribution to the philosophy of personalism was his unrelenting application of its principles to what he considered to be the chief social problems of his day: racism, poverty/economic exploitation, and militarism. In this regard, he was the quintessential *social activist personalist* or *theologian of nonviolent resistance*. In this, he transcended his personalist teachers at Boston University.

Defining Personalism

Personalism is the philosophy that was systematically developed by Bowne at Boston University from the time he began teaching there in 1876, until he collapsed from a stroke in the classroom on April 1, 1910, and died later that day. I like to tell my students that, simply put, personalism is any philosophy that stresses God as personal, and human beings—all human beings or none!—as inherently and inviolably sacred. I then follow by telling them that having said that, it took me 256 pages of text to unpack the meaning of that statement in my *Personalism: A Critical Introduction* (1999). Truthfully, personalism really is a philosophy around which one can easily wrap her mind, if she remembers the two fundamental tenets just cited. One who believes in God as personal and the dignity of all persons is in the personalist camp, if only a minimalist. Martin Luther King, of course, was a maximalist or thoroughgoing personalist, since he argued personalism out to its logical conclusions, especially regarding its relevance for addressing social evils.

Personalists in the tradition of Martin Luther King believe that ultimate reality (read "God") is personal and that persons (those beings who are at least self-conscious, rational, self-directed, and possess and can articulate an inborn sense of worth) are the highest (not the only!) intrinsic values. They believe that the universe is a society of interacting and intercommunicating persons, and thus is fundamentally social or relational. This is why King frequently declared the interrelatedness of all life. "We are all caught in an inescapable network of mutuality, tied in a single garment of destiny," he liked to remind his contemporaries. "Whatever affects one directly, affects all indirectly. We are made to live together because of the interrelated structure of reality."[6] As a type of idealism, the King type of personalism maintains that there is an objective moral order in the universe to which human beings ought to conform. Because of his fundamental belief in the existence of such an order, King insisted that the universe itself has the texture of justice, and thus is on the side of justice and right. Acts of injustice on any level, then, contradict what the universe requires. When such contradictions exist, the world does not operate the way God intends. This conviction enhanced King's faith that evil and wrongdoing cannot, indeed will not, have the last word in such a universe. It also gave him strong reason to believe that those who struggle for justice and freedom throughout the world have cosmic and divine companionship, which means they are never alone in the struggle.

The foregoing paragraph referenced four personalistic ideas: (1) *reality is personal*; (2) *persons are the highest (but not the only) intrinsic values*; (3) *reality is social or relational*; and (4) there is *an objective moral order at the seat of the universe*, the violation of which opens the door to severe consequences. Suffice it to say that the rudiments of these ideas were instilled in King long before he learned the word *personalism* (quite possibly while he was a student at Morehouse College), was formally introduced to it at Crozer Theological Seminary, and later studied it systematically as a doctoral student at Boston University. Indeed, that King so easily and readily adhered to personalism as his basic philosophical point of departure, through which to make deeper sense of his faith in a personal God and his belief that all persons are absolutely sacred, is a testament to the family and religious values instilled in him during his childhood and adolescent years. Before proceeding, it is important to establish *which* King is the subject of this discussion.

Martin Luther King, Jr.: Post-1966

It is not my intention to suggest that Martin Luther King was a kind of split person-ality. He was not, at least no more so than any other "normal" human being. For the sake of what I want to get across, however, it is important to be clear about *which* King is at the center of this discussion. Is one talking about the early, idealistic King of the Mont-gomery, Birmingham, and Selma Alabama campaigns (roughly 1955–1965)? Or, is one talk-ing about the mature, more politically astute King of the post–Chicago campaign (roughly 1965–1968)?

The disintegration of the so-called "War on Poverty" in the mid–1960s, the escalation of the war in Vietnam, and the failed Chicago campaign of 1966 forced King to engage in a deeper social analysis of the socio-economic and political structures of this society. In my esti-mation, the aforementioned events and King's ensuing critical social analysis, led to the emer-gence of a more militant King—a King who, near the end of his life, was calling for a radical rebirth of the entire nation, and he was not referring to the more traditional idea of spiritual rebirth, as if the focus was to be on the souls of individuals only. In his last SCLC presidential address, King called on the entire human rights movement to "address itself to the question of restructuring the whole of American society,"[7] which means both demanding a broader dis-tribution of economic wealth, and of recognizing the interconnections between social prob-lems. King continued: "Now, when I say question the whole society, it means ultimately coming to see that the problem of racism, the problem of economic exploitation, and the problem of war are all tied together. These are the triple evils that are interrelated.... What I am saying today is that we must go from this convention and say, 'America, you must be born again!'"[8] In that same address, King admonished that blacks needed to stop being ashamed of their blackness (a point to which I return below).

The King of this period, post–1966, was much more interested in getting to the root causes of major social maladies. And while he continued to focus on the moralization of the attitudes of individuals, he now had a more pronounced interest and zeal for the moralization of societal structures so that all persons would be treated with dignity and respect. So militant was the King of this period that not only did his public stance against the war in Vietnam put in jeopardy the support of many liberals, but such support eroded because of his efforts to organize a massive Poor People's Campaign whereby the poor of all races and ethnic back-grounds in this country would go the nation's capital and camp out until lawmakers heard and responded appropriately to their plea for a real war on poverty that would at least generate "jobs or income for all" the nation's poor.[9] Indeed, many, including King's daughter Yolanda, have speculated that although he might well have been murdered eventually, he was likely assassinated when he was because of the radical ramifications of the impending Poor People's Campaign.[10] King discovered that all the talk about the right of U.S. citizens to life, liberty, and the pursuit of happiness meant nothing if a person did not have a living wage job, or no income at all. Indeed, in his last Sunday morning sermon, preached at the National Cathedral (Episcopal) in Washington, D.C., on March 31, 1968 (four days before he was assassinated), King made it clear that one without a job or income "has neither life nor liberty nor the pos-sibility for the pursuit of happiness. He merely exists."[11]

For our purpose then, this is the Martin Luther King I have in mind as I consider his mes-sage and meaning for the black community today. I begin by naming a specific social issue. Although it has taken on a different form today, it is an issue that came to King's attention when he took the Movement north, to Chicago.

Intra-Community Black Violence and Murder

By the end of the 1980s, a definitive study concluded: "*In American society today, no single group is more vulnerable, more victimized, and more violated than young black males in the age range of 15 to 24.*"[12] It was argued that it was a well-documented fact that the leading cause of death among young black males was homicide. Indeed, Andrew Billingsley tells us that by the end of the decade of 1989 "homicide had become the leading cause of death among young black men and women between the ages of fifteen and thirty-four."[13] A 1985 federal government study concluded that "after heart disease, 'homicide accounts for more excess mortality among black Americans than any other cause of death.'"[14] Blacks are twelve percent of the nation's population, but account for an alarming 44 percent of all murder victims. "Black men were more than six times as likely as white men to be victims of homicide, and black women were four times as likely as white women to be such victims."[15] Most of the murder victims are young black males between fifteen and twenty years of age. Most of the perpetrators are also young black males in that age range. As serious and tragic as this phenomenon is, "it has been estimated that for every homicide there are approximately one hundred other serious assaults or attempted homicides"[16] in the black community. Approximately 84 percent of all violent crimes committed against blacks in the 1980s were committed by other blacks.[17] At this writing, there is no evidence of a decline in this percentage.

King's method did not only include naming the specific social maladies, but identifying their causes. Indeed, two of the three social problems he focused on most are culprits in the phenomenon of black-on-black violence and murder. These include racism in its individual and institutional forms, and massive poverty that is the result of economic exploitation. King himself saw that these are interrelated problems which feed on, and fuel each other.

When it can be said that the high school drop-out rate for black males in a major metropolitan center is 71 percent in a given year, and that unemployment among black male youth ranges from 46 percent to 52 percent,[18] it should not be difficult to see the link to racism and economic deprivation, past and present. The only reasonable conclusion to draw is that this is the worst of times—with worse times in the making for *all* black boys. And as Gwendolyn Rice reminds us: it is the worst of times for "those doing okay and those who are not." She cites cases where even the brightest, most promising young black males are endangered. Either they become victims of violence because of their refusal to join gangs, or they become victims of the prison system when they have to resort to violence in attempts to enforce their NO to gang members and drug dealers.

Much of the intra-community violence among young black males is a reaction to outside forces due to no fault of their own. These are systemic forces due to racism and economic injustice. This is by no means to be taken as an excuse for black-on-black violence or any other crimes in the black community, for there is also the matter of moral agency which should be taken seriously, as well as the importance of owning responsibility for specific acts of violence in the black community. King himself pointed to the need to address both the external environmental causes, as well as the matter of individual choice. I return to this important matter momentarily. For now, it is important to observe that *racism and economic exploitation are among the dominant causes of the conditions that have caused the escalation of intra-community violence among blacks.* And there are no grounds for pretending that there has been a significant decline in racism since the civil rights movement, no matter what the likes of William J. Wilson[19] and Shelby Steele[20] have said! Racism is still alive and well in far too many individuals and in every institution in the United States. One need only read Cornel West's *Race Matters*[21] and *Democracy Matters*,[22] Andrew Hacker's *Two Nations: Black and White, Separate, Hostile, Unequal*,[23] and Joe R. Feagin's *Systemic Racism: A Theory of Oppression*[24] and *Racist America: Roots, Current Realities, and Future Reparations*[25] for verification. And although he does not address the issue of moral agency, Amos Wilson is emphatic in the claim that the fundamental cause of intra-community black violence is white supremacy. Wilson puts it in quite a poignant way.

> White supremacy by its very nature and intent requires the continuing oppression and subordination of African peoples and, in time, may require their very lives. Subordination of a people requires that that people in some way or ways be violated, dehumanized, humiliated, and that some type of violence be perpetrated against them. The violently oppressed react violently to their oppression. *When their reactionary violence, their retaliatory or defensive violence, cannot be effectively directed at their oppressors or effectively applied to their self-liberation, it then will be directed at and applied destructively to themselves.* This is the essence of Black-on-Black violence.[26]

There are those, especially of a previous generation, who will point out that there has always been black-on-black violence, and thus the problem which I have named is not a new thing under the sun. But it is important to point out that what *is* new is both the *randomness* and the *staggering numbers* of the acts of violence and murder in the black community today, and there is no evidence on the horizon that this will change any time soon. And what is striking is that historically, blacks exhibited a much higher appreciation for black dignity and worth. Indeed, historically, there is nothing in the value system of black Americans that explains the present-day low estimate of the worth and value of black personhood among so many young black males.

Yet, there is no question that the level of *lovelessness, hopelessness, aimlessness*, and sheer *mean-spiritedness* among many young black males today has reached epic proportion.[27] In part, this state of affairs exists because as a group, young black males have few alternatives that make any sense at all. This means that far too often, no matter what choice they make, the result will be life-threatening rather than life-enhancing.

Martin Luther King was aware that the quantity and quality of choices for some groups are so limited that no matter what they choose, the result is self-defeating and demeaning. King had a sense that this was the case when he spoke of the many blacks who, because they had known nothing in their lives but oppression, racial, and economic dehumanization, "...are so devoid of pride and self-respect that they have resigned themselves to segregation."[28] When King took the Movement to Chicago he intentionally rented and lived in a slum apartment and had the opportunity to meet and talk with many of the angry young black males who had no sense of hope or purpose because this society offered them nothing of substance. Many of these resorted to violence, frequently against each other and other members of the Chicago black ghetto. Reflecting on this experience King said:

> I met these boys and heard their stories in discussion we had on some long, cold nights last winter at the slum apartment I rent in the West Side ghetto of Chicago. I was shocked at the venom they poured out against the world. At times I shared their despair and felt a hopelessness that these young Americans could ever embrace the concept of nonviolence as the effective and powerful instrument of social reform.
>
> All their lives, boys like this have known life as a madhouse of violence and degradation. Some have never experienced a meaningful family life. Some have police records. Some dropped out of the incredibly bad slum schools, then were deprived of honorable work, then took to the streets.
>
> To the young victim of the slums, this society has so limited the alternatives of his life that the expression of his manhood is reduced to the ability to defend himself physically. No wonder it

appears logical to him to strike out, resorting to violence against oppression. That is the only way he thinks he can get recognition.

And so, we have seen occasional rioting—and, much more frequently and consistently, brutal acts and crimes by Negros against Negroes. In many a week in Chicago, as many or more Negro youngsters have been killed in gang fights as were killed in the riots here last summer.[29]

Indeed, as far back as the late 1950s, King expressed concern about the high rate of crime in black communities.[30] A southerner himself, King also knew that black men, especially in the Deep South, generally owned guns and sharp knives and were not hesitant to use them in defense of self and loved ones. As well, they would just as quickly use these weapons against each other. This is why King could say in 1967 that the spirit of violence was too high among blacks. As proof of this, he said that a visit to local emergency rooms in inner city hospitals on the weekends will reveal large numbers of blacks being treated for gunshot and stab wounds inflicted by other blacks.[31] Were King alive today, he would undoubtedly further accentuate his concerns by saying that not only do the limited quality alternatives reduce expressions of young black males' manhood to resorting to proactive and reactive violence against each other and innocent bystanders in the community, but to engaging in teen baby making, long before either parent has had a chance to live and mature into responsible adulthood.

Self-Love and Other-Regarding Love

Although Martin Luther King appealed to both the Law of Individualism and the Law of Altruism,[32] John J. Ansbro suggests that he identified more with the latter law, which implies that there was in King's ethics a strong other-regarding sentiment. The Law of Individualism, on the other hand, focuses on the idea of the individual as the basic moral unit, and thus the importance of self-love or the self-regarding sentiment. It expresses the idea that no person should ever be used as fuel to warm society.[33] King accepted the validity of this Law, although the early King seemed to place less emphasis on the principle of self-love. He seemed to focus more on other-regarding love, or the ethics of altruism or agape.[34]

According to King, agape "is the love of God working in the lives of men. When we love on the *agape* level," said King, "we love men not because we like them, not because their attitudes and ways appeal to us, but because God loves them."[35] It is this understanding of love which led King to the provocative conviction that "unearned suffering is redemptive."[36] But King went further. "Now I pray that, recognizing the necessity of suffering, the Negro will make of it a virtue. To suffer in a righteous cause," he said, "is to grow to our humanity's full stature."[37] King was clear that there is nothing redemptive about suffering as such. Rather, suffering is *made* to be redemptive through organized relentless nonviolent struggle against it.

The evidence suggests that King "was convinced that *agape* may at times demand even the suspension of the law of self-preservation so that through our self-sacrifice we can help create the beloved community."[38] King did not believe that such self-sacrifice necessarily precludes self-respect and self-love, although one surely wonders about this when it is remembered how many times he seemed to place the moral onus of bearing suffering on those who are already suffering from seemingly endless oppression and injustice. In one place, for example, he said that "there will be no permanent solution to the race problem until oppressed men develop the capacity to love their enemies."[39] King believed that in the best interest of the redemption of others and the establishment of the beloved community, it is sometimes necessary for oppressed people to sacrifice all for such an end. His application of the Law of Altruism, i.e., of loving others, was more open to self-sacrifice.[40] But why not require the same of oppressors, and those who benefit mightily from human oppression?

Although Martin Luther King surely did not intend it, an implication of his stance about the self-sacrifice of the oppressed might be that the self, especially the oppressed self, is not as valuable as others. Even the later King would continue to stress self-sacrifice, but as a result of the Black Consciousness Movement he emphasized more and more the significance of blacks loving themselves and being proud of who they are as a people. This was a way of acknowledging *both* the infinite worth of oneself as well as that of others. In this, King was being consistent not only with the values he received through his family and the black church upbringing, but with his training in the philosophy of personalism. Personalistic ethics maintains that just as the individual is not to disregard the needs and interests of society, nor should society unduly sacrifice the individual and her interests. Both the individual and society have values that ought to be respected.[41]

Indeed, nowhere was the later King's emphasis on the dignity and worth of the self more evident than his insistence that blacks learn to love and respect themselves and their heritage. This King urged blacks to stand up and say for all the world to hear: "I'm black and I'm beautiful."[42] Such an awareness is needed if blacks are to be able to transform a sense of powerlessness into one of creative power. King urged that blacks identify and proudly and courageously affirm and agree with the positive contributions of Black Power. In this regard he said: "We are in desperate need to find our identity. We need to be proud of our heritage. We need to be proud of being black and not ashamed of it."[43]

It stands to reason that, if I have little or no regard for myself, I will not likely have a healthy regard for others, let alone for those who oppress me and demean my humanity. And while it may be conceded that it is difficult to maintain a healthy balance between self-love and other-regarding love, I would say that it behooves groups like young black males to place more emphasis on healthy regard for self. This is especially important in light of the alarmingly high incidence of intra-community black violence and murder.

Freedom and Moral Agency

King stressed not only the centrality of the person, and thus the absolute dignity and worth of persons as such. He also emphasized the primacy of freedom. For King, the personalist, all being is characterized by freedom. This means that to be is to be free, and to act or have the potential to do so. Indeed, at bottom, to be free is what it means to be a person; to be a person is to be free. This fundamental freedom has important implications for the ethical and political freedom of human beings in the world and what they ought to be willing to do to assert their freedom.

According to King, persons come into existence as free beings and with the capacity to be self-determining moral agents. Some persons lack moral agency, i.e., the capacity to act freely, responsibly, and maturely, because they are mentally challenged or otherwise deprived. This may raise the theodicy question, or it may prompt us to consider whether some persons are so deprived socio-politically and economically that they cannot make responsible moral choices. Nevertheless, it is because of this fundamental freedom that *all* persons who are moral agents are morally obligated to resist fiercely anybody and anything that undermines or seeks to deny that freedom. Here it is important to make a distinction between *moral subject* and *moral agent*.

Every conscious being, from an amoeba to a human being, is a moral subject, and thus a self. But not every moral subject is a moral agent. That is, not all moral subjects are capable of making, abiding by, and living with the consequences of responsible moral choices. Although moral subjects, they lack ability to be moral agents. As noted previously, some human persons fall into this category, e.g., the mentally challenged, those suffering from drug induced memory loss, Alzheimer's disease, and other forms of dementia.

In addition, it seems to me that another group which comes dangerously close to being in this category are those who are systematically denied opportunity for meaningful and adequate education, meaningful and gainful employment, decent housing in reasonably "safe" neighborhoods, etc. Many—not all—young blacks and Latinos/as may comprise such a group. Many of these do not have quality life-chances and often dropout of high school. They exhibit low self-esteem and sense of self, which frequently leads to a lack of consideration and respect for the worth of other persons, especially in their respective communities. Many of these young men are confused and embittered by the lack of quality life-chances and seem to launch out against the perceived enemy (frequently their own powerless peers and other community members!) in the only way they think is available to them, namely, through violence. When they commit acts of violence and murder, in what sense—other than legal—can it be said that they are responsible for their acts? Responsibility implies freedom and moral agency, which at best seem to be dormant in them, primarily for reasons already cited.

In any event, moral agency implies the capacity to act freely, responsibly, maturely, and reasonably. In addition, the moral agent is able to critically examine the process of moral decision making and apply what is learned to new situations as they arise. It is assumed that the moral agent acts reasonably or with reason. To be a moral agent one must be both reasonable and capable of responsible moral choices. Furthermore, the moral agent always owes responsibilities to moral subjects,[44] i.e., to those life forms not capable of responsible moral choice. This point has important ethical implications for issues pertaining to abortion and our thinking and behavior toward nonhuman life forms. To say that there is one God, who creates and sustains all life, is to also say that all life is loved by God and thus has intrinsic value or worth. Their worth is, in this sense, not dependent upon human judgment and behavior. They possess intrinsic worth because created, sustained, and loved by God.

King said several things about the fundamental freedom that characterizes all being. First, freedom is the capacity to be self-determined and self-directed. Second, it is "the capacity to deliberate or weigh alternatives." This means that once I choose a particular alternative I necessarily cut off other choices. And thirdly, King said that freedom implies responsibility. Once I make a choice I am responsible for that choice and the most foreseeable consequences of it.[45]

Any practice that threatens my freedom is a threat to my personhood and impinges on my ability to weigh alternatives, to make decisions, and to be responsible for my choices. Therefore, King too distinguished between moral subject and moral agent. This distinction is significant regarding the issue of black-on-black violence and murder among young black males. Indeed, in light of the socio-political, economic, and racial factors that have produced the conditions which cause them to react toward each other as they do, in what sense can we say they are morally responsible for their actions?

So important was freedom for King that he concluded that without it persons cannot exist. Furthermore, consistent with personalist philosophy, King emphasized both the ethical and the speculative significance of freedom. Without freedom neither morality nor knowledge is possible, since both depend on the capacity to deliberate and choose. To possess the capacity to do these things implies dependence upon, and the important place of, reason in this process.

As a doctoral student, King wrote an essay on the personalism of the British philosopher, John M.E. McTaggart (1866–1925), in which he argued against McTaggart's rejection of freedom. King concluded that freedom is "the most important characteristic of personality."[46] Therefore, one who rejects freedom rejects human beings.

King's Message for Today

Martin Luther King would say many things to us today regarding the tragedy that is intra-community black violence and homicide. Although the mature King developed a strong global or internationalist perspective—the roots of which date back to his years as pastor of the Dexter Avenue Baptist Church in Montgomery, Alabama[47]—I submit that were he here today his attention would be drawn to addressing the issue before us. As mentioned earlier, his experience in Chicago brought him face to face with the phenomenon of black-on-black violence among young black males. King would be appalled that this problem has escalated to the point that young black males are on the endangered species list, but he would not be surprised at this reality. For, near the end of his life, King was calling for radical change in the structures of this society, recognizing that piecemeal changes were not adequate. And he called for "a revolution of values" which would make human beings more important than the profit motive, and would cause citizens to "soon look uneasily on the glaring contrast of poverty and wealth."[48] Such a revolution of values would force all to see that a system that produces beggars, homeless people, unemployed and underemployed people, needs radical restructuring.

Nevertheless, I think that King's audience today would be the black community. He would want to emphasize at least three things that necessarily must happen if we expect realistically to put a stop to the immediate day to day incidents of black-on-black violence. And while King would most assuredly have a message for the powerful and privileged who control and benefit from the structures of this society, he would want to specifically send three interrelated messages to black Americans.

First, King would point out that because God is the Creator and sustainer of *all* persons or of *no* persons, every person, regardless of gender or race, class or health, age or sexual orientation has been stamped with the image, fragrance, and voice of God. Because God willingly creates persons, all have absolute and infinite value, which means that all owe respect to each other and to self. It means that no person or group should be easily sacrificed for the wellbeing of another; that one should love self and other persons because God loves us.

So King would remind black adults (many of whom have forgotten), and inform scores of black youths (many of whom have never known!) that they possess infinite worth. He would emphasize that it is not merely the spiritual aspect or the soul of the black self that is so precious to God, but the *whole* self; that mind and body are as two sides of a single coin, and that both needs the other in order for either to exist in human form. King would stress the sacredness of the whole black person—mind *and* body. Human beings are at once spiritual and biological beings. Therefore, it is the whole person who is sacred. Because early Christian anthropology became tainted by the Platonic, Cartesian, Kantian, and post–Kantian idealistic view that the mind is far superior to the body, which presumably imprisons it, Christian teaching has sometimes placed more emphasis on caring for the soul than the body. But influenced both by the Bible and values instilled in him by his parents and the black church, King was convinced that everything that God makes is good, and that includes the body. Accordingly, King maintained that the body is neither evil nor inherently depraved.

Therefore, King would say to young black males today that "the body in Christianity is sacred and significant."[49] Indeed, it is through the body that we come to know and understand life; that we know about emotions; that we are able to see, hear, touch, receive, give, separate, fuse, procreate, etc. The human person has no better means, no better instrument for communicating love (or anything else for that matter!) than the body. Although King was influenced by that form of idealism that seemed to make the soul or spirit superior to the body,[50] he would agree with those who maintain that "a human being is not essentially a soul inhabiting a body, but a body made to live by God."[51] God is the fundamental cause of both body and soul, and thus both are intrinsically good and warrant respect and care. Indeed, none understood the importance of stressing the dignity of the human body, especially black bodies, better than King. As we saw earlier, King knew that the high incidence of intra-community violence and homicide in black communities was clear evidence of low self-esteem and sense of self-worth among blacks, particularly young black males. King was certain that young blacks needed to be taught that their whole self, mind and body, is precious and sacred before God, and should be treated as such in daily living. After all, God created all that there is, and declared that it was very good (Gen. 1:31). Having created the human body, God breathed into it the breath of life. Both body and soul are sacred. The human person is always at once a body *and* a soul—an embodied self. Justo González has put it nicely, and were King alive he would agree. "The entire human being is body, and the same human being is soul. A disembodied soul is not a human being, just as a 'dis-souled' body is no longer a human being."[52]

King would drive home the point that the bodies of black people have an inviolable sacredness of their own, and therefore should be cared for and protected. He would plead with black youths to love, care for, and respect not only their own bodies, but those of others in the black community. Indeed, King would join with Toni Morrison's character, Baby Suggs, in praising the dignity of black bodies and admonishing that they love their bodies, no matter what.[53] For it is blacks themselves who must love, respect, protect, and preserve the sacredness of their bodies. LOVE YOUR BODIES! That is what King would say to young black males today.

The body is sacred, and as such, is infinitely precious to God. King came to reject the long history of Platonic idealism that viewed the body as little more than a covering or shell over the "real" self, as if the body had no significance or value in itself. In the sermon, "What is Man?," King argued persuasively against that form of idealism that undermined the value of the body. He saw the biblical perspective as more consistent with his best religious views and his own experience and awareness of the systematic mistreatment of black bodies. King reasoned that if it is true that the mind or more spiritual aspects of the person is sacred, the body must be as well, since God created human beings attached to a body. Moreover, he knew that the Genesis creation story was quite adamant that God created the world and all in it, and declared not only that it was good, but *very* good. God created human beings with bodies, which must also be very good. King reasoned:

> Since this is true, there is nothing essentially wrong with man's created nature, for we read in the Book of Genesis that everything God made is good. There is nothing derogatory in having a body. This assertion is one of the things that distinguish the Christian doctrine of man from the Greek doctrine. Under the impetus of Plato, the Greeks came to feel that the body is inherently evil and that the soul will never reach its full maturity until it is freed from the prison of the body. Christianity, on the other hand, contends that the will, and not the body, is the principle of evil. The body is both sacred and significant in Christian thought.[54]

The second point King would make is necessarily related to the first. Influenced by the best he perceived in the Black Power Movement, King would admonish that black youths be proud of their heritage and their race. If they possess a healthy sense of the sacredness of their mind-body, this will open the way to being proud, and not ashamed of, their blackness. This can only lead to a heightened sense of self-love, which will mean less temptation to violate one-self or others. No one who truly loves self, people, and heritage seeks their own, or the destruction of others. In his final presidential address to SCLC staff members, King said "... we must massively assert our dignity and worth. We must stand up amidst a system that still oppresses us and develop an unassailable and majestic sense of values. We must no longer be ashamed of being black."[55] This admonition implies the need to make a conscious effort to learn about black history, including both African and American contributions. Reminiscent of W.E.B. DuBois's reference to blacks' sense of double-consciousness, ever feeling their "twoness—an American, a Negro; two souls, two thoughts, two unreconciled strivings; two warring ideals in one dark body...,"[56] King insisted that whether we like it or not, blacks are an amalgam of Africa and America; of black and white; "the child of two cultures..., neither totally African nor totally Western..., a little bit colored and a little bit white."[57] It is a challenging, but not insurmountable task, for blacks to learn all they can about the African and American side of their heritage. As I say this, it is also important to point out what we do not often hear, namely, that white people also have a great deal of learning to do in this regard. For, by having been intricately and inextricably intermingled with blacks since the period of enforced enslavement in this country, white people too, are essentially children of two cultures; an amalgam of white America and of Africa. There is so much white in blacks, and so much African in whites, that it is impossible for either group to ever again claim to be anything other than what King referred to (in referencing blacks) as a "true hybrid."[58] And yet, knowing the American educational system as I do, we can be certain that black youth, and white youth alike (who are lucky), will not learn about their intermingled heritage and history there. For black Americans, this means that the responsibility of so educating black youths falls to black churches, civic, and other organizations in the black community. Something similar needs to happen in the white community, but at this time I have less reason to be optimistic that it will.

King's admonition to be proud of being black also implies the capacity for developing such pride. In order to possess such pride, one must aggressively assert the will and the effort to develop and sustain it. In addition, what is important is not what those outside the black community think about blacks. On this point, King would join with Malcolm × in saying that it is necessary that blacks look to themselves, first and foremost. "We've got to change our own minds about each other," declared Malcolm. "We have to see each other with new eyes. We have to see each other as brothers and sisters. We have to come together with warmth so we can develop unity and harmony that's necessary to get this problem solved ourselves."[59] King himself acknowledged the difficulty of reversing in blacks the tendency of many to hate everything about Africa and what it means to be black in the United States, and to believe what those outside the black community say about them. "The job of arousing manhood within a people that have been taught for so many centuries that they are nobody is not easy,"[60] King said. But he was just as adamant that people of African descent have in them what is needed to turn this around. Indeed, this idea of taking their own destiny and self-definition into their own hands points to the third thing that King would likely say to black youth and the black community today.

As we saw before, King would insist on the need for the black community to own responsibility for all that happens and is allowed to happen therein. This raises the issue of *moral agency* that has been so difficult for blacks to discuss openly and publicly for fear that whites will use what is said to appease their own consciences, and to diminish their sense of responsibility for creating the socio-economic and political conditions that have made young black males an endangered species. Yet, I think that one who is consistent in following King's ideas, witness, and example would have to say that there is too much at stake for blacks to continue to remain silent about moral agency and the failure to own up to responsibility for the many specific acts of violence and murder that still occur in the black community.

Blacks can and *should* blame (perhaps even hate)[61] the powerful and privileged who manage, control, and benefit from the racist institutions that have caused the conditions that have created in so many black youths a sense of hopelessness, lovelessness, and sheer mean-spiritedness to the extent that many will take the life of another black youth at the drop of a pen. But as for the specific acts of violence, blacks must find in themselves the courage and the wherewithal to say that inasmuch as black boys pull the trigger of the gun that maims or takes the lives of others in the black community, they must answer—*not to white America!*—but to their own community. For both the perpetrators and their victims belong to the black community. On the other hand, inasmuch as black adults allow incidents of black-on-black violence and murder to continue unabated, without vociferous outcries and strong steps to eradicate the problem, they must be able to say: *WE* are responsible, and we alone can—indeed must!—put a stop to the violence.

No matter how bad things get, we are at bottom the "masters of our own destiny," said Malcolm. We may not be responsible for what has caused our condition, but we are responsible for the response we give to it. In this regard, the late Rabbi Abraham Joshua Heschel's adage is apropos: "Few are guilty, all are responsible."[62] Although blacks did not create the conditions that led to the tragic phenomenon of intra-community black violence and murder on a massive scale, it is still within their power (as moral agents) to respond to the consequences of it one way or another. Not guilty of the causes of the tragedy, blacks are morally responsible for how they respond to it. Moreover, King—influenced by existentialist philosophers such as Martin Heidegger, Karl Jaspers, and Jean Paul Sartre—reminds us emphatically that, not to choose is in fact a choice made. King expressed the point this way: "The existentialists say we must choose, that we are choosing animals...."[63] King was surely influenced by Sartre's argument that human beings are "condemned to be forever free"[64]; condemned to choose; and when one claims not to have chosen, she is guilty of "bad faith."[65]

During an interview with Kenneth Clark, Malcolm said emphatically that no one framed him when he was arrested and incarcerated prior to joining the Nation of Islam. "I went to prison," he said, "for what I did...."[66] "FOR WHAT *I* DID"! Malcolm owned responsibility for what he did, even though he knew the American judicial and prison systems to be unjust and racist. Indeed, were Martin Luther King here today he would say that until blacks come to terms with their own responsibility for intra-community black violence and murder among black boys, the problem, tragically, will be with them for many years to come.

As far back as 1958, King said: "We must not let the fact that we are the victims of injustice lull us into abrogating responsibility for our own lives."[67] In his "Advice for Living" column in *Ebony* magazine, also in 1958, King addressed the question of how to reduce the crime rate in black communities. In doing so, he stressed the role of individual choice or decision, *as well as* the role of systemic causes outside the control of blacks. Acknowledging the role that poverty and ignorance play in breeding crime, regardless of the racial-ethnic group, King went on to say: "So we must work to remove the system of segregation, discrimination and the existence of economic injustice if we are to solve the problem of crime in the Negro community. For these external factors are causally responsible for crime. On the other hand, the Negro must work within the community to solve the problem while the external cause factors are being removed."[68]

There is no question that Martin Luther King would encourage his people to believe that they are capable of ending the practice of black-against-black violence and homicide among young black males. There are still large segments of the black community that possesses the historic values of belief in a personal God who loves, cares for, and empowers them to fight to end the threats to their personhood and communities. Many still cling to the African, Jewish, and Christian doctrines of the sacredness of persons and the importance of strong families and communities. King would say that we need not leave either our community or the world the way they were when we were born. Each member can make a difference, and we are only being naive if we think that all we need do is pray and the problem of violence and murder will vanish. Instead, King would agree with James Baldwin: "Now, this country is going to be transformed. It will not be transformed by an act of God, but by all of us, by you and me. I don't believe any longer that we can afford to say that it is entirely out of our hands. We made the world we're living in and we have to make it over."[69] In other words, King would call for both a radical ethic of black dignity, and black self-determination, as the two chief elements in the fight against intra-community violence and murder among young black males.

15

White Moderates, White
Liberals and King's Dream[1]

Martin Luther King was profoundly committed to transformative social change and there-fore demanded nothing short of determined social action from people of good will, regardless of race-ethnicity. He most certainly expected this of both religious and secular well-meaning southern white people. King held all institutions accountable for their stance and behavior regarding race, but he was adamant that the church was responsible for being a powerful beacon for social justice and peace. This, in part, is why he was so critical of the self-help religion of Norman Vincent Peale,[2] and those preachers who preach sermons on "How to be Happy" and "How to Relax,"[3] as well as sermons on how to essentially grow mega-churches. The term "mega-church" was not yet in usage in King's day, so he used the term "jumboism."[4] Such ser-mons were not the answer to midnight in the moral order. Just as King was critical of white moderates and white liberals for their failure to speak and act against racial discrimination in all of its forms, he was also critical of blacks who conformed or adjusted to segregation and second class citizenship.[5]

This chapter seeks to show that Martin Luther King's view of religious white moderates and liberals changed significantly from the beginning of the civil rights movement of the mid–1950s to approximately his time of incarceration in the Birmingham jail in 1963, and even more so after the Chicago campaign in 1966. Initially believing—even hoping—that his people could depend on the support of moderates and liberals, King was later forced to the harsh realization that many of these persons were spineless and did not support proposals for deep-rooted, radical changes in the structures of American society. Even when liberals supported such policies, he discovered that they frequently lacked the moral courage to support them. Despite his frustration and deep disappointment, however, King continued to be hopeful that the beloved commu-nity—a community wherein every person would be respected and treated like the precious entity she is—would eclipse the existent American community in which varying degrees of racism and white supremacy reigned supreme. And yet in his hope for the beloved community, King's deepest hope and faith was not in white moderates and liberals, nor in his own people. Rather, his deepest faith was in the God of the Hebrew prophets and Jesus Christ, the God of his par-ents and grandparents who he discovered as his own. His deepest faith was in God's relentless faithfulness, care, and concern for the wellbeing of every person, regardless of race-ethnicity. Although King experienced periods of deep despair and discouragement, his hope to the very end was that the racist American community would be eclipsed by the beloved community.

Martin Luther King was not only critical of the lack of courage among white moderates, and white liberals of the South. Reflecting on white liberals in the North In January 1958 he made it clear that the type of liberalism that pretends to be for everything and everybody, was useless. "What we find too often in the North," he said, " is a sort of quasi-liberalism which is based on the philosophy of looking sympathetically at all sides, and it becomes so involved in seeing all sides that it doesn't get committed to either side."[6] What King called for was "a 'positive, genuine liberalism' that would result in committed action to insure all people have 'justice and freedom.'"[7] Six months after King made this statement at Beth Emet the Free Synagogue in Evanston, Illinois, he told a newly formed United Presbyterian Church that he rejected the tendency of liberals to fail to take a stance against racism. He also denounced their inclination toward gradualism and moderation in race relations. "But if moderation means slowing up in the move for justice and capitulating to the whims and caprices of the guardians of a deadening status quo," he said, "then moderation is a tragic vice which all men of goodwill must condemn."[8] King knew that many well-meaning white moderates and liberals sincerely opposed segregation and discrimination behind closed doors (or to him privately), but never took a serious public stance against it because of fear of standing alone and being ostracized.[9] Notwithstanding this, King also acknowledged that there were white people—South and North—who make a courageous public witness and stand against racism and discrimination; who dare to stand up for justice.[10] The true Christians among these, he contended, are white people who not only worship Christ emotionally, but more importantly, morally.[11]

The Martin Luther King of the post–Chicago campaign was also close to Malcolm X's attitude toward white liberals, namely that they should not be trusted uncritically. To be sure, King had had doubts about both white liberals and moderates during the Birmingham campaign. After his experience in Chicago and the suburb of Marquette Park in 1966, King emphatically announced a very different opinion of these groups than he previously held. An examination of King's changing perspective reveals that although he did not use the same kind of language that Malcolm used, he clearly held a similar position.[12] Right up to the time of his assassination, King believed that there were some genuinely committed white liberals. He saw this most clearly in the contributions of white youths, many who had been influenced by the leadership of black youths during the sit-ins in 1960, and the Freedom Rides the following year, and the voter education projects before and after Freedom Summer in the Mississippi Delta in 1964. Nevertheless, one gets a sense that at least by 1967, King was not convinced that there were as many as he had previously thought and hoped.

King and Racism

To begin this discussion it is important to clarify King's stance on racism in the United States. This is important, because King himself was aware after 1965 that large numbers of whites seemed to believe that racism was no longer a significant factor in American life. After all, had not Congress passed the Civil Rights Act of 1964 and the Voting Rights Act the following year? However, we will see that there was absolutely no question that right up to the time he was brutally murdered, King believed this to be a racist nation (See *Where Do We Go from Here*, 75, 77, 69, 88–9, 173, 176; re: Jefferson/Lincoln, 80, 83; See Washington, ed., 314, 316, 375, 385). As late as 1967, King declared color prejudice to be the "most despicable expression of man's inhumanity to man."[13] Moreover, there is no question that King concurred with Swedish economist and social scientist, Gunnar Myrdal, that racism was the nation's "greatest moral dilemma."[14] In the massive classic study, *An American Dilemma: The Negro Problem and Modern Democracy* (1944), Myrdal wrote that his book devoted significant space to socio-economic and political matters relative to the race question, but that fundamentally the race problem was the "moral dilemma" of the nation.[15]

Despite the fact that he had grown up in a middle class, relatively safe and protected environment, King, like most blacks, met the ugly face of racism early and often in life. In later years he recalled that he could never get used to segregation; to the idea of going to the rear of busses and to the rear of stores to be served. He could not get used to sitting in the balcony of movie houses, or sitting in the segregated section of trains and other means of public transportation. "The first time that I had been seated behind a curtain in a dining car," he wrote, "I felt as if the curtain had been dropped on my selfhood."[16] King knew that all blacks, regardless of class and level of educational attainment, suffer from the sting of racism. In the last few months of his life he lamented: "It doesn't matter where we are individually in the scheme of things, how near we may be either to the top or to the bottom of society; the cold facts of racism slap each of us in the face."[17] King knew that if one is black, especially in the south, there is nowhere to run to escape direct and indirect influences of racism. He knew racism to be endemic to the fabric of this society.

While a sociology major at Morehouse College, King learned that racism and economic exploitation are "twin evils." During summers he had occasion to experience this on various jobs he worked. King therefore developed a strong sense that poor blacks suffered almost insurmountable pain and agony. Few expressed better than King what it means to be black in America.

> The central quality in the Negro's life is pain—pain so old and so deep that it shows in almost every moment of his existence. It emerges in the cheerlessness of his sorrow songs, in the melancholy of his blues and in the pathos of his sermons. The Negro while laughing sheds invisible tears that no hand can wipe away. In a highly competitive world, the Negro knows that a cloud of persistent denial stands between him and the sun, between him and life and power, between him and whatever he needs.[18]

Poor whites were exploited in the job market just like blacks. King knew that. He had seen it with his own eyes when he worked some of those summer jobs. However, he was aware that blacks experienced greater pain because of the prevalence of racism in virtually every facet of American society. Blacks are victims not only of economic exploitation, but of racism as well. King therefore rejected the argument that if white ethnic immigrant groups could pull themselves up by the bootstraps, blacks should be able to do so as well. He understood that by and large white ethnic groups came to these shores by choice; that they were not ripped from their homelands, enslaved, and subjected to cruel, inhumane attempts to strip them of their socio-cultural heritage. Instead, and unlike blacks, they were given land and other resources and the opportunity to make a decent living. He also knew that by virtue of their white skin, white ethnics were able to blend in with the dominant group of whites. King did not attempt to downplay the suffering and difficulty that these groups experienced, however. He just wanted it to be absolutely clear that one could not reasonably compare their experience to that of black Americans. "When white immigrants arrived in the United States in the late nineteenth century," he said, "a beneficent government gave them free land and credit to build a useful, independent life."[19] White immigrant groups did confront many obstacles, but King was convinced that "none was so brutally scorned or so consistently denied opportunity and hope as was the Negro."[20]

Although the famous Emancipation Proclamation (1863) ostensibly freed blacks from the bondage of slavery, King knew that theirs was at best an abstract freedom—a freedom in word only. Landless and without property for over two hundred years, blacks were "freed" from slavery and given no means to start a new life of freedom. The ten years of "reconstruction" (1867–1877) that followed Lincoln's famous Proclamation was not radical enough, nor were resources allocated, to make a significant difference in the lives of the masses of blacks during that period. The "freedom" of the Emancipation Proclamation was at best a nebulous gesture. Looking back on this situation, King further clarified the difference between the abstract freedom of blacks, and the more substantive freedom of white ethnics during the nineteenth century.

> In 1863 the Negro was given abstract freedom expressed in luminous rhetoric. But in an agrarian economy he was given no land to make liberation concrete. After the war the government granted white settlers, without cost, millions of acres of land in the West, thus providing America's new white peasants from Europe with an economic floor. But at the same time its oldest peasantry, the Negro, was denied everything but a legal status he could not use, could not consolidate, could not even defend.[21]

King knew that blacks had been freed from physical slavery only to be continued in economic and psychological slavery. Unlike white ethnics, then, they were never given a chance to start a new life.

This, in part, is why the mature (post–1965) King could refer to the black man as "the twice forgotten man."[22] King asserted that one of the moral imperatives of the late 1960s was the challenge of working "all over the world with unshakable determination to wipe out the last vestiges of racism."[23] Clearly, for King, racism was one of the most pressing social evils in existence. King was greatly disappointed that nearly seven decades after W. E. B. DuBois's prophecy that the problem of the twentieth century is the problem of the color line, the nation and the world were no closer to eradicating this problem in 1967. For King, racism was "the hound of hell which dogs the tracks of ... civilization."[24] More than four decades after King's death this remains true.

After the Chicago campaign in 1966, King operated under no illusions regarding the cause(s) of black deprivation and pain. He wrote about this in *Where Do We Go from Here: Chaos or Community?*

> It is time for all of us to tell each other the truth about who and what have brought the Negro to the condition of deprivation against which he struggles today. In human relations the truth is hard to come by, because most groups are deceived about themselves. Rationalization and the incessant search for scapegoats are the psychological cataracts that blind us to our individual and collective sins.[25]

By this time, King did not hesitate to name names. He seemed less willing to do this in earlier years, perhaps because of his unwillingness to offend white moderates, and particularly white liberals, who might serve the cause of civil rights and racial equality as allies. King still wanted them as allies, but after Chicago he realized that many of them were not as committed to racial equality as he had once believed. Indeed, had he not written in "Letter from Birmingham Jail" of "the appalling silence of the good people?"[26] This was clearly a reference to white moderates and liberals. King considered, even in 1963, that he might well have expected too much of these groups. "I suppose I should have realized that few members of the oppressor race can understand the deep groans and passionate yearnings of the oppressed race," he said, "and still fewer have the vision to see that injustice must be rooted out by strong, persistent and determined action."[27] He believed just as fervently that the genuinely committed whites were "still all too few in quantity, but they are big in quality."[28] Some of these, King said, included Ralph

McGill, Lillian Smith, Harry Golden, James McBride Dabbs, Ann Braden and Sarah Patton Boyle, all who had written in an enlightened way about the black struggle in the South.

In any case, King came to the point that he insisted on the necessity of distinguishing between fact and fiction, reality and intention, regarding the race question. In "A Testament of Hope" he said:

> It is time that we stopped our blithe lip service to the guarantees of life, liberty and pursuit of happiness. These fine sentiments are embodied in the Declaration of Independence, but that document was always a declaration of intent rather than of reality. There were slaves when it was written; there were still slaves when it was adopted; and to this day, black Americans have not life, liberty nor the privilege of pursuing happiness....[29]

King admonished that at the bare minimum any who are serious about solving the race problem must be committed to honesty and open recognition and examination of the problem of racism wherever it exists. I examine proposed solutions in the conclusion of this chapter.

Chicago taught King that racism was not only deeply entrenched and embedded in the structures of the white South, but in the North as well. He was more familiar with racism in the South because it was there that he experienced it in its most blatant and subtle forms as a child and adult. Not having had much experience with racism in the North previously, after the march through Chicago's Marquette Park area, he remarked that he had never in his life experienced such hatred expressed by whites against blacks. Indeed, he was convinced that the people of Mississippi and Alabama could learn much about racial hatred in Chicago. "I've never seen anything like it," King said of the march that day. "I've been in many demonstrations all across the south, but I can say that I have never seen—even in Mississippi and Alabama—mobs as hostile and as hate-filled as I've seen in Chicago."[30] He was convinced that racism was the underlying cause of the "massive outpouring of hatred" he experienced in Chicago and other places.[31] King was sorely disturbed by the "blinders," "indifference," and "silence" of northern whites in general and white liberals in particular. His experience in Chicago and the overall reaction of Chicago's white leadership convinced him that most whites did not want full equality and integration for blacks. Prior to Chicago, King believed differently, although he expressed suspicions as a result of his experiences in Albany and Birmingham. Chicago forced him to conclude that only a very small percentage of whites, primarily young college students, were totally committed to the cause of eliminating racism in all its forms. This was a point that Malcolm X made as well.[32]

King knew that racism persisted after the first decade of the civil rights struggle. The reason, he believed, was because "America is deeply racist and its democracy is flawed both economically and socially."[33] King was disturbed by white moderates' and liberals' indifference to racism and economic exploitation that sought to systematically dehumanize blacks. He held that the greatest peril is that whites are "infected with racism."[34]

According to King, all things considered, the status of blacks in the United States had nothing to do with bogus charges of racial inferiority, laziness, or blacks' refusal to raise their level of achievement in all areas of life. Blacks' status was due primarily to the intentional efforts of the white majority to keep them out, by insuring that they have no easy access to the means to make a life that is worth living. Although there were times when King was rightly critical of blacks for not doing all they could to help their own cause,[35] and admonished that they have a key role to play in the liberation process,[36] he was equally convinced that at bottom blacks were not to blame for their unearned suffering.

According to King, then, racism was not a black problem, but a white problem, particularly in the sense that whites gave birth to it, and they alone have the power to continue to perpetuate it. Of course, as a theological social ethicist, King knew full well that racism is, fundamentally, a moral problem. As such, it is a problem for all people, regardless of gender, race, class, etc. In order to locate the roots of black pain and suffering, it is necessary to "turn to the white man's problem,"[37] he said. King would not have disagreed with Lerone Bennett, Jr., in this regard.

> The problem of race in America, insofar as that problem is related to packets of melanin in men's skins, is a white problem. And in order to solve that problem we must seek its source, not in the Negro but in the white American ... and in the structure of the white community.
>   When we say that the causes of the race problem are rooted in the white American and the white community, we mean that the power is the white American's and so is the responsibility. We mean that the white American created, invented the race problem and that his fears and frailties are responsible for the urgency of the problem.[38]

Blacks did not invent the race problem, and, by and large, are not responsible for its continued existence. In order for one to adequately understand the predicament of blacks, it is necessary to understand something about the white man's world—about his general tendency to espouse the lofty ideals of democracy and equality, while making little to no effort to be consistent with these ideals in practice. White America has always had an ambivalent attitude toward blacks, "causing America to take a step backward simultaneously with every step forward on the question of racial justice,"[39] said King. This led him to conclude that, "There has never been a solid, unified and determined thrust to make justice a reality for Afro-Americans."[40] He rejected the early claim that this is a nation whose dominant ideology is based on democracy and equality for all, while racism is merely a deviation from this norm by a few white racists. The racism to which blacks were subjected was not simply about a small number of diehard bigots. Influenced by George Kelsey's view of racism as a faith, or form of idolatry, and Ruth Benedict's definition of it "as 'the dogma that one ethnic group is condemned by nature to hereditary inferiority and another group is destined to hereditary superiority,'"[41] King offered his own definition.

> Racism is a philosophy based on a contempt for life. It is the arrogant assertion that one race is the center of value and object of devotion, before which other races must kneel in submission. It is the absurd dogma that one race is responsible for all the progress of history and alone can assure the progress of the future. Racism is total estrangement. It separates not only bodies, but minds and spirits. Inevitably it descends to inflicting spiritual or physical homicide upon the out-group.[42]

By 1968, Martin Luther King was convinced that no presidential administration had really done much for blacks, although Presidents Kennedy and Johnson received what he once described as "much undeserved credit" for helping them.[43] When one considers the various reports on the status of black America from economic, educational, housing, and health perspectives over the past decades, it is clear that over forty years after the assassination of King, there is still no evidence of a systematic, unified, and relentless thrust to make justice and equality a reality for blacks.[44] If white liberals were genuinely committed to black liberation, one cannot help but wonder how it is possible for the previous sentence to be true. What did King think about white moderates and liberals?

White Moderates and Liberals

From around 1963 onward, Martin Luther King was in agreement with many blacks' perception that the white liberal, not the Ku Klux Klan, John Birch Society, or White Citizens

Councils, was blacks' "most troublesome adversary."[45] He discovered during the Birmingham campaign that white moderates and liberals were more devoted to law and order, and tranquility than to justice and equality.[46] King did not name Evangelist Billy Graham, but his criticism most assuredly included him, particularly in light of Graham's very public counsel that the civil rights activists needed to slow down. During the Birmingham campaign, for example, Graham called for a "cooling off" period, and asked for "a period of quietness in which moderation prevails."[47] Without question, King had become deeply disturbed and disappointed about such advice from white moderates, and most especially, religious ones.

Although King acknowledged his disappointment with religious white moderates and liberals he also knew that blacks could not solve the problem of racial discrimination alone. They needed the support of genuine, committed white liberals. Even though it had become clear to him by 1967 that many liberals had disguised and latent prejudices, King insisted that a "sound resolution of the race problem in America will rest with those white men and women who consider themselves as generous and decent human beings."[48] I return to this important point subsequently. For now, suffice it to say that notwithstanding King's deep disappointment in white moderates and liberals, he was convinced that the problem of racism could not be solved without their relentless and bold contributions toward this end. King was aware that these—moderates and liberals—were but two types of racially prejudiced white people. Generally, King only distinguished between moderates and liberals in his speeches and writings, but there is no question that he was aware that there were types of moderates and types of liberals. He sometimes hints at this, but more often he does not.

Social scientists are aware that the advantage of acknowledging the existence of multiple types of racially prejudiced moderates and liberals is that one can then see that the solution to one type may not be as effective for another, and that one type of prejudiced person may even be effective in helping to alter the attitude and practice of another. Before focusing on King's concern about white moderates, followed by a discussion on some of his specific concerns regarding white liberals, it will be instructive to briefly discuss some types of racial moderates and liberals and the relation to the types that King frequently encountered and reacted to in his speeches and writings. In what follows I will consider four specific types. In social science lingo these are ideal types—ideal not in the normative or ethical sense, but only as a means of classification in the world of ideas. It is a way of helping to identify typical characteristics of say, the "unprejudiced discriminator." A problem with the ideal type is that it is so concerned about acknowledging similarities that it gives little to no attention to nuanced differences. In actual experience there may be differences between "unprejudiced discriminator" A, and "unprejudiced discriminator" B. In any case, we should be aware that because these are ideal types, there will not likely be a perfect example in everyday experience. I see the four types as part of a continuum, with other types in between.

When social scientist Robert K. Merton devised a four classification model of prejudiced white people he did so with the intention of suggesting strategies that might effectively address and solve each type. To characterize each type, Merton used language that was popular during the era of the civil rights movement, e.g., "all-weather liberal" (the "unprejudiced nondiscriminator") and "fair-weather liberal" (the "unprejudiced discriminator"). Merton rounds out the typology with the "fair-weather illiberal" (what he calls the "prejudiced nondiscriminator"), and the "all-weather illiberal" (or "prejudiced discriminator").[49]

King had serious encounters with representatives in each type, including the group that was the smallest, i.e., the all-weather liberal. Examples of the latter include white SNCC and CORE activists such as Jim Zwerg, Bob Zellner, Michael and Rita Schwerner, Jane Stembridge, as well as many of the white college volunteers who participated in the Freedom Summer Project in the Mississippi Delta in 1964, and those who participated in the equally dangerous SCLC sponsored SCOPE, the Summer Community Organization and Political Education Project in Wilcox County, Alabama and other parts of the Deep South in 1965. Many of these white youths suffered savage beatings by white racists (prejudiced discriminators), and even when some were murdered, their peers were determined to stay the course. King had firsthand acquaintance with some of these youths. Moreover, he expressed his awareness of the existence of all-weather liberals in his famous "I Have a Dream" speech when he referred to those white people present at the March "who are as concerned that we be free, as we are to be free." Such ones are a necessary ingredient of any efforts to radically reduce or eliminate racial prejudice and discrimination.

Generally, the weakness of all-weather liberals is the tendency to essentially preach to the choir about matters of race, or to somehow feel it necessary to make their witness in the presence of blacks, rather than whites who are prejudiced on various levels of the racism continuum. Merton refers to their weakness as the "fallacy of group soliloquies.... Ethnic liberals are busily engaged in talking to themselves. Repeatedly, the same groups of like-minded liberals seek each other out, hold periodic meetings in which they engage in mutual exhortation, and thus lend social and psychological support to one another."[50] When one relentlessly preaches to the choir about something as serious as racial prejudice and discrimination, little to no progress is made toward actually remedying the problem. The real work of the all-weather liberal, as King surely knew, is among other whites on the racism continuum, not among like-minded liberals, and most certainly not among blacks. Their work is within places where racism and discrimination emanates. "The all-weather liberal mistakes discussion in like-minded groups for effective action and overestimates the support for his position."[51] Moreover, we will see that King was aware that liberals, regardless of where they were on the racism-discrimination continuum, frequently failed to publicly voice their criticism of racial injustice, even when they themselves were against it. Relentless criticism and pressure of various kinds from blacks may be enough to get the all-weather liberal to see and change his tendency to preach to the choir. The all-weather liberal who has already been liberated from this practice can play a significant role as well.

The white moderate that King frequently referred to and criticized exhibited the traits of the fair-weather liberal and the fair-weather illiberal. At times, the moderate was unprejudiced but was not opposed to discriminating against blacks if she could see advantages of doing so. For King, these included such people as the eight Birmingham clergymen who wrote an open letter (while he was in Birmingham jail) accusing him of being an outsider, and stirring things up. They also included people such as Selma, Alabama director of public safety, Wilson Baker. Baker, like some of the ministers, at times behaved like a prejudiced-nondiscriminator. The tendency of the fair-weather liberal to avoid discriminating against blacks, whether because of a court order, or their respect for "law and order," keeps them in the category of the moderate.

Although the fair-weather liberal tends not to be prejudiced, he may discriminate if he believes that doing so is easier or more profitable. "He may show the expediency of silence or timidity, or discriminate to seize an advantage."[52] If he thinks that hiring blacks or other people of color will hurt his business in any way, he will not hire them. And yet, such one tends to experience pangs of conscience for his discriminatory actions, which makes him a prime candidate to be worked on by all-weather liberals.[53]

The fair-weather illiberal is not entirely different from the fair-weather liberal, although he does not—like the latter—suffer pangs of conscience. He is, however, "the reluctant conformist, the employer who discriminates until a fair employment practices law puts the fear of punishment and loss into him, the trade-union official who, though prejudiced himself, abolishes Jim Crow because the rank and file of his membership demands it."[54] He may be a reluctant conformist, but he will likely conform if he can see that discrimination is both "costly and painful." Initially, challenges to his prejudice may cause him to resist, but over time there will likely be a reduction in his propensity to discriminate.

Moderates, both fair-weather liberals and fair-weather illiberals, were among the largest group of whites with whom King and other civil rights activists had to contend. These were often people who had a good sense of right and wrong in race relations, but had not the character and courage to behave accordingly. King frequently characterized these as white people of good will[55] who were generally afraid[56] to speak and stand publicly against racism and segregation. King believed that many of these were sincerely opposed to segregation and discrimination. They simply lacked the moral spine needed to stand up against it. They scarred the dream of the beloved community by their silence and fear. They were guilty of what King referred to as a conspiracy of silence and apathy.[57] They were otherwise good people who disapproved of the tactics of hardcore racists such as Bull Connor. They were "decent white citizens who privately deplored the maltreatment of Negroes. But they remained publicly silent…. The ultimate tragedy of Birmingham," said King, "was not the brutality of the bad people, but the silence of the good people."[58] The other group, the all-weather illiberal, or the prejudiced discriminator, was also a very large group. This type was nothing short of a racist personality, and thus could be counted on to behave as a racist, whether as an individual or in a group. Looked at psychologically, the prejudice of such a one is a trait of personality. Gordon Allport taught that the most serious form of prejudice is lockstitched into the fabric of one's personality structure. "In such cases it cannot be extracted by tweezers. To change it, the whole pattern of life would have to be altered."[59] As important as this claim is, it does not go far enough. For example, I would say that racial prejudice is also lockstitched into the very fabric of American society, and this only exacerbates the difficulty of removing it. Virtually the entire society (or personality as the case may be) would need to be entirely made over, which, in the nature of the case, would be quite a revolutionary undertaking.

Depending on the location, the all-weather illiberal might well have been the largest group of whites that King had to deal with. I think of the state of Mississippi (especially in the Delta region) and certain parts of Alabama (such as Lowndes County and Wilcox County), in this regard. In such places, the vast majority of whites made it crystal clear that blacks had no rights that they were bound by law, or otherwise, to respect. Indeed, in such places blacks were not even considered to be human beings. Rather, they were considered to be subhuman at best. All-weather illiberals included such people as Roy Bryant and J.W. Milam (murderers of fourteen-year-old Emmett Louis Till in 1955), Birmingham's police commissioner Bull Connor, Byron de la Beckwith (murderer of NAACP activist Medgar Evers), the Mississippi Delta's deputy sheriff Cecil Price (co-murderer of James Chaney, Michael Schwerner, and Andrew Goodman at the beginning of Freedom Summer), and Selma, Alabama's sheriff Jim Clark. Of course, the list would also include Mississippi governor Ross Barnett, Alabama governor George Wallace, and Arkansas governor Orval Faubus.

The all-weather illiberal is a hardcore racist; one for whom there is consistency between belief and behavior. (In this she is similar to the all-weather liberal, except that her beliefs and behavior are not consistent with the claims of human rights documents such as the Declaration of Independence and the Constitution of the United States.) Because the all-weather illiberal believes that blacks are less human than whites, she sees nothing wrong with treating them different than she would treat people of her own race who share her way of thinking and behaving. Such one "believes that differential treatment of minority groups is not discrimination, but discriminating."[60] The hardcore racist who lives among similar whites will, if somehow made to change, experience a deep sense of alienation from the group. If such a one lived among large numbers of fair-weather liberals and illiberals and had inclinations to being open to integrating among them, she might be successfully turned. The exposure of the hardcore racist to all-weather liberals, however, will not likely have the desired effect, any more than exposure to blacks, since they are thought to be the scum of the earth. Although Martin Luther King often spoke and wrote about solution to the race problem in more general terms, he surely knew that because of the different types of racists any solution would have to be adapted to the particular type in question; that one solution would not be appropriate for all types. What did King say and think about white moderates and white liberals?

WHITE MODERATES

In light of what was said above, this discussion on white moderates includes both fair-weather liberals and fair-weather illiberals. The fair-weathers (liberal and illiberal) are actually moderates. Unless otherwise noted, references to "liberal" are to fair-weather liberal, since it seems to me that generally when King spoke and wrote about liberals he was actually referring to the fair-weather, rather than the much smaller group of all-weather liberals. This helps to explain why, near the end of his life, he seemed to collapse moderates and liberals into one group. The actions of the two groups exhibited little difference because most of King's references to white liberals had actually been to the fair-weather liberal, a type of moderate.

Martin Luther King urged both white moderates and liberals to be firm in their efforts to demand justice and equality for blacks. Reflecting on the Montgomery bus boycott, King recalled how deeply he wanted to believe that white ministers would do the right thing regarding the race question and the issue of justice. He recalled that the least thing they asked of white ministers proved fruitless.

> We tried to get the white ministerial alliance to make a simple statement calling for courtesy and Christian brotherhood, but in spite of the favorable response of a few ministers, Robert Graetz [one of the truly committed white ministers] reported that the majority "dared not get involved in such a controversial issue." This was a deep disappointment. Although the white ministers as a group had been appallingly silent throughout the protest, I had still maintained the hope that they would take a stand once the decision was rendered.[61]

Although in the earlier years of the civil rights movement he expected much more from white moderates, King later confessed that he was simply naïve to think that by merely pointing out to white moderate Christians that racism was a serious problem confronting the church and society that this alone would guarantee their support in eradicating racism and discrimination. In the *Playboy* interview of 1965, Alex Haley asked him what his most serious mistake had been in his leadership role in the movement. He responded by saying:

> Well, the most pervasive mistake I have made was in believing that because our cause was just, we could be sure that the white ministers of the South, once their Christian consciences were challenged, would rise to our aid. I felt that white ministers would take our cause to the white power structures. I ended up, of course, chastened and disillusioned. As our movement unfolded, and direct appeals were made to white ministers, most folded their hands—and some even took stands against us.[62]

In "Letter from Birmingham Jail," King pointed out that he was very disappointed with the reaction of white moderate Christians to the nonviolent civil rights demonstrations. He was also disappointed that he had been so naïve as to expect so much from white moderate ministers, who, in the end, gave very little.[63] King realized that members of the dominant oppressor group seldom understand and respond appropriately to the deep pain and hurt suffered by their victims.

In his famous Letter, King reflected more deeply on his disappointment with the white moderate.

> I have almost reached the regrettable conclusion that the Negro's great stumbling block in his stride toward freedom is not the White Citizen's Counciler or the Ku Klux Klanner, but the white moderate, who is more devoted to "order" than to justice; who prefers a negative peace which is the absence of tension to a positive peace which is the presence of justice; who constantly says: "I agree with you in the goal you seek, but I cannot agree with your methods of direct action"; who paternalistically believes he can set the timetable for another man's freedom; who lives by a mythical concept of time and who constantly advises the Negro to wait for a "more convenient season."[64]

King had hoped that the white moderate would see the need, indeed the moral obligation, to address injustice, rather than speak of law and order as if they have nothing to do with the establishment of justice. Failing to acknowledge this connection makes it easy for law and order to "become the dangerously structured dams that block the flow of social progress."[65]

King was also deeply disappointed that in regards to the race problem and the establishment of justice, the religious white moderate naively believed with social Darwinism that given enough time any social problem will work itself out. King wrote that just this type of idea was expressed in a letter he received from a white Texan. The letter chided King for insisting on the need for freedom and justice now, rather than some time in the distant future (which would be more satisfactory to many whites). "All Christians know that the colored people will receive equal rights eventually," the letter said, "but it is possible that you are in too great a religious hurry. It has taken Christianity almost two thousand years to accomplish what it has. The teachings of Christ take time to come to earth."[66] King concluded that there is nothing about time as such that, given enough of it, there will be automatic or inevitable progress. "Human progress never rolls in on wheels of inevitability; it comes through the tireless efforts of men willing to be co-workers with God, and without this hard work, time itself becomes an ally of the forces of social stagnation."[67]

White Liberals

Recognizing that many white moderates had become indifferent toward the struggle for racial equality during the mid–1960s, King stressed the importance of the *committed* white liberal (read fair-weather liberal) and the need to "...escalate his support for the struggle of racial justice rather than de-escalate it.... The need for commitment," he said, "is greater today than ever."[68] King believed that blatant forms of injustice existed and would continue as long as there was a deterioration of commitment on the part of otherwise well-meaning white people, or liberals. As long as there is shallow commitment—even in areas such as theological schools, where such white liberals may have significant influence—the plight of blacks will not be much better than in areas where they have little or no influence at all. King observed that many liberals had "fallen into the trap of seeing integration in merely aesthetic terms, where a token number of Negroes adds color to a white-dominated power structure."[69] This is why liberals could frequently be heard boasting that, by finally hiring one black on a previously all-white seminary faculty, for example, theirs is now an "integrated" faculty, committed to racial inclusiveness! By hiring one token black on their lily white faculty, many are often satisfied that they have effectively done their Christian duty and that "the problem" has been solved. They then insist that because of their ongoing commitment to inclusiveness and pluralism, as well as their desire to "treat all persons and groups fairly," they cannot in good Christian conscience give priority to any one racial-ethnic, or religious group as they seek new additions to their faculty and executive staff. They now contend that it is immoral to preference blacks over others, e.g., gay and lesbian people, who have also been traditionally excluded from their faculty and top administrative staff.

King's position toward such a stance is clear. Recognizing even in 1963 that many white liberals were troubled by the concept of compensatory or preferential treatment for blacks,[70] he said in 1967 that in light of more than three centuries of forced deprivation and denial of human rights, doing justice to blacks means giving them "special treatment." He went on to say: "A society that has done something special against the Negro for hundreds of years must now do something special for him, in order to equip him to compete on a just and equal basis."[71]

King maintained that it was simply too early for whites to insist on a policy of "race neutrality" in the mid to late 1960s. Were he alive today to consider the progress in race relations since 1968, King would undoubtedly declare that no institution in America—secular or religious—is in position to support race neutral policies. There must be adequate compensation to blacks for the long years of deprivation if the ideal of justice and equality means anything. King would be deeply disappointed to find that affirmative action policies have at best been taken lightly, and at worse have been dismantled after existing for such a brief period of time.

Aware in 1963 that white liberals questioned the justice and fairness of affirmative action policies, King reflected on an experience he had during his visit to India in 1959. Prime Minister Jawaharlal Nehru explained to him and Lawrence Reddick that because of the long years of forced deprivation experienced by the so-called "untouchables" (now known as "dalits"), the Indian government was committed to doing something special for them as a way of compensating them for the many years of mistreatment and exclusion from socio-economic privilege. When Reddick asked whether this was a form of discrimination in reverse, Nehru responded that this may very well be the case. He went further, saying: "But this is our way of atoning for the centuries of injustices we have inflicted upon these people."[72] King was more than satisfied with this response, which is one reason he began declaring that the United States must devise creative ways of compensating blacks for the long years of enslavement and discrimination. Unlike many whites and some blacks today, King clearly did not want to just forget the many years of past injustices endured by his people by insisting on race neutral policies.

Although the commitment of white liberals was on the decline, King was at best ambivalent as to whether it was advisable to completely dismiss and exclude them from black civil rights organizations. Believing that most blacks were still committed to the principle of black and white cooperation in the civil rights struggle, and that there was a need for a change in the relationship between blacks and whites in the context of the movement in terms of who should now occupy the leadership positions, he wrote that, "white liberals must be prepared to accept a transformation of their role. Whereas it was once a primary and spokesman role, it must now become a secondary and supportive role. This does not mean that whites must work only with whites and blacks with blacks; such an approach is always in danger of polarizations that can only intensify distrust and despair."[73] King therefore insisted on an interracial staff at SCLC. "By insisting on racial openness in our organizations, we are setting a pattern for the racially integrated society toward which we work."[74]

And yet, during a conversation with Jewish rabbis ten days before he was assassinated, King made it unequivocally clear that there may be situations in which the temporary separation of the races may be necessary. In contradistinction to many black militants who advocated absolute and permanent separatism as the ultimate goal, King came to see that in the short term separation may be a necessary step *on the way to full equality and liberation*. By this time he believed that this was the stance of many blacks as well. "They see it as a temporary way-station," he said, "to put them into a truly integrated society where there is a shared power."[75] He went on: "I must honestly say that there are points at which I share this view. There are points at which I see the necessity for temporary segregation in order to get to the integrated society."[76] Too often an institution's claim to want to integrate the minority element into its structure has meant integrating the minority group out of any power and influence it may otherwise have had as an organized bloc. King would have been supportive of the development and existence of a powerful black caucus in the predominantly white institution. An important point to acknowledge and remember here is Lewis Baldwin's reminder that when King spoke of the temporary separation of the races this was a strategic or tactical statement, not an ethical imperative.[77]

King was not interested in the aesthetic side of integration as much as the political aspect. He wanted blacks to be integrated into power, not out of it. Liberals frequently seemed to be unaware of the significance of this, or in any case, did not willingly support the socio-economic and political empowerment of blacks.

Near the end of his life, King wrote of "the millions who have morally risen above prevailing prejudices," and who "...are willing to share power and to accept structural alterations of society even at the cost of traditional privilege."[78] However, to his credit, King was realistic enough to know that there were not just a few white bigots in the United States, and that for the good of all it is necessary to point out that racism is not just an occasional departure from the alleged norms of freedom and equality. Rather, King maintained that, "To live with the pretense that racism is a doctrine of a very few is to disarm us in fighting it frontally as scientifically unsound, morally repugnant and socially destructive. The prescription for the cure rests with the accurate diagnosis of the disease."[79] King was making a clear-cut distinction between the majority of uncommitted whites, i.e., the fair-weather liberals, and the much smaller group of genuine whites that he once described as the "creative minority of whites absolutely committed to civil rights..."[80] These were the all-weather liberals, e.g., many of the white college volunteers who participated in Freedom Summer and SCOPE in 1964 and 1965, respectively. The commitment of fair-weather liberals was too shallow and unpredictable. Although such liberals often gave their support, in too many instances they did not do so for the right reasons. Because racism was fundamentally a theological and moral problem in King's view,[81] he was disturbed that so many white ministers, particularly in the South, admonished their congregants to abide by civil rights laws not because blacks are their brothers and sisters, and because it is the morally right thing to do, but because they had an obligation to obey the law of the land.[82]

Martin Luther King believed that prior to the Chicago campaign in 1966 there was a much higher degree of commitment on the part of white liberals.[83] However, by 1967 there was a noticeable shift in his position. He no longer made a real distinction between white moderate and white liberal. He now said things about white liberals that he once said about moderates. It was no longer just the moderates who were held suspect and viewed as half-committed and devoted only to law and order. It was not only the moderates who insisted that the nonviolent protest marches incited white violence and produced a white backlash.[84]

By 1967, King seemed to use the terms "white moderate" and "white liberal" interchangeably, as if he no longer recognized a significant difference between them, especially in terms of commitment to full racial equality. King now seemed to acknowledge the existence of three groups of whites that blacks had to contend with in the struggle. The first, a very large group, especially in the Deep South, but also in the north in places like the Chicago suburb of Cicero, included professed white supremacists. The second included what Thomas Pettigrew calls "conforming bigots" or "latent liberals" (fair-weather liberals and illiberals). Pettigrew placed approximately three-fifths of all whites in this category.[85] King referred to white Christians in this category as "un-Christian Christians."[86] These are people who are kind and loving, but only in superficial ways; who have good intentions in terms of treating all persons with respect, but who do not seem to know how to respond to the race question in ways that would be consistent with an ethic that requires that all persons be treated with dignity and respected because they have the image of God etched into their very being.

According to Pettigrew, latent liberals comprise the largest group of whites that blacks have to contend with. The great sin of this group is the failure to do what it can to eliminate racist practices in the religious institutions with which they are affiliated. These are the fair-weather liberals and illiberals. The third group that the mature King recognized was that very small minority of totally committed whites upon whom he believed rested a great responsibility. These are the all-weather liberals. They seemed to be few and far between during King's day. Unfortunately, this appears to be the case today as well, and there is no indication that a major change is on the horizon.

Conclusion

An important component of King's method of theological social ethics was to include in most of his speeches and writings suggestions of what can be done to eradicate social problems such as racism, economic exploitation, and militarism (the trilogy of social problems he vowed in seminary to address throughout his ministry). Therefore, in this concluding section I will include, among other things, suggestions as to what both whites and blacks will need to do if they are truly hopeful to move beyond racism.

Martin Luther King had little time and peace of mind to engage in leisurely critical reflection. He spoke of this in January 1965. "I feel urgently the need for even an hour of time to get away, to withdraw, to refuel. I need more time to think through what is being done, to take time out from the mechanics of the movement, to reflect on the meaning of the movement."[87] King was absolutely committed to the struggle for the full liberation and empowerment of his people, and yet there were times when he longed for the day when he could leave the pastorate and teach theology in the university. He was not superhuman, but was, through and through, a human being with feelings and emotions, hopes, aspirations, etc.

There is much resistance among religious and non-religious persons about acknowledging that racism is still a significant socio-moral and political factor in the United States. Neo conservatives such as George Gilder, William J. Wilson, Shelby Steele, and Stephen Carter have been declaring "the declining significance of race" at least since the 1980s. Such persons are generally supporters of the basic socio-economic structure of this nation, believing that, but for the need of a minor reform here and there, such structure is essentially sound. King clearly was not among this group, but rather was in agreement with social scientists like Manning Marable, Joe Feagin, and C. Eric Lincoln. These maintain that the basic structure of this country is corrupt and unjust. Their view is that racism remains deeply embedded in the very fabric of the nation.

King himself said that racism "is so embedded in the white society that it will take many years for color to cease to be a judgmental factor."[88] The preponderance of the evidence and the testimonies of most blacks suggest that racism is still alive and well in the United States.

King pointed the way to the elimination of the dreaded evil of racism. The fundamental prerequisite for genuine racial equality, he said, is "a humble acknowledgement of guilt." Honest confession serves to begin the process of purging the self and preparing one to participate in the liberation process. If there is to be hope of solving the problem of racism, there must first be acknowledgement by whites that it exists, and that by virtue of their white skin they are the recipients of countless unearned benefits and privileges. Since King was a Christian, he believed that individual white Christians and churches should take the lead. He expressed similar sentiments to Jewish rabbis at the meeting of the Rabbinical Assembly on March 25, 1968. "However difficult it is to hear, however shocking it is to hear, we've got to face the fact that America is a racist country. We have got to face the fact that racism still occupies the throne of our nation. I don't think we will ultimately solve the problem of racial injustice until this is recognized, and until this is worked on.... I think religious institutions in society must really deal with racism."[89] White Christians in particular need to take this seriously, even as blacks develop the courage to be honest and forthright about their experience of racism and stop placating whites, causing many to feel that significant progress is being made in matters of race when this is not the case. Indeed, what is needed from both groups is a display of openness and honesty regarding their true feelings on the subject. Malcolm × expressed this concern, and King would have concurred. "Raw, naked truth exchanged between the black man and the white man is what a whole lot more of is needed in this country—to clear the air of the racial mirages, clichés, and lies that this country's very atmosphere has been filled with for four hundred years."[90]

In addition to confession, the smaller number of sincere whites (all-weather liberals) will need to make greater efforts to help the much larger number of fair-weather liberals and illiberals to effectively turn the corner in the area of race relations. They can do this best by taking every opportunity to be outspoken and prophetic on this issue in the white religious and secular institutions and communities to which they belong. They can form organizations to deal with racism in their own communities and institutions. In addition, genuinely committed whites should be prophetic in those institutions where there is evidence of tokenism in employment practices.

Those who take the gospel ethic of love seriously must be committed enough to the ideal of racial equality, that they recognize that the cost of liberation will not be cheap. King spoke of this cost near the end of his life.

> When millions of people have been cheated for centuries, restitution is a costly process.... Justice so long deferred has accumulated interest and its cost for this society will be substantial in financial as well as human terms. This fact has not been fully grasped, because most of the gains of the past decade were obtained at bargain prices. The desegregation of public facilities cost nothing; neither did the election and appointment of a few black public officials.[91]

Neither the government nor churches and their institutions have been as committed in their attempts to eliminate individual and institutional racism as they have been to other interests. King was rightly convinced that although America did not have a sufficient amount of wealth to adequately compensate black Americans for their long years of forced deprivation and dehumanization, every conceivable effort should be made to devise, implement, and enforce policies and programs that would atone for some of the past injustices.

Since King thought of himself first and foremost as a Christian minister,[92] he was not unmindful of the church's role in eliminating racism and racial discrimination. For King, the church had a divine mandate to take the lead in removing racism from the churches and providing moral and spiritual leadership for the rest of the nation and world. The church "must lead men along the path of true integration, something the law cannot do."[93] Civil law can insure justice between persons, but only moral law can insure love between them.

Martin Luther King firmly believed that as autonomous moral beings, blacks must take their destiny into their own hands. They must not make the mistake of passively waiting for whites to take up their cause, nor should they uncritically trust the moral sense of whites. In this, King accepted the teaching of theological social ethicist Reinhold Niebuhr (who he studied in seminary and during doctoral studies), that "the Negro will never win his full rights in society merely by trusting the fairness and sense of justice of the white man. Whatever increase in the sense of justice can be achieved will mitigate the struggle between the white man and the Negro, but it will not abolish it."[94] King held that blacks must work unceasingly toward the development of a deeper sense of self-esteem and pride, even as they relentlessly resist injustice. Although they are Americans, they are also Africans. This, said King, is their great inescapable dilemma—at once an amalgam of African and American.[95]

Unfortunately, blacks have too frequently emphasized the American side of their dilemma at the expense of the African. If they expect to gain full liberation it is necessary to begin to highlight the African religious, socio-cultural side of their heritage. They must work in their homes, schools, and churches to rid themselves of self-doubt and of enough of their repressed rage and anger that they are able to recapture the true meaning of that now forgotten slogan of the late 1960s, "I'm black and I'm proud." Indeed, King himself counseled that "...we must stand up and say, 'I'm black and I'm beautiful,' and this self-affirmation is the black man's need, made compelling by the white man's crimes against him."[96] This sense of black pride must be intentionally instilled in black children from the time they are able to recognize the meaning of symbols and words. It must be an on-going process until it becomes so deeply woven into their psyche that, when they are older, they naturally pass it on to others in and out of the immediate family.

Black Americans must not depend on white moderates and fair-weather liberals to do for them what they alone can and must do. There are some things that blacks and whites must strive to do together, and some things they must do separately, if liberation is to be a real possibility. This may mean that blacks will periodically and strategically need to separate themselves into political caucuses that will present a formidable challenge to the dominant power.

From Montgomery to Memphis, Martin Luther King struggled against white moderates (fair-weather liberals and illiberals), as well as all-weather illiberals (hardcore racists). Although he exhibited an amazing sense of patience with such people, he was equally (if not more so) impatient with individual and systemic racism against his people. As a little boy he vowed to help his father to fight racism, and when he entered seminary he renewed that vow. No matter what else demanded his attention—whether poverty or the war in Vietnam—his entire civil rights ministry always focused on ridding this nation and the world of racism. We cannot know for certain whether King believed that racism would be entirely eradicated. What we do know is that his staunch, relentless faith in the God of the Hebrew prophets and Jesus Christ, and his sense of what was possible through cooperative endeavor between human beings and God caused him to retain a high degree of hope in the possibility. In any case, whatever we intend to do about racial injustice we had best get on with it. "Black Americans have been patient people," said King, "and perhaps they could continue patient with but a modicum of hope; but everywhere, 'time is winding up ... corruption in the land, people take your stand; time is winding up.'"[97]

Chapter Notes

Introduction

1. I have shown in an earlier book that there are at least a dozen types of personalisms. See my *Personalism: A Critical Introduction* (St. Louis: Chalice Press, 1999), Chapters 2, 3.

2. See Martin Luther King, Jr., "Pilgrimage to Nonviolence," in *A Testament of Hope: The Essential Writings of Martin Luther King, Jr.* ed. James M. Washington (New York: Harper & Row, 1986), 37.

3. See Martin Luther King, Jr., *Stride Toward Freedom* (New York: Harper & Row, 1958), 100.

4. See Lewis V. Baldwin, *To Make the Wounded Whole: The Cultural Legacy of Martin Luther King, Jr.* (Minneapolis: Fortress Press, 1992), 155–56.

5. King, "A Knock at Midnight," in his *Strength to Love* (New York: Harper & Row, Publishers, 1963), 47.

6. King, *Why We Can't Wait* (New York: Harper & Row, Publishers, 1964), 95.

7. Ibid.

8. Fyodor Dostoevsky, *The Brothers Karamazov* (New York: Bantam Books, 1981), 65.

Chapter 1

1. This chapter was originally published as "Martin Luther King, Jr. and the Objective Moral Order: Some Ethical Implications," in *Encounter*, vol. 61, no. 2, Spring 2000. It has undergone substantial revision for this book.

2. Royce discussed the beloved community concept at length in *The Problem of Christianity*, one volume edition (Washington, D.C.: The Catholic University of America Press, 2001) [originally published by Macmillan Company, 1913, two volumes], 125, 129–31, 141, 196–98, 268–70, 318, 381.

3. Ibid., 199.

4. Ibid., 200.

5. Walter Rauschenbusch, *Christianizing the Social Order* (New York: Macmillan, 1926) [1912], 93.

6. Martin Luther King, Jr., *Stride Toward Freedom* (New York: Harper & Row, 1958), 91.

7. Lawrence N. Jones, "Black Christians Antebellum America: In Quest of the Beloved Community," *The Journal of Religious Thought*, Vol. 38, No. 1, Spring-Summer 1981, 12.

8. Ibid., 14.

9. King, *Stride*, 19, 20.

10. Martin Luther King, Sr., *Daddy King: An Autobiography,* with Clayton Riley (New York: William Morrow and Company, 1980), 82.

11. Quoted in Leo Sandon, Jr., "Boston University Personalism and Southern Baptist Theology," *Foundations*, Vol. 20 (April-June 1977), 105.

12. King, *Stride*, 100.

13. See King, "The Personalism of J.M.E. McTaggart Under Criticism." King wrote this paper in Brightman's course on philosophy of religion in 1951. See Clayborne Carson et al. eds., *The Papers of Martin Luther King, Jr.* (Berkeley: University of California Press, 1994), 2:61–76.

14. See King, "A Comparison and Evaluation of the Philosophical Views Set Forth in J.M.E. McTaggart's *Some Dogmas of Religion* and William E. Hocking's *The Meaning of God in Human Experience* with Those Set Forth in Edgar S. Brightman's Course on 'Philosophy of Religion,'" in *The Papers*, 2:76–92.

15. Clayborne Carson, ed., *The Autobiography of Martin Luther King, Jr.* (New York: Warner Books, 1998), 32.

16. See King's doctoral dissertation, "A Comparison of the Conceptions of God in the Thinking of Henry Nelson Wieman and Paul Tillich," (Ph. D. dissertation, Boston University 1955). Here King opts for a doctrine of God similar to that of Bowne and DeWolf.

17. See David J. Garrow, ed., *Martin Luther King, Jr. and the Civil Rights Movement* (New York: Carlson Publishing Inc., 1989), 1:xiv. Garrow also argues that King often used the phrase "the dignity and worth of all human personality" in sermons and speeches because "it was the consonance between King's already-developed views and the principal theme of personalism that led King to adopt and give voice to that tenet so firmly and consistently" (Garrow, "The Intellectual Development of Martin Luther King, Jr.: Influences and Commentaries," Garrow, ed., *Martin Luther King, Jr. and the Civil Rights Movement*, 2:445). In addition, Garrow complains in an endnote that King's teachers and mentors at Boston University "have badly overstated the formative influence their instruction and personalism had on King" (Ibid., 2:451n23). He then invites the reader to examine writings by DeWolf ("Martin Luther King, Jr., as Theologian," *Journal of the Interdenominational Theological Center*, 4 (Spring 1977), 1–11, and Muelder ("Communitarian Christian Ethics: A Personal Statement and a Response," in *Toward a Discipline of Social Ethics* ed. Paul Deats, Jr. (Boston: Boston University Press, 1972), 295–320, at 299 and 314; and "Martin Luther King, Jr.'s Ethics of Nonviolent Action," unpublished Paper, 1985, King Center.

18. See Keith D. Miller, *Voice of Deliverance: The Language of Martin Luther King, Jr. and Its Sources* (New York: The Free Press, 1992), 7, 17.

19. King, *The Trumpet of Conscience* (New York: Harper & Row, 1968), 72.

20. Garrow, "The Intellectual Development of Martin Luther King, Jr.: Influences and Commentaries" in *Martin Luther King, Jr.: Civil Rights Leader, Theologian, Orator* ed. Garrow (New York: Carlson Publishing, Inc., 1989), 5.

21. Taylor Branch, *Parting the Waters: America in the King Years 1954–63* (New York: Simon & Schuster, 1988), 918.

22. Garrow, "The Intellectual Development of Martin Luther King, Jr.," 6.

23. Coretta Scott King, *My Life with Martin Luther King, Jr.* (New York: Holt Rinehart and Winston, 1969), 92.

24. *The Papers* (1992), 1:390.

25. King, "A Comparison of the Conceptions of God...," 269.

26. Ibid., 270. The claim that complete and perfect personality inheres only in God was the view of Bowne's teacher, Rudolph Hermann Lotze, a view that Bowne himself adopted. In an early book, *Studies in Theism* (New York: Phillips & Hunt, 1879) Bowne credited Lotze with this idea. Here he wrote that, "we must say with Lotze that full personality is possible only to the infinite. It alone is in full possession and knowledge of itself.... Full personality exists only where the nature is transparent to itself, and where all the powers are under absolute control. Such personality is not ours; it can belong only to the infinite, while ours is but its faint and imperfect image" (275). Lotze argued similarly in his massive *Microcosmus : An Essay Concerning Man and His Relation to the World* trans. Elizabeth Hamilton and E. E. Constance Jones, in Two Volumes (Edinburgh: T&T Clark, 1885) [published originally as three volumes 1856–1864], 2:688. God is perfect consciousness, selfhood, will, and wisdom.

27. King, "A Comparison of the Conception of God...," 270. See also Bowne, *Personalism* (Boston: Houghton Mifflin, 1908) where he characterizes essential person as selfhood, self-consciousness, self-control, and the power to know (266).

28. Quoted in Ibid., 268 (taken from Albert C. Knudson, *The Doctrine of God* [Nashville: Abingdon Press, 1930], 300).

29. See Edgar S. Brightman's illuminating discussion on the objectivity of value in *An Introductuon to Philosophy* Third Edition, Revised by Robert N. Beck (New York: Holt Rinehart Winston, 1964), Chapter 7.

30. Quoted in Renée D. Turner, "Remembering the Young King: Classmates and Friends Recall Fun-Loving Youth in 'Big Apple' Hat," *Ebony*, vol. 43, January 1988, 42.

31. Brightman, *Moral Laws* (Nashville: Abingdon, 1933), 286.

32. See *The Papers* (1994), 2:88n44, 89n45, 92 (where he includes *Moral Laws* in the bibliography of a paper written for Brightman.

33. King, "Our God Is Able," in his *Strength to Love* (New York: Harper & Row, 1963), 105.

34. Ibid., 103.

35. King, "Love, Law, and Civil Disobedience," in *A Testament of Hope*, 52. Theodore Parker actually said: "I do not pretend to understand the moral universe; the arc is a long one, my eye reaches but little ways; I cannot calculate the curve and complete the figure by the experience of sight; I can divine it by conscience. And from what I see I am sure it bends towards justice" [Parker, "Of Justice and the Conscience," in *The Collected Works of Theodore Parker* ed.

Frances Power Cobbe (London: Trübner & Company, Ludgate Hill, 1879), 2:48]. The specific rendering of King's oft quoted line was given by John Haynes Holmes who was clearly aware of Parker's statement. In the December 1956 issue of *Liberation* Holmes, along with Harry Emerson Fosdick and others gave a salute to the participants in the Montgomery bus boycott. Holmes declared that "the forces of righteousness" were on the side of those struggling for justice in Montgomery. Afterward he said, clearly influenced by Parker: "The victory may seem slow in coming. The waiting for it may seem interminable. We perhaps may not live to see the hour of triumph. But the great Theodore Parker, abolitionist preacher in the days before the Civil War, answered this doubt and fear when he challenged an impatient world. 'The arc of the moral universe is long, but it bends toward justice'" [Holmes, "Salute to Montgomery," *Liberation* (December 1956), 5].

36. Carson, ed., *The Autobiography*, 33.

37. Ibid.

38. J. DeOtis Roberts, *A Black Political Theology* (Philadelphia: Westminster Press, 1974), 200.

39. See King, *Stride*, 169, 209; and King, *Why We Can't Wait* (New York: Harper & Row, 1964), 94.

40. Carson, *The Autobiography*, 69.

41. Ibid., 70.

42. King, "Letter from Birmingham Jail," in his *Why We Can't Wait*, 87–89.

43. Ibid.

44. Roberts, *A Black Political Theology*, 200–201.

45. See Rufus Burrow, Jr., and Jimmy L. Kirby, "Conceptions of God in the thinking of Martin Luther King, Jr. and Edgar S. Brightman," *Encounter*, Vol. 60, No. 3, Summer 1999.

46. King, "The Death of Evil upon the Seashore," in *Strength to Love*, 64.

47. See Branch, *Parting the Waters*, 221–22.

48. King, "The Answer to a Perplexing Question," in *Strength to Love*, 124.

49. See King, "A New Sense of Direction," *Worldview*, April 1972, 11; and King, "Where Do We Go from Here?," in *A Testament of Hope*, 250.

50. King, "A Christmas Sermon on Peace," in *A Testament of Hope*, 255.

51. King, "The Ethical Demands for Integration," in *A Testament of Hope*, 122.

52. Borden P. Bowne, *Principles of Ethics* (New York: Harper & Brothers, 1892), 190–91.

53. King, "A Knock at Midnight" in *A Knock at Midnight* eds. Clayborne Carson and Peter Holloran (New York: Warner Books, 1998), 88.

54. Bowne, *Principles of Ethics*, 305.

55. King, "Remaining Awake Through a Great Revolution," in *A Testament of Hope*, 270.

56. King, "Letter from Birmingham Jail," in *Why We Can't Wait*, 89.

Chapter 2

1. This chapter is a revised version of my article, "Martin Luther King, the Church, and a Value-Fused Universe," published in *Encounter*, Vol. 66, No. 3, Summer 2005, 199–220. The article itself was adapted from a speech I gave on the occasion of the Twentieth Annual Service of Repentance & Reconciliation, hosted by Plymouth Congregational Church (UCC) and sponsored by The Associated Churches and the Interdenominational Ministerial Alliance in Fort Wayne, Indiana, January 16, 2005.

2. Immanuel Kant, *Critique of Practical Reason* trans. Lewis White Beck (Indianapolis: The Bobbs-Merrill Company, Inc., 1956) [1788], 166.

3. Martin Luther King, Jr., "Rediscovering Lost Values," in *A Knock at Midnight* eds. Clayborne Carson and Peter Holloran (New York: Warner Books, 1998), 10.

4. In his "Advice for Living" column in *Ebony* magazine, King responded to a reader who asked whether he believed that God approves of the death penalty for heinous crimes such as murder and rape. He responded that God disapproves of the death penalty for any crime whatever. "God's concern is to improve individuals and bring them to the point of conversion.... Capital punishment is against the best judgment of modern criminology and, above all, against the highest expression of love in the nature of God." See Clayborne Carson, et al., eds., *The Papers of Martin Luther King, Jr.* (Berkeley: University of California Press, 2000), 4:305.

5. Eberhard Bethge, *Dietrich Bonhoeffer: A Biography*, ed. Victoria J. Barnett, revised edition (Minneapolis: Fortress Press, 2000), 830.

6. Dietrich Bonhoeffer, *Ethics* ed. Clifford J. Green, in *Dietrich Bonhoeffer Works*, Vol. 6 (Minneapolis: Fortress Press, 2005), 282–83 (my emphasis).

7. See Desmond Tutu, *God Has a Dream: A Vision of Hope for Our Time* (New York: Doubleday, 2004), 20.

8. Ibid., 22.

9. Ibid., 23–24.

10. King, "The Un-Christian Christian," *Ebony*, August 1965, 77.

11. King, "A Time to Break Silence," in *A Testament of Hope: The Essential Writings of Martin Luther King, Jr.*, ed. James M. Washington (New York: Harper & Row, Publishers, 1986), 232.

12. King, "Why Jesus Called a Man a Fool," in *A Knock at Midnight*, 146.

13. King, "A Knock at Midnight," in his *Strength to Love* (New York: Harper & Row, 1963), 44.

14. King, "Transformed Nonconformist," in *Strength to Love*, 12.

15. Ibid., 11.

16. King, "A Knock at Midnight," in *Strength to Love*, 47.

17. Ibid.

18. King, "Letter from Birmingham Jail," in his *Why We Can't Wait* (New York: New American Library, 1964), 95.

19. Ibid.

20. King, "I've Been to the Mountaintop," in *A Call to Conscience* eds. Clayborne Carson and Kris Shepherd (New York: Warner Books, 2001), 213–14.

21. Abraham J. Heschel, *The Prophets* (New York: Harper & Row, Publishers, 1962), 204.

22. Ibid.

23. Ibid., 204–205.

24. Ibid., 167.

25. King, et al., Face to Face Television News Interview, in *A Testament of Hope*, 408.

26. King, "The Un-Christian Christian," 80.

27. Ibid.

28. King, "Where Do We Go from Here," in *A Call to Conscience*, 192.

29. King, "Our God is Able," in *Strength to Love*, 103.

30. Ibid., 105.

31. James Russell Lowell, "The Present Crisis," in *The Complete Poetical Works of James Russell Lowell* (Boston: Houghton Mifflin Company, 1925), 67.

32. Theodore Parker, "The State of the Nation," in *The Collected Works of Theodore Parker* ed. Frances Power Cobbe (London: Trübner and Company, 1863), 4:263.

33. Ibid., 4:264.

34. King, *Where Do We Go from Here: Chaos or Community?* (Boston: Bantam Books, 1968), 222.

35. King, "A Christmas Sermon on Peace," in *A Testament of Hope*, 257.

36. King, "Facing the Challenge of a New Age," in *A Testament of Hope*, 141.

37. Ibid.

38. Thomas Jefferson, *Notes on Virginia*, Query XVIII, in *The Life and Selected Writings of Thomas Jefferson* eds. Adrienne Koch and William Peden (New York: Modern Library, 1972), 278–79.

39. King, "Love, Law, and Civil Disobedience," in *A Testament of Hope*, 52.

40. Parker, "The State of the Nation," 4:265.

41. Ibid.

42. King, "A Time to Break Silence," in *A Testament of Hope*, 240, 629.

43. Heschel, "No Religion Is an Island," in *Moral Grandeur and Spiritual Audacity* ed. Susannah Heschel (New York: Farrar, Straus, Giroux, 1996), 253.

44. King, "A Time to Break Silence," in *A Testament of Hope*, 242.

45. Ibid.

46. Heschel, *The Prophets*, 4.

47. King, "Negroes Are Not Moving Too Fast," in *A Testament of Hope*, 180.

48. Heschel, *The Prophets*, 16.

49. King, "The Answer to a Perplexing Question," in *Strength to Love*, 123.

Chapter 3

1. Clayborne Carson, et al. eds., *The Papers of Martin Luther King, Jr.* (Berkeley: University of California Press, 2007), 6:407–410.

2. Fred Standley and Louis Pratt, eds., *Conversations with James Baldwin* (Jackson: University Press of Mississippi, 1989), 226.

3. Martin Luther King, Jr., *Stride Toward Freedom* (New York: Harper & Row, 1958), 19, 20.

4. *The Papers* (1992), 2:362; also King, *Stride*, 18–19.

5. Clayborne Carson, ed., *The Autobiography of Martin Luther King, Jr.* (New York: Warner Books, 1998), 9.

6. King, *Stride*, 90.

7. Carson, ed., *The Autobiography*, 10.

8. Carson, ed., *The Autobiography*, 11–12.

9. King, *Stride*, 90.

10. *The Papers*, 6:162n10.

11. Ibid., 6:110.

12. Stephen B. Oates, *Let the Trumpet Sound: The Life of Martin Luther King, Jr.* (New York: Harper & Row, 1982), 35.

13. Clayborne Carson and Peter Holloran, eds., *A Knock at Midnight* (New York: Warner Books, 1998), 146.

14. Cornel West, *Race Matters* (Boston: Beacon Press, 1993), Chapter 1.

15. Christine King Farris, "The Young Martin: From Childhood through College," *Ebony*, Vol. xli, No. 3 (January 1986), 56–58.

16. Carson and Holloran, eds., *A Knock at Midnight*, 88.

17. See Lewis V. Baldwin's excellent discussion of these and related matters in *There Is a Balm in Gilead: The Cultural Roots of Martin Luther King, Jr.* (Minneapolis: Fortress Press, 1991), Chapter 2. See also Baldwin and Amiri YaSin Al-Hadid, *Between Cross and Crescent: Christian and Muslim Perspectives on Malcolm and Martin* (Gainesville:

University Press of Florida, 2002), Chapters 1, 3, 5, 9. See also Michael Eric Dyson, *I May Not Get There with You: The True Martin Luther King, Jr.* (New York: The Free Press, 2000), Introduction, Chapters 7–10; David Garrow, *Bearing the Cross: Martin Luther King, Jr. and the SCLC* (New York: William Morrow and Company, Inc., 1986), 375–376; Taylor Branch, *Parting the Waters: America in the King Years 1954–63* (New York: Simon & Schuster, 1988), 239, 860. Theodore Pappas has written most systematically on King's plagiarism. See his *Plagiarism and the Culture War: The Writings of Martin Luther King, Jr. and Other Prominent Americans,* Revised and Expanded Edition (Tampa, FL: Hallberg Publishing Corporation, 1998). Also see "Becoming Martin Luther King, Jr.—Plagiarism and Originality: A Round Table," in *The Journal of American History,* Volume 78, Number 1 (June 1991), 11–123.

18. *Playboy* Interview: Martin Luther King, Jr. in *A Testament of Hope: Essential Writings of Martin Luther King, Jr.,* ed. James M. Washington (New York: Harper & Row, 1986), 372.

19. Ibid., 375.

20. King, "A Challenge to Churches and Synagogues," in *Race: Challenge to Religion,* ed. Mathew Amann (Chicago: Henry Regnery Company, 1963), 164.

21. See Garth Baker-Fletcher, *Somebodyness: Martin Luther King, Jr., and the Theory of Dignity* (Minneapolis: Fortress Press, 1993).

22. In *Stride,* King wrote of his people having "won new dignity" (161), and of their recognition that they are "somebody" (190), as a result of the Montgomery struggle. He wrote further that with this growing sense of somebodyness and dignity came also a growing self-respect which inspired them "with a new determination to struggle and sacrifice until first-class citizenship becomes a reality" (190).

23. Baker-Fletcher, *Somebodyness,* 48.

24. *The Papers,* 6:315.

25. King, "The Ethical Demands for Integration" in *A Testament of Hope,* 122.

26. For example, we must consider whether persons, by virtue of their capacity for rationality, morality, and humanity, have value because of this, quite apart from their being valued by God. In other words, might there be philosophical or ethical grounds for human worth as well as theistic or religious ones? This is certainly suggested in the second form of Immanuel Kant's categorical imperative: "Act so that you treat humanity, whether in your own person or in that of another, always as an end and never as a means only" [Immanuel Kant, *Foundations of the Metaphysics of Morals,* trans. by Lewis White Beck (Indianapolis: Bobbs-Merrill, 1959) [1785], 47.

27. King, "The Ethical Demands for Integration," in *A Testament of Hope,* 122.

28. King, "Where Do We Go from Here?," in *A Testament of Hope,* 251.

29. John Wright Buckham, *Christianity and Personality* (New York: Round Table Press, 1936), 166.

30. Ibid.

31. See Buckham, *Personality and the Christian Ideal* (Boston: The Pilgrim Press, 1909), 20.

32. Borden P. Bowne, *The Principles of Ethics* (New York: American Book Company, 1892), 190–91.

33. Ibid., 199.

34. John S. Mbiti, *African Religions and Philosophy,* Second Edition (Portsmouth, NH: Heinemann Publishers, 1982) [1969], 106.

35. Aylward Shorter, *African Christian Theology* (Maryknoll, NY: Orbis Books, 1977), 35.

36. Bowne, *Philosophy of Theism* (New York: Harper & Brothers, 1887), 52–53.

37. For example, see Benjamin Ewuku Oguah, "African and Western Philosophy: A Comparative Study," in *African Philosophy: An Introduction,* 3rd Edition, ed. Richard A. Wright (New York: University Press of America, 1984), 220–221; Ifeanyi A. Menkiti, "Person and Community in African Traditional Thought," in Ibid., 171–181.

38. Desmond Tutu, *God Has A Dream: A Vision of Hope for Our Time* (New York: Doubleday, 2004), 25.

39. Ibid., 25–26.

40. King, "The Ethical Demands for Integration," in *A Testament of Hope,* 122.

41. James Baldwin, "A Talk to Teachers," in his *The Price of the Ticket: Collected Nonfiction 1948–1985* (New York: St. Martin's/Marek, 1985), 690.

42. King, "A Christmas Sermon on Peace," in *A Testament of Hope,* 255.

43. King, "The Ethical Demands for Integration," in *A Testament of Hope,* 119.

44. Frederick Douglass, "The Constitution of the United States: Is it Pro-Slavery or Anti-Slavery?" in *The Life and Writings of Frederick Douglass,* ed. Philip S. Foner (New York: International Publishers, 1975), 2:477.

45. Alexis de Tocqueville, *Democracy in America* (New York: Vintage Books, 1945), 1:372 (my emphasis).

46. Ibid., 1:388–89.

47. Henry Steele Commager, *Documents of American History* Seventh Edition (New York: Appleton-Century-Crofts, Division of Meredith Publishing Company, 1963), 342.

48. Andrew Hacker, *Two Nations: Black and White, Separate, Hostile, Unequal* (New York: Ballantine Books, 1992), 23 (my emphasis).

49. See William J. Wilson, *The Declining Significance of Race: Blacks and Changing American Institutions* (Chicago: University of Chicago Press, 1978).

50. Dinesh D'Souza, *The End of Racism: Principles for a Multiracial Society* (New York: The Free Press, 1995).

51. Manning Marable, *Black Liberation in Conservative America* (Boston: South End Press, 1997), 188–205.

52. Joe R. Feagin, *Racist America: Roots, Current Realities, and Future Reparations* (New York: Routledge, 2000).

53. C. Eric Lincoln, *Race, Religion, and the Continuing American Dilemma* rev. ed. (New York: Hill and Wang, 1999).

54. This is the argument of Marable, Feagin, and Lincoln throughout the corpus of each man's voluminous writing and lecturing on the subject of systemic racial discrimination.

55. King, *Where Do We Go from Here: Chaos or Community?* (Boston: Beacon Press, 1967), 173–76.

56. King, "A Testament of Hope," in *A Testament of Hope,* 314.

57. Ibid.

58. King, "Where Do We Go from Here?," in *A Testament of Hope,* 251.

59. King, "Showdown for Nonviolence," in *A Testament of Hope,* 71.

60. King, "A Time to Break Silence," in *A Testament of Hope,* 240.

61. King, "Where Do We Go from Here?," in *A Testament of Hope,* 250.

62. "A Conversation with Martin Luther King," in *A Testament of Hope* (1991), 676.

63. See Erazim Kohák, "Selves, People, Persons: An Essay in American Personalism," in *Selves, People, and Persons: What Does it Mean to be a Self?* ed. Leroy S. Rouner (Notre Dame: University of Notre Dame Press, 1992), 17–35. What Kohák and environmentalists seem to want is a

way of thinking about persons that does not imply the worthlessness or devaluation of other life forms. He seems to think that the best way to do this is to characterize all conscious life forms as persons. The assumption is that human persons will feel obligated to treat non-human life forms with more respect than has heretofore been the case. Not only do I think this not likely to occur, but I think the same hoped for outcome can be achieved by acknowledging that all conscious life forms are moral subjects, and therefore warrant respect. Since not all moral subjects have moral agency, those that do, e.g., human persons, owe duties to those who do not. At the bear minimum this means treating them with respect. For all moral subjects have intrinsic worth or value (although in varying degrees). Thus they ought to be respected.

64. King went to Boston University to earn his doctorate precisely because he wanted to study personalism under its leading authority, Edgar S. Brightman. While in seminary he studied Brightman's classic work, *A Philosophy of Religion* under George W. Davis. He then had the privilege of studying the same text under Brightman. In that text Brightman wrote: "There is no reason on the basis of known evidence to draw the line sharply and say that only human beings are persons; pigs, dogs, apes, and horses seem to be at least elementary persons" [See his *A Philosophy of Religion* (New York: Prentice-Hall, Inc., 1940), 350].

65. Jewelle Taylor Gibbs, ed., *Young, Black, and Male in America: An Endangered Species* (New York: Auburn House Publishing Company, 1988), Chapters 1, 4, 7, 8.

66. C. Birch, *Regaining Compassion for Humanity and Nature* (St. Louis: Chalice Press, 1993), 105.

67. Ibid., 103.

68. Edith Hamilton and Huntington Cairns, ed., *Plato: The Collected Dialogues Including the Letters* (Princeton: Princeton University Press, 1971), 699.

69. Francis M. Cornford, *The Republic of Plato* (New York: Oxford University Press, 1945), 160n2.

70. Ibid., 161.

71. Ernest Barker, *The Politics of Aristotle* (New York: Oxford University Press, 1946), 9–18, 35.

72. Ibid., 35, 36. See also R. McKeon, ed., *The Basic Works of Aristotle* (New York: Random House, 1941), 665–680.

73. Ibid., 36.

74. Bowne, *The Principles of Ethics*, 161, 193. See also Etienne Gilson, *The Spirit of Medieval Philosophy* (New York: Charles Scribner's Sons, 1940). Gilson writes: "Neither Plato nor Aristotle, although they held all the necessary metaphysical principles in their hands, ever had a sufficiently high idea of the worth of the individual as such..." (190). They lacked a metaphysic of the person.

75. Ralph Tyler Flewelling, *Philosophy and the War* (New York: Abingdon Press, 1918), 33.

76. Ibid., 33–34.

77. Immanuel Kant, *Observations on the Feeling of the Beautiful and Sublime,* trans. John T. Goldthwaith (Berkeley: University of California Press, 1973), 110–111.

78. David Hume, "Of National Characters" in *Philosophical Historian,* eds. David Fate Norton and Richard H. Popkin (Indianapolis: Bobbs-Merrill Company, Inc., 1965), 47n, 48.

79. Pauline Kleingeld has argued that although Kant held a hierarchical and inegalitarian view of the races in the 1780s, he dropped the hierarchical view for a more egalitarian one in the 1790s. See her provocative essay, "Kant's Second Thoughts on Race," *The Philosophical Quarterly,* Vol. 57, No. 229, October 2007, 573–92.

80. Bowne, *The Principles of Ethics.*

81. Helmut Thielicke, *Theological Ethics: Foundations,* ed. W. H. Lazareth (Philadelphia: Fortress Press, 1966), 1:609, and 578.

82. Ibid., 1:594.

83. Ibid., 1:666.

84. Ibid., 1:590.

85. This was the experience of James W.C. Pennington in the first third of the nineteenth century. See "Great Moral Dilemma," in *Afro-American Religious History: A Documentary Witness,* ed. Milton C. Sernett (Durham: Duke University Press, 1985), 81–87.

86. Thielicke, *Theological Ethics,* 1:590.

87. Alice Walker develops this theme wonderfully in her *Anything We Love Can Be Saved: A Writer's Activism* (New York: Random House, 1997).

88. Toni Morrison, *Beloved* (New York: Alfred A. Knopf, 1987), 88.

89. King, "Who Are We?," Sermon preached at Ebenezer Baptist Church in Atlanta, February 5, 1966, King Library and Archives, 3. See also his sermon, "The Christian Doctrine of Man," in *The Papers,* 6:332. This sermon was preached at the Detroit Council of Churches' Noon Lenten Services on March 12, 1958.

90. *The Papers,* 6:332.

91. Ibid., 6:410.

92. Reinhold Niebuhr, *Moral Man and Immoral Society* (New York: Scribner's, 1932), 252.

93. Baldwin, "A Talk to Teachers," in his *The Price of the Ticket,* 330.

94. W. E. B. DuBois, *The Souls of Black Folk* (New York: Dodd, Mead & Company, 1961) [1903], 3.

95. King, *Where Do We Go from Here: Chaos or Community?* (Boston: Beacon Press, 1967), 53; and "A Testament of Hope," in *A Testament of Hope,* 318.

96. King, "Where Do We Go from Here?," in *A Testament of Hope,* 246.

97. King, "Showdown for Nonviolence," in *A Testament of Hope,* 71.

98. James Baldwin, "Falukner and Desegregation" in his *Nobody Knows My Name* (New York: Dell, 1961), 106.

99. King, "A Time to Break Silence," in *A Testament of Hope,* 243.

100. Baldwin, "Notes for a Hypothetical Novel," in *Nobody Knows My Name,* 126.

101 Baldwin, *The Fire Next Time* (New York: Dial Press, 1963), 119–120.

Chapter 4

1. See "Fragment of Application to Boston University" in *The Papers of Martin Luther King, Jr.,* eds. Clayborne Carson et al. (Berkeley: University of California Press, 1992), 1:390.

2. See Kenneth Clark, *King, Malcolm, Baldwin: Three Interviews* (Wesleyan University Press, 1985), 21.

3. L. Harold DeWolf, "Martin Luther King, Jr., As Theologian," *The Journal of the Interdenominational Theological Center,* Vol. 4, No. 2, Spring 1977, 10. In light of the charge of plagiarism lodged against King posthumously, one wonders whether DeWolf's statement that, "occasionally I find his language following closely the special terms of my own lectures and writings," might have been an implied concern that King bordered dangerously on plagiarism in some of the written work for DeWolf's courses.

4. See Martin Luther King, Jr., "A New Sense of Direction," *Worldview,* April 1972, 11; and King, "Where Do We Go from Here?" in *A Testament of Hope: The Essential Writings of Martin Luther King, Jr.,* ed. James M. Washington (New York: Harper & Row, 1986), 250.

5. See Rufus Burrow, Jr., "John Wesley Edward Bowen:

First Afrikan American Personalist," *Encounter*, Vol. 56, No. 3 (Summer 1995), 241–260. Bowen actually studied personalism under Borden P. Bowne (1847–1910), "the father of American Personalism." Indeed, at that time Bowne was not using the term personalism, but *objective idealism* and *transcendental empiricism*. But his emphasis at each stage in the movement toward personalism was on the centrality of the self or person.

6. See David J. Garrow, "The Intellectual Development of Martin Luther King, Jr.: Influences and Commentaries" in *Martin Luther King, Jr.: Civil Rights Leader, Theologian, Orator*, ed. Garrow (New York: Carlson Publishing, Inc., 1989), 2:451n23.

7. See King, *Stride Toward Freedom* (New York: Harper & Row, 1958), 100.

8. Susan Harlow was a Master of Divinity student at Christian Theological Seminary. With her permission, this quote was taken from a paper she submitted in my class, Theological Ethics of Martin Luther King, Jr., in April 1997.

9. King, *Stride*, 100.

10. Ibid.

11. These include the Englishman John Grote and the Americans Walt Whitman and A. Bronson Alcott.

12. Borden P. Bowne, *The Philosophy of Herbert Spencer* (New York: Phillips & Hunt, 1874).

13. See Rufus Burrow, Jr., "Borden Parker Bowne's Doctrine of God," *Encounter*, Vol. 53, No. 4 (Autumn 1992), 381–400.

14. Albert C. Knudson, *The Philosophy of Personalism* (New York: Abingdon Press, 1927), 85, 433.

15. However, it should be noted that there was a similar movement afoot at the University of California under the leadership of George Holmes Howison (1836–1916). Unlike Bowne, who came to consider himself "a Personalist, the first of the clan in any thoroughgoing sense," Howison named his philosophy Personal Idealism. There are several differences between their philosophies, the chief of which is that Howison was a non-creationist, believing that God is the Final, not the First Cause. Bowne, on the other hand, was a creationist. He insisted that God is the fundamental cause of all things. I have discussed at length some similarities and dissimilarities between Bowne and Howison in my *Personalism: A Critical Introduction* (St. Louis: Chalice Press, 1999), Chapter 3.

16. The types of personalisms include (but may not be limited to): Atheistic Personalism, Pantheistic Personalism, Absolutistic Personalism, Relativistic Personalism, Ethical Personalism, Theistic Personalism, Realistic Personalism, Political Personalism, Panpsychistic Personalism, Anthropormorphic Personalism, and Afrikan American Personalism.

17. King, "The Ethical Demands for Integration" in *A Testament of Hope*, 122.

18. Ibid., 119.

19. See Bowne, *The Principles of Ethics* (New York: American Book Company, 1892), 97, 203, 216–17.

20. Bowne, *Studies in Theism* (New York: Phillips & Hunt, 1879), 411–12.

21. Ibid., 4.

22. King, "Pilgrimage to Nonviolence," in his *Strength to Love* (New York: Harper & Row, 1963), 141.

23. King, "An Experiment in Love," in *A Testament of Hope*, 20. I find it interesting that King does not characterize God's power as absolute or omnipotent, but as "matchless." This seems to me a subtle qualification of the classical view of divine omnipotence. Even Brightman, whose doctrine of God King both appreciated and criticized, would appreciate the idea of the "matchless" power of God. For this idea does not mean that God possesses absolute power

in the classical sense, and thus has affinity with Brightman's doctrine of the finite-infinite God.

24. Here I follow the distinction that Paul W. Taylor makes between "moral subjects" and "moral agents." Any conscious being is a moral subject, even if unable to make responsible moral choices. In any event they are beings to whom moral agents owe responsibilities. Moral agents, on the other hand, are moral subjects whose faculties are such that they are capable of making responsible moral choices, anticipating the consequences of those choices, willing to take responsibility for these, and able to assess the outcome and apply what is learned in new situations calling for moral choice. See Taylor, *Respect for Nature: A Theory of Environmental Ethics* (Princeton: Princeton University Press, 1986), 14–16.

25. King, "The Ethical Demands for Integration," in *A Testament of Hope*, 120.

26. King, "The Personalism of J.M.E. McTaggart Under Criticism," in *The Papers* (1994), 2:73. This paper was presented to DeWolf on December 4, 1951, in his class on Personalism.

27. King, "The Ethical Demands for Integration," in *A Testament of Hope*, 120.

28. King, "What Is Man?," in *Strength to Love*, 90.

29. King, "How Should a Christian View Communism," in *Strength to Love*, 95.

30. Edgar S. Brightman, *Nature and Values* (New York: Abingdon, 1945), 117.

31. John S. Pobee, *Toward an African Theology* (Nashville: Abingdon, 1979), 49.

32. Francis J. McConnell, *Personal Christianity* (New York: Fleming H. Revell Company, 1914), 48.

33. Walter G. Muelder, *Moral Law in Christian Social Ethics* (Richmond, VA: John Knox Press, 1966), 124.

34. Brightman, *An Introduction to Philosophy*, 3rd ed., rev. by Robert N. Beck (New York: Holt Rinehart Winston, 1963), 353.

35. Knudson, *The Principles of Christian Ethics* (New York: Abingdon Press, 1943), 118.

36. King, "Paul's Letter to American Christians," in *Strength to Love*, 133. See also his "The Most Durable Power," in *A Testament of Hope*, 11, for a slightly different version of this.

37. King, "The Ethical Demands for Integration," in *A Testament of Hope*, 122.

38. King, "A Christmas Sermon on Peace," in *A Testament of Hope*, 254.

39. Brightman, *Moral Laws* (New York: Abingdon Press, 1933), 94.

40. These include Peter A. Bertocci and Richard M. Millard, Walter G. Muelder, L. Harold DeWolf, Paul Deats, Jr., and J. Philip Wogaman.

41. Brightman, *Moral Laws*, 49.

42. Ibid., 35–45.

43. Ibid., 45.

44. Ibid.

45. Ibid., 204.

46. Ibid., 242.

47. See Stephen B. Oates, *Let the Trumpet Sound: The Life of Martin Luther King, Jr.* (New York: Harper & Row, 1982), 35.

48. John J. Ansbro, *Martin Luther King, Jr.: The Making of a Mind* (Maryknoll, NY: Orbis Books, 1982), 15.

49. Quoted in Leo Sandon, Jr., "Boston University Personalism and Southern Baptist Theology," *Foundations*, Vol. 20 (April-June 1977), 105. King wrote about Brightman's influence in a 1957 publication in *Bostonia* (Spring 1957), 7. He also mentioned in his application to Boston University Graduate School that he had been influenced by Brightman's ideas while a student at Crozer Theological

Seminary (See *The Papers*, 1:390). King noted Brightman's presence at Boston University as one of the two reasons that institution appealed to him.

50. King, "The Personalism of J.M.E. McTaggart under Criticism" in *The Papers*, 2:72.

51. See Bowne, *Theory of Thought and Knowledge* (New York: Harper & Brothers, 1897), 239.

52. Quoted in *The Papers*, 2:72–73. It should be noted that this quote is not exact. King both omits and adds words and phrases without alerting his readers. Brightman's exact words are: "...without it we are not even free to think, to say nothing of making other moral choices. The power to think means that the individual can impose on himself the ideal of logic or scientific method and hold it through thick and thin" (Brightman, *Moral Laws*, 282).

53. Brightman, *Moral Laws*, 286.

54. King, "Our God Is Able," in *Strength to Love*, 103.

55. King, "How Should a Christian View Communism?," in *Strength to Love*, 95.

56. King, "The Power of Nonviolence," in *A Testament of Hope*, 14.

57. See *The Papers*, 4:280. In *Moral Laws*, Brightman wrote that "moral experience and moral laws are just as real as sense experience and physical laws" (Ibid., 285).

58. See King, "Love, Law, and Civil Disobedience," in *A Testament of Hope*, 48.

59. See Kenneth Smith and Ira Zepp, Jr., *Search for the Beloved Community: The Thinking of Martin Luther King, Jr.* (Valley Forge: Judson Press, 1974), 110–113.

60. In 1983 Muelder addressed this topic in a paper he read at Morehouse College, "Martin Luther King, Jr. and the Moral Laws."

61. Bowne, *The Principles of Ethics* (New York: American Book Company, 1892), 199.

62. King, "An Experiment in Love," in *A Testament of Hope*, 19.

63. King, "Nonviolence and Racial Justice," in *A Testament of Hope*, 8–9.

64. King, "Suffering and Faith," in *A Testament of Hope*, 41. See also King, *Stride*, 103.

65. *The Papers* (2005), 5:369 (my emphasis). See also 5:371, 444.

66. King, "An Experiment in Love," in *A Testament of Hope*, 18.

67. Quoted in King, "An Experiment in Love," in *A Testament of Hope*, 18.

68. Quoted in Ibid.

69. Ansbro, Martin Luther King, Jr., 85.

70. King, "Loving Your Enemies," in *Strength to Love*, 39–40.

71. Ansbro, Martin Luther King, Jr., 86.

72. See Bowne, *The Principles of Ethics*, 113.

73. Ibid., 209 (my emphasis).

74. Ibid., 197–98.

75. King, *Stride*, 223. See also *The Papers*, 4:398, 471.

76. King, *Where Do We Go from Here: Chaos or Community?* (Boston: Beacon Press, 1967), 64.

77. Ibid., 125.

78. King, "A Gift of Love," in *A Testament of Hope*, 62–63.

79. King, *The Measure of a Man* (Philadelphia: Fortress Press, 1988) [1959], 13–14.

80. Robert Bruce McLaren, *Christian Ethics: Foundations and Practice* (Englewood Cliffs, NJ: Prentice Hall, 1994), 109.

81. Alice Walker, "From an Interview," in her *In Search of Our Mothers' Gardens* (New York: Harcourt Brace Jovanovich, 1983), 245.

82. Maya Angelou, from "Maya Angelou Raps," in *Conversations with Maya Angelou,* ed. Jeffrey M. Elliot (Jackson: University Press of Mississippi, 1989), 96.

83. King, "Where Do We Go from Here?," in *A Testament of Hope*, 245.

84. King, "A Testament of Hope," in *A Testament of Hope*, 318. See also King, *Where Do We Go from Here*, 53.

85. Malcolm X, "The Ballot or the Bullet," in *Malcolm X Speaks,* ed. George Breitman (New York: Pathfinder Press, 1989) [1965], 40 (my emphasis).

86. Clark, ed., *King, Malcolm, Baldwin: Three Interviews*, 38.

Chapter 5

1. On October 11, 2011, I delivered a much shorter version of this chapter at the University of Northern Iowa in Professor Michael Blackwell's course on Martin Luther King, Jr. There were approximately 35 junior and senior students present in the Center for Multicultural Education where the class met. The present form of the chapter has been enhanced, expanded, and otherwise altered for publication.

2. Clayborne Carson et al., eds., *The Papers of Martin Luther King, Jr.* (Berkeley: University of California Press, 1992), 1:391.

3. Ibid., 1:89.

4. Ibid., 1:390.

5. See Josiah Royce, *The Problem of Christianity* (Washington, D.C.: The Catholic University of America Press, 2001) [first published in 1913 by Macmillan], 125, 129–31, 141, 268–70, 318, 381.

6. The verbatim quote is found in Martin Luther King, Jr., "Facing the Challenge of a New Age," in *A Testament of Hope: The Essential Writings of Martin Luther King, Jr.,* ed. James M. Washington (New York: Harper & Row, Publishers, 1986), 144. Originally published in *Phylon* 28 (April 1957): 24–34.

7. See King, "Pilgrimage to Nonviolence," in *Stride Toward Freedom* (New York: Harper & Row, 1958), Chapter VI, and also in his *Strength to Love* (New York: Harper & Row, 1963), Chapter XVII.

8. *The Papers* (2007), 6:110, 111.

9. Albert C. Knudson, *The Philosophy of Personalism* (New York: The Abingdon Press, 1927), 80.

10. John Wright Buckham, *Christianity and Personality* (New York: Round Table Press, Inc., 1936), 33. A. E. Garvie even described Christianity as personalism. See Garvie, *The Expository Times*, June, 1933, 398.

11. Buckham, *Personality and the Christian Ideal* (Boston: The Pilgrim Press, 1909), 3.

12. King, *Stride*, 100.

13. See my *Personalism: A Critical Introduction* (St. Louis: Chalice Press, 1999), 76–84.

14. Benjamin E. Mays, *Seeking to Be Christian in Race Relations,* Revised Edition (New York: Friendship Press, 1952) [1946], 15.

15. Mays, "His Goodness Was Not Enough," in *Dr. Benjamin E. Mays Speaks,* ed. Freddie C. Colston (Lanham, NY: University Press of America, Inc., 2002), 211.

16. Martin Luther King, Jr., *Why We Can't Wait* (New York: Harper & Row, Publishers, 1964), 79.

17. King, "A Christmas Sermon on Peace," in his *The Trumpet of Conscience* (New York: Harper & Row, Publishers, 1968), 69.

18. Borden P. Bowne, *Philosophy of Theism* (New York: Harper & Brothers, 1887), 52–53.

19. King, "The American Dream," in *A Testament of Hope*, 210.

20. Ibid.

21. See Lewis V. Baldwin and Paul R. Dekar, eds., *"In an Inescapable Network of Mutuality": Martin Luther King, Jr. and the Globalization of an Ethical Ideal* (Eugene, OR: Cascade Books, 2013).

22. See Thomas Mulhall, *A Lasting Prophetic Legacy: Martin Luther King, Jr., The World Council of Churches, and the Global Crusade Against Racism and War* (Eugene, OR: Cascade Books, 2014).

23. Baldwin, *To Make the Wounded Whole: The Cultural Legacy of Martin Luther King, Jr.* (Minneapolis: Fortress Press, 1992), Chapter 4. Baldwin's excellent book, *Toward the Beloved Community: Martin Luther King, Jr. and South Africa* (Cleveland: The Pilgrim Press, 1985), stresses the idea of King as internationalist or globalist (dating back to his years in Montgomery in the mid to late 1950s), who emphasized the theme of global inhabitants, "the worldwide neighborhood," and the great "world house" (see 2, 57, and throughout). In *Between Cross and Crescent: Christian and Muslim Perspectives on Malcolm and Martin* (Gainesville: University Press of Florida, 2002), Baldwin and co-author, Amiri Ya Sin Al-Hadid, contends that King, like Malcolm, stressed the international dimensions of the social struggle, a point that Baldwin agreed with (264). See also the excellent anthology edited by Baldwin for the King Legacy Series for Beacon Press, *"In a Single Garment of Destiny": A Global Vision of Justice* (Boston: Beacon Press, 2012).

24. King, "Remaining Awake Through a Great Revolution," in *A Testament of Hope*, 269.

25. Bowne, *Personalism* (Boston: Houghton Mifflin, 1908), 277.

26. Bowne, *The Immanence of God* (Boston: Houghton Mifflin, 1905), 32.

27. Clayborne Carson, ed., *The Autobiography of Martin Luther King, Jr.* (New York: Warner Books, 1998), 20.

28. See Buckham, *Personality and the Christian Ideal*, vii. Here Buckham quoted from a letter from George A. Gordon regarding this book: "I have been prepared for the appreciation of the value of your essay by the fact that for many years Personality has been to me the key of our world and our universe. It is the key or there is none."

29. Bowne, *Personalism*, 105.

30. Ibid., 104.

31. Francis J. McConnell, "Bowne and Personalism," in *Personalism in Theology: A Symposium in Honor of Albert C. Knudson*, ed. Edgar S. Brightman (Boston: Boston University Press, 1943), 21.

32. Bowne, *The Immanence of God* (Boston: Houghton, Mifflin and Company, 1905), 32.

33. Picking up from where the late Warren Steinkraus (a fourth generation personalist) left off this writer has been searching for the whereabouts of any extant unpublished papers of Bowne for nearly two decades, but to no avail. Documents in my possession from Boston University reveal that Bowne's library and papers went to Drew University in Madison, New Jersey. Communications with the librarian at Drew, and a copy of the deed of Bowne materials that went to Drew reveal that only Bowne's library and some magazines were received. It might well be that Bowne's biographer and former student, Francis J. McConnell, has left a significant clue regarding the whereabouts of Bowne's papers and letters. McConnell writes that "one Christmas day shortly before he died," Bowne burned "a mass of papers and correspondence," presumably "to prevent giving data for any biography that might be written." See McConnell, *Borden Parker Bowne* (New York: Abingdon Press, 1929), 30. In his autobiography, McConnell reports that Bowne read to him "passages from letters and other papers that would have been interesting" for biography purposes, but unfortunately these were not available after Bowne died, as they presumably were consumed in the fire set by Bowne. See McConnell, *By the Way: An Autobiography* (New York: Abingdon-Cokesbury Press, 1952), 258–59.

34. Bowne, *The Principles of Ethics* (New York: Harper & Brothers, 1892), 190–91.

35. Ibid., 199.

36. Quoted in Fyodor Dostoevsky, *The Brothers Karamazov* (New York: Bantam Book, 1981), 65.

37. Dostoevsky, The Brothers Karamazov, 66.

38. See my *Personalism: A Critical Introduction* (St. Louis: Chalice Press, 1999), 78–80.

39. The late Warren Steinkraus reproduced the two Bowne letters in "The Eucken-Bowne Friendship," *The Personalist*, Vol. 51, (1970), 402–403. At this writing, however, I have not been able to locate a response(s) from Eucken. From Eucken's essay, "The Work of Borden P. Bowne," we know that he had much admiration for Bowne and his work, although they had not met. Eucken's introductory essay appears in Ralph Tyler Flewelling, *Personalism and the Problems of Philosophy* (New York: The Methodist Book Concern, 1915), 17–31.

40. Larry O. Rivers, "James Hudson: Tallahassee Theologian and Campus Activist," *The AME Church Review*, Vol. CXXIII No. 408 (October-December 2007), 49.

41. Ibid. 49.

42. Carson, ed., *The Autobiography*, 14.

43. King, "Pilgrimage to Nonviolence," in *Strength to Love*, 141.

44. Ibid., 141–42 (my emphasis).

45. Bowne, *Personalism*, 266 (my italics).

46. Ibid., 267.

47. *The Papers*, 6:268.

48. King, *Stride*, 134.

49. Ibid., 134–35.

50. King, "Why Jesus Called a Man a Fool," in *A Knock at Midnight*, eds. Clayborne Carson and Peter Holloran (New York: Warner Books, 1998), 161.

51. *The Papers* (2000), 4:298. See also 367.

52. Quoted in Seth Cagin and Philip Dray, *We Are Not Afraid: The Story of Goodman, Schwerner, and Chaney, and the Civil Rights Campaign for Mississippi* (New York: Nation Books, 2006) [1989], 382.

53. Quoted in Cagin and Dray, *We Are Not Afraid*, 382.

54. Quoted in Ibid.

55. *The Papers*, 4:298.

56. David J. Garrow, *Bearing the Cross: Martin Luther King, Jr., and the Southern Christian Leadership Conference* (New York: William Morrow & Company, Inc., 1986), 57; also 89.

57. King, "Pilgrimage to Nonviolence," in *Strength to Love*, 141.

58. King, "A Tough Mind and a Tender Heart," in *Strength to Love*, 7.

59. King, "The Death of Evil Upon the Seashore," in *Strength to Love*, 65.

60. King, "Pilgrimage to Nonviolence," in *Strength to Love*, 142.

61. Alfred North Whitehead, *Process and Reality*, Corrected Edition, ed. David Ray Griffin and Donald W. Sherburne (New York/London: The Free Press, 1978) [1929, 1957], 351.

62. King, "Why Jesus Called a Man a Fool," in *A Knock at Midnight*, 163.

63. Ibid., 164.

64. *The Papers* (1994), 2:110.

65. King, "The Ethical Demands for Integration," in *A Testament of Hope*, 119–120.

66. Bowne, *Metaphysics,* rev. ed. (New York: Harper & Brothers Publishers, 1898), 405.

67. See Bowne, *The Theory of Thought and Knowledge* (New York/London: Harper & Brothers Publishers, 1899), 244.

68. See Bowne's provocative discussion in *The Theory of Thought and Knowledge,* Chapter XI.

69. This is my spin on Joseph Butler's (1692–1752) famous sermon, "Upon the Natural Supremacy of Conscience," where he writes: "Had it strength, as it had right; had it power, as it had manifest authority, it would absolutely govern the world" [in *Ethical Theories: A Book of Readings,* Second Edition, ed. A.I. Melden (Englewood Cliffs, NJ: Prentice-Hall, Inc., 1955) [1950], 227.

70. King, "The Ethical Demands for Integration," in *A Testament of Hope,* 120.

71. Bowne, *Metaphysics,* 405.

72. Ibid., 406.

73. King, "Why a Movement," address to SCLC Staff Retreat at Frogmore, SC, November 28, 1967, King Center Library and Archives, 6.

74. See King, "A Comparison of the Conceptions of God in the Thinking of Paul Tillich and Henry Nelson Wieman," Ph. D. diss., Boston University, 1955.

75. *The Papers,* 6:574n2.

76. King, "What Is Man?," in *Strength to Love,* 90. In *The Protestant Era,* Tillich wrote: "Personality is that being which has the power of self-determination, or which is free; for to be free means to have power over one's self, not to be bound to one's given nature" [Tillich, *The Protestant Era,* trans. James Luther Adams (Chicago: The University of Chicago Press, 1948), 115].

77. King, "Pilgrimage to Nonviolence," in *Strength to Love,* 137.

78. *The Papers* (2005), 5:339.

79. Ibid., 6:356.

80. Jean Paul Sartre, *Existentialism and Human Emotions* (New York: Philosophical Library, 1957), 23. See also his *The Age of Reason,* trans. Eric Sutton (New York: Bantam Books, 1967), 276.

81. Ibid., 41.

82. King, "The Ethical Demands for Integration," in *A Testament of Hope,* 120.

83. *The Papers,* (2005), 5:339.

84. *The Papers,* 4:156.

85. Bowne, *Personalism,* 300–301.

86. *The Papers,* 6:178.

87. Ibid., 1:281.

88. Ibid., (2000), 4:124.

89. Ibid., 6:410.

90. Edgar S. Brightman, *Nature and Values* (New York: Abingdon-Cokesbury Press, 1945), 117.

91. King, *Why We Can't Wait,* 79. As noted previously, these are essentially words that King borrowed from Benjamin E. Mays without attribution. See notes 14 and 15.

92. King, *The Trumpet of Conscience* (New York: Harper & Row, Publishers, 1968), 69–70. In *The Papers* (6:416n13) we find that these are actually words appropriated from Leslie Weatherhead without attribution. See the latter's book, *Why Do Men Suffer?* (New York: Abingdon-Cokesbury, 1936), 69–70.

93. King, *Why We Can't Wait,* 79.

94. *The Papers,* 6:454.

95. King, "Facing the Challenge of a New Age," in *A Testament of Hope,* 141.

96. *The Papers,* 4:398.

97. King, "Remaining Awake Through a Great Revolution," in *A Testament of Hope,* 277.

98. Bowne, *The Principles of Ethics,* 173.

99. King, "Rediscovering Lost Values," in *A Knock at Midnight,* 10.

100. King, "Our God Is Able," in *Strength to Love,* 103.

101. Bowne, *The Principles of Ethics,* 251.

102. Although most of the wording is Professor Rivers,' I have altered some of the wording for my purpose. In the original Rivers uses plural forms since he was talking about both King and the personalist James Hudson. I use singular forms, as my focus is on King. I received Professor Rivers' permission via email on October 6, 2011, to paraphrase his statements.

103. For Professor Rivers' verbatim account see his article, "James Hudson: Tallahassee Theologian and Campus Activist," 50–51.

Chapter 6

1. This chapter was written solely for this book.

2. Gary Dorrien, *Social Ethics in the Making: Interpreting an American Tradition* (Malden, MA: Wiley-Blackwell, 2009), 391.

3. Ibid., 2.

4. James DeOtis Roberts, *Bonhoeffer and King: Speaking Truth to Power* (Louisville: Westminster John Knox, 2005).

5. Ibid., 111, 112.

6. Ibid., 125.

7. Ibid., 111.

8. Baldwin actually began this emphasis in a brilliant way when he introduced what may be referred to as the southern black cultural genre in King studies in his first two books on King: *There Is a Balm in Gilead: The Cultural Roots of Martin Luther King, Jr.,* and *To Make the Wounded Whole: The Cultural Legacy of Martin Luther King, Jr.,* both published by Fortress Press, 1991 and 1992, respectively.

9. It is significant that in a number of his books, renowned personalist Edgar S. Brightman places Ladd in the personalist tradition. My reading of a number of Ladd's books confirms the legitimacy of Brightman's action. See Brightman's books, *Religious Values* (New York: Abingdon Press, 1925), 167, and *Person and Reality: An Introduction to Metaphysics,* ed. Peter A. Bertocci, in collaboration with Jannette Elthina Newhall and Robert Sheffield Brightman (New York: The Round Table Press Company, 1958), 206. Ladd was a contemporary of Borden Parker Bowne (1847–1910), the father of American personalism. The president of Yale tried to induce Bowne to join the faculty there [Francis J. McConnell, *Borden Parker Bowne: His Life and His Philosophy* (New York: Abingdon Press, 1929), 91].

10. Martin Luther King, Jr., "An Autobiography of Religious Development," in *The Papers of Martin Luther King, Jr.,* ed. Clayborne Carson et al. (Berkeley: University of California Press, 1992), 1:361. See also Clayborne Carson, ed., *The Autobiography of Martin Luther King, Jr.* (New York: Warner Books, 1998), 15–16.

11. Carson, ed., *The Autobiography,* 15.

12. Ibid., 16.

13. Coretta Scott King, *My Life with Martin Luther King, Jr.* (New York: Holt, Rinehart and Winston, 1969), 59. Here it appears that King may have been influenced by Reinhold Niebuhr, who said something similar in volume two of *The Nature and Destiny of Man:* "It is unwise for Christians to claim any knowledge of either the furniture of heaven or the temperature of hell; or to be too certain about any details of the Kingdom of God in which history is consummated" (New York: Charles Scribner's Sons, 1949 one volume edition), 2:294.

14. I am here influenced by the definition given by E. Clinton Gardner. See his *Biblical Faith and Social Ethics* (New York: Harper & Row, Publishers, 1960), 9.

15. See my *God and Human Dignity: The Personalism, Theology, and Ethics of Martin Luther King, Jr.* (Notre Dame: University of Notre Dame Press, 2006), 20.

16. Martin Luther King, Jr., "Letter from Birmingham Jail," in his *Why We Can't Wait* (New York: Harper & Row Publishers, 1964), 79. The other steps include negotiation with the powers; self-purification; and nonviolent direct action.

17. King, *Why We Can't Wait*, 49–50.

18. Carson, ed., *The Autobiography*, 159.

19. Ibid., 241–42.

20. Keith A. Roberts, *Religion in Sociological Perspective*, Third Edition (Belmont, CA: Wadsworth Publishing Company, 1995), 32, 33.

21. See Joseph Butler, *The Analogy of Religion: Natural and Revealed, to the Constitution and Course of Nature* (New York: Newman and Ivison, 1852) [1736], 30.

22. King made this statement on "Face to Face" Television News Interview in 1967. See *A Testament of Hope: The Essential Writings of Martin Luther King, Jr.,* ed. James M. Washington (New York: Harper & Row, 1986), 408.

23. King, "The Power of Nonviolence," in *A Testament of Hope*, 13.

24. Carson, ed., *The Autobiography*, 179. It is of interest to note that King evidences the influence of his father and maternal grandfather when he reminds the black ministers that they are freer and more independent than others in the black community. See Martin Luther King, Sr., *Daddy King: An Autobiography,* with Clayton Riley (New York: William Morrow and Company, Inc., 1980), 125.

25. King, "Paul's Letter to American Christians," in *A Knock at Midnight*, eds. Clayborne Carson and Peter Holloran (New York: Warner Books, 1998), 28.

26. King, "A View of the Cross Possessing Biblical and Spiritual Justification," in *The Papers*, 1:267.

27. See Anders Nygren, *Agape and Eros,* trans. Philip S. Watson (Philadelphia: The Westminster Press, 1953 single volume edition), 726–41.

28. The reference here is to Walter Marshall Horton, *Contemporary Continental Theology: An Interpretation for Anglo-Saxons* (New York: Harper, 1938), 163–65, as documented in *The Papers* (1994), 2:127n32–33.

29. King, "An Experiment in Love," in *A Testament of Hope*, 19.

30. See Sören Kierkegaard, *Works of Love: Some Christian Reflections in the Form of Discourses,* trans. Howard and Edna Hong (New York: Harper Torchbook, 1964), 320–29; and Paul Ramsey, *Basic Christian Ethics* (New York: Charles Scribner's Sons, 1952), Ch. III, "The Meaning of Christian Love."

31. King, "An Experiment in Love," in *A Testament of Hope*, 19.

32. Ibid.

33. King, "Loving Your Enemies," in his *Strength to Love* (New York: Harper & Row, 1963), 36.

34. Ibid.

35. Ibid., 36–37.

36. King, "How Should a Christian View Communism?," in *Strength to Love*, 95.

37. King, "Three Dimensions of a Complete Life," in *Strength to Love*, 69.

38. Nygren, *Agape and Eros*, 217.

39. Ibid., 222.

40. Ibid.

41. See Edgar S. Brightman, *Moral Laws* (New York: Abingdon Press, 1933).

42. King, *Where Do We Go from Here: Chaos or Community?* (Boston: Beacon Press, 1967), 180.

43. King, "How Should a Christian View Communism?," in *Strength to Love*, 95.

44. King, "Three Dimensions of a Complete Life," in *Strength to Love*, 71.

45. See Brightman, *Moral Laws*, Ch. XVI, "The Autonomy of Moral Law."

46. Quoted in Walter G. Muelder, *Moral Law in Christian Social Ethics* (Richmond, VA: John Knox Press, 1966), 60.

47. King, "Three Dimensions of a Complete Life," in *Strength to Love*, 73.

48. Ervin Smith, *The Ethics of Martin Luther King, Jr.* (New York: Mellen Press, 1981), 89.

49. Ibid., 90.

50. The poet-philosopher-romanticist Novalis (pseudonym of Friedrich Leopold Freiherr von Hardenberg, 1772–1801) is credited with having eulogized Spinoza this way. Although God was the chief subject of much of Spinoza's philosophizing, many felt that his impersonal God essentially left him godless. And yet, philosophers, following the short lived Novalis, characterized him as "the God-intoxicated man" [Quoted in Radoslav A. Tsanoff, *The Moral Ideals of Our Civilization* (New York: E. P. Dutton & Company, 1947, 1942), 350.

51. Peter J. Paris, *Black Religious Leaders: Conflict in Unity,* Revised (Louisville: Westminster John Knox Press, 1991 [1978]), 100.

52. See King, "Pilgrimage to Nonviolence," in *Stride*, 91, and Carson, ed., *The Autobiography*, 19.

53. See James Goodman, *Stories of Scottsboro* (New York: Pantheon Books, 1994), 278–83.

54. Charles Marsh, *God's Long Summer: Stories of Faith and Civil Rights* (Princeton: Princeton University Press, 1997), 121.

55. See "List of Courses at Boston University," in *The Papers* (1994), 2:18.

56. King, *Stride*, 100.

57. Walter G. Muelder, "An Autobiographical Introduction: Forty Year of Communitarian Personalism," in his *The Ethical Edge of Christian Theology* (Lewiston, NY: Mellen Press, 1983), 25.

58. "*Playboy* Interview: Martin Luther King, Jr.," in *A Testament of Hope*, 344.

59. H. Richard Niebuhr, *The Social Sources of Denominationalism* (New York: Henry Holt Company, 1929), 9.

60. King, *Stride*, 207.

61. King, "Letter from Birmingham Jail," in *Why We Can't Wait*, 96.

62. King, "Transformed Nonconformist," in *Strength to Love*, 11.

63. See Michael G. Long's excellent and provocative book, *Martin Luther King, Jr., Homosexuality, and the Early Gay Rights Movement,* Afterword by Archbishop Desmond Tutu (New York: Palgrave Macmillan, 2012).

64. See King, "Pilgrimage to Nonviolence," in *Strength to Love*, 137.

65. King, *Stride*, 69.

66. King, "Pilgrimage to Nonviolence," in *Strength to Love*, 137.

67. Martin Luther King, Sr., *Daddy King: An Autobiography,* with Clayton Riley (New York: William Morrow & Company, Inc., 1980), 109.

68. King, *Stride*, 207.

69. King, *Where Do We Go from Here: Chaos or Community?* (Boston: Beacon Press, 1967), 155.

70. Plato, *Euthyphro, Apology, Crito,* rev., trans. Robert D. Cumming (Indianapolis/New York: The Bobbs-Merrill Company, Inc., 1956) [1948], 37.

71. King, *Stride*, 210.

72. King, "Transformed Nonconformist," in *Strength to Love*, 14.

73. Quoted in David J. Garrow, "Martin Luther King, Jr., and the Spirit of Leadership," in *We Shall Overcome: Martin Luther King, Jr. and the Black Freedom Struggle*, eds. Peter J. Albert and Ronald Hoffman (New York: Da Capo Press, 1993), 28.

Chapter 7

1. This chapter was originally given as an address on King Day (Sunday, January 20, 2002) at a program sponsored by Iglesia Christiana Hermandad, Faith United, Northwood, and University Park Christian Churches (DoC). The program was hosted by Faith United and University Park Christian Churches in Indianapolis, Indiana. The address was revised for publication in *Encounter*, vol. 64, no. 2 (Spring 2003), and has been significantly revised for this volume.

2. See Lewis V. Baldwin's informative discussion on the King Holiday controversy in his book, *To Make the Wounded Whole: The Cultural Legacy of Martin Luther King, Jr.* (Minneapolis: Fortress Press, 1992), 286–301.

3. See Christine King Farris, "The Young Martin: From Childhood through College," *Ebony*, Vol. 41, No. 3, January 1986.

4. Christine King Farris, *Through It All: Reflections on My Life, My Family, and My Faith* (New York: Atria Paperback, 2009), 3.

5. The first official King Day was the third Monday in January 1986. The annual celebration is the third Monday in January.

6. David J. Garrow, *Bearing the Cross: Martin Luther King, Jr. and the Southern Christian Leadership Conference* (New York: William Morrow and Company, 1986), 375.

7. Quoted in Ibid., 312.

8. Garrow, *Bearing the Cross*, 375.

9. Ibid., 376.

10. In fairness to Branch, it should be said that he later seemed to tone down his discussions regarding this matter.

11. Michael Eric Dyson, *I May Not Get There with You: The True Martin Luther King, Jr.* (New York: The Free Press, 2000), 177.

12. See Lewis Baldwin's excellent and informative discussion of womanists and other black feminist scholars' stance on the sexism of Martin and Malcolm, as well as Martin's extra-marital affairs. See Baldwin's chapter, "The Character of Womanhood," in his and Amiri Ya Sin Al-Hadid's *Between Cross and Crescent: Christian and Muslim Perspectives on Malcolm and Martin* (Gainesville: University Press of Florida, 2002), Chapter 5. See also Kirk-Duggan's chapter, "Drum Major for Justice or Dilettante of Dishonesty: Martin Luther King, Jr., Moral Capital, and Hypocrisy of Embodied Messianic Myths," in *The Domestication of Martin Luther King, Jr.: Clarence B. Jones, Right-Wing Conservatism, and the Manipulation of the King Legacy*, eds. Lewis V. Baldwin and Rufus Burrow, Jr. (Eugene, OR: Cascade Books, 2013), Chapter 5.

13. Bertrand Russell, *A History of Western Philosophy* (New York: Simon & Schuster, 1945), p. 366, also Book Two, Part I, Chapters III, IV.

14. Garrow, *Bearing the Cross*, 587. Here Garrow quotes King as saying: "I make mistakes tactically. I make mistakes morally, and get down on my knees and confess it and ask God to forgive me."

15. It is estimated that by the time this project is completed there will be fourteen large volumes of King's papers. At this writing six volumes have been published.

16. Martin Luther King, Jr., "The un–Christian Christian," *Ebony*, August 1965, 77.

17. King, "A Time to Break Silence," in *A Testament of Hope: The Essential Writings of Martin Luther King, Jr.,* ed. James M. Washington (New York: Harper & Row, Publishers, 1986), 231.

18. "Conversation with Martin Luther King," *Conservative Judaism*, Volume XXII, No. 3 (Spring 1968), 17.

19. See Garrow, *Bearing the Cross*, 543.

20. Clayborne Carson, ed., *The Autobiography of Martin Luther King, Jr.* (New York: Warner Books, 1998), 335.

21. Garrow, *Bearing the Cross*, 555 (my emphasis).

22. King did not live long enough to include "sexual orientation" in his mantra, but I have argued that given his personalism and doctrine of human dignity, and his propensity to change and expand his moral field to include concerns previously unacknowledged when the evidence requires it, he would most likely have included sexual orientation, as well as gay rights in his field of moral concern.

23. See Josiah Royce, *The Problem of Christianity* (Washington, D.C.: The Catholic University of America Press, single volume edition, 2001) [originally published by The Macmillan Company in 2 volumes, 1913], 125, 129–31, 141, 197, 199, 200, 268–70, 318, 381.

24. King, "A Christmas Sermon on Peace," in *A Testament of Hope*, 257.

25. Ibid.

26. Ibid.

27. See King, "A Testament of Hope," in *A Testament of Hope*, 326.

28. Ibid., 327.

29. Ibid.

30. Quoted in Baldwin, *To Make the Wounded Whole*, 259.

31. Quoted in Idid., 262.

32. Quoted in Ibid.

33. Baldwin, *To Make the Wounded Whole*, 307–312.

34. Paul M. Sniderman and Thomas Piazza argued that racism is not built into the ethos and fabric of American society. See their book, *The Scar of Race* (Cambridge: Harvard University Press, 1993), 5, 175.

35. Dinesh D'Sousa, *The End of Racism: Principles for a Multiracial Society* (New York: Free Press, 1995).

36. Alice Walker, "A Talk: Convocation 1972," in her *In Search of Our Mothers' Gardens* (New York: Harcourt Brace Jovanovich, 1983), 37.

37. Baldwin, *To Make the Wounded Whole*, 307.

38. King, *The Trumpet of Conscience* (New York: Harper & Row, Publishers, 1968), xi, 45–47, 49.

39. King, "Letter from Birmingham Jail," in his *Why We Can't Wait* (New York: Harper & Row, Publisher, 1964), 89.

40. In this regard, King agreed with the statement frequently attributed to Edmund Burke: "The only thing necessary for the triumph of evil is for good men to do nothing." See *The Merriam-Webster Dictionary of Quotations* (Springfield: Merriam-Webster, Publishers, 1992), 126.

41. W.E.B. DuBois, "Sex and Racism," in *W.E.B. DuBois: A Reader,* ed. David Levering Lewis (New York: Henry Holt and Company, 1995), 313.

42. Ibid.

Chapter 8

1. An earlier version of this chapter was published as "The Beloved Community: Martin Luther King, Jr. and

Josiah Royce" in *Encounter*, Vol. 73, No. 1, Fall 2012, 37–64.

2. Randy Auxier, professor of philosophy at the University of Southern Illinois at Carbondale extended the invitation, and was also the convener of the session.

3. Tunstall is a fulltime faculty member in the department of religion and philosophy at Grand Valley State College near Grand Rapids, Michigan. He is fast becoming an expert in Personalist, King, and Royce studies.

4. Gary Herstein teaches philosophy at Ellis University in Carbondale, Illinois.

5. Josiah Royce, letter to Edgar S. Brightman, July 16, 1913, in *The Letters of Josiah Royce*, ed. John Clendenning (Chicago: The University of Chicago Press, 1970), 604.

6. Martin Luther King, Jr., *Stride Toward Freedom* (New York: Harper & Row, Publishers, 1958), 100.

7. See Josiah Royce, *The World and the Individual* (Second Series) Nature, Man, and the Moral Order (New York: The Macmillan Company, 1908), 418, 425. See entirety of Lectures VI-VIII, X for Royce's discussion on these.

8. See Clayborne Carson, et al. ed., *The Papers of Martin Luther King, Jr.* (Berkeley: University of California Press, 1994), 2:61–75, 110–113.

9. See his dissertation, "A Comparison of the Conceptions of God in the Thinking of Paul Tillich and Henry Nelson Wieman," in *The Papers*, 2:339–544.

10. Howard Thurman, "Desegregation, Integration, and the Beloved Community," unpublished, undated article. Internal evidence in the article indicates that it was likely written in 1966. See 5, 6, 18.

11. See Stewart Burns, *To the Mountaintop: Martin Luther King, Jr.'s Sacred Mission to Save America 1955–1968* (New York: HarperSanFrancisco, 2004), 260–61, 264, 280, 287, 346, 406, 429.

12. Lewis Baldwin is presently compiling a small book of King's jokes and humorous sayings.

13. See Lewis V. Baldwin, *Toward the Beloved Community: Martin Luther King, Jr. and South Africa* (Cleveland: The Pilgrim Press, 1995).

14. Peter J. Ling, *Martin Luther King, Jr.* (London/New York: Routledge, 2002), 52.

15. See Martin Luther King, Jr., *Where Do We Go from Here: Chaos or Community?* (Boston: Beacon Press, 1967), 43.

16. W.E.B. DuBois, *The Souls of Black Folk* (New York: The New American Library, 1969), 45.

17. King, *Where Do We Go*, 53.

18. Ibid.

19. See David Thelen, ed., "Becoming Martin Luther King, Jr.—Plagiarism and Originality: A Round Table," in *The Journal of "American History*, vol. 78, no. 1 (June 1991), 11–123.

20. King reflects on his call in *The Autobiography of Martin Luther King, Jr.*, ed. Clayborne Carson (New York: Warner Books, 1998), 13, 14–16. See also King, "Autobiography of Religious Development," in *The Papers* (1992), 1:363.

21. Conley Hughes, Foreword to Symposium #2, "The Philosophical and Theological Influences in the Thought and Action of Martin Luther King, Jr.," in *Debate & Understanding*, Vol. 1, No. 3, Semester II, 1977, iii (my emphasis).

22. King, "Letter from Birmingham Jail," in his *Why We Can't Wait* (New York: Harper & Row, Publishers, 1964), 78.

23. This is John Haynes Holmes' paraphrase of the nineteenth-century preacher-abolitionist Theodore Parker. Parker actually said in 1852: "I do not pretend to understand the moral universe; the arc is a long one, my eye reaches but little ways; I cannot calculate the curve and complete the figure by the experience of sight; I can divine it by conscience. And from what I see I am sure it bends towards justice" [In *The Collected Works of Theodore Parker* ed. Frances Power Cobbe (London: Tribner & Company, 1879), 2:48].

24. See Reinhold Niebuhr, "The Relevance of an Impossible Ethical Ideal," in his *An Interpretation of Christian Ethics* (New York: Harper & Brothers, 1935), Ch. IV.

25. King, "The Case Against 'Tokenism,'" in *A Testament of Hope: The Essential Writings of Martin Luther King, Jr.*, ed. James M. Washington (New York: Harper & Row, 1986), 110.

26. Dwayne Tunstall, "Royce and King on *Agape* and the Beloved Community," 12.

27. See Josiah Royce, "Race Questions and Prejudices," in his *Race Questions, Provincialism, and other American Problems* (New York: The Macmillan Company, 1908), 3–53. Royce also wrote on the race question in 1905. See Thomas F. Powell, *Josiah Royce* (New York: Washington Square Press, Inc., 1967), 113.

28. See Robert V. Hine, *Josiah Royce: From Grass Valley to Harvard* (Norman: University of Oklahoma Press, 1992), 159.

29. David L. Lewis, *W.E.B. DuBois: Biography of Race 1868–1919* (New York: Henry Holt and Company, 1993), 88.

30. See W.E.B. DuBois, *The Autobiography of W.E.B. DuBois: A Soliloquy on Viewing My Life from the Last Decade of Its First Century* (New York: International Publishers, 1968), 144. Here DuBois wrote: "Naturally my English instructors had no idea nor interest in the way in which Southern attacks on the Negro were scratching me on the raw flesh." Herbert Aptheker identifies the English instructors as Josiah Royce and two assistants, Ernest L. Conant and George P. Baker, Jr. [See Herbert Aptheker, ed., *W.E.B. DuBois: Against Racism, Unpublished Essays, Papers, Addresses 1887–1961* (Amherst: The University of Massachusetts Press, 1985), 16.]

31. Ibid., 148.

32. Lewis, *W.E.B. DuBois*, 517.

33. See my *God and Human Dignity: The Personalism, Theology, and Ethics of Martin Luther King, Jr.* (Notre Dame, IN: University of Notre Dame Press, 2006), Ch. 5.

34. See Edgar S. Brightman, *Religious Values* (New York: Abingdon Press, 1925), where Brightman mentions Royce and the Beloved Community (221).

35. *The Papers*, 2:88–89.

36. Quoted in Benjamin E. Mays and Joseph William Nicholson, *The Negro's Church* (Salem, NH: Ayer Company, Publishers, Inc., 1988) [1933], 64.

37. Quoted in Ibid., 65.

38. Martin Luther King, Jr., "A Christian View of the World," in *The Papers*, 2:283.

39. Ibid., 2:284.

40. King, "Facing the Challenge of a New Age," in *A Testament of Hope*, 140.

41. See August Meier, Elliott Rudwick, and Francis L. Broderick, eds., *Black Protest Thought in the Twentieth Century*, Second Edition (Indianapolis and New York: The Bobbs-Merrill Company, Inc., 1971) [1965], 306.

42. Clayborne Carson, ed., *The Autobiography of Martin Luther King, Jr.* (New York: Warner Books, Inc., 1998), 125.

43. Anders Nygren, *Agape and Eros*, single volume, ed. and trans. by Philip S. Watson (Philadelphia: The Westminster Press, 1953), 57.

44. King, *Where Do We Go*, 186.

45. Royce, *The Problem of Christianity* (Washington,

D.C.: The Catholic University of America Press, 2001, one volume edition) [originally published by The Macmillan Company, 1913], 199.

46. King, *Where Do We Go*, 190.

47. King, "Love, Law, and Civil Disobedience," in *A Testament of Hope*, 45.

48. Carson, ed., *The Autobiography of Martin Luther King, Jr.*, 109.

49. Lawrence N. Jones, "Black Christians in Antebellum America: In Quest of the Beloved Community," *The Journal of Religious Thought*, Vol. 38, No. 1 (Spring-Summer 1981), 12–19.

50. See John J. Ansbro, *Martin Luther King, Jr.: The Making of a Mind* (Maryknoll, NY: Orbis, 1982), 319n152.

51. Ira G. Zepp, Jr., "The Social Vision of Martin Luther King, Jr.," (Ph. D. diss.), in *Martin Luther King, Jr., and the Civil Rights Movement*, ed. David J. Garrow (Brooklyn: Carlson Publishing, 1989), 209.

52. John H. Cartwright, "Foundations of the Beloved Community," *Debate and Understanding*, Vol. 1, No. 3, Semester II, 1977, 171.

53. Ibid.

54. Ibid., 172.

55. Walter Rauschenbusch, *A Theology for the Social Gospel* (New York: The Macmillan Company, 1917), 70–71.

56. Ibid., 127.

57. See *The Papers* (2007), 6:629–55. It is important to note, however, that the editors point out that this selection of books does not include those that are "unrelated to homiletics such as school textbooks" (629). Consequently, a definitive answer as to whether *The Problem of Christianity* may be in King's personal library must await a thorough examination of the entire collection.

58. Edgar S. Brightman, "Religion as Truth," in *Contemporary American Theology: Theological Autobiographies*, ed. Vergilius Ferm (New York: Round Table Press, 1932), 1:57.

59. There are also references to Royce in others of Brightman's books, but there is no indication that King read or studied them. Nor is there reference to "the beloved community" nomenclature of Royce. See *A Philosophy of Ideals* (New York: Henry Holt and Company, 1928; *The Finding of God* (New York: Abingdon Press, 1931); *Personality and Religion* (New York: Abingdon Press, 1934); and *The Spiritual Life* (New York/Nashville: Abingdon-Cokesbury Press, 1942. There are also many references to Royce in Brightman's posthumously published book, *Person and Reality: An Introduction to Metaphysics*, ed. Peter A. Bertocci, Jannette E. Newhall, and Robert S. Brightman (New York: The Ronald Press, 1958). The book was published three years after King graduated from Boston University.

60. Jannette E. Newhall, "Edgar Sheffield Brightman," *Philosophical Forum*, Vol. 12 (1954), 14.

61. See Clendenning, ed., *The Letters of Josiah Royce*, 603n1.

62. Edgar S. Brightman, *Religious Values* (New York: The Abingdon Press, 1925), 221 (my emphasis).

63. King, "Comparison and Evaluation of the Philosophical Views Set Forth in J.M.E. McTaggart's *Some Dogmas of Religion*, and William E. Hocking's *The Meaning of God in Human Experience* with Those Set Forth in Edgar S. Brightman's Course on Philosophy of Religion," in *The Papers*, 2:88, 89n45. It is important to note that King did not include *Religious Values* in the bibliography for this paper, although he did include Brightman's *The Problem of God, Moral Laws*, and *A Philosophy of Religion* (2:92).

64. See Rufus Burrow, Jr., "Moral Laws in Borden P. Bowne's *Principles of Ethics*," *The Personalist Forum* Vol. VI, No. 2, Fall 1990.

65. See Thomas Jefferson, *Notes on the State of Virginia*, ed. William Peden (Chapel Hill: The University of North Carolina Press, 1982), 139.

66. See Alexis de Tocqueville, *Democracy in America* (New York: Vintage Books, 1945), 1:370–394.

67. See Andrew Hacker, *Two Nations: Black and White, Separate, Hostile, Unequal*, Expanded and Updated (New York: Ballantine Books, 1995) [1992].

68. Bowne had many of the right sentiments and a strong social justice outlook. He staunchly argued for the rights of (white) women and for child labor laws. As dean of the graduate school he admitted John Wesley Edward Bowen, the first black man, to the Ph.D. program in historical theology. Bowen was much influenced by classes he took with Bowne. I have long wondered whether Bowne might have written on the humanity, dignity, and rights of blacks in his unpublished papers and lectures. An extensive search for these papers has, to this point, proved futile. It seems that when Bowne died his wife, angry with Boston University officials because she felt they tried to cheat her out of insurance money, sold his personal library and papers to Drew University. I requested and received a copy of the deed. This document referenced books and magazines, but no papers of any kind. Initially there was a separate room that housed Bowne's library. However, librarians at Drew informed me in the early 1990s that Bowne's books were eventually integrated into the larger library collection. In addition, I was told of a fire that destroyed the old library, implying that many of his books were destroyed.

Chapter 9

1. This chapter was presented as a keynote address at Messiah College, Grantham, Pennsylvania, January 17, 2006, while I was on a year-long research leave. It has been substantially revised for this book.

2. Royce discussed the beloved community concept at length in *The Problem of Christianity*, Single Volume Edition (Washington, D.C.: The Catholic University of America Press, 2001) [originally published by The Macmillan Company, 1913, in two volumes), 125, 129–31, 141, 196–98, 268–70, 318, 381.

3. Ibid., 199.

4. Ibid., 200.

5. Walter Rauschenbusch, *Christianizing the Social Order* (New York: Macmillan, 1926) [1912], 93.

6. Martin Luther King, Jr., *Stride Toward Freedom* (New York: Harper & Row, 1958), 91.

7. Lawrence N. Jones, "Black Christians Antebellum America: In Quest of the Beloved Community," *The Journal of Religious Thought*, Vol. 38, No. 1 (Spring-Summer 1981), 12.

8. Ibid., 14.

9. Stephen B. Oates, *Let the Trumpet Sound: The Life of Martin Luther King, Jr.* (New York: Harper & Row, Publishers, 1982), 413, 418.

10. Martin Luther King, Jr., "A New Sense of Direction," *Worldview*, April 1972, 7.

11. See Lewis V. Baldwin, *To Make the Wounded Whole: The Cultural Legacy of Martin Luther King, Jr.* (Minneapolis: Fortress Press, 1992), 286–301.

12. See Ibid., 292.

13. Martin Luther King, Jr., "Unfulfilled Dreams," in *A Knock at Midnight*, eds. Clayborne Carson and Peter Holloran (New York: Warner Books, 1998), 198–99.

14. Ibid., 196.

15. King, "The Un-Christian Christian," *Ebony*, August 1965, 77.

16. King, "Why Jesus Called a Man a Fool," in *A Knock at Midnight*, 146.

17. King, "A Time to Break Silence," in *A Testament of Hope: The Essential Writings of Martin Luther King, Jr.*, ed. James M. Washington (New York: Harper & Row, Publishers, 1986), 231.

18. "Conversation with Martin Luther King," *Conservative Judaism*, Volume XXII, No. 3 (Spring 1968), 17.

19. See David Garrow, *Bearing the Cross: Martin Luther King, Jr., and the Southern Christian Leadership Conference* (New York: William Morrow and Company, 1986), 543.

20. King, *The Autobiography of Martin Luther King, Jr.*, ed. Clayborne Carson (New York: Warner Books, 1998), 335.

21. Garrow, *Bearing the Cross*, 555. (my emphasis)

22. Desmond Tutu, *God Has a Dream: A Vision of Hope for Our Time* (New York: Doubleday, 2004), 20.

23. See Taylor Branch, *At Canaan's Edge: America in the King Years 1965–68* (New York: Simon & Schuster, 2006), 34–35.

24. In his 1970 publication David L. Lewis reported that no member of the Birmingham white community attended the funerals. See his *King: A Critical Biography* (New York: Praeger Publishers, 1970), 205.

25. King, "Eulogy for the Martyred Children," in *A Testament of Hope*, 221.

26. King, "Eulogy of the Young Victims of the Sixteenth Street Baptist Church Bombing," in *A Call to Conscience: The Landmark Speeches of Dr. Martin Luther King, Jr.*, eds. Clayborne Carson and Kris Shephard (New York: Warner Books, 2001), 98.

27. Ibid., 99.

28. King, "A Christmas Sermon on Peace," in *A Testament of Hope*, 257.

29. Ibid.

30. Ralph Luker makes the fantastic claim that in the waning years of King's life he placed less and less emphasis on the beloved community ideal, and for good reason. There was little evidence of the abatement of institutional racism; the war in Vietnam was escalating; and the plight of the nation's poor was worsening. It is therefore true that in the last two years of his life, King saw fewer and fewer signs of the beloved community on the horizon. Luker is right about much of this, but he most assuredly misses the mark when he suggests that the post–1965 King was losing hope that the beloved community would be established or more nearly approximated. It seems preposterous that because King did not actually use the beloved community nomenclature after a certain period, one should conclude that it was no longer central to his thinking, and that he no longer had faith in its possibility. King was enough of a realist to know that various manifestations of human sin, e.g., racism, economic exploitation, and militarism would always be impediments to establishing the beloved community once and for all. As a human being, it is understandable that King would be more discouraged and depressed about this some days than others. Moreover, that he did not invoke the beloved community terminology as frequently during the last two years of his life is not in itself proof that his faith in its possible establishment was declining. Indeed, King was an avid personalist, but we know only of a couple of places in his post-graduate school writings and speeches where he specifically uses that term. The truth is, his written expressions and his behavior were consistently personalistic. A similar argument can be made regarding his fundamental commitment to the ideal of the beloved community, even as he seemed to use the term much less frequently near the end of his life. (See Luker, "Kingdom of God and Beloved Community in the Thought of Martin Luther King, Jr.," in *The Role of Ideas in the Civil Rights South*, ed. Ted Ownby (Jackson: University Press of Mississippi, 2002, 39–54.) Remember, King told his staff at the retreat at Frogmore, South Carolina, in 1967 that while he was not totally optimistic, nor was he a defeatist. This was just a few months before he was assassinated. Furthermore, it should be recalled that on the night before he was assassinated, King spoke optimistically about his people getting to the Promised Land, although he was less than optimistic that he himself would get there with them. Therefore, contrary to Luker's claim, I do not see the evidence that the beloved community ideal became less prominent in King's thinking during the last two years of his life, despite the fact that he seldom used that terminology during that period.

31. King, "Rediscovering Lost Values," in *A Knock at Midnight*, 10.

32. See King, "An Autobiography of Religious Development," in *The Papers of Martin Luther King, Jr.*, ed. Penny Russell and Ralph Luker (Berkeley: University of California Press, 1992), I:360.

33. King would have agreed with the likes of Josiah Royce and Reinhold Niebuhr that the reality and depth of sin in persons and communities is what makes it difficult to impossible for them to establish the beloved community on their own. According to Royce individuals cannot—on their own—extricate themselves from this deeply ingrained "disease" or "curse," or sin (See Royce, *The Problem of Christianity*, 127). Unlike King and Niebuhr, however, Royce believed that individuals could escape the disease through Loyalty, i.e., the utter love and devotion that one has for her or his community (Ibid., 128). King and Niebuhr believed, on the other hand, that the curse or sin exists on every level of human achievement. As long as there are human beings, Niebuhr argued, it is virtually impossible to envisage a society of pure love and free of sin (See Niebuhr, "Must We Do Nothing," in *The Christian Century Reader*, ed. Harold E. Fey and Margaret Frakes [New York: Association Press, 1962], 226.) Therefore, there is for King and Niebuhr no total escape from sin, even with the aid of divine grace. In addition, both men would reject Royce's view that Loyalty can extricate the individual from the disease or sin once for all.

34. Words from the gospel hymn, "You Can't Do Wrong and Get By," written by Lethal Albert Ellis (1929).

35. Tutu, *God Has a Dream*, 2.

36. Transcription of interview that Carl Stern did with Heschel a few days before the latter died. "A Conversation with Dr. Abraham Joshua Heschel," copyright National Broadcasting Company, Inc., 1973, prepared under the auspices of The Jewish Theological Seminary of America, 14.

37. Ibid.

38. Quoted in King, "Facing the Challenge of a New Age," in *A Testament of Hope*, 143.

39. See Lewis Mumford, *Ralph Waldo Emerson: Essays and Journals* (Selected with an Introduction) (Garden City, NY: Doubleday & Company, 1968), 293.

40. King, "The Purpose of Education," in *The Papers*, 1:124.

41. King, *Stride Toward Freedom* (New York: Harper & Row, Publishers, 1958), 33.

42. King, *Where Do We Go from Here: Chaos or Community?* (Boston: Beacon Press, 1967), 155.

43. James Baldwin, "A Talk to Teachers," in his *The Price of the Ticket: Collected Nonfiction 1948–1985* (New York: St. Martin's/Marek, 1985), 326.

44. Ibid., 331.

45. Quoted in Lewis Baldwin, *There Is a Balm in Gilead: The Cultural Roots of Martin Luther King, Jr.* (Minneapolis: Fortress Press 1991), 46.

46. King, *Where Do We Go*, 122.

47. Ibid., 123.

48. Ibid., 122, 123.

49. Ibid., 123.

50. Ibid.

51. Naomi Wolf, "The Racism of Well-Meaning White People," in *Skin Deep: Black and White Women Write About Race,* ed. Marita Golden and Susan Richards Shreve (New York: Doubleday, 1995), 43–44.

52. *Playboy* Interview: Martin Luther King, Jr., in *A Testament of Hope*, 375.

53. King, *Where Do We Go*, 176.

54. Quoted in Baldwin, *To Make the Wounded Whole*, 262.

55. King, *Where Do We Go*, 173.

56. Paul M. Sniderman and Thomas Piazza argue that racism is not built into the ethos and fabric of American society. See their book, *The Scar of Race* (Cambridge: Harvard University Press, 1993), 5, 175.

57. Dinesh D'Sousa, *The End of Racism: Principles for a Multiracial Society* (New York: Free Press, 1995).

58. King, "A Testament of Hope" in *A Testament of Hope*, 316.

59. Ibid., 314.

60. *Playboy* Interview: Martin Luther King, Jr., in *A Testament of Hope*, 375.

61. King, "The Crisis in America's Cities," SCLC, Atlanta, August 15, 1967, King Library and Archives, 3.

62. King, *Where Do We Go*, 173

63. Ibid., 176.

64. Ibid.

65. James Baldwin, "Here Be Dragons," in *The Price of the Ticket*, 690.

66. See King, "Where Do We Go from Here?," in *A Testament of Hope*, 251.

67. It is important for the reader to know that when I presented this address at the inauguration of the Annual Dr. Martin Luther King, Jr., Commemoration Week at Messiah College in Grantham, Pennsylvania, on January 17, 2006, I included the following three sentences: "The blood of every white and Afrikan American person in this audience flows in the veins of each other. When we remember the rapes of black women by their white captors during American slavery, it should not be difficult to see that it is a theological, historical, and sociological fact that black and white people in this country are inescapably a part of each other. We are left only with futile attempts of denial." Reflecting on the lecture, Dr. Larry Burnley, then Associate Dean of Multicultural Programs at Messiah, and my former student, reminded me that there were other persons of color in the audience who were not blacks, but who might well have felt made to appear invisible in light of those three sentences. I concurred, and told him that I would correct this tendency in my work. Although the lecture had already been given, it seemed reasonable to me to begin the process of correction, since I promised to permit selections from the lecture to appear on the Messiah web page and am publishing it in this collection. By so doing, I am hopeful that non-black persons of color who read this may know not only of my error, but of my willingness to correct it forthwith, and to say in a public way that I erred.

68. Royce, *The Problem of Christianity*, 88.

69. Ibid.

70. James Baldwin, *The Fire Next Time* (New York: The Modern Library, 1995) [1963], 82.

71. King, "A Christmas Sermon on Peace," in his *The Trumpet of Conscience* (New York: Harper & Row, Publishers, 1968), 69.

72. King, "The American Dream," in *A Testament of Hope*, 213.

73. Tutu, *God Has a Dream*, 62.

74. Lewis Baldwin, *To Make the Wounded Whole*, 307.

75. King, *The Trumpet of Conscience*, xi, 45–47, 49.

76. Royce, *The Problem of Christianity*, 200.

77. Ibid.

Chapter 10

1. This chapter is a much expanded version of a lecture I gave at the 50th Anniversary Celebration of the March on Washington for Jobs and Freedom and the "I Have a Dream" Speech. The celebration was held at Christian Theological Seminary, Indianapolis, Indiana on April 12, 2013. The other three lecturers were Allan Boesak (former president of World Alliance of Reformed Churches and moderator of the Dutch Mission Church in Southern Africa), Frank Thomas (professor of homiletics at Christian Theological Seminary), and Walter Brueggemann (William Marcellus McPheeters Professor of Old Testament Emeritus at Columbia Theological Seminary). I name these other presenters because during the question-response period after my lecture a woman in the audience asked why there were no women presenters on the program. Aware that the four lecturers were males I was not at all surprised that the question was raised. While I responded forthrightly by thanking the woman for the question, saying that she was right on target, and that the all-male make-up of the cast of presenters is a limitation in which we celebrate this occasion, I was truly embarrassed because I knew that as an institution we are better than what was on display during that day and evening of celebration. I also shared with the audience an experience that the late Coretta Scott King had at a 1986 conference on Martin Luther King, Jr.'s legacy and leadership. At the end of the conference, after all presentations had been made, Mrs. King addressed those assembled and said that although they had come to the end of the conference they still had not addressed the issue of Martin Luther King, Jr., and the role of women in leadership. She was also troubled by the fact that of the large number of presenters only one was a woman, Professor Mary Frances Berry. Mrs. King then said: "The next time we have a conference on him I want to see more women scholars" [Coretta Scott King, "Thoughts and Reflections" in *We Shall Overcome: Martin Luther King, Jr. and the Black Freedom Struggle,* eds. Peter J. Albert and Ronald Hoffman (New York: DA CAPO Press, 1993), 255].

2. Henry Hampton and Steve Fayer (with Sarah Flynn), *Voices of Freedom: An Oral History of the Civil Rights Movement from the 1950s through the 1980s* (New York: Bantam Books, 1990), 159–60.

3. George Brown Tindall and David E. Shi, *America: A Narrative History,* 4th Edition (New York: W.W. Norton & Company, 1996), 1243.

4. Hampton and Fayer, *Voices of Freedom*, 161.

5. Jim Hoft, "Bummer...Martin Luther King, Jr. Stole 'I Have a Dream' Speech," http://www.thegatewaypundit.com/2008/01/bummer-martin-luther-king-jr-stole-i-have-a-dream-speech-from-black-republican/.

6. Cited in Hoft, "Bummer...," 1.

7. Martin Luther King, Jr., "I Have a Dream," in *A Call to Conscience: The Landmark Speeches of Dr. Martin Luther King, Jr.,* eds. Clayborne Carson and Kris Shepherd (New York: Warner Books, 2001), 86–87.

8. Clayborne Carson et al., eds., *The Papers of Martin Luther King, Jr.* (Berkeley: University of California Press, 2000), 4:88–89 (my italics). At one point the wording in the April 10 speech is slightly different: "As I heard a powerful orator say not long ago, that must become literally true" (*The Papers*, 4:178–79).

9. Ibid., (1997), 3:93.

10. Ibid., 3:95.

11. Ibid., 3:140.

12. Ibid., 4:343.

13. John Lewis, Introduction to "Address at the Conclusion of the Selma to Montgomery March," in *A Call to Conscience*, 112.

14. Ellen Levine, *Freedom's Children: Young Civil Rights Activists Tell Their Own Stories* (New York: G. P. Putnam's, 1993), 86.

15. Quoted in Aldon D. Morris, *The Origins of the Civil Rights Movement: Black Communities Organizing for Change* (New York: The Free Press, 1984), 98. From Septima Clark interview, November 17, 1978, Charleston, S.C.

16. Morris, *The Origins of the Civil Rights Movement*, 98.

17. See Clayborne Carson, *Martin's Dream: My Journey and the Legacy of Martin Luther King, Jr., A Memoir* (New York: Palgrave Macmillan, 2013), 129.

18. Morris, *The Origins of the Civil Rights Movement*, 59.

19. Ibid., 98.

20. Ibid., 60.

21. Drew Hansen, *The Dream: Martin Luther King, Jr. and the Speech that Inspired a Nation* (New York: HarperCollins, 2003), 110.

22. At this writing the speech has not been reproduced by the King Papers Project or in any other source of King's speeches. However, an earlier version of the speech (December 1956), without the "I have a dream" sections, appears in James M. Washington, ed., *A Testament of Hope: The Essential Writings of Martin Luther King, Jr.* (New York: Harper & Row, 1986), 135–44.

23. Hansen, *The Dream*, 110–111.

24. King, Address at the Freedom Rally in Cobo Hall, in *A Call to Conscience*, 61.

25. *The Papers* (2005), 5:202.

26. Ibid., 5:508.

27. Quoted in Hansen, *The Dream*, 250. See Hansen's interesting discussion on possible SNCC connections to the emergence of the "I have a dream" refrain. Hansen's discussion is based on interviews with a number of former SNCC activists in the Albany movement, including SCLC staff member Dorothy Cotton, who remembered a white woman SNCC activist using the phrase. Cotton said that she told King about it and he later began using the phrase (114). Hansen's is an interesting discussion, but even he agrees that the information from the interviews is not sufficient to say with certainty how the phrase emerged. See Chapter 3 of his book.

28. Hansen, *The Dream*, 250.

29. Quoted in Dorothy F. Cotton, *If Your Back's Not Bent: The Role of the Citizenship Education Program in the Civil Rights Movement* (New York: Atria Books, 2012), 220.

30. Ibid.

31. Ibid.

32. Quoted in Hansen, *The Dream*, 110, 111.

33. Quoted in Cotton, *If Your Back's Not Bent*, 220.

34. *The Papers* (1992), 1:354.

35. The other speech advisors included: Cleveland Robinson, Reverends Walter Fauntroy, Bernard Lee, and Ralph Abernathy; King biographer Lawrence Reddick, and Bayard Rustin. See Clarence B. Jones with Stuart Connerly, *Behind the Dream: The Making of the Speech that Transformed a Nation* (New York: Palgrave Macmillan, 2011), 55.

36. Jones, *Behind the Dream*, 67.

37. See Anna Hedgeman, *The Trumpet Sounds: A Memoir of Negro Leadership* (New York: Holt, Rinehart and Winston, 1964), 178–80.

38. Pauli Murray, "The Negro Woman in the Quest for Equality," reprinted from *The Acorn* [official publication of Lamda Kappa Mu sorority] (June 1964), 2.

39. Dorothy Height, "We Wanted the Voice of a Woman to be Heard" (Black Women and the 1963 March on Washington), in *Sisters in the Struggle: African American Women in the Civil Rights-Black Power Movement*, eds. Bettye Collier-Thomas and V.P. Franklin (New York: New York University Press, 2001), 86–87.

40. Ibid., 87, 88.

41. Jones, *Behind the Dream*, 101.

42. In the printed text of the speech the following sentence was to have been read just after the words from the prophet Amos about justice rolling down like waters and righteousness like a mighty stream: "And so today, let us go back to our communities as members of the international association for the advancement of creative dissatisfaction" [Quoted in Taylor Branch, *Parting the Waters: America in the King Years 1954–63* (New York: Simon & Schuster, 1988), 882]. This sentence was clearly out of rhythm, and to King's credit as orator, he recognized this and omitted speaking it, extemporizing instead.

43. Branch, *Parting the Waters*, 882, 1000.

44. See the photo of Jackson's proximity to King in Herb Boyd, *We Shall Overcome*, Narrated by Ossie Davis and Ruby Dee (Naperville, IL: Sourcebooks, 2004), 153.

45. Ted Kennedy, *True Compass: A Memoir* (New York: Twelve/Hachette Book Group, 2009), 201.

46. See Hansen, *The Dream*, 243.

47. Jones, *Behind the Dream*, 112.

48. Ibid., 112, 113. The italics are Jones's.

49. Ibid., 112.

50. King, "I Have a Dream," in *A Call to Conscience*, 85.

51. Ibid.

52. Quoted in Carson, *Martin's Dream*, 194.

53. Quoted in Branch, *Parting the Waters*, 882, 1000.

54. Marquis Childs, "Triumphal March Silences Scoffers," *Washington Post*, August 30, 1963, A-18.

55. Quoted in Peter Goldman, *The Death and Life of Malcolm X*, 2nd ed. (Urbana: University of Illinois Press, 1979) [1973], 107.

56. King, "A Christmas Sermon on Peace," in *A Testament of Hope: The Essential Writings of Martin Luther King, Jr.*, ed. James M. Washington (New York: Harper & Row, 1986), 257. See also *Playboy* Interview: Martin Luther King, Jr., in Ibid. 351.

57. Hebrew Bible scholar Walter Brueggemann cautioned that we not think that the nightmare only began after King's famous speech. Blacks and the nation were already living in the nightmare, even as King delivered his speech. Brueggemann made this observation at The Dream Today: Celebrating the 50th Anniversary of the March on Washington and Dr. Martin Luther King, Jr.'s "I Have a Dream" Speech at Christian Theological Seminary, April 12, 2013.

58. King, "Eulogy for the Victims of the Sixteenth Street Baptist Church Bombing," in *A Call to Conscience*, 95. A separate service was held for Carole Robertson, who was eulogized by Rev. Fred Shuttlesworth.

59. Brian Ward, *Radio and the Struggle for Civil Rights in the South* (Gainesville: University Press of Florida, 2004), 207.

60. Ibid.

61. Hampton and Fayer, *Voices of Freedom*, 175.

62. King, "Where Do We Go from Here?," in *A Testament of Hope*, 252. In "Of Justice and the Conscience" (1852), Parker actually said: "Look at the facts of the world. You see a continual and progressive triumph of the right. I do not pretend to understand the moral universe; the arc is a long one, my eye reaches but little ways; I cannot calculate the curve and complete the figure by the experience of sight; I can divine it by conscience. And from what I see I am sure it bends towards justice" [in *The Collected Works of Theodore Parker,* Sermons and Prayers, ed. Frances Power Cobbe (London: Trübner & Company, 1879), 2:48]. It was actually John Haynes Holmes who, in his salute to those who had been involved in the Montgomery bus boycott, offered the popular version of Parker's statement when he said: "The victory may seem slow in coming. The waiting for it may seem interminable. We perhaps may not live to see the hour of triumph. But the great Theodore Parker, abolitionist preacher in the days before the Civil War, answered this doubt and fear when he challenged an impatient world. '*The arc of the moral universe is long, but it bends toward justice*'" [Holmes, "Salute to Montgomery," *Liberation* (December 1956): 5].

63. Bruce Watson, *Freedom Summer: The Savage Season that Made Mississippi Burn and Made America a Democracy* (New York: Viking, 2010), 295, 296.

64. See Coretta Scott King, *My Life with Martin Luther King, Jr.* (New York: Holt, Rinehart and Winston, 1969), 244.

65. Hampton and Fayer, *Voices of Freedom*, 168.

66. See Charles C. Brown, *Niebuhr and His Age: Reinhold Niebuhr's Prophetic Role in the Twentieth Century* (Philadelphia: Trinity Press International, 1992), 220.

67. King, "Where Do We Go from Here?," in *A Call to Conscience*, 199 (my emphasis).

Chapter 11

1. An earlier version of this chapter was delivered as an address at the University of Northern Iowa during its King Day celebration in 2011. A later, revised version was given at Wabash College during Black History Month that year. The present chapter has undergone major revisions for this book.

2. King, "The Future of Integration." Speech given at Manchester College (Indiana), February 1, 1968, 17.

3. See E. Cook and L. Racine, "The Children's Crusade and the Role of Youth in the African American Freedom Struggle," *OAH Magazine of History* 19, 1 (2005), 31–36; Dwight Hopkins, "The Last Testament of Martin Luther King, Jr.," *Theology Today* 65, 1 (2008), 67–80.

4. Martin Luther King, Jr., "Face to Face" television news interview, in *A Testament of Hope: The Essential Writings of Martin Luther King, Jr.,* ed. James M. Washington (New York: Harper & Row, Publishers, 1986), 408.

5. Clayborne Carson et al., eds., *The Papers of Martin Luther King, Jr.* (Berkeley: University of California Press, 2007), 6:169.

6. Ibid., (2000), 4:125.

7. Ibid., 4:366.

8. Paraphrase from King, "The Drum Major Instinct," in *A Knock at Midnight,* eds. Clayborne Carson and Peter Holloran (New York: Warner Books, 1998), 171.

9. King's first full-length speech devoted to Vietnam was delivered on February 25, 1967, at the *Nation* Institute in Los Angeles. See Stephen B. Oates, *Let the Trumpet Sound: The Life of Martin Luther King, Jr.* (New York:

Harper & Row, Publishers, 1982), 431. This was followed by the famous Riverside Church speech against the war in Vietnam on April 4, 1967.

10. King, "Why Jesus Called a Man a Fool," in *A Knock at Midnight*, 146.

11. Ibid. (emphasis added).

12. This is also the stance that Michael G. Long takes in his seminal excellent book, *Martin Luther King, Jr., Homosexuality, and the Early Gay Rights Movement* (New York: Palgrave/Macmillan, 2013).

13. King, "Rediscovering Lost Values," in *A Knock at Midnight*, 10.

14. King, "A Christmas Sermon on Peace," in *The Trumpet of Conscience* (New York: Harper & Row, 1968), 69.

15. King, "Second Anniversary of Protest: President's Address," Montgomery, Alabama, December 5, 1957, King Library and Archives, 12.

16. King, *Stride Toward Freedom* (New York: Harper & Row, Publishers, 1958), 223.

17. *The Papers*, 4:471.

18. King, "Second Anniversary of Protest: President's Address," Montgomery, Alabama, December 5, 1957, King Library & Archives, 11.

19. Two excellent books inform the remainder of this discussion: Ellen Levine, *Freedom's Children: Young Civil Rights Activists Tell Their Own Stories* (New York: G. P. Putnam's Sons, 1993), and David Halberstam, *The Children* (New York: Random House, 1998).

20. See the provocative book by Miles Wolff, *Lunch at the 5 & 10,* Revised and Expanded (Chicago: Ivan R. Dee, 1990) [1970].

21. "Sit-Ins," in Clayborne Carson et al., *The Martin Luther King, Jr. Encyclopedia* (Westport, CT: Greenwood Press, 2008), 307.

22. Kwame Anthony Appiah and Henry Louis Gates, eds., "Sit-Ins," in *Africana: Civil Rights* (Philadelphia/London: Running Press, 2004), 369.

23. See Washington's introductory statement on King, "Love, Law, and Civil Disobedience" in *A Testament of Hope*, 43.

24. King, "Nonviolence: The Only Road to Freedom," in *A Testament of Hope*, 58.

25. King, "The Burning Truth in the South," in *A Testament of Hope*, 94.

26. Ibid.

27. Ibid., 97.

28. Ibid., 97–98.

29. King, "The Time for Freedom Has Come," in *A Testament of Hope*, 162.

30. Ibid., 165.

31. Quoted in Seth Cagin and Philip Dray, *We Are Not Afraid: The Story of Goodman, Schwerner, and Chaney, and the Civil Rights Campaign for Mississippi* (New York: Nation Books, 2006) [1988], 120.

32. Cagin and Dray, *We Are Not Afraid*, 120.

33. Quoted in Fred Powledge, *Free at Last?: The Civil Rights Movement and the People Who Made It* (New York: HarperPerennial, 1991), 262.

34. Diane Nash, "Inside the Sit-Ins and Freedom Rides: Testimony of a Southern Student," in *The New Negro,* ed. Mathew H. Ahmann (New York: Biblo and Tannen, 1961), 58–59.

35. Halberstam, *The Children*, 337–38.

36. Cagin and Dray, *We Are Not Afraid*, 121.

37. James Lawson, who was one of the riders, was critical of the protection provided by state police and National Guardsmen, arguing that this was inconsistent with the philosophy and practice of nonviolence. See Cagin and Dray, *We Are Not Afraid*, 122.

38. *The Papers* (2005), 5:466.

39. Ibid., 5:467.

40. Ibid.

41. Ibid., 5:450.

42. Ibid., 5:569.

43. Shuttlesworth and others founded the ACMHR when Circuit Judge Walter B. Jones banned the NAACP from civil rights activity in Alabama in 1956. The ACMHR was a direct action organization. Under the strong leadership of Shuttlesworth there were demonstrations against bus segregation, segregation in the public schools, and in other places in Birmingham.

44. King, "Letter from Birmingham Jail," in his *Why We Can't Wait* (New York: Harper & Row, Publishers, 1963), 79.

45. King, *Why We Can't Wait*, 37.

46. Ibid.

47. This college is affiliated with the Christian Methodist Episcopal Church. At the time, its president was Dr. Lucius Pitts, who participated in early negotiations with the White Senior Citizens Committee to eradicate segregation.

48. King was aware that local and state courts in Alabama were notorious for issuing injunctions to hamper demonstrations for freedom and civil rights. He saw that "the courts of Alabama had misused the judicial process in order to perpetuate injustice and segregation" (*Why We Can't Wait*, 69). Conscience forbade him and SCLC to obey such injunctions.

49. Levine, *Freedom's Children*, 82.

50. Ibid., 88.

51. King, *Why We Can't Wait*, 101.

52. Levine, *Freedom's Children*, 69.

53. King, *The Trumpet of Conscience*, 46.

54. Clayborne Carson, ed., *The Autobiography of Martin Luther King, Jr.* (New York: Warner Books, 1998), 207.

55. Quoted in Diane McWhorter, *Carry Me Home: Birmingham, Alabama the Climactic Battle of the Civil Rights Revolution* (New York: Simon & Schuster, 2001), 371.

56. McWhorter, *Carry Me Home*, 386.

57. Quoted in Ibid., 371.

58. Quoted in Henry Hampton and Steve Fayer, ed. (with Sarah Flynn), *Voices of Freedom: An Oral History of the Civil Rights Movement from the 1950s Through the 1980s* (New York: Bantam Books, 1990), 133.

59. Powledge, *Free at Last?*, 308.

60. McWhorter, *Carry Me Home*, 390.

61. Quoted in Hampton and Fayer, ed., *Voices of Freedom*, 132.

62. Brian Ward, *Radio and the Struggle for Civil Rights in the South* (Gainesville: University Press of Florida, 2004), 203.

63. Ibid., 204.

64. Ibid., 204.

65. Halberstam, *The Children*, 441.

66. Levine, *Freedom's Children*, 78, 79.

67. Powledge, *Free at Last?*, 511–12, and McWhorter, *Carry Me Home*, 339–41.

68. McWhorter, *Carry Me Home*, 385.

69. Gene Roberts and Hank Klibanoff, *The Race Beat: The Press, the Civil Rights Struggle, and the Awakening of a Nation* (New York: Alfred A. Knopf, 2007), 332–33.

70. Quoted in Hampton and Fayer, ed., *Voices of Freedom*, 133.

71. Lerone Bennett, Jr., *Confrontation: Black and White* (Chicago: Johnson Publishing Company, 1965), 280.

72. This is Maya Angelou's neologism. See *Conversations with Maya Angelou*, ed. Jeffrey M. Elliot (Jackson: University Press of Mississippi, 1989), 112.

73. Quoted in Jack Gilbert (News Editor), "King Urges Youth Join in New Order," King Library & Archives, December 1959, 1.

74. King, speech to the American Federation of State, County and Municipal Employees (AFSCME) in Memphis, Tennessee, March 18, 1968, in *"All Labor Has Dignity,"* ed. Michael K. Honey (Boston: Beacon Press, 2011), 172.

75. King, speech to AFSCME, in Ibid., 171.

76. King, "Youth and Social Action," in *The Trumpet of Conscience*, 47.

77. Ibid., 45.

78. King, *Stride*, 218.

79. King, "A Time to Break Silence," in *A Testament of Hope*, 243.

Chapter 12

1. An earlier version of this chapter was published as "The Doctrine of Unearned Suffering," in *Encounter*, vol. 63, nos. 1–2 (Winter/Spring 2002).

2. See Joanne Carlson Brown and Rebecca Parker, "For God So Loved the World," in *Christianity, Patriarchy, and Abuse: A Feminist Critique,* eds. Carole R. Bohn and Joanne Carlson Brown (Cleveland: The Pilgrim Press, 1989), 1–30; Carol J. Adams and Marie M. Fortune, eds., *Violence against Women and Children: A Christian Theological Sourcebook* (New York: Continuum Publishing Company, 1995); M. Shawn Copeland, "Wading Through Many Sorrows: Toward a Theology of Suffering," in *A Troubling in My Soul: Womanist Perspectives on Evil & Suffering,* ed. Emilie M. Townes (Maryknoll, NY: Orbis Books, 1993), 109–129; and Jacquelyn Grant, "The Sin of Servanthood," in Ibid., 199–218.

3. See Copeland, "Wading Through Many Sorrows," 124.

4. Martin Luther King, Jr., "Love, Law, and Civil Disobedience," in *A Testament of Hope: The Essential Writings of Martin Luther King, Jr.,* ed. James M. Washington (New York: Harper & Row, 1986), 47.

5. Cheryl A. Kirk-Duggan, "Drum Major for Justice or Dilettante of Dishonesty: Martin Luther King, Jr., Moral Capital, and Hypocrisy of Embodied Messianic Myths," in *The Domestication of Martin Luther King, Jr.: Clarence B. Jones, Right-Wing Conservatism, and the Manipulation of the King Legacy,* eds. Lewis V. Baldwin and Rufus Burrow, Jr. (Eugene, OR: Cascade Books, 2013), 118.

6. Delores Williams, *Sisters in the Wilderness: The Challenge of Womanist God-Talk* (Maryknoll, NY: Orbis Books, 1993), 200.

7. Brian Kane, "The Influence of Boston Personalism on the Thought of Martin Luther King, Jr." (MTS thesis, Boston University, 1985), 57.

8. See Martin Luther King, Jr., *Stride Toward Freedom* (New York: Harper & Brothers, 1958), 102–107.

9. Clayborne Carson, ed., *The Autobiography of Martin Luther King, Jr.* (New York: Warner Books, 1998), 29. See also Clayborne Carson et al., eds., *The Papers of Martin Luther King, Jr.* (Berkeley: University of California Press, 2007), 6:594

10. King, *Stride*, 103.

11. Ibid.

12. Quoted in Ibid., 103.

13. King, *Stride*, 102, 172, 213, 221.

14. M.K. Gandhi, *Non-Violent Resistance* (New York: Schocken Books, 1961), 364–365.

15. Ibid., 88.

16. Ibid., 89.

17. King, *Stride*, 106.

18. King, "An Autobiography of Religious Development," in *The Papers of Martin Luther King, Jr.*, ed. Clayborne Carson (Berkeley: University of California Press, 1992), 1:360.

19. This is how King's teacher, Brightman, characterized God, and King accepted this view as his own. See Edgar S. Brightman, *A Philosophy of Religion* (New York: Prentice-Hall, 1940), 204n4, 209n9, 217, 230.

20. King, *Stride*, 106.

21. Kane, "The Influence of Boston Personalism on the Thought of Martin Luther King, Jr.," 52 (my emphasis).

22. Copeland, "Wading Through Many Sorrows," 121.

23. Ibid.

24. L. Harold DeWolf, *A Theology of the Living Church* (New York: Harper & Brothers, 1960) [1953], 140.

25. Ibid., 141.

26. See Rufus Burrow, Jr., and James L. Kirby, "Conceptions of God in the Thinking of Martin Luther King, Jr. and Edgar S. Brightman," *Encounter*, Volume 60, Number 3 (Summer 1999), 283–305.

27. *The Papers*, 1:426. This was King's reaction in a paper written for Davis while in seminary. See also *The Papers* (1994), 2:84–85, where he acknowledges that there are both limitations and strengths in Brightman's doctrine.

28. *The Papers*, 2:109. One might question the sincerity of King here, since he expressed this stance in a final examination on philosophy of religion written for Brightman. Students often find it difficult to disagree with the views of a favorite teacher, or any teacher if the assignment is to be graded.

29. Brightman, *A Philosophy of Religion*, 338.

30. Walter Wink, *Engaging the Powers: Discernment and Resistance in a World of Domination* (Minneapolis: Fortress Press, 1992), 161.

31. King, "Suffering and Faith," *The Christian Century* 77:17 (27 April 1960), 510.

32. King, "No Vengeance," unpublished sermon, King Library and Archives, February 13, 1958.

33. Brown and Parker, "For God So Loved the World?," in *Christianity, Patriarchy, and Abuse*, 20.

34. Lewis V. Baldwin, *The Voice of Conscience: The Church in the Mind of Martin Luther King, Jr.* (New York: Oxford University Press, 2010), 245.

35. Ibid.

36. Carson, ed., *The Autobiography of Martin Luther King, Jr.*, 25–27

37. King, *Stride*, 99.

38. King, "Love, Law, and Civil Disobedience," in *A Testament of Hope: The Essential Writings of Martin Luther King, Jr.*, ed. James M. Washington (New York: Harper & Row, 1986), 47 (emphasis added).

39. Quoted in Stephen B. Oates, *Let the Trumpet Sound: The Life of Martin Luther King, Jr.* (New York: Harper & Row, Publishers, 1982), 413.

40. Oates, *Let the Trumpet Sound*, 418.

41. Ibid.

42. Edgar S. Brightman, *The Finding of God* (New York: The Abingdon Press, 1931), 141.

43. *The Papers* (2007), 6:288–89.

Chapter 13

1. A much shorter version of this chapter was published as "Some Reflections on King, Personalism, and Sexism," *Encounter*, Vol. 65, No. 1 (2004), 9–38.

2. The term "recovering sexist" is not one to be used lightly. One must earn the label. He does so by first admitting to himself (first and foremost) and others that he is in fact a sexist, and that he benefits from sexism (even if he himself is not a sexist!). It is important that he think through how it feels to be a sexist, and one who benefits mightily from it; what he intends to do about it, how, and when. He then must vow to intentionally and relentlessly work to identify sexist elements in his thought and practice and how these are manifested in myriad ways. He should also be willing, at every step, to be assisted in this by women. It is important that he remain open to critique and suggestions about how he can extricate himself of his own sexist tendencies, as well as be a champion women's rights and opportunities throughout society. To be a recovering sexist means that one is always cognizant of his sexism and the fact that he is a beneficiary of it, even if he is consciously working on liberating himself and others from it.

3. Clayborne Carson et al., eds., *The Papers of Martin Luther King, Jr.* (Berkeley: University of California Press, 2007), 6:88.

4. Ibid., 6:327.

5. Michael K. Honey, "Introduction," in Martin Luther King, Jr., *"All Labor Has Dignity,"* ed. Honey (Boston: Beacon Press, 2011), XXXI.

6. See King's address to American Federation of State, County and Municipal Employees (AFSCME), Memphis, Tennessee, March 8, 1968, in *"All Labor Has Dignity,"* 174.

7. See "Face to Face" television news interview, in *A Testament of Hope: The Essential Writings of Martin Luther King, Jr.*, ed. James M. Washington (New York: Harper & Row, 1986), 408.

8. *The Papers* (2000), 4:368.

9. Stewart Burns, *To the Mountaintop: Martin Luther King, Jr.'s Sacred Mission to Save America 1955–1968* (New York: HarperSanFrancisco, 2004), 373.

10. See James H. Cone, *Martin & Malcolm & America: A Dream or a Nightmare* (Maryknoll, NY: Orbis Books, 1991), 273–280.

11. See Lewis V. Baldwin and Amiri YaSin Al-Hadid, *Between Cross and Crescent: Christian and Muslim Perspectives on Malcolm and Martin* (Gainsville: University Press of Florida, 2002), Chapter 5, "The Character of Womanhood: The Views of Malcolm and Martin." It should be noted, however, that Al-Hadid, the Muslim co-author and scholar, rejects any claims that either King or Malcolm was sexist (6, 137, 141, 156).

12. See Paula Giddings, *When and Where I Enter: The Impact of Black Women on Race and Sex in America* (New York: William Morrow & Company, 1984), 312–14.

13. Cheryl A. Kirk-Duggan, *Refiner's Fire: A Religious Engagement with Violence* (Minneapolis: Fortress Press, 2001), 90–92.

14. See Andrew Billingsley, *Mighty Like a River: The Black Church and Social Reform* (New York: Oxford University Press, 1999), 142–43.

15. King appealed to and discussed Bowne's views in essays and exams under Brightman. See his paper, "The Personalism of J.M.E. McTaggart Under Criticism," in *The Papers* (1994), 2:73; "Final Examination Answers, Philosophy of Religion" in Ibid., 110–111; and his doctoral dissertation, "A Comparison of the Conceptions of God in the Thinking of Paul Tillich and Henry Nelson Wieman" in Ibid., 511.

16. See Albert C. Knudson, *The Philosophy of Personalism: A Study in the Metaphysics of Religion* (New York: Abingdon Press, 1927), 85, 87, 433. According to Edgar S. Brightman, another of Bowne's students, the book was originally given the title, *Bowne and Personalism*. See Brightman, *An Introduction to Philosophy* (New York: Henry Holt, 1925), 374.

17. John S. Mbiti, *African Religions and Philosophy*, Second Edition (Portsmouth, NH: Heinemann, 1989) [1969], 106.

18. John Wright Buckham, *Personality and the Christian Ideal* (Boston: The Pilgrim Press, 1909), 21.

19. Inasmuch as there is no evidence in Bowne's published writings that he wrote explicitly against racism and the denial of political rights to black women, I am not inclined to presume that when he argues for suffrage for women he also means black women.

20. Efforts by this writer, as well as the late Warren Steinkraus, to locate the unpublished papers of Bowne where he *might* have addressed racism have failed to date. Bowne's wife implied in a letter to their godson, Borden Bowne Kessler (January 6, 1912), that her husband left behind both books, papers, and magazines. It therefore seems logical to conclude that whichever institution received Bowne's book and magazine collection also received the papers to which Mrs. Bowne referred. It is known that Bowne's library and magazines went to Drew University Library in 1912. Unfortunately, library officials then have insisted that his papers were not included with his library. Moreover, a copy of the Drew University Librarian's Report in 1912 reveals nothing of unpublished papers being included with Bowne's library and unbound magazines. Moreover, the deed to the Bowne materials (of which I have a copy in my possession) does not list unpublished papers as part of the collection.

21. See Bowne, *The Principles of Ethics* (New York: Harper & Brothers, 1892), 286–88; and "Woman and Democracy," *North American Review* 191 (April 1910), 527–36.

22. See Gerda Lerner, ed., *Black Women in White America: A Documentary History* (New York: Vintage Press, 1973), 440.

23. Bowne, *The Principles of Ethics*, 161.

24. Bowne, *The Philosophy of Theism* (New York: Harper & Brothers, 1887), 248–49.

25. Ibid., 249.

26. Ibid. (emphasis added)

27. See my *Personalism: A Critical Introduction* (St. Louis: Chalice Press, 1999), 85–86, 106–108.

28. Bowne writes: "No logical subtlety would enable a man to judge in the court of aesthetics, who was lacking in the aesthetic sense. Such an one would likely decide that there is no proof that the Hottentot Venus is any less fair than the Venus of Milo; and he might even boast of the acumen and impartiality of his decision" [Bowne, *Theism* (New York: American Book Company, 1902), 260]. I would be interested to know what an educated black person in Bowne's day would say about this (e.g., Frederick Douglass and Anna Julia Cooper), since the Hottentots were dark-skinned Africans.

29. See Gary Dorrien, *The Making of American Liberal Theology: Idealism, Realism, and Modernity 1900–1950* (Louisville: Westminster John Knox Press, 2003), 305–355.

30. S. Paul Schilling, "Albert Cornelius Knudson: Person and Theologian," in *The Boston Personalist Tradition in Philosophy, Social Ethics, and Theology*, eds. Paul Deats, Jr., and Carol Robb (Macon, GA: Mercer University Press, 1986), 102–103.

31. See Francis J. McConnell, *Borden Parker Bowne: His Life and His Philosophy* (New York: The Abingdon Press, 1929), 176, 259.

32. See King's letter to Sankey Lee Blanton at Crozer Theological Seminary, January 1951, in *The Papers* (1992), 1:391.

33. David J. Garrow, *Bearing the Cross: Martin Luther King, Jr., and the Southern Christian Leadership Conference* (New York: William Morrow and Company, 1986), 44.

34. See "Fragment of Application to Boston University," 1951, in *The Papers*, 1:390.

35. Martin Luther King, Jr., *Stride Toward Freedom: The Montgomery Story* (New York: Harper & Row, Publishers, 1958), 100.

36. King, "A Time to Break Silence," in *A Testament of Hope*, 232–33.

37. See Chapter 3 of this book for a discussion on King's doctrine of dignity.

38. We get a sense of this in a paper King wrote during his first year in seminary, "An Autobiography of Religious Development," in *The Papers*, 1:360.

39. *The Papers*, 6:123.

40. Coretta Scott King, *My Life with Martin Luther King, Jr.* (New York: Holt Rinehart Winston, 1969), 60.

41. Cone, *Martin & Malcolm & America*, 277–78.

42. See Clayborne Carson, ed., *The Autobiography of Martin Luther King, Jr.* (New York: Warner Books, 1998), 160–65.

43. Mary Fair Burks, close friend and predecessor of Robinson's, reminds us that the boycott was not solely the latter's idea, and that in any case the important thing is that it occurred and had a successful outcome. See Burks, "Trailblazers: Women in the Montgomery Bus Boycott," in *Women in the Civil Rights Movement: Trailblazers and Torchbearers 1941–1965*, eds. Vicki L. Crawford, Jacqueline Anne Rouse, and Barbara Woods (Bloomington and Indianapolis: Indiana University Press, 1993), 75.

44. King, *Stride*, 30, 34, 118. See also Taylor Branch, *Parting the Waters: America in the King Years, 1955–63* (New York: Simon & Schuster, 1988), 132n.

45. See Lewis V. Baldwin, *There Is a Balm in Gilead: The Cultural Roots of Martin Luther King, Jr.* (Minneapolis: Augsburg Fortress Press, 1991), 184. Here Baldwin is influenced by King, "Unknown Heroes," *The New York Amsterdam News* (May 12, 1962), 1ff.

46. Ibid., 270n137.

47. See King's letter to Mrs. Katie E. Whickam, King Library and Archives, July 7, 1958, 1.

48. I address this at length in my *God and Human Dignity: The Personalism, Theology, and Ethics of Martin Luther King, Jr.* (Notre Dame: University of Notre Dame Press, 2006), 131–39.

49. My unpublished essay, "Martin Luther King, Jr.: The Person," has an extensive discussion of this and related matters. This manuscript is located in my personal files.

50. See Clarence B. Jones, *Behind the Dream: The Making of the Speech that Transformed a Nation,* with Stuart Connelly (New York: Palgrave/Macmillan, 2011), 55.

51. Pauli Murray, *Song in a Weary Throat* (New York: Harper & Row, 1987), 377.

52. Quoted in Lynne Olson, *Freedom's Daughters: The Unsung Heroines of the Civil Rights Movement from 1830–1970* (New York: A Touchstone Book, Published by Simon & Schuster, 2001), 129.

53. Quoted in Rosa Parks, *Rosa Parks: My Story,* with Jim Haskins (New York: Dial Books, 1992), 139.

54. Parks, *Rosa Parks*, 139.

55. Olson, *Freedom's Daughters*, 116 (my emphasis).

56. See Anna Hedgeman, *The Trumpet Sounds: A Memoir of Negro Leadership* (New York: Holt, Rinehart and Winston, 1964), 178–80. See also Jones, *Behind the Dream*, 100–102.

57. Quoted in Douglas Brinkley, *Rosa Parks* (New York: Viking Penguin, 2000), 185.

58. Brinkley, *Rosa Parks*, 186.

59. Barbara Ransby, *Ella Baker and the Black*

Freedom Movement: A Radical Democratic Vision (Chapel Hill: University of North Carolina Press, 2003), 173.

60. Baker exhibited characteristics of what Alice Walker would describe as a "womanish." See her "Coming Apart," in *Take Back the Night: Women on Pornography,* ed. Laura Lederer (New York: William Morrow and Company, Inc., 1980), 100.

61. Ransby, *Ella Baker and the Black Freedom Movement,* 35.

62. Coretta Scott King, *My Life with Martin Luther King, Jr.,* rev. ed. (New York: Henry Holt and Company, 1993) [1969], 142 (emphasis added).

63. See Malcolm X, *The Autobiography of Malcolm X,* as told by Alex Haley (New York: Ballantine Books, 1992) [1965], 101–103, 246, 322.

64. Michael Eric Dyson reports that King "allegedly got physical with at least one woman...." See his *I May Not Get There With You: The True Martin Luther King, Jr.* (New York: The Free Press, 2000), 177. This is likely the incident to which King's best friend, Ralph David Abernathy, refers in his autobiography, *And the Walls Came Tumbling Down* (New York: Harper & Row, 1989), 436.

65. See Garrow, *Bearing the Cross,* 655n12. See also Andrew Young, *An Easy Burden: The Civil Rights Movement and the Transformation of America* (New York: HarperCollins Publishers, 1996), 137.

66. G.W.F. Hegel, *The Phenomenology of Mind,* trans. J.B. Baillie (New York: Harper Torch Books/The Academy Library, 1967), 81.

67. Alice Walker, "Coretta King: Revisited," in her *In Search of Our Mothers' Gardens* (New York: Harcourt Brace Jovanovich, 1983), 155.

68. See my discussion of this criterion of truth in my *Personalism,* Chapter 5.

69. King, "Letter from Birmingham Jail," in his *Why We Can't Wait* (New York: Harper & Row, 1964), 79.

70. See his Nobel Prize acceptance speech, in *A Testament of Hope,* 226.

71. Baldwin chronicles King's development in this regard in his book, *Toward the Beloved Community: Martin Luther King, Jr. and South Africa* (Cleveland: The Pilgrim Press, 1995). Chapter One, "The Politics of Race: Viewing South Africa in Context in the 1950s," traces his development toward an international perspective from the earliest period of his leadership. Baldwin also addresses King's developing internationalism in *To Make the Wounded Whole: The Cultural Legacy of Martin Luther King, Jr.* (Minneapolis: Fortress Press, 1992), 247–57, and entirety of Chapter Four, "Caught in an Inescapable Network: A Vision of World Community."

72. See Carson, ed., *The Autobiography of Martin Luther King, Jr.,* 335.

73. King, *Where Do We Go from Here: Chaos or Community?* (Boston: Beacon Press, 1967), 97.

74. Ibid., 98. This idea comes from Tillich, *The Protestant Era* (Chicago: The University of Chicago Press, 1948), 115. It is also important to point out that this is a basic idea in the philosophy of personalism. See Bowne, *Metaphysics,* rev. ed. (New York: Harper & Brothers, 1898), 406.

75. Benjamin E. Mays, *The Negro's God as Reflected in His Literature* (New York: Atheneum, 1969), Chapter VI.

76. King, "The Ethical Demands for Integration," in *A Testament of Hope,* 122.

77. *The Papers,* 6:212.

78. See Walter Rauschenbusch, *Christianity and the Social Crisis* (New York: Macmillan, 1907), 150.

79. Philip S. Foner, ed., *Frederick Douglass on Women's Rights* (New York: Da Capo Press, 1992), 119. Douglass characterized himself as a "radical woman suffrage man" (Ibid).

80. *The Papers,* 6:432.

81. King, "Letter from Birmingham Jail," in *Why We Can't Wait,* 79.

Chapter 14

1. This chapter was originally published as "Martin Luther King, Jr., Personalism, and Intra-community Violence," *Encounter,* Vol. 58, No. 1 (Winter 1997).

2. See Garth Baker-Fletcher's instructive study on King's doctrine of dignity in his *Somebodyness: Martin Luther King, Jr. and the Theory of Dignity* (Minneapolis: Fortress Press, 1993).

3. See my article, "John Wesley Edward Bowen: First Afrikan American Personalist," *Encounter,* Vol. 56, No. 3 (Summer 1995), 241–260.

4. John Wesley Edward Bowen, "Apology for Higher Education of the Negro," *Methodist Review* (1897), 730.

5. Bowen, *An Appeal for Negro Bishops, But No Separation* (New York: Eaton & Mains, 1912), 66.

6. King, "A Christmas Sermon on Peace," in *A Testament of Hope: The Essential Writings of Martin Luther King, Jr.,* ed. James M. Washington (New York: Harper & Row, 1986), 255.

7. King, "Where Do We Go from Here?," in *A Testament of Hope,* 250.

8. Ibid.

9. Carson, ed., *The Autobiography of Martin Luther King, Jr.* (New York: Warner Books, 1998), 346.

10. Yolanda King made this observation during a keynote address to Christian Church (Disciples of Christ) youths at Christian Theological Seminary, Indianapolis, Indiana, in late March 1986.

11. King, "Remaining Awake Through a Great Revolution," in *A Testament of Hope,* 274.

12. See Jewelle Taylor Gibbs, "Health and Mental Health of Young Black Males," in *Young, Black, and Male in America: An Endangered Species,* ed. Gibbs (Dover, MA: Auburn House, 1988), 219 (my emphasis).

13. Andrew Billingsley, *Climbing Jacob's Ladder: The Enduring Legacy of African-American Families* (New York: Simon & Schuster, 1992), 160.

14. Quoted in Ibid., 162.

15. Billingsley, *Climbing Jacob's Ladder,* 162.

16. Ibid. Here Billingsley cites a study by Carl C. Bell and Esther J. Jenkins, "Preventing Black Homicide," in *The State of Black America 1990,* ed. Janet DeWart.

17. See Amos N. Wilson, *Black-on-Black Violence* (New York: Afrikan World Infosystems, 1990), xi.

18. See Gwendolyn Rice, "Young Black Men, the Church, and Our Future," *The Chicago Theological Seminary Register,* Vol. LXXVIII, No. 2 (Spring 1988), 11.

19. William J. Wilson, *The Declining Significance of Race* (Chicago: University of Chicago Press, 1978).

20. Shelby Steele, *The Content of Our Character: A New Vision of Race in America* (New York: Harper Perennial, 1990).

21. Cornel West, *Race Matters* (Boston: Beacon Press, 1993).

22. West, *Democracy Matters: Winning the Fight Against Imperialism* (New York: The Penguin Press, 2004).

23. Andrew Hacker, *Two Nations: Black and White, Separate, Hostile, Unequal,* Expanded and Updated Edition (New York: Ballantine Books, 1995) [1992].

24. Joe R. Feagin, *Systemic Racism: A Theory of Oppression* (New York: Routledge, 2006).

25. Feagin, *Racist America: Roots, Current Realities, and Future Reparations* (New York: Routledge, 2000).

26. Wilson, *Black-on-Black Violence*, xiii (emphasis added).

27. See Cornel West's important chapter, "Nihilism in Black America," in his *Race Matters*, Chapter 1.

28. *Playboy* Interview: Martin Luther King, Jr., in, *A Testament of Hope*, 370.

29. King, "A Gift of Love," in *A Testament of Hope*, 62–63.

30. King, *Stride Toward Freedom* (New York: Harper & Row, 1958), 223.

31. King, *Where Do We Go from Here: Chaos or Community?* (Boston: Beacon Press, 1967), 64.

32. These are two of the eleven principles in the moral law system of the personalist Edgar S. Brightman (1884–1953) who was King's academic advisor and teacher. See Brightman, *Moral Laws* (Nashville: Abingdon Press, 1933). King was influenced by this book during his doctoral studies.

33. Borden P. Bowne, *The Principles of Ethics* (New York: American Book Company, 1892), 199.

34. King, "An Experiment in Love," in *A Testament of Hope*, 19.

35. King, "Nonviolence and Racial Justice," in *A Testament of Hope*, 8–9.

36. King, "Suffering and Faith," in *A Testament of Hope*, 41.

37. Clayborne Carson et al., eds., *The Papers of Martin Luther King, Jr.* (Berkeley: University of California Press, 2005), 5:369.

38. John J. Ansbro, *Martin Luther King, Jr.: The Making of a Mind* (Maryknoll, NY: Orbis Books, 1982), 85.

39. King, "Loving Your Enemies," in his *Strength to Love* (New York: Harper & Row, 1963), 39.

40. Ansbro, *Martin Luther King, Jr.*, 86.

41. Bowne, *The Principles of Ethics*, 197–98.

42. King, "Where Do We Go from Here?," in *A Testament of Hope*, 246.

43. King, "A New Sense of Direction," *Worldview*, April 1972, 11.

44. Paul W. Taylor, *Respect for Nature: A Theory of Environmental Ethics* (Princeton: Princeton University Press, 1986), 14–16.

45. King, "The Ethical Demands for Integration," in *A Testament of Hope*, 120.

46. *The Papers*, "The Personalism of J.M.E. McTaggart Under Criticism," (1994), 2:73. This paper was presented to L. Harold DeWolf on December 4, 1951, in his class on Personalism.

47. Lewis Baldwin was among the first to point out that King began exhibiting a global or internationalist vision from the beginning of his civil rights ministry, and continued to unfold it throughout that ministry. See Baldwin, *To Make the Wounded Whole: The Cultural Legacy of Martin Luther King, Jr.* (Minneapolis: Fortress Press, 1992), Chapter 4, "Caught in an Inescapable Network: A Vision of World Community." Baldwin develops this theme even more fully in *Toward the Beloved Community: Martin Luther King, Jr. and South Africa* (Cleveland: The Pilgrim Press, 1995). In yet another master stroke, Baldwin, along with co-editor Paul R. Dekar, has recently published *"In An Inescapable Network of Mutuality": Martin Luther King, Jr. and the Globalization of an Ethical Ideal* (Eugene, OR: Cascade Books, 2013). It is also of interest to note that Thomas Mulhall has recently written a book manuscript that also focuses on the globalization theme in King. See

his, *A Lasting Prophetic Legacy: Martin Luther King, Jr., The World Council of Churches, and the Global Crusade Against Racism and War* (Eugene, OR: Cascade Books, 2014). I read Mulhall's manuscript and wrote an endorsement of his book.

48. King, *Where Do We Go*, 188.

49. King, *The Measure of a Man* (Philadelphia: Fortress Press 1988) [1959], 13–14.

50. See his discussion of the nature of person in Ibid. And although this seems to be the emphasis, it is also clear that he wishes to highlight the dignity and sacredness of the body (13–14).

51. Robert Bruce McLaren, *Christian Ethics: Foundations and Practice* (Englewood Cliffs, NJ: Prentice Hall, 1994), 109.

52. Justo González, *Mañana: Christian Theology from a Hispanic Perspective* (Nashville: Abingdon Press, 1990), 127.

53. Toni Morrison, *Beloved* (New York: Alfred A. Knopf, 1987), 88.

54. King, "What Is Man?," in *Strength to Love*, 89.

55. King, "Where Do We Go from Here?," in *A Testament of Hope*, 245.

56. W.E.B. DuBois, "Of Our Spiritual Strivings," in his *The Souls of Black Folk* (New York: Dodd, Mead & Company, 1961) [1903], 3.

57. King, *Where Do We Go*, 53.

58. Ibid.

59. George Brietman, ed., *Malcolm X Speaks* (New York: Pathfinder Press, 1989) [1965], 40.

60. King, "Where Do We Go from Here?," in *A Testament of Hope*, 245.

61. As I write these words I am remembering a provocative statement made by Alice Walker. The statement has haunted me for a long time (and still does!), for when I first read it, it resonated with me, and still does. At some point I know I must grapple with her statement and the theological and moral consequence of it. For now, I cite Walker's statement without further comment. "I've found, in my own writing, that a little hatred, keenly directed, is a useful thing. Once spread about, however, it becomes a web in which I would sit caught and paralyzed like the fly who stepped into the parlor. The artist must remember that some individual men, like Byron de la Beckwith [who murdered NAACP civil rights leader Medgar Evers] or Sheriff Jim Clark [whose men instigated the tragic 'Bloody Sunday' incident during the Selma, Alabama, voter registration campaign in 1965], should be hated, and that some corporations like Dow and General Motors should be hated too. Also the Chase Manhattan Bank and the Governor of Mississippi" [Alice Walker, "Duties of the Black Revolutionary Artist," in her *In Search of Our Mothers' Gardens: Womanist Prose* (New York: Harcourt Brace Jovanovich, 1983), 137]. Walker also reminds her readers that there are some people and organizations that should be loved.

62. Abraham J. Heschel, *The Prophets* (New York: Harper & Row, 1962), 16.

63. King, "The Ethical Demands for Integration," in *A Testament of Hope*, 120.

64. Jean Paul Sartre, *The Age of Reason* (New York: Bantam, 1968), 276.

65. Sartre, *Being and Nothingness: An Essay on Phenomenological Ontology,* trans. Hazel E. Barnes (New York: Philosophical Library, 1956), 47–70.

66. Kenneth Clark, ed., *King, Malcolm, Baldwin: Three Interviews* (Wesleyan University Press: 1985) [1963], 38.

67. King, *Stride*, 223.

68. *The Papers* (2000), 4:471.

69. James Baldwin, *Nobody Knows My Name* (New York: Dell, 1963), 126.

Chapter 15

1. This chapter is a thorough revision of the very first article I wrote on Martin Luther King, titled "Martin Luther King, Jr., Racism, the White Moderates and White Liberals." Two years after I submitted it, the article was accepted for publication (with minor revisions) by the *Journal of Negro History* in the late 1980s. I did not make the proposed revisions and returned the article to the editor, who kept a copy in the files. When Lewis V. Baldwin was researching his second of many books on King, he had occasion to go through the files of the *Journal* where he located and read my unpublished article (which I had completely forgotten about). Baldwin cited the article in *To Make the Wounded Whole: The Cultural Legacy of Martin Luther King, Jr.* (Minneapolis: Fortress Press, 1992), 155–56. Upon seeing this when I read the book, I decided that because of Baldwin's favorable review of my article, I might well have something to offer to King Studies. At that time, I made the decision to begin devoting much of my scholarly time and energy to working in this area.

2. Clayborne Carson et al., eds., *The Papers of Martin Luther King, Jr.* (Berkeley: University of California Press, 2007), 6:30n130.

3. Martin Luther King, Jr., "A Knock at Midnight," in his *Strength to Love* (New York: Harper & Row, 1963), 43.

4. Ibid., 44.

5. The Papers, 6:376.

6. Ibid., 6:29.

7. Ibid.

8. Ibid., 6:343.

9. See Ibid., 6:197, 252, 253, 289.

10. Ibid., 6:302.

11. Ibid., 6:232.

12. In *The Autobiography of Malcolm X*, Malcolm made clear what his attitude toward white liberals was. He felt that most could not be trusted. He criticized Northern white liberals, saying: "Snakes couldn't have turned on me faster than the liberal. Yes, I will pull off that liberal's halo that he spends such efforts cultivating! The North's liberals have been for so long pointing accusing fingers at the South and getting away with it that they have fits when they are exposed as the world's worst hypocrites." See *The Autobiography of Malcolm X*, as told to Alex Haley (New York: Ballantine Books, 1992) [1965], 296.

13. See Martin Luther King, Jr., *Where Do We Go from Here: Chaos or Community?* (Boston: Beacon Press, 1967), 110.

14. King, *Stride Toward Freedom* (New York: Harper & Row, 1958) 205.

15. Gunnar Myrdal, *An American Dilemma: The Negro Problem and Modern Democracy,* with the assistance of Richard Sterner and Arnold Rose (New York: Harper & Brothers Publishers, 1944), xlvii.

16. King, *Stride*, 20.

17. King, "A Testament of Hope," in *A Testament of Hope: The Essential Writings of Martin Luther King, Jr.*, ed. James M. Washington (New York: Harper & Row, Publishers, 1986), 322. This article was published posthumously.

18. King, *Where Do We Go*, 102–103.

19. King, *The Trumpet of Conscience* (New York: Harper & Row, Publishers, 1968), 12.

20. Ibid.

21. King, *Where Do We Go*, 79.

22. Ibid., 139.

23. Ibid., 173.

24. Ibid.

25. Ibid., 67.

26. King, "Letter from Birmingham Jail," in his *Why We Can't Wait* (New York: Harper & Row, 1964), 89.

27. Ibid., 93.

28. Ibid.

29. King, "A Testament of Hope," in *A Testament of Hope*, 315.

30. Quoted in Stephen B. Oates, *Let the Trumpet Sound: The Life of Martin Luther King, Jr.* (New York: Harper & Row, Publishers, 1982), 413.

31. King, "Meet the Press" television news interview, in *A Testament of Hope*, 385.

32. See George Breitman, ed., *Malcolm X Speaks* (New York: Pathfinder Press, 1965, 1989), 136.

33. King, "A Testament of Hope," in *A Testament of Hope*, 314.

34. King, "Showdown for Nonviolence," in *A Testament of Hope*, 71.

35. King, *Where Do We Go*, 20, 124.

36. King, *Stride*, 211.

37. King, *Where Do We Go*, 67.

38. Lerone Bennett, Jr., "The White Problem in America," in *White Racism: Its History, Pathology and Practice*, ed. Barry Schwartz and Robert Disch (New York: Dell, 1970), 251, 252.

39. King, *Where Do We Go*, 68.

40. Ibid.

41. Quoted in Ibid., 69.

42. Ibid., 70.

43. King, "A Testament of Hope," in *A Testament of Hope*, 320. King's relationship with Kennedy and Johnson was complex, to say the least. Blacks had suffered a great deal in the South before President Kennedy finally declared that racism is a moral problem, and proposed a comprehensive civil rights bill (that would be passed posthumously during the Johnson administration). For much too long, Kennedy and his brother, Attorney General Robert Kennedy, was more concerned with protecting the nation's image on the international stage than protecting civil rights workers during the sit-in movement, Freedom Rides, and during voter education-registration projects in the dangerous Mississippi Delta and other places in the Deep South. Johnson was the leading politician to push through Kennedy's Civil Rights Act in 1964, followed by the Voting Rights Act the next year. In addition, Johnson pushed through the Economic Opportunity Act of 1964 which opened the way to the War on Poverty. Initially thrilled by this promising idea, King would see by 1966 that Johnson's commitment to escalating the war in Vietnam meant the destruction of the War on Poverty. When his conscience no longer allowed him to be silent on Vietnam, King lost all favor with the Johnson administration. Nevertheless, this did not deter him from criticizing the Administration's war policy.

44. For discussions on this idea see Marable, *How Capitalism Underdeveloped Black America*, 1983; Leslie W. Dunbar, ed., *Minority Report* (New York: Pantheon, 1984); James D. Williams, ed., *The State of Black America: 1985* (New York: National Urban League, 1985); *Facts on Institutional Racism* (compiled by The Council on Interracial Books for Children, Inc., New York City, 1984).

45. King, *Where Do We Go*, 88.

46. King, *Why We Can't Wait*, 87.

47. "Billy Graham Urges Restraint in Sit-Ins," *New York Times*, April 18, 1963, 21.

48. King, *Where Do We Go*, 89.

49. Sociologists J. Milton Yinger and George Eaton Simpson discuss Merton's typology in their classic study, *Racial and Cultural Minorities: An Analysis of Prejudice and Discrimination,* Fourth Edition (New York: Harper & Row, Publishers, 1972) [1958, 1965], 658–63. Merton's typology first appeared in his essay, "Discrimination and the American Creed," in *Discrimination and National Welfare,* ed. Robert M. MacIver (New York: Harper & Row, 1949).

50. Quoted in Yinger and Simpson, *Racial and Cultural Minorities,* 658–59.

51. Yinger and Simpson, *Racial and Cultural Minorities,* 659.

52. Ibid.

53. Ibid.

54. Ibid.

55. *The Papers,* 6:302, 344.

56. Ibid., 6:168, 197, 252.

57. Ibid. (2005), 5:509.

58. Clayborne Carson, ed., *The Autobiography of Martin Luther King, Jr.* (New York: Warner Books, 1998), 173.

59. Gordon Allport, *The Nature of Prejudice,* 25th Anniversary Edition (Reading, MA: Addison-Wesley Publishing Company, 1982) [1954], 408.

60. Yinger and Simpson, *Racial and Cultural Minorities,* 660.

61. King, *Stride,* 169.

62. King, *Playboy* "Interview: Martin Luther King, Jr.," in *A Testament of Hope,* 344–345.

63. King, *Stride,* 209.

64. King, "Letter from Birmingham Jail," in *Why We Can't Wait,* 87.

65. Ibid., 88.

66. Ibid., 89.

67. Ibid.

68. King, *Where Do We Go,* 91.

69. Ibid., 88.

70. King, *Why We Can't Wait,* 134, 135.

71. King, *Where Do We Go,* 90.

72. Quoted in King, *Why We Can't Wait,* 147.

73. King, *Where Do We Go,* 94.

74. Ibid.

75. See "Conversation with Martin Luther King, Jr.," *Conservative Judaism,* Vol. 22, No. 3 (Spring 1968), 8.

76. Ibid. Unfortunately, King here used "separation" and "segregation" interchangeably. Separation implies that which one (or a group) decides on its own to do, whereas segregation as practiced in the United States historically had the force of civil law behind it. In this sense, blacks have never willfully segregated from whites, nor have they had the power to do so if they wanted to. Nevertheless, King's view that there may be need for temporary separation of the races in some situations parallels Malcolm X's view that whites who are sincere about helping in the struggle could make their greatest contribution not by joining black organizations, but by developing their own organizations to deal with racism in their own communities, churches, and other institutions. See *The Autobiography of Malcolm X,* 411–412.

77. See Baldwin in *Between Cross and Crescent,* 308–309.

78. King, *The Trumpet of Conscience* (New York: Harper & Row, 1968), 8; also *Where Do We Go,* 69.

79. King, *Where Do We Go,* 83.

80. Ibid., 95, 11.

81. Ibid., 99.

82. King, *Why We Can't Wait,* 90.

83. Ibid., 89.

84. King, *Where Do We Go,* 91.

85. See Thomas F. Pettigrew, *Racially Separate or Together?* (New York: McGraw-Hill Book Company, 1971), 139–140, 205–206, 208n-209n.

86. See his article, "The Un-Christian Christian," *Ebony,* August 1965, 77–80.

87. King, *Playboy* "Interview," in *A Testament of Hope,* 372.

88. Ibid., 375.

89. See "Conversation with Martin Luther King," 16, 17.

90. Malcolm X, *The Autobiography of Malcolm X,* 298.

91. King, "A Testament of Hope," in *A Testament of Hope,* 314–315. King realized, much like Malcolm X, that in a real sense there was no way that the United States could ever fully repay blacks for the long years of injustice and deprivation. He would not have objected to Malcolm's query: "Indeed, how *can* white society atone for enslaving, for raping, for unmanning, for otherwise brutalizing *millions* of human beings, for centuries? What atonement would the God of Justice demand for the robbery of the black people's labor, their lives, their true identities, their culture, their history—and even their human dignity? A desegregated cup of coffee, a theater, public toilets—the whole range of hypocritical 'integration'—these are not atonement" (*The Autobiography of Malcolm X,* 405). However, King did believe that America should make an effort toward reparations.

92. King, "Un-Christian Christians," 77.

93. King, *Where Do We Go,* 100.

94. Reinhold Niebuhr, "Can the Church Give 'a Moral Lead'?," in *Essays in Applied Christianity,* ed. D.B. Robertson (New York: Meridian Books, 1965), 81.

95. King, *Where Do We Go,* 53.

96. King, "Where Do We Go from Here?," in *A Testament of Hope,* 246.

97. King, "Showdown for Nonviolence," in *A Testament of Hope,* 71.

Bibliography

Abernathy, Ralph D. *And the Walls Came Tumbling Down: An Autobiography*. New York: Harper & Row, 1989.

Albert, Peter J., and Ronald Hoffman, eds. *We Shall Overcome: Martin Luther King, Jr. and the Black Freedom Struggle*. New York: DaCapo Press, 1993.

Allport, Gordon. *The Nature of Prejudice*. 25th Anniversary Edition. Reading, MA: Addison-Wesley, 1982 [1954].

Ansbro, John J. *Martin Luther King, Jr.: The Making of a Mind*. Maryknoll, NY: Orbis, 1982.

Appiah, Kwame Anthony, and Henry Louis Gates. *Africana: Civil Rights*. Philadelphia: Running Press, 2004.

Baker-Fletcher, Garth. *Somebodyness: Martin Luther King, Jr. and the Theory of Dignity*. Minneapolis: Fortress Press, 1993.

Baldwin, James. *The Fire Next Time*. New York: Dial Press. 1963.

_____. *Nobody Knows My Name*. New York: Dell, 1961.

_____. *The Price of the Ticket: Collected Nonfiction 1948–1985*. New York: St. Martin's/Marek, 1985.

Baldwin, Lewis V., and Paul R. Dekar, eds. *"In an Inescapable Network of Mutuality": Martin Luther King, Jr. and the Globalization of an Ethical Ideal*. Eugene, OR: Cascade, 2013.

_____ and _____. *Never to Leave Us Alone: The Prayer Life of Martin Luther King, Jr*. Minneapolis: Fortress Press, 2010.

_____ and _____. *The Voice of Conscience: The Church in the Mind of Martin Luther King, Jr*. New York: Oxford University Press, 2010.

Baldwin, Lewis V., and Amiri YaSin Al-Hadid. *Between Cross and Crescent: Christian and Muslim Perspectives on Malcolm and Martin*. Gainesville: University Press of Florida, 2000.

_____ and _____. *There Is a Balm in Gilead: The Cultural Roots of Martin Luther King, Jr*. Minneapolis: Fortress Press, 1991.

_____ and _____. *To Make the Wounded Whole: The Cultural Legacy of Martin Luther King, Jr*. Minneapolis: Fortress Press, 1992.

_____ and _____. *Toward the Beloved Community: Martin Luther King, Jr. and South Africa*. Cleveland: The Pilgrim Press, 1995.

Barker, Ernest, ed. *The Politics of Aristotle*. New York: Oxford University Press, 1946.

Bennett, Lerone. *Confrontation: Black and White*. Chicago: Johnson, 1965.

Bethge, Eberhard. *Dietrich Bonhoeffer: A Biography*. Revised Edition. Ed. Victoria J. Barnett. Minneapolis: Fortress Press, 2000.

Billingsley, Andrew. *Climbing Jacob's Ladder: The Enduring Legacy of African-American Families*. New York: Simon & Schuster, 1992.

_____. *Mighty Like a River: The Black Church and Social Reform*. New York: Oxford University Press, 1999.

Birch, C. *Regaining Compassion for Humanity and Nature*. St. Louis: Chalice Press, 1993.

Bonhoeffer, Dietrich. *Ethics*. Ed. Clifford J. Green, in *Dietrich Bonhoeffer Works*, Vol. 6. Minneapolis: Fortress Press, 2005.

Bowen, John Wesley Edward. "Apology for Higher Education of the Negro." *Methodist Review*. 1897.

_____. *An Appeal for Negro Bishops, But No Separation*. New York: Eaton & Mains, 1912.

Bowne, Borden P. *The Immanence of God*. Boston: Houghton Mifflin, 1905.

_____. *Metaphysics*. Rev. ed. New York: Harper & Brothers, 1898.

_____. *Personalism*. Boston: Houghton Mifflin, 1908.

_____. *The Philosophy of Herbert Spencer*. New York: Phillips & Hunt, 1874.

_____. *Philosophy of Theism*. New York: Harper & Brothers, 1887.

_____. *Principles of Ethics*. New York: Harper & Brothers, 1892.

_____. *Studies in Theism*. New York: Phillips & Hunt, 1879.

_____. *Theory of Thought and Knowledge*. New York: Harper & Brothers, 1897.

Branch, Taylor. *At Canaan's Edge: America in the King Years 1965–68*. New York: Simon & Schuster, 2006.

_____. *Parting the Waters: America in the King Years 1954–63*. New York: Simon & Schuster, 1988.

_____. *Pillar of Fire: America in the King Years 1963–65*. New York: Simon & Schuster, 1998.

Breitman, George, ed. *Malcolm X Speaks*. New York: Pathfinder Press, 1989 [1965].

Brightman, Edgar S. *The Finding of God*. New York: The Abingdon Press, 1931.

_____. *An Introduction to Philosophy*. Third Edition, Rev. by Robert N. Beck. New York: Holt Rinehart Winston, 1964.

_____. *Moral Laws*. Nashville: Abingdon Press, 1933.

_____. *Nature and Values*. New York: Abingdon Press, 1945.

_____. *Person and Reality: An Introduction to Metaphysics*. Ed. Peter A. Bertocci, in collaboration with Jannette Elthina Newhall and Robert Sheffield Brightman. New York: The Round Table Press Company, 1958.

_____. *Personality and Religion*. New York: Abingdon Press, 1934.

_____. *A Philodophy of Ideals*. New York: Henry Holt and Company, 1928.

_____. *A Philosophy of Religion*. New York: Prentice-Hall, 1940.

_____. "Religion as Truth." In *Contemporary American Theology: Theological Autobiographies*. Ed. Vergilius Ferm. New York: Round Table Press, 1932. 1:53–81.

_____. *Religious Values*. New York: Abingdon Press, 1925.

_____. *The Spiritual Life*. New York: Abingdon-Cokesbury Press, 1942.

Brinkley, Douglas. *Rosa Parks*. New York: Viking Penguin, 2000.

Brown, Charles C. *Niebuhr and His Age: Reinhold Niebuhr's Prophetic Role in the Twentieth Century*. Philadelphia: Trinity Press International, 1972.

Brown, Joanne Carlson, and Rebecca Parker. "For God So Loved the World." In *Christianity, Patriarchy, and Abuse: A Feminist Critique*. Ed. Carole R. Bohn and Joanne Carlson Brown. Cleveland: The Pilgrim Press, 1989. 1–30.

Buckham, John Wright. *Christianity and Personality*. New York: Round Table Press, 1936.

_____. *Personality and the Christian Ideal*. Boston: The Pilgrim Press, 1909.

Burks, Mary Fair. "Trailblazers: Women in the Montgomery Bus Boycott." In *Women in the Civil Rights Movement: Trailblazers and Torchbearers 1941–1965*. Eds. Vicki L. Crawford, Jacqueline Anne Rouse, and Barbara Woods. Bloomington: Indiana University Press, 1993. 71–83.

Burns, Stewart. *To the Mountaintop: Martin Luther King, Jr.'s Sacred Mission to Save America 1955–1968*. New York: HarperSanFrancisco, 2004.

Burrow, Rufus, Jr. "Borden Parker Bowne's Doctrine of God." *Encounter*. Vol. 53, No. 4, Autumn 1992. 381–400.

_____. *God and Human Dignity: The Personalism, Theology, and Ethics of Martin Luther King, Jr.* Notre Dame: University of Notre Dame Press, 2006.

_____. "John Wesley Edward Bowen: First Afrikan American Personalist." *Encounter*. Vol. 56, No. 3, Summer 1995. 241–260.

_____. "Moral Laws in Borden P. Bowne's *Principles of Ethics*." *The Personalist Forum*. Vol. VI, No. 2, Fall 1990.

_____. *Personalism: A Critical Introduction*. St. Louis: Chalice Press, 1999.

Burrow, Rufus, Jr., and Jimmy Kirby. "Conceptions of God in the Thinking of Martin Luther King, Jr. and Edgar S. Brightman." *Encounter*, Vol. 60, No. 3, Summer 1999.

Cagin, Seth, and Philip Dray. *We Are Not Afraid: The Story of Goodman, Schwerner, and Chaney, and the Civil Rights Campaign for Mississippi*. New York: Nation, 2006 [1989].

Carson, Clayborne. "King Scholarship and Iconoclastic Myths." *Reviews in American History*. Vol. 16, No. 1, March 1988.

_____. *Martin's Dream: My Journey and the Legacy of Martin Luther King, Jr.: A Memoir*. New York: Palgrave Macmillan, 2013.

Carson, Clayborne, et al., eds. *The Papers of Martin Luther King, Jr.* 6 Volumes. Berkeley: University of California Press, 1992, 1994, 1997, 2000, 2005, 2007.

Carson, Clayborne, ed. *The Autobiography of Martin Luther King, Jr.* New York: Warner, 1998.

Carson, Clayborne, and Peter Holloran, eds., *A Knock at Midnight*. New York: Warner, 1998.

_____ and _____. "Martin Luther King, Jr.: The Crozer Years." *The Journal of Blacks in Higher Education*. Vol. 16, Summer 1997. 123–28.

_____ and _____. "Martin Luther King, Jr.: The Morehouse Years." *The Journal of Blacks in Higher Education*. Vol. 15, Spring. 121–25.

_____ and _____. "Sit-Ins." In Clayborne Carson et al. *The Martin Luther King, Jr. Encyclopedia*. Westport, CT: Greenwood Press, 2008. 307–308.

Carson, Clayborne, and Kris Shepherd, eds. *A Call to Conscience*. New York: Warner, 2001.

Childs, Marquis. "Triumphal March Silences Scoffers." *Washington Post*. August 30, 1963. A-18.

Clark, Kenneth. *King, Malcolm, Baldwin: Three Interviews*. Boston: Beacon Press, 1963.

Cole, Johnnetta Betsch, and Beverly Guy-Sheftall. *Gender Talk: The Struggle for Women's Equality in African American Communities*. New York: One World/Ballantine, 2003.

Commager, Henry Steele, ed. *Documents of American History*. Seventh Edition. New York: Appleton-Century-Crofts, Division of Meredith, 1963.

Cone, James H. *Martin & Malcolm & America: A Dream or a Nightmare*. Maryknoll, NY: Orbis, 1991.

Cook, E., and L. Racine. "The Children's Crusade and the Role of Youth in the African American Freedom Struggle." *OAH Magazine of History*, Vol. 19, No. 1, 2005. 31–36.

Copeland, M. Shawn. "Wading Through Many Sorrows: Toward a Theology of Suffering in Womanist Perspective." In *A Troubling in My Soul: Womanist Perspectives on Evil & Suffering*. Ed. Emilie M. Townes. Maryknoll, NY: Orbis, 1993. 109–29.

Cornford, Francis M. *The Republic of Plato*. New York: Oxford University Press, 1945.

Cotton, Dorothy F. *If Your Back's Not Bent: The Role of the Citizenship Education Program in the Civil Rights Movement*. New York: Atria, 2012.

Day, Dorothy. *The Long Loneliness: The Autobiography of the Legendary Catholic Social Activist*. New York: HarperSanFrancisco, 1952.

DeWolf, L. Harold. "Martin Luther King, Jr., as Theologian." *Journal of the Interdenominational Theological Center*, Vol. 4, Spring 1977. 1–11.

_____. *A Theology of the Living Church*. New York: Harper & Brothers, 1960 [1953].

Dorrien, Gary. *The Making of American Liberal Theology: Idealism, Realism, and Modernity 1900–1950*. Louisville: Westminster John Knox Press, 2003. 305–55.

_____. *Social Ethics in the Making: Interpreting an American Tradition*. Malden: MA: Wiley-Blackwell, 2009.

Douglass, Frederick. "The Constitution of the United States: Is It Pro-Slavery or Anti- Slavery?" In *The Life and Writings of Frederick Douglass*. Ed. Philip S. Foner. New York: International Publishers, 1975. 2:467–80.

D'Souza, Dinesh. *The End of Racism: Principles for a Multiracial Society*. New York: The Free Press, 1995.

DuBois, W.E.B. *The Autobiography of W.E.B. DuBois: A Soliloquy on Viewing My Life from the Last Decade of Its First Century*. New York: International Publishers, 1968.

_____. "Sex and Racism." in *W.E.B. DuBois: A Reader*. Ed. David Levering Lewis. New York: Henry Holt and Company, 1995. 313–14.

_____. *The Souls of Black Folk*. New York: The New American Library, 1969 [1903].

Dunbar, Leslie W. ed. *Minority Report*. New York: Pantheon, 1984.

Dyson, Michael Eric. *I May Not Get There With You: The True Martin Luther King, Jr.* New York: The Free Press, 2000.

Elliot, Jeffrey M., ed. *Conversations with Maya Angelou*. Jackson: University Press of Mississippi, 1989.

Fairclough, Adam. Foreword to *The Domestication of Martin Luther King, Jr.: Clarence B. Jones Right-Wing Conservatism, and the Manipulation of the King Legacy*. Eds. Lewis V. Baldwin and Rufus Burrow, Jr. Eugene, OR: Cascade, 2013.

_____. *To Redeem the Soul of America: The Southern Christian Leadership Conference and Martin Luther King, Jr.* Athens: The University of Georgia Press, 2001 [1987].

Farris, Christine King. *Through It All: Reflections on My Life, My Family, and My Faith*. New York: Atria Paperback, 2009.

_____. "The Young Martin: From Childhood through College." *Ebony*. Vol. xli, No. 3, January 1986. 56–58.

Feagin, Joe R. *Racist America: Roots, Current Realities, and Future Reparations*. New York: Routledge, 2000.

_____. *Systemic Racism: A Theory of Oppression*. New York: Routledge, 2006.

Flewelling, Ralph Tyler. *Personalism and the Problems of Philosophy*. New York: The Methodist Book Concern, 1915.

_____. *Philosophy and the War*. New York: Abingdon Press, 1918.

Foner, Philip S., ed. *Frederick Douglass on Women's Rights*. New York: Da Capo Press, 1992.

Friedly, Michael, and David Gallen. *Martin Luther King, Jr.: The FBI File*. New York: Carroll & Graf, 1993.

Gandhi, M.K. *Non-Violent Resistance*. New York: Schocken, 1961.

Garrow, David J. *Bearing the Cross: Martin Luther King, Jr. and the Southern Christian Christian Leadership Conference*. New York: William Morrow, 1986.

_____. *The FBI and Martin Luther King, Jr.: From "Solo" to Memphis*. New York: W.W. Norton, 1981.

_____. "The Intellectual Development of Martin Luther King, Jr.: Influences and Commentaries." In *Martin Luther King, Jr.: Civil Rights Leader, Theologian, Orator*. Ed. David J. Garrow. New York: Carlson, 1989.

Garrow, David J., ed. *Martin Luther King, Jr. and the Civil Rights Movement*. New York: Carlson, 1989.

Gibbs, Jewelle Taylor, ed. *Young, Black, and Male in America: An Endangered Species*. New York: Auburn House, 1988.

Giddings, Paula. *When and Where I Enter: The Impact of Black Women on Race and Sex in America*. New York: William Morrow, 1984.

Gilbert, Jack. "King Urges Youth Join in New Order." King Library and Archives, December 1959.

Gilson, Etienne. *The Spirit of Medieval Philosophy*. New York: Charles Scribner's Sons, 1940.

Golden, Marita, and Susan Richards Schreve, eds. *Skin Deep: Black and White Women Write About Race*. New York: Doubleday, 1995.

Goldman, Peter. *The Death and Life of Malcolm X*. 2nd Edition. Urbana: University of Illinois Press, 1979 [1973].

González, Justo. *Mañana: Christian Theology from a Hispanic Perspective*. Nashville: Abingdon Press, 1990.

Grant, Jacquelyn. "The Sin of Servanthood." In *A Troubling in My Soul: Womanist Perspectives on Evil & Suffering*. Ed. Emilie M. Townes. Maryknoll, NY: Orbis, 1993. 199–218.

Hacker, Andrew. *Two Nations: Black and White, Separate, Hostile, Unequal*. New York: Ballantine, 1992.

Halberstam, David. *The Children*. New York: Random House, 1998.

Hamilton, E., and H. Cairns, eds. *Plato: The Collected Dialogues Including the Letters*. Princeton: Princeton University Press, 1971.

Hampton, Henry, and Steve Fayer (with Sarah Flynn). *Voices of Freedom: An Oral History of the Civil Rights Movement from the 1950s through the 1980s*. New York: Bantam, 1990.

Hansen, Drew. *The Dream: Martin Luther King, Jr. and the Speech that Inspired a Nation*. New York: HarperCollins, 2003.

Hedgeman, Anna. *The Trumpet Sounds: A Memoir of Negro Leadership*. New York: Holt, Rinehart and Winston, 1964.

Height, Dorothy. "We Wanted the Voice of a Woman to Be Heard" (Black Women and the 1963 March on Washington). In *Sisters in the Struggle: African American Women in the Civil Rights-Black Power Movement*. Eds. Bettye Collier-Thomas and V. P. Franklin. New York: New York University Press, 2001. Ch. 6.

Heschel, Abraham J. *Man's Quest for God: Studies in Prayer and Symbolism*. New York: Charles Scribner's Sons, 1954.

_____. "No Religion Is an Island." In *Moral Grandeur and Spiritual Audacity*. Ed. Susannah Heschel. New York: Farrar, Straus, Giroux, 1996. 235–50.

_____. *The Prophets*. New York: Harper & Row, 1962.

_____. "The Religious Basis of Equality of Opportunity—The Segregation of God." In *Race: Challenge to Religion*. Ed. Mathew Ahmann. Chicago: Henry Regenery Company, 1963. 55–71.

Hine, Darlene Clark, and Kathleen Thompson. *A Shining Thread of Hope: The History of Black Women in America*. New York: Broadway, 1998.

Hine, Robert V. *Josiah Royce: From Grass Valley to Harvard*. Norman: University of Oklahoma Press, 1992.

Hoft, Jim. "Bummer...Martin Luther King, Jr. Stole 'I Have a Dream' Speech." http://www.thegatewaypundit.com/2008/01/bummer-martin-luther-king-jr-stole-i-have-a-dream-speech-from-black-republican/.

Hume, David. "Of National Characters." In *Philosophical Historian*. Eds. David Fate Norton and Richard H. Popkin. Indianapolis: Bobbs-Merrill Company, 1965.

Jones, Clarence B., and Stuart Connelly. *Behind the Dream: The Making of the Speech that Transformed a Nation*. New York: Palgrave Macmillan, 2011.

Jones, Lawrence N. "Black Christians Antebellum America: In Quest of the Beloved Community." *The Journal of Religious Thought*, Vol. 38, No. 1, Spring-Summer 1981. 12–19.

Kane, Brian. "The Influence of Boston Personalism on the Thought of Martin Luther King, Jr." MTS thesis, Boston University, 1985.

Kant, Immanuel. *Critique of Practical Reason*. Trans. Lewis White Beck. Indianapolis: Bobbs-Merrill Company, 1956 [1788].

_____. *Foundations of the Metaphysics of Morals*. Trans. by Lewis White Beck. Indianapolis: Bobbs-Merrill, 1959 [1785].

_____. *Observations on the Feeling of the Beautiful and Sublime*. Trans. John T. Goldthwaith. Berkeley: University of California Press, 1973.

Kennedy, Ted. *True Compass: A Memoir*. New York: Twelve/Hachette Book Group, 2009.

Kierkegaard, Sören. *Works of Love: Some Christian Reflections in the Form of Discourses*. Trans. Howard and Edna Hong. New York: Harper Torchbook, 1964.

King, Coretta Scott. *My Life with Martin Luther King, Jr.* New York: Holt Rinehart and Winston, 1993 [1969].

_____. "Thoughts and Reflections." In *We Shall Overcome: Martin Luther King, Jr. and the Black Freedom Struggle*. Eds. Peter J. Albert and Ronald Hoffman. New York: Dacapo Press, 1993.

King, Martin Luther, Jr. *"All Labor Has Dignity."* Ed. Michael K. Honey. Boston: Beacon Press, 2011.

_____. "A Challenge to the Churches and Synagogues," in

Race: Challenge to Religion. Ed. Mathew Ahmann. Chicago: Henry Regenery Company, 1963. 155–73.

_____. "A Comparison of the Conceptions of God in the Thinking of Henry Nelson Wieman and Paul Tillich." Ph.D. diss., Boston University, 1955.

_____. "The Future of Integration." Speech given at Manchester College (Indiana), February 1, 1968.

_____. *"In a Single Garment of Destiny": A Global Vision of Justice.* Ed. Lewis V. Baldwin. Boston: Beacon Press, 2012.

_____. *The Measure of a Man.* Philadelphia: Fortress Press, 1988 [1959].

_____. "No Vengeance." Unpublished sermon. King Library and Archives, February 13, 1958.

_____. "Second Anniversary of Protest: President's Address." Montgomery, Alabama. December 5, 1957. King Library and Archives.

_____. *Strength to Love.* New York: Harper & Row, 1963.

_____. *Stride Toward Freedom.* New York: Harper & Row, 1958.

_____. *"Thou, Dear God": Prayers that Open Hearts and Spirits.* Ed. Lewis V. Baldwin. Boston: Beacon Press, 2012.

_____. *The Trumpet of Conscience.* New York: Harper & Row, 1968.

_____. "The Un-Christian Christian." *Ebony,* August 1965. 77–80.

_____. "Unfulfilled Dreams." In *A Knock at Midnight.* Eds. Clayborne Carson and Peter Holloran. New York: Warner, 1998.

_____. *Where Do We Go from Here: Chaos or Community?* Boston: Beacon Press, 1967.

_____. "Who Are We?" King Library and Archives.

_____. *Why We Can't Wait.* New York: Harper & Row, 1964.

King, Martin Luther, Sr., with Clayton Riley. *Daddy King: An Autobiography.* New York: William Morrow, 1980.

Kirk-Duggan, Cheryl A. "Drum Major for Justice or Dilettante of Dishonesty: Martin Luther King, Jr., Moral Capital and Hypocrisy of Embodied Messianic Myths." In *The Domestication of Martin Luther King, Jr.: Clarence B. Jones, Right-Wing Conservatism, and the Manipulation of the King Legacy.* Eds. Lewis V. Baldwin and Rufus Burrow, Jr. Eugene, OR: Cascade, 2013. Ch. 5.

_____. *Refiner's Fire: A Religious Engagement with Violence.* Minneapolis: Fortress Press, 2001.

Kleingeld, Pauline. "Kant's Second Thoughts on Race." *The Philosophical Quarterly.* Vol. 57, No. 229, October 2007. 573–92.

Knudson, Albert C. *The Philosophy of Personalism.* New York: Abingdon Press, 1927.

_____. *The Principles of Christian Ethics.* New York: Abingdon Press, 1943.

Kohak, Erazim. "Selves, People, Persons: An Essay in American Personalism." In *Selves, People, and Persons: What Does It Mean to Be a Self?* Ed. Leroy S. Rouner. Notre Dame: University of Notre Dame Press, 1992. 17–35.

Lerner, Gerder, ed. *Black Women in White America: A Documentary History.* New York: Vintage Press, 1973.

Levine, Ellen. *Freedom's Children: Young Civil Rights Activists Tell Their Own Stories.* New York: G. P. Putnam's, 1993.

Lewis, David L. *King: A Critical Biography.* New York: Praeger Publishers, 1970.

_____. *W.E.B. DuBois: Biography of Race 1868–1919.* New York: Henry Holt, 1993.

Lincoln, C. Eric. *Race, Religion, and the Continuing American Dilemma.* Rev. ed. New York: Hill and Wang, 1999.

Ling, Peter J. *Martin Luther King, Jr.* London: Routledge, 2002.

Long, Michael G. *Against Us, But for Us: Martin Luther King, Jr. and the State.* Macon: Mercer University Press, 2002.

_____. *Martin Luther King, Jr., Homosexuality, and the Early Gay Rights Movement.* Afterword by Archbishop Desmond Tutu. New York: Palgrave Macmillan, 2012.

Lotze, Rudolph Hermann. *Microcosmus: An Essay Concerning Man and His Relation to the World.* Trans. Elizabeth Hamilton and E. E. Constance Jones, in Two Volumes. Edinburgh: T&T Clark, 1885 [originally published in three volumes 1856–1864].

Marable, Manning. *Black Liberation in Conservative America.* Boston: South End Press, 1997.

_____. *How Capitalism Underdeveloped Black America.* Boston: South End Press, 1983.

Marsh, Charles. *God's Long Summer: Stories of Faith and Civil Rights.* Princeton: Princeton University Press, 1997.

Martínez, Elizabeth, ed. *Letters from Mississippi: Reports from Civil Rights Volunteers & Poetry of the 1964 Freedom Summer.* Brookline, MA: Zephyr Press, 2007.

Mays, Benjamin E. *The Negro's God as Reflected in His Literature.* New York: Atheneum, 1969.

_____. *Seeking to be Christian in Race Relations.* Rev. ed. New York: Friendship Press, 1952 [1946].

_____, and Joseph William Nicholson. *The Negro's Church.* Salem, NH: Ayer Company, 1988 [1933].

Mbiti, John S. *African Religions and Philosophy.* Second Edition. Portsmouth, NH: Heinemann, 1989.

McConnell, Francis J. *Borden Parker Bowne.* New York: Abingdon Press, 1929.

_____. "Bowne and Personalism." In *Personalism in Theology: A Symposium in Honor of Albert C. Knudson.* Ed. Edgar S. Brightman. Boston: Boston University Press, 1943. Ch. II.

_____. *Personal Christianity.* New York: Fleming H. Revell Company, 1914.

McLaren, Robert Bruce. *Christian Ethics: Foundations and Practice.* Englewood Cliffs, NJ: Prentice Hall, 1994.

McWhorter, Diane. *Carry Me Home: Birmingham, Alabama the Climactic Battle of the Civil Rights Revolution.* New York: Simon & Schuster, 2001.

Miller, Keith D. *Voice of Deliverance: The Language of Martin Luther King, Jr. and Its Sources.* New York: The Free Press, 1992.

Morris, Aldon D. *The Origins of the Civil Rights Movement: Black Communities Organizing for Change.* New York: The Free Press, 1984.

Morrison, Toni. *Beloved.* New York: Alfred A. Knopf, 1987.

Muelder, Walter G. "Communitarian Christian Ethics: A Personal Statement and a Response." In *Toward a Discipline of Social Ethics.* Ed. Paul Deats, Jr. Boston: Boston University Press, 1972. 295–320.

_____. *The Ethical Edge of Christian Theology: Forty Years of Communitarian Personalism.* Lewiston, NY: Mellen Press, 1983.

_____. "Martin Luther King, Jr.'s Ethics of Nonviolent Action." Unpublished paper. King Center Archives and Library.

_____. *Moral Law in Christian Social Ethics.* Richmond: John Knox Press, 1966.

Mulhall, Thomas. *A Lasting Prophetic Legacy: Martin Luther King, Jr., The World Council of Churches, and the Global Crusade Against Racism and War.* Eugene: OR: Cascade, 2014.

Murray, Pauli. *Song in a Weary Throat.* New York: Harper & Row, 1987.

Nash, Diane. "Inside the Sit-Ins and Freedom Rides: Testimony of a Southern Student." In *The New Negro.* Ed. Mathew H. Ahmann. New York: Biblo and Tannen, 1961. 43–60.

Niebuhr, Reinhold. *An Interpretation of Christian Ethics.* New York: Harper & Brothers, 1935.

_____. *Moral Man and Immoral Society.* New York: Scribner's, 1932.

Nygren, Anders. *Agape and Eros.* Single volume edition. Trans. Philip S. Watson. Philadelphia: The Westminster Press, 1953.

Oates, Stephen B. *Let the Trumpet Sound: The Life of Martin Luther King, Jr.* New York: Harper & Row, 1982.

Olson, Lynne. *Freedom's Daughters: The Unsung Heroines of the Civil Rights Movement from 1830 to 1970.* New York: Scribner, 2001.

Pappas, Theodore. *Plagiarism and the Culture War: The Writings of Martin Luther King, Jr. and Other Prominent Americans.* Revised and Expanded Edition. Tampa: FL: Hallberg, 1998.

Paris, Peter J. *Black Religious Leaders: Conflict in Unity.* Rev. Louisville: Westminster John Knox, 1991 [1978].

Parker, Theodore. "Of Justice and the Conscience." In *The Collected Works of Theodore Parker.* Ed. Frances Power Cobbe. London: Trübner and Company, 1879. 2:37–57.

_____. "The State of the Nation." in *The Collected Works of Theodore Parker.* Ed. Frances Power Cobbe. London: Trübner and Company, 1879. 4:235–65.

Parks, Rosa, with Jim Haskins. *Rosa Parks: My Story.* New York: Dial, 1992.

Pettigrew, Thomas. *Racially Separate or Together?* New York: McGraw-Hill, 1971.

Pobee, John S. *Toward an African Theology.* Nashville: Abingdon, 1979.

Powers, Georgia Davis. *I Shared the Dream: The Pride, Passion and Politics of the First Black Woman Senator from Kentucky.* Far Hills, NJ: New Horizon Press, 1995.

Powledge, Fred. *Free at Last? The Civil Rights Movement and the People Who Made It.* New York: HarperPerennial, 1991.

Ramsey, Paul. *Basic Christian Ethics.* New York: Charles Scribner's Sons, 1952.

Ransby, Barbara. *Ella Baker and the Black Freedom Movement: A Radical Democratic Vision.* Chapel Hill: University of North Carolina Press, 2003.

Rauschenbusch, Walter. *Christianity and the Social Crisis.* New York: Macmillan, 1907.

_____. *Christianizing the Social Order.* New York: Macmillan, 1926 [1912].

_____. *A Theology for the Social Gospel.* New York: Macmillan, 1917.

Rice, Gwendolyn. "Young Black Men, the Church, and Our Future." *The Chicago Theological Seminary Register,* Vol. LXXVIII, No. 2, Spring 1988.

Roberts, Gene, and Hank Klibanoff. *The Race Beat: The Press, the Civil Rights Struggle, and the Awakening of a Nation.* New York: Alfred A. Knopf, 2007.

Roberts, J. DeOtis. *A Black Political Theology.* Philadelphia: Westminster Press, 1974.

_____. *Bonhoeffer and King: Speaking Truth to Power.* Louisville: Westminster John Knox, 2005.

Royce, Josiah. *The Problem of Christianity.* One Volume Edition. Washington, D.C.: The Catholic University of America Press, 2001. Originally published by Macmillan, 1913, two volumes.

_____. *Race Questions, Provincialism, and Other American Problems.* New York: Macmillan, 1908.

_____. *The World and the Individual: Nature, Man, and the Moral Order.* Second Series. New York: Macmillan, 1908.

Russell, Bertrand. *A History of Western Philosophy.* New York: Simon & Schuster, 1945.

Sanders, Leo, Jr. "Boston University Personalism and Southern Baptist Theology." *Foundations.* Vol. 20, April–June, 1977.

Sartre, Jean Paul. *Being and Nothingness: An Essay on Phenomenological Ontology.* Trans. Hazel E. Barnes. New York: Philosophical Library, 1956. 47–70.

_____. *Existentialism and Human Emotions.* New York: Philosophical Library, 1957.

Schilling, S. Paul. "Albert Cornelius Knudson: Person and Theologian." In *The Boston Personalist Tradition in Philosophy, Social Ethics, and Theology.* Eds. Paul Deats, Jr., and Carol Robb. Macon: Mercer University Press, 1986. 81–102.

Schwartz, Barry, and Robert Disch. *White Racism: Its History, Pathology and Practice.* New York: Dell, 1970.

Sernett, Milton, ed. *Afro-American Religious History: A Documentary Witness.* Durham: Duke University Press, 1985.

Simpson, George, and J. Milton Yinger. *Racial and Cultural Minorities: An Analysis of Prejudice and Discrimination.* Fourth Edition. New York: Harper & Row, 1972 [1958, 1965].

Smith, Ervin. *The Ethics of Martin Luther King, Jr.* New York: Mellen Press, 1981.

Smith, Kenneth, and Ira Zepp, Jr. *Search for the Beloved Community: The Thinking of Martin Luther King, Jr.* Valley Forge: Judson Press, 1974.

Sniderman, Paul M., and Thomas Piazza. *The Scar of Race.* Cambridge: Harvard University Press, 1993.

Standley, Fred, and Louis Pratt, eds. *Conversations with James Baldwin.* Jackson: University Press of Mississippi, 1989.

Steele, Shelby. *The Content of Our Character: A New Vision of Race in America.* New York: Harper Perennial, 1990.

Stern, Carl. "A Conversation with Dr. Abraham Joshua Heschel." National Broadcasting Company, prepared under the auspices of The Jewish Theological Seminary of America, 1973.

Taylor, Paul W. *Respect for Nature: A Theory of Environmental Ethics.* Princeton: Princeton University Press, 1986.

Thelen, David, ed. "Becoming Martin Luther King, Jr.— Plagiarism and Originality: A Round Table." *The Journal of American History,* Vol. 78, No. 1, June 1991. 11–123.

Thielicke, Helmut. *Theological Ethics: Foundations.* Ed. W.H. Lazareth. Philadelphia: Fortress Press, 1966. Vol. 1.

Tindall, George Brown, and David E. Shi. *America: A Narrative History.* 4th Edition. New York: W. W. Norton, 1996.

Tocqueville, Alexis de. *Democracy in America.* New York: Vintage, 1945. Vol. 1.

Tsanoff, Radoslav A. *The Great Philosophers.* 2nd Edition. New York: Harper & Row, 1964 [1953].

_____. *The Moral Ideals of Our Civilization.* New York: E. P. Dutton, 1947.

Tutu, Desmond. *God Has a Dream: A Vision of Hope for Our Time.* New York: Doubleday, 2004.

Walker, Alice. *Anything We Love Can Be Saved: A Writer's Activism.* New York: Random House, 1997.

_____. "Coming Apart." In *Take Back the Night: Women on Pornography.* Ed. Laura Lederer. New York: William Morrow, 1980. 95–104.

_____. *In Search of Our Mothers' Gardens.* New York: Harcourt Brace Jovanovich 1983.

Ward, Brian. *Radio and the Struggle for Civil Rights in the South.* Gainesville: University Press of Florida, 2004.

Washington, James M., ed. *A Testament of Hope: The Essential Writings of Martin Luther King, Jr.* New York: Harper & Row, 1986.

Watson, Bruce. *Freedom Summer: The Savage Season that Made Mississippi Burn and Made America a Democracy.* New York: Viking, 2010.

West, Cornel. *Democracy Matters: Winning the Fight Against Imperialism.* New York: Penguin, 2004.

_____. *Race Matters.* Boston: Beacon Press, 1993.

West, Traci C. "Gay Rights and the Misuse of Martin." In *The Domestication of Martin Luther King, Jr.: Clarence B. Jones, Right-Wing Conservatism, and the Manipulation of the King Legacy.* Eds. Lewis V. Baldwin and Rufus Burrow, Jr. Eugene, OR: Cascade, 2013. Ch. 7.

Williams, James D., ed. *The State of Black America: 1985.* New York: National Urban League, 1985.

Wilson, Amos N. *Black-on-Black Violence.* New York: Afrikan World Infosystems, 1990.

Wilson, William J. *The Declining Significance of Race: Blacks and Changing American Institutions.* Chicago: University of Chicago Press, 1978.

Wink, Walter. *Engaging the Powers: Discernment and Resistance in a World of Domination.* Minneapolis: Fortress Press, 1992.

Wolff, Miles. *Lunch at the 5 & 10.* Revised and Expanded. Chicago: Ivan R. Dee, 1990 [1970].

Wright, Richard A., ed. *African Philosophy: An Introduction.* 3rd Edition. New York: University Press of America, 1984.

X, Malcolm, with Alex Haley. *The Autobiography of Malcolm X.* New York: Ballantine, 1992 [1965].

Young, Andrew. *An Easy Burden: The Civil Rights Movement and the Transformation of America.* New York: HarperCollins, 1996.

Zepp, Ira G. "The Social Vision of Martin Luther King, Jr." Ph.D. diss. In *Martin Luther King, Jr. and the Civil Rights Movement.* Ed. David J. Garrow. Brooklyn: Carlson, 1989.

Index